KT-157-111

The English Spenserians

The English Spenserians

The Poetry of Giles Fletcher, George Wither
Michael Drayton, Phineas Fletcher
and Henry More

Edited by William B. Hunter, Jr.

THE UNIVERSITY OF UTAH PRESS

Salt Lake City, Utah 84112
Library of Congress Catalog Card Number 75-30155
International Standard Book Number 0-87480-110-9
Printed in the United States of America

To Margaret

For Every Reason

Contents

Illustrations

The agent was claimed to be a witch, Jane Brooks (1657). In the bottom picture a boy named Richard Jones is shown as he was found "sometimes strangely hanging above the ground." He claimed that the agent was the same Jane Brooks, who was executed on March 26, 1658. The top illustration of the right column depicts Elizabeth Styles and three other women meeting a man dressed in black who was the devil himself (note the cloven feet). He "baptized" a wax image of a child, Elizabeth Hill, and then stuck thorns into various parts of it. Styles was tried later, "but she prevented execution, by dying in Gaol" in 1664. The bottom two pictures seem to be more general, contrasting a devil and an angel who are in attendance at death.

The English Spenserians

The English Spenserians

Literary history has not been kind to most of the poets who published during the first quarter of the seventeenth century. One thinks at once, of course, of such men who were writing then as John Donne, George Herbert, Ben Jonson, and Robert Herrick; but their major poetic collections all appeared after 1630. Literary staples earlier in the century are represented instead by epigrams like those of Jonson (1616) and translations such as Chapman's *Iliad* (1609 and later) and Sylvester's *Divine Weekes* (1605). Of original English poetry one notes otherwise only Daniel's *Civil Wars* (1609 and 1623), the thirteen short poems of Jonson's *Forrest* (1616), and the work of Spenser and his followers, who indeed dominate the first generation of poets under the Stuarts.

Spenser had died in London in 1599. Perhaps because of his isolation on his estate in Ireland during his later years he left few immediate literary heirs despite an outpouring of works during the last decade of his life. The decisive event for the remarkable growth of his posthumous influence was the reprinting of the entire *Faerie Queene* with the added Mutabilitie Cantos in 1609, followed in 1611 by the publication of a full collection of his works which was so successful that a new edition was called for in 1617. The young Giles Fletcher responded at once to the 1609 volume with his *Christs Victorie, and Triumph*, which appeared the next year and is clearly indebted to the *Faerie Queene*. The *Epithalamion*, reprinted in the 1611 collection, evoked imitations by Donne and Jonson (the epithalamion seems to be the only aspect of Spenser to have interested them), and George Wither promptly adapted it to celebrate the marriage of Princess Elizabeth. Minding the *Shepheards Calendar*, now a generation old, which was reprinted in the same collection, several "Shepheard" poems quickly appeared, including Wither's *Shepheards Hunting* (1615) and William Browne's *Shepheards Pipe* (1614). Browne's *Britannia's Pastorals* (1613 and 1616) was the most extended application of the pastoral form, which Phineas Fletcher was also imitating in his *Piscatory Eclogues*, though they were not to appear until almost a generation later. A major expansion of the physiological allegory of the Castle of Alma in the *Faerie Queene*, 2. 9, was the dozen cantos of Phineas Fletcher's *Purple Island*, though it too was not to be printed for years. Biggest of all these early imitations was Michael Drayton's *Poly-Olbion* (1612 and

1622), inspired in part by the geographical allegory of the marriage of the Thames and the Medway in the *Faerie Queene*, 4. 11, and of the Irish countryside in the description of Father Mole in 7. 6.

Thus Spenserianism dominated English poetry until well into the reign of Charles; it was the literary milieu in which Milton was educated and came to maturity, as is evidenced in one way or another by all of his early English poetry. There were indeed almost no other contemporary English models for him to follow. Yet these Spenserians are almost completely forgotten today, an unfortunate fact of literary history in that they are remarkably interesting writers for both style and content as well as for the challenge which they make that one develop a critical response to them.

The reader confronts at once the highly artificial style which they all employ. The literary tastes which had so emphasized artifice in the prose styles of euphuism and of arcadianism dominate this poetry, which always tends to be retrospective in its expression: the artificial is the artistic. Thus these works abound in the rhetorical patterning and archaisms of diction which Spenser had explored to produce, especially in his earlier poems, a language such as has never been heard on sea or land. As "E.K." had annotated the *Shepheards Calendar*, these writers express some pedantry in marginal notes. The realistic syntax which Donne employed so effectively seems to have begun to develop especially in the satires with which he and others like Jonson were experimenting early in the century, but this style is generally avoided by the Spenserians in favor of an artificial, literary grammar; the more natural form appears in this collection only in some of the verse epistles of Drayton. Most readers today prefer the more natural medium.

An even more serious critical problem in reading these poems is the scope which they typically encompass. Like their master these poets were most at home in the long work. In contrast, Donne has only one poem (the *Second Anniversary*) of over five hundred lines, a length which Jonson and Herbert do not approach; Herrick does not reach even a hundred lines. The other poets who were active before the Restoration and who are widely read today, like Vaughan, Traherne, Marvell, Suckling, or Lovelace, are also typically represented by shorter pieces. Because of the overwhelming influence of the anthology upon modern American education, the Spenserians have accordingly suffered for their discursiveness, for it is impossible to present them adequately through excerpts. Even Milton has had difficulties in this respect. The metaphysicals and Jonsonians, on the other hand, are well represented in their lyrics, satires, and other shorter pieces.

The experience of reading a long poem seems to differ fundamentally from that of reading a short one. Just what constitutes this difference is very hard to define, nor has it figured in modern critical theory. Perhaps a start may be made in explaining the differences between the responses to the two forms by appeal to the different kinds of learning and memory which each appears to involve. Psychologists for a century have distinguished two kinds of memory, the short term and the long term. Such experimental psychologists as Wilhelm Wundt, Ernst Meumann, and William James recognized a profound difference between thoughts currently present in one's consciousness and those which are brought back to consciousness after a memory search which in itself may be laborious. Since the early 1950s the subject has received further consideration by such investigators as Donald Broadbent, D. O. Hibb, and George A. Miller. They have discovered that information stored in the short-term or working memory remains there if unattended for perhaps fifteen seconds and then may be permanently forgotten. It may, however, be retained in awareness by *rehearsal*, a voluntary reviewing and retention of information for an indefinite length of time. Short-term memory is under the immediate control of the subject, who by rehearsal can, however, sustain only a limited number of items in it. From this short-term phase the information may or may not enter the long-term store. Input into the long-term store is only partly under the control of the subject, and recall from it may likewise not be optional. The capacity of the long-term memory is enormously larger than that of the short-term one.

These two different kinds of memory may offer an explanation of, or at least an analogy to, the profound difference between reading short poems and long ones which everyone experiences. The short poem is certainly "rehearsed": it is read and reread so as to consciously establish its contents in the short-term memory until its reader comprehends it as a whole. During the process it may or may not enter his long-term memory. Because the experience employs the same memory as that which is concerned with the environment, the short poem may have something of the same immediacy as that provided by the environment. This seems to be the view of the literary experience which Poe was describing when he argued that a poem of more than a hundred lines could not exist.

But one should also recognize that another kind of literary response may exist which depends upon the long-term memory. It will differ from that associated with the short-term one in that it will not possess the same immediacy of environmental experience (though individual parts of it may, of course) and in that the experience of the whole will require more or less conscious recall of that whole which could never be perceived immediately and as a whole by the limited process of rehearsal. Furthermore, to aid the process of recall the writer must employ some overall principle of organization to facilitate it — an architectonic which enables the reader to retrieve from his long-term memory the ordered details which constitute a whole and unified work. Narrative line is one obvious way to achieve this. By contrast, a long poem not so ordered cannot be reconstructed from unaided memory. It is thus doubtful whether anyone can recall the consecutive details of either of Donne's *Anniversaries* without reference to a text because they do not have an obvious organizing principle. Size alone, that is, seems to make a fundamental difference in artistic perception as it employs different memorial processes. One does not view a Vermeer in the same way as a Rubens.

Because there seems to be no architectonic principle which must be recognized in order to appreciate fully the individual poems which constitute them, such collections as Donne's *Songs and Sonets*, Herbert's *Temple*, Herrick's *Hesperides*, and Vaughan's *Silex Scintillans* may be profitably read as individual poems and anthologized — a principle not so evident in the sonnet cycles, which have, however, been freely pillaged. Giles Fletcher, on the other hand, narrates at length in *Christs Victorie, and Triumph* elements of the story of the Son of God from incarnation to ascension, which he divides into four contrasting but mutually supportive genres. To follow the narrative and finally perceive the whole work the reader must employ his long-term memory, with relatively little rehearsal in the short-term memory as he proceeds; he may, of course, pause to reflect on and rehearse certain details — the reason, perhaps, that the poem is divided into stanzas. The five movements of Wither's *Shepheards Hunting* find their unity amidst the more subjective reactions by the author to his imprisonment and to his literary career, though one may question how successful he was in unifying the whole. Drayton's *Nimphidia* subsumes in its formal plot of Queen Mab's infidelity to King Oberon the details of its author's witty display of fairy lore and human failings. Phineas Fletcher's story in *The Apollyonists* is that of the Guy Fawkes Plot, which the reader must rely upon to organize the vast amount of supporting allegorical and historical material. Finally, More's *Præexistency of the Soul* is based not upon a narrative structure but upon a logical one, that the soul may be separated from the body and that the existence of witches proves the case — a theory which orders his interesting excursions into Satanic lore. To appreciate properly these works and others like them it seems then necessary for the reader to develop for himself the techniques of memorial recall, supported by recognition of whatever organizing framework the author chooses to employ, rather than to rehearsal alone, which will prove unequal to the task. A less sophisticated critic may limit himself to the latter experience.

But one need not select these writers who normally employed the long poem because of their achievements in that form alone. All of them also wrote lyrics — some of the best in the language, as one will quickly discover in Wither's "Christmas Carroll," for instance, or Drayton's "Love's Conquest" or Phineas Fletcher's "Vast Ocean of light," to mention three which are almost unknown today. Short pieces whose appreciation depends upon rehearsal in the short-term memory have been included in this collection to show how well their authors could handle the lyric forms as well as longer ones. In reading them, however, one will discover at once that this "School of Spenser" was well aware of other contemporary literary developments. It is apparent, for instance, that some of Phineas Fletcher's shorter poems exhibit familiarity with the "metaphysicals." Wither's short poems share many characteristics with Jonson, Herrick, and the later Cavaliers, and many of Drayton's epistles suggest the same genre as it was practiced by both Donne and Jonson. It is a mistake to divide the literary trends of the early Stuart period too neatly into "schools."

The principle of selection of the poems in this collection has been to represent fairly the immense diversity of Spenser's various followers in works which continue to be delightful to read today. In every case they are printed in their entirety. The long narrative form which developed from the model of the *Faerie Queene* is represented by *Christs Victorie, and Triumph* and *The Apollyonists* by the Fletcher brothers. The former includes the kinds of allegorical set pieces in which Spenser delighted, their characters, generally endowed with non-English names, being ultimately the ancestors of Comus; the latter is closer to the native English allegory of the *Induction* to *The*

Mirror for Magistrates, whose characters find descendants in Sin and Death in *Paradise Lost*.

Wither provides a good example of the Stuart pastoral in his *Shepheards Hunting*, but he has modified the mode from the relative objectivity of the *Shepheards Calendar* to a personal plaint and expostulation with society for his imprisonment. Also from Wither is the example of the wide influence of Spenser's *Epithalamion*, though the later poem lacks the constructive skill evident in its model.

Drayton's *Odes*, *Epistles*, and *Nimphidia* are included to represent the diverse kinds of literary expression possible for this group of writers. Some of the *Epistles* evince the same social criticism found in parts of the *Shepheards Calendar* and in *Mother Hubberds Tale* (Drayton's *The Owle* would have been an alternative possibility, but its social satire is to a large extent not yet clearly understood). The *Odes* try to recapture what Drayton thought was genuine English history and poetic style (that of the Welsh British, that is) in the same spirit as that in which Spenser turned to the Welsh legends of Arthur. *Nimphidia*, by way of contrast, employs native folklore with closer analogues in Shakespeare than in Spenser. Drayton is the only poet of this group who could have been levied on for a sonnet sequence like the *Amoretti*, but the intrinsic interest of his complete cycle did not seem to warrant its inclusion here.

Finally, More's long argument to prove the pre-existence of the soul is an example of the direction in which the Mutabilitie Cantos of the *Faerie Queene* might lead writers. These two sections from an unfinished book 7 are a medieval debate concerned with the abstract subject of the extent to which mutability or change permeates the universe so as to provide a basis for philosophical skepticism. More's pen turns this kind of poetry into a logical disquisition almost totally lacking in any of the characteristics usually associated with literature. From his model he retains more than anyone else the diction and the stanza of Spenser — exterior trappings within which the poetic has been replaced by the logical. With this self-defeating tendency formal Spenserianism disappeared from English writing until it was revived by a new generation in the next century.

Because of the length of their major poems it was not possible to print here examples of the poetry of all the writers whom Spenser influenced during the early part of the seventeenth century. *Britannia's Pastorals* by William Browne, Wither's friend, comes to mind at once as an important omission, as may the lesser work of William Drummond, Drayton's friend. Francis Quarles' various publications, both emblematic and pastoral, do not seem so important today as the poetry which is printed here. To have included Joseph Beaumont's *Psyche, or Love's Mystery* (1648) would have required another volume, its contents of questionable merit.

The editorial principle which has been followed is to reproduce the first text in which the author's work came to maturity; the introductions to the individual writers state the editions of each which have been followed, with all changes from them given in the footnotes. Only *i–j* and *u–v* have been normalized to modern practice. Besides surveys of the Spenserians in histories of English literature and occasional excerpts in anthologies, one should consult Joan Grundy's fine study, *The Spenserian Poets* (New York: St. Martin's Press, 1969), and William Wells' recent collection, *Spenser Allusions in the Sixteenth and Seventeenth Centuries*, a supplement to *Studies in Philology: Texts and Studies* (Chapel Hill: University of North Carolina, 1971 and 1972).

In conclusion I wish to express my deep appreciation to the staff of the University of Utah Press, and especially to Paula Roberts, for the careful editing and imaginative treatment this work has received in publication.

IOHN 5:6
MAR 9:4
IOH: 9:1
IOH: 8:6
Tis written. Thus the tempter saught (And thus
by scriptures wrack'd he oft preuailes on vs
weake flesh and blood) But that he thus did dare
by Moses, and the prophets to insnare
the sonne of God: thinck it not strange that he
became confounded in his policie
for sure it could but slender hopes afford
he by the scriptures should orecome ye word
G: yate sti

Giles Fletcher

Giles Fletcher, Elizabethan courtier, ambassador, and man of letters, gave his second son his own name. The younger Giles was born in London about 1586, brother of the poet Phineas and cousin to the dramatist John. He was educated at Westminster School and went on to Trinity College, Cambridge, where he earned a B.A. in 1606 and in due time became a fellow. He remained at Cambridge until 1618, when he moved to a parsonage in Sussex where he died in 1623. His original writing in English had all been done much earlier and consists, aside from poems commemorating the deaths of Elizabeth and of Prince Henry, only of *Christs Victorie, and Triumph* (1610).

Fletcher found it necessary to defend poetry in his address "To the Reader," which establishes the literary expression of the religious tradition from such early medieval writers as Juvencus, Prudentius, and Sedulius through the Italian renaissance poet Sannazaro, the Frenchman du Bartas, and finally Spenser. In fact, his poem is not a close imitation of any of these models. It narrates the story of Christ from his incarnation to his ascension, but each of the four parts into which it is divided is a different literary genre, as Grundy observes (p. 194): consecutively medieval debate, Spenserian allegory, a mourning plaint, and a beatific vision. And yet the whole remains a unit. Fletcher invented the stanza form, an eight-line modification of the Spenserian rhyming *a b a b b c c c*, the final line being an alexandrine. But he avoids Spenser's pastoral mode, his employment of Spenserian archaisms is not very extensive, and as J. S. Dees observes, Fletcher's narrator has a different function from Spenser's ("The Narrator's Voice in *The Faerie Queene*, *Christs Victorie, and Triumph*, and *The Locusts, or Apollyonists*," Ph.D. dissertation, University of Illinois, 1962). Instead *Christs Victorie, and Triumph* is built upon extreme rhetorical artifice. It opens, for instance, with a traditional paradoxical treatment of Christ expressed in the classical pattern known as chiasmus. Thus in the first stanza, *birth* : *beginning*::*beginning* : *borne*; or *greater* : *grew*::*growing* : *less*; or *worthily* : *died*::*died* : *unworthily*—

> The birth of him that no beginning knewe,
> Yet gives beginning to all that are borne,
> And how the Infinite farre greater grewe,
> By growing lesse, . . .
> How worthily he died, that died unworthily.

The final stanza of the poem is equally remarkable but its effect is achieved in a different way. It repeats a word from the end of each line early in the next line to produce a poetically coherent statement despite its extreme artifice:

> Impotent words, weake sides, that strive in vaine,
> In vaine, alas, to tell so heav'nly sight,
> So heav'nly sight, as none can greater feigne,
> Feigne what he can, that seemes of greatest might,
>   Might any yet compare with Infinite?
>   Infinite sure those joyes, my words but light,
> Light is the pallace whear she dwells. O blessed wight!

Between these two stanzas the poem is constantly marked by attention to rhetorical artifice, affording a fine example of the literary baroque. Despite this artifice its author's insights may be profound as when, for instance, he observes man's "Want of knowledge how to use/ Abundance" (1. 13. 2–3) or in the description of how trees, the sons of the mountains, "Dandled the mornings childhood in their armes" (4. 3. 3).

Fletcher seems to have conceived of *Christs Victorie, and Triumph* as in some sense two different works; at least it has two title pages, one for the whole and a second for the last two cantos. The first two of the four deal with the "Victorie," apparently the events in which Christ was an active participant, choosing to become incarnate and choosing to resist Satan's temptation. The "Triumph," on the other hand, seems to be the full revelation of the meaning of his passive acquiescence in his death and resurrection. Only the first two cantos directly imitate Spenser: the first is in the medieval debate form which governs the Cantos of Mutability in which the subject is not a narrative, like much of the rest of the *Faerie Queene*, but an argument that mutability or change governs the universe, an argument answered (briefly but decisively) by Dame Nature. In a similar way Fletcher dichotomizes Justice and Mercy, a traditional polarity developed from the "four daughters of God" in Ps. 85:10 and probably best known today in Shakespeare's treatment of it in *The Merchant of Venice* and *Measure for Measure*. In theological terms the polarity exists between the exercise of justice based on the Law of the Old Testament, which is exemplified by the Ten Commandments and is not subject to amelioration, and Mercy, based upon the inner light or conscience of the New Testament which modifies the externally imposed law and leads one to be merciful in his exercise of justice. But a just God's mercy can be evidenced to man only when a sacrifice has been made to atone for man's sinfulness, and accordingly the debate is resolved by the appearance of his incarnate Son, who almost casually appears in stanza 84. This is the "Victorie in Heaven" — the supplanting of Old Testament justice by New Testament mercy. Like Spenser's treatment of his characters in the Mutability Cantos, which had been published only a year earlier, Justice and Mercy here are purely allegorical, and Justice is accompanied by such figures as Sickness, Famine, and War. Mercy's symbolic dress is described at length, in the terms used by Alanus de Insulis in his *De Planctu Naturæ*, as Grundy observes (p. 188). The implication for Fletcher is that Mercy is inherent in all of creation whereas we today would see Law operating there instead.

The second canto, detailing the Temptation in the Wilderness, is the closest literary analogue to *Paradise Regained*, and yet one should recognize that differences may outweigh similarities. Milton follows the order of temptations found in Luke, whereas Fletcher uses that of Matthew (4:1–11). Satan indeed appears in the same disguise in both poems (Spenser's Archimago is in the background of both too), and like Satan in *Paradise Regained* the Tempter falls from the pinnacle of the temple after the failure of that test. For further similarities see H. E. Cory in *University of California Publications in Modern Philology*, 2 (1912): 362–67. But the differences are profound: as Jesus appears in Fletcher's wilderness it becomes a new Eden (2. 3–5), and the allegory of Despair (2. 23ff.) has no counterpart in Milton's work. Most startling in Fletcher is the extreme sensuality of his description of Jesus and of the temptation of Vaine Glory. Excusing himself by the authority of the biblical Song of Songs, he presents Jesus in excessive Petrarchan terms usually reserved for women:

> His cheekes as snowie apples, sop't in wine,
> Had their red roses quencht with lillies white,
> And like to garden strawberries did shine,
> Wash't in a bowle of milke, or rose-buds bright
> Unbosoming their brests against the light:
>   Here love-sicke soules did eat.
>
> [2. 11. 1–6]

His legs (bare) are described

> As two white marble pillars that uphold
> Gods holy place whear he in glorie sets, . . .
> Vein'd every whear with azure rivulets.
> [2. 13. 1–5]

Such sensuality had indeed appeared briefly in the description of Mercy in canto 1. 50. But these details are only preliminary to the description of Pangloretta's temptations in stanzas 39–59, modeled upon Acrasia and the Bower of Bliss in the *Faerie Queene* 2. 12. In a beautiful, sensual garden shaped like a woman and surrounded with drunken trees is a fountain running with rose water in which Pangloretta has intercourse; Circean men-beasts surround it and all participate in drinking orgies leading to "Luxurie." In the second stage of this temptation we move from this "false Eden" to Panglory's throne, surrounded by self-arching columns (they are thus likely to fall) which reflect the person within their circumference. This temptation is figured as pride or self-centeredness; even Panglory's crown is her own hair. In her hand she holds the world, a glossy soap bubble. The climax of the temptation is a song in rhyming tetrameters (stanza 59), praising sexual love which is acclaimed as the source of order in the universe; the carpe diem theme is well handled in its second stanza. The underlying temptation is that man forgets his creator as he enjoys the created universe. As the refrain of the song urges,

> Onely bend thy knee to mee,
> Thy wooing shall thy winning bee.

This is indeed a very different wilderness from that of *Paradise Regained*, though Milton implies some of its aspects.

The third canto is much quieter, a plaint mourning the Passion; Milton's own abortive "The Passion" was conceived in quite similar terms. In general, unlike canto 2, this is a paraphrase, without expansion, of the biblical story. After a long account of Judas' attempts to escape his guilt through suicide, the canto quietly concludes with the mourning of the world and of the poet, summarized by a powerful description of the destruction by mowers of a lark's nest.

The final part, *Christs Triumph after Death*, is ostensibly a pæan of rejoicing over the resurrection and ascension; as Christ is raised from the dead, nature comes back to life — the vernal associations of Easter are here remembered. From the Book of Revelation (not from the Gospels) comes the anachronistic account of the rejoicing of saints, martyrs, and virgins accompanying the event (stanzas 18 and 19). But it turns out that Fletcher's real goal is to parallel the entire story of Christ's mission with his conception of England as the new Eden which is saved by the Son of God and is now led by His minister James (stanza 21) with moralizing comparisons made between English and continental societies. Accordingly James is the "Deere Prince" of 24. 1, the vessel of everything good; and he is compared with the resurrected Son of God. After such adulation, which Phineas shares in *The Apollyonists*, the poem concludes with an idealized vision of heaven, a place, Fletcher believes, where appetites and sensations are still experienced (stanzas 32 and 34). But he is primarily interpreting Revelation here, the final Christian goal of the entire story of *Christs Victorie, and Triumph* which is expressed for him throughout eternity in the Church, the Bride of Christ (stanza 48).

The poem was published at Cambridge in 1610 with two quite different title pages. This was the only edition to appear during Fletcher's lifetime and is the one reproduced here. It has been accurately reprinted by Frederick S. Boas in *Giles and Phineas Fletcher: Poetical Works* (Cambridge: At the University Press, 1908), 2 vols., along with variants of the editions of 1632 which Giles' brother Phineas probably oversaw, and of its reprint in 1640. Nigel Alexander includes it in his *Elizabethan Narrative Verse* (London: Edward Arnold, 1967).

Christs Victorie, and Triumph.

To the Right
Worshipfull, and Reverend
M^r. Doctour Nevile, Deane of Canterburie,
and the Master of Trinitie Colledge
in Cambridge.

Right worthie, and reverend Syr:

As I have alwaies thought the place wherein I live, after heaven, principally to be desired, both because I most want, and it most abounds with wisdome, which is fled by some with as much delight, as it is obtained by others, and ought to be followed by all: so I cannot but next unto God, for ever acknowledge myselfe most bound unto the hand of God, (I meane yourselfe) that reacht downe, as it were out of heaven, unto me, a benefit of that nature, and price, then which, I could wish none, (onely heaven itselfe excepted) either more fruitfull, and contenting for the time that is now present, or more 10 *comfortable, and encouraging for the time that is alreadie past, or more hopefull, and promising for the time that is yet to come.*

For as in all mens judgements (that have any judgement) Europe *is worthily deem'd the Queene of the world, that Garland both of Learning, and pure Religion beeing now become her crowne, and blossoming upon her head, that hath long since laine withered in* Greece *and* Palestine*; so my opinion of this Island hath alwaies beene, that it is the very face, and beautie of all* Europe, *in which both true Religion is faithfully professed without superstition, and (if on earth) true Learning sweetly flourishes without ostentation: and what are the* 20 *two eyes of this Land, but the two Universities; which cannot but prosper in the time of such a Prince, that is a Prince of Learning, aswell as of People: and truly I should forget myselfe, if I should not call* Cambridge *the right eye: and I thinke (King* Henrie *the* 8. *beeing the uniter,* Edward *the* 3. *the Founder, and your selfe the Repairer*

Address: *Worshipfull* : *Worshipull* 1610. *Doctour Nevile*: Thomas Nevile (d. 1615), bitter enemy of Gabriel Harvey, was Master of Trinity College during Fletcher's entire association with it. He was a great benefactor of the College, having many of its buildings renovated.

24 Henrie: Trinity College was founded by Henry VIII in December 1546 from two antecedent colleges, Michaelhouse and King's Hall. Although the two colleges had begun in 1324 and 1326 under Edward II, Edward III gave its first building to King's Hall.

of this Colledge, wherein I live) none will blame me, if I esteeme the same, since your polishing of it, the fairest sight in Cambridge*: in which beeing placed by your onely favour, most freely, without either any meanes from other, or any desert in my selfe, beeing not able to*
30 *doe more, I could doe no lesse, then acknowledge that debt, which I shall never be able to pay, and with old* Silenus, *in the Poet (upon whome the boyes* — injiciunt ipsis ex vincula sertis, *making his garland, his fetters) finding my selfe bound unto you by so many benefits, that were given by your selfe for ornaments, but are to me as so many golden cheines, to hold me fast in a kind of desired bondage, seeke (as he doth) my freedome with a song, the matter whereof is as worthie the sweetest Singer, as my selfe, the miserable Singer, unworthie so divine a subject: but the same favour, that before rewarded no desert, knowes now as well how to pardon all faults, then which*
40 *indulgence, when I regard my selfe, I can wish no more; when I remember you, I can hope no lesse.*

So commending these few broken lines unto yours, and your selfe into the hands of the best Physitian, Jesus Christ, *with whome, the most ill affected man, in the midst of his sicknes, is in good health, and without whome, the most lustie bodie, in his greatest jollitie, is but a languishing karcase, I humbly take my leave, ending with the same wish, that your devoted Observer, and my approoved Friend doth, in his verses presently sequent, that your passage to heaven may be slow to us, that shall want you here, but to your selfe, that cannot want*
50 *us there, most secure and certeyne.*

Your Worships, in all
dutie, and service
G. Fletcher.

31 *Poet*: Virgil, who in Eclogue 6 describes two youths, Chromis and Mnasylos, who came upon Silenus, an old companion of Bacchus, asleep after a night of revelry. They bound him with his garland (the Latin, l. 19 of the poem, which Fletcher translates) and got him to sing about the creation of the universe and some of its subsequent mythology.

47 *Friend*: Sir Francis Nethersole (1587–1659), a friend of Fletcher's at Trinity who contributed an English and a Latin dedicatory poem to his volume (not reprinted here). Like Fletcher, he wrote verses on the death of Prince Henry two years later.

To the Reader.

Thear are but fewe of many that can rightly judge of Poetry, and yet thear ar many of those few, that carry so left-handed an opinion of it, as some of them thinke it halfe sacrilege for prophane Poetrie to deale with divine and heavenly matters, as though David *wear to be sentenced by them, for uttering his grave matter upon the harpe: others something more violent in their censure, but sure lesse reasonable (as though Poetrie corrupted all good witts, when, indeed, bad witts corrupt Poetrie) banish it with* Plato *out of all well-ordered Commonwealths. Both theas I will strive rather to satisfie, then refute.*

And of the first I would gladlie knowe, whither they suppose it 10 *fitter, that the sacred songs in the Scripture of those heroicall Sainɑts,* Moses, Deborah, Jeremie, Mary, Simeon, David, Salomon, *(the wisest Scholeman, and wittiest Poet) should bee ejeɑted from the canon, for wante of gravitie, or rather this erroure eraced out of their mindes, for wante of truth. But, it maye bee, they will give the Spirit of God leave to breath through what pipe it please, & will confesse, because they must needs, that all the songs dittied by him, must needs bee, as their Fountaine is, most holy: but their common clamour is, who may compare with God? true; & yet as none may compare without presumption, so all may imitat, and not without commenda-* 20 *tion: which made* Nazianzen, *one of the Starrs of the Greeke Church, that nowe shines as bright in heaven, as he did then on earth, write so manie divine Poems of the Genealogie, Miracles, Parables, Passion of Christ, called by him his χριστὸς πάσχων, which when* Basil, *the Prince of the Fathers, and his Chamberfellowe, had seene, his opinion of them was, that he could have devised nothing either more fruitfull to others: because it kindely woed them to Religion, or more honour-*

8 Plato: in the *Republic*, 607.

12 Moses, etc.: All have poetry attributed to them in the Bible.

21 Nazianzen: Gregory of Nazianzus, fourth century bishop of the Eastern Church. Among his many works are over sixteen thousand lines of poetry, both theological and historical. They were printed several times in the sixteenth century and were included in the *Opera* (Paris, 1609, 1611) being published when Fletcher was writing his poem.

24 χριστὸς πδσχιον: *Christus Patiens, The Suffering Christ*, attributed formerly to Gregory but now considered spurious.
Basil: fourth century Eastern bishop and close friend of Gregory.

able to himselfe, οὐδὲν γὰρ μακαριώτερόν ἐστι τοῦ τὴν ἀγγέλων χορείαν ἐν γῇ μιμεῖσθαι, *because by imitating the singing Angels in heav'n,*
30 *himselfe became, though before his time, an earthly Angel. What should I speake of* Juvencus, Prosper, *& the wise* Prudentius*? the last of which living in* Hieroms *time, twelve hundred yeares agoe, brought foorth in his declining age, so many, & so religious poems, straitly charging his soule, not to let passe so much as one either night or daye without some divine song,* Hymnis continuet dies, Nec nox ulla vacet, quin Dominum canat. *And as sedulous* Prudentius, *so prudent* Sedulius *was famous in this poeticall divinity, the coetan of* Bernard, *who sung the historie of* Christ *with as much devotion in himself, as admiration to others; all which wear followed by the choicest witts of*
40 Christendome*:* Nonnius *translating all Sainct* Johns *Ghostpel into Greek verse,* Sanazar, *the late-living Image, and happy imitator of* Virgil, *bestowing ten yeares upon a song, onely to celebrat that one*

28-29 οὐδὲν etc.: There is nothing more blessed than to imitate on earth the chorus of angels. Basil, Letter 2 (Loeb edition, 1:13).

31 Juvencus: early fourth century Spanish priest who paraphrased the Gospel (mostly Matthew) in Latin hexameters which were very popular in the Middle Ages as well as the Renaissance.

Prosper: fifth century lay theologian who wrote poems in Latin hexameters on such subjects as *On Those Lacking Grace.* He composed a number of religious epigrams too.

Prudentius: the greatest Christian Latin poet, fourth century, who remained popular well into the seventeenth century.

32 Hieroms: St. Jerome's.

35-36 Hymnis, etc.: He occupied his days with songs nor did any night pass when he did not sing to the Lord.

37 Sedulius: fifth century Christian poet whose major work was *Paschale Carmen.* Book 2 narrates the baptism of Christ, the temptation in the wilderness, and the beginning of the ministry. The remaining three books continue the story through the Passion and Resurrection.

coetan of Bernard: contemporary of St. Bernard (though the famous father of Clairvaux was a twelfth century French abbot).

40 Nonnius: Nonnius of Panopolis, Egyptian Christian of the early fifth century who wrote a pagan epic, *Dionysiaca,* and a Christian *Paraphrase of St. John's Gospel* in hexameter poetry.

41 Sanazar: Jacopo Sannazaro (1458–1530), Italian writer most famous for his pastoral allegory, the *Arcadia* (1504). His *De partu virginis* (1526), to which Fletcher refers, narrates the events from the Annunciation to the Nativity, earning him the title of "the Christian Virgil."

day when Christ was borne unto us on earth, & we (a happie change) unto God in heav'n: thrice-honour'd Bartas, *& our (I know no other name more glorious then his own) Mr.* Edmund Spencer *(two blessed Soules) not thinking ten years inough, layeing out their whole lives upon this one studie: Nay I may justly say, that the Princely Father of our Countrey (though in my conscience, God hath made him of all the learned Princes that ever wear the most religious, and of all the religious Princes, the most learned, that so, by the one, hee might oppose him against the Pope, the peste of all Religion, and by the other, against* Bellarmine *the abuser of all good Learning) is yet so far enamour'd with this celestiall Muse, that it shall never repent mee —* calamo trivisse labellum, *whensoever I shall remember* Hæc eadem ut sciret quid non faciebat Amyntas? *To name no more in such plenty, whear I may finde how to beginne, sooner then to end, Saincte Paule, by the Example of Christ, that wente singing to mounte Olivet, with his Disciples, after his last supper, exciteth the Christians to solace themselves with hymnes, and Psalmes, and spirituall songs; and thearefore, by their leav's, be it an error for* Poets *to be Divines, I had rather err with the Scripture, then be rectifi'd by them: I had rather adore the stepps of* Nazianzen, Prudentius, Sedulius, *then followe their steps, to bee misguided: I had rather be the devoute Admirer of* Nonnius, Bartas, *my sacred Soveraign, and others, the miracles of our latter age, then the false sectarie of these, that have nothing at all to follow, but their own naked opinions: To conclude, I had rather with my Lord, and his most divine Apostle sing (though I sing sorilie) the love of heaven and earthe, then praise God (as they doe) with the woorthie guift of silence, and sitting still, or think I*

44 Bartas: Guillaume Salluste du Bartas, whose one major poem, *La Semaine*, paraphrasing the creation stories in Genesis, was translated into English as *Divine Weekes and Works* by Joshua Sylvester. The complete translation had appeared in 1605, to great acclaim.

47 *Father*: James I in his youth had published a number of short poems and some literary criticism.

52 Bellarmine: Robert Bellarmine (1542–1621), Italian Jesuit and leader of Counter Reformation thinking who disputed with, among others, James I.

54-55 calamo . . . Amyntas: to have frayed (my) lips with (learning to play) the reed — i.e., to write poetry. Amyntas tried in vain to learn how to play it. Quoted from Virgil, *Eclogues* 2. 34–35.

57 Below in canto 3, stanza 1, Fletcher again alludes to the story that Christ and his followers sang a hymn before going to the Mount of Olives (Matt. 26:30). Paul commends church singing in Eph. 5:19.

70 *dispraisd him with this poetical discourse. It seems they have either not read, or clean forgot, that it is the dutie of the Muses (if wee maye beeleeve* Pindare, *and* Hesiod*) to set allwaies under the throne of* Jupiter, ejus & laudes, & beneficia *ὑμνειούσας, which made a very worthy German writer conclude it* Certò statuimus, proprium atque peculiare poetarum munus esse, Christi gloriam illustrare, *beeing good reason that the heavenly infusion of such Poetry, should ende in his glorie, that had beginning from his goodnes,* fit orator, nascitur Poeta.

For the secound sorte thearfore, that eliminat Poets out of their 80 *citie gates; as though they wear nowe grown so bad, as they could neither growe woorse, nor better, though it be somewhat hard for those to bee the onely men should want cities, that wear the onely causers of the building of them, and somewhat inhumane to thrust them into the woods, to live among the beasts, who wear the first that call'd men out of the woods, from their beastly, and wilde life, yet since they will needes shoulder them out for the onely firebrands to inflame lust (the fault of earthly men, not heavenly Poetrie) I would gladly learne, what kind of professions theas men would bee intreated to entertaine, that so deride and disaffect Poesie: would they admit of* 90 *Philosophers, that after they have burnt out the whole candle of their life in the circular studie of Sciences, crie out at length,* Se nihil prorsus scire*? or should Musitians be welcome to them, that* Dant sine mente sonum — *bring delight with them indeede, could they aswell expresse with their instruments a voice, as they can a sound? or would they most approve of Soldiers that defend the life of their countrymen either by the death of themselves, or their enemies? If Philosophers please them, who is it, that knowes not, that all the lights of Example, to cleare their precepts, are borowed by Philosophers from Poets; that without* Homers *examples,* Aristotle *would be as blind as* Homer*:* 100 *If they retaine Musitians, who ever doubted, but that Poets infused the verie soule into the inarticulate sounds of musique; that without*

73 ejus, etc.: hymning his praises and benefits.

74-75 Certò, etc.: Truly we believe that it is the proper and peculiar office of poets to make famous the glory of Christ.

77-78 fit, etc.: The orator is made, the poet is born.

82 *men*: men who.

91-92 Se, etc.: whether one can know anything for certain.

92-93 Dant, etc.: give forth sound without thought.

Pindar, & Horace *the Lyriques had beene silenced for ever: If they must needes entertaine Soldiers, who can but confesse, that Poets restore againe that life to soldiers, which they before lost for the safetie of their country; that without* Virgil, Æneas *had never beene so much as heard of. How then can they for shame deny commonwealths to them, who wear the first Authors of them; how can they denie the blinde Philosopher, that teaches them, his light; the emptie Musitian that delights them, his soule; the dying Soldier, that defends their life, immortalitie, after his owne death; let Philosophie, let* Ethiques, *let all the Arts bestowe upon us this guift, that we be not thought dead men, whilest we remaine among the living: it is onely Poetrie that can make us be thought living men, when we lie among the dead, and therefore I thinke it unequall to thrust them out of our cities, that call us out of our graves, to thinke so hardly of them, that make us to be so well thought of, to deny them to live a while among us, that make us live for ever among our Posteritie.* 110

So beeing nowe weary in perswading those that hate, I commend my selfe to those that love such Poets, as Plato *speakes of, that sing divine and heroical matters.* οὐ γὰρ οὗτοι εἰσὶν, οἱ ταῦτα λέγοντες, ἀλλ' ὁ Θεὸς, αὐτός ἐστιν ὁ λέγων, *recommending theas my idle howers, not idly spent, to good schollers, and good Christians, that have overcome their ignorance with reason, and their reason, with religion.* 120

120-21 *οὐ*, etc.: for it is not they (the poets) who say these things but God himself (through them). *Ion* 534D.

A new way here that prophets text may pass
for truth: the oxe his owner knew, the ass
his masters crib. thus thus incradled lay
your King, your Lord, your Christ; there fix there stay
thy stoopinge low, deified thoughts shall I
since he lay thus depressd, care where I lie.
Geo: yate, sculp.
Esay: 1.3.

Christs Victorie, and Triumph.

Christs Victorie in Heaven.

1

The birth of him that no beginning knewe,
Yet gives beginning to all that are borne,
And how the Infinite farre greater grewe,
By growing lesse, and how the rising Morne,
That shot from heav'n, did backe to heaven retourne,
    The obsequies of him that could not die,
    And death of life, ende of eternitie,
How worthily he died, that died unworthily;

The Argument propounded in generall: Our redemption by Christ.

2

How God, and Man did both embrace each other,
Met in one person, heav'n, and earth did kiss,
And how a Virgin did become a Mother,
And bare that Sonne, who the worlds Father is,
And Maker of his mother, and how Bliss
    Descended from the bosome of the High,
    To cloath himselfe in naked miserie,
Sayling at length to heav'n, in earth, triumphantly,

3

Is the first flame, wherewith my whiter Muse
Doth burne in heavenly love, such love to tell.
O thou that didst this holy fire infuse,
And taught'st this brest, but late the grave of hell,
Wherein a blind, and dead heart liv'd, to swell
    With better thoughts, send downe those lights that lend
    Knowledge, how to begin, and how to end
The love, that never was, nor ever can be pend.

The Authors Invocation, for the better handling of it.

4

Ye sacred writings in whose antique leaves
The memories of heav'n entreasur'd lie,

3.3-6 recount his conversion through action of God's grace.

3.8 pend: written, perhaps with pun: limited.

Say, what might be the cause that Mercie heaves
The dust of sinne above th' industrious skie;
And lets it not to dust, and ashes flie?
  Could Justice be of sinne so over-wooed,
  Or so great ill be cause of so great good,
That bloody man to save, mans Saviour shed his blood?

5

The Argument, Mans redemption, expounded from the cause. Mercie

Or did the lips of Mercie droppe soft speech
For traytrous man, when at th' Eternalls throne
Incensed Nemesis did heav'n beseech
With thundring voice, that justice might be showne
Against the Rebells, that from God were flowne;
  O say, say how could Mercie plead for those
  That scarcely made, against their Maker rose?
Will any slay his friend, that he may spare his foes?

6

Dwelling in heaven

There is a place beyond that flaming hill
From whence the starres their thin apparance shed,
A place, beyond all place, where never ill,
Nor impure thought was ever harboured,
But Sainctly Heroes are for ever s'ed
  To keepe an everlasting Sabbaoths rest,
  Still wishing that, of what th' ar still possest,
Enjoying but one joy, but one of all joyes best.

7

And pleading for man now guiltie,

Here, when the ruine of that beauteous frame,
Whose golden building shin'd with everie starre
Of excellence, deform'd with age became,
MERCY, remembring peace in midst of warre,
Lift up the musique of her voice, to barre
  Eternall fate, least it should quite erace

6.1 place: the heaven of heavens as distinguished from the visible sky.

7 gloss: guiltie, : guiltie. 1610.

7.1 frame: the created universe.

7.5 lift: lifted.

That from the world, which was the first worlds grace,
And all againe into their nothing, Chaos, chase.

8

For what had all this All, which Man in one
Did not unite; the earth, aire, water, fire,
Life, sense, and spirit, nay the powrefull throne
Of the divinest Essence, did retire,
And his owne Image into clay inspire:
So that this Creature well might called be
Of the great world, the small epitomie,
Of the dead world, the live, and quicke anatomie.

9

But Justice had no sooner Mercy seene — with Justice, described
Smoothing the wrinkles of her Fathers browe,
But up she starts, and throwes her selfe betweene.
As when a vapour, from a moory slough,
Meeting with fresh Eous, that but now
Open'd the world, which all in darkenesse lay,
Doth heav'ns bright face of his rayes disaray,
And sads the smiling orient of the springing day.

10

She was a Virgin of austere regard, — by her qualities.
Not as the world esteemes her, deafe, and blind,
But as the Eagle, that hath oft compar'd
Her eye with heav'ns, so, and more brightly shin'd
Her lamping sight: for she the same could winde
Into the solid heart, and with her eares,
The silence of the thought loude speaking heares,
And in one hand a paire of even scoals she weares.

7.8 their nothing, Chaos, chase. : their, nothing, Chaos chase. 1610.

8.1 Man: i.e., as microcosm.

8.4 retire: re-attire.

8.8 quicke: living.

9.5 Eous (three syllables): dawn goddess.

10.3 The eagle traditionally looked at the sun to sharpen its sight.

10.8 scoals: scales. weares: bears.

11

No riot of affection revell kept
Within her brest, but a still apathy
Possessed all her soule, which softly slept,
Securely, without tempest, no sad crie
Awakes her pittie, but wrong'd povertie,
  Sending his eyes to heav'n swimming in teares,
  With hideous clamours ever struck her eares,
Whetting the blazing sword, that in her hand she beares.

12

Her Retinue.

The winged Lightning is her Mercury,
And round about her mightie thunders sound:
Impatient of himselfe lies pining by
Pale Sicknes, with his kercher'd head upwound,
And thousand noysome plagues attend her round,
  But if her clowdie browe but once growe foule,
  The flints doe melt, and rocks to water rowle,
And ayrie mountaines shake, and frighted shadowes howle.

13

Famine, and bloodles Care, and bloodie Warre,
Want, and the Want of knowledge how to use
Abundance, Age, and Feare, that runnes afarre
Before his fellowe Greefe, that aye pursues
His winged steps; for who would not refuse
  Greefes companie, a dull, and rawebon'd spright,
  That lankes the cheekes, and pales the freshest sight,
Unbosoming the cheerefull brest of all delight;

14

Before this cursed throng, goes Ignorance,
That needes will leade the way he cannot see:
And after all, Death doeth his flag advaunce,
And in the mid'st, Strife still would roaguing be,

12.1 Mercury: i.e., messenger.

12.6 foule: harsh.

13.7 lankes: makes thin.

14.4 roaguing: acting like a rogue.

Whose ragged flesh, and cloaths did well agree:
    And round about, amazed Horror flies,
    And over all, Shame veiles his guiltie eyes,
And underneth, Hells hungrie throat still yawning lies.

15

Upon two stonie tables, spread before her,
She lean'd her bosome, more then stonie hard,
There slept th' unpartiall judge, and strict restorer
Of wrong, or right, with paine, or with reward,
There hung the skore of all our debts, the card
    Whear good, and bad, and life, and death were painted:
    Was never heart of mortall so untainted,
But when that scroule was read, with thousand terrors fainted.

Her Subject.

16

Witnes the thunder that mount Sinai heard,
When all the hill with firie clouds did flame,
And wandring Israel, with the sight afeard,
Blinded with seeing, durst not touch the same,
But like a wood of shaking leaves became.
    On this dead Justice, she, the Living Lawe,
    Bowing herselfe with a majestique awe,
All heav'n, to heare her speech, did into silence drawe.

17

Dread Lord of Spirits, well thou did'st devise
To fling the worlds rude dunghill, and the drosse
Of the ould Chaos, farthest from the skies,
And thine owne seate, that heare the child of losse,
Of all the lower heav'n the curse, and crosse,
    That wretch, beast, caytive, monster Man, might spend,
    (Proude of the mire, in which his soule is pend)
Clodded in lumps of clay, his wearie life to end.

Her accusation of Mans sinne.

15.1 tables: of the Mosaic law.

15.3 There: where.

15.5 skore: record.

16 from Exodus, the giving of the Old Testament law on Mount Sinai.

17.4 heare: here.

18

And 1. of Adams first sinne.

His bodie dust: whear grewe such cause of pride?
His soule thy Image: what could he envie?
Himselfe most happie: if he so would bide:
Now grow'n most wretched, who can remedie?
He slewe himselfe, himselfe the enemie.
    That his owne soule would her owne murder wreake,
    If I were silent, heav'n and earth would speake,
And if all fayl'd, these stones would into clamours breake.

19

How many darts made furrowes in his side,
When she, that out of his owne side was made,
Gave feathers to their flight? whear was the pride
Of their newe knowledge; whither did it fade,
When, running from thy voice into the shade,
    He fled thy sight, himselfe of sight bereav'd;
    And for his shield a leavie armour weav'd,
With which, vain man, he thought Gods eies to have deceav'd?

20

And well he might delude those eyes, that see,
And judge by colours: for who ever sawe
A man of leaves, a reasonable tree?

Then of his posterities, in all kinde of Idolatrie.

But those that from this stocke their life did drawe,
Soone made their Father godly, and by lawe
    Proclaimed Trees almightie: Gods of wood,
    Of stocks, and stones with crownes of laurell stood
Templed, and fed by fathers with their childrens blood.

21

The sparkling fanes, that burne in beaten gould,
And, like the starres of heav'n in mid'st of night,
Blacke Egypt, as her mirrhours, doth behould,
Are but the denns whear idoll-snakes delight

18.6 her: the soul's.

19.2 she: Eve. The rest of the stanza is from Genesis 3, narrating the fall of man.

21.1 fanes: temples.

Againe to cover Satan from their sight:
    Yet these are all their gods, to whome they vie
    The Crocodile, the Cock, the Rat, the Flie.
Fit gods, indeede, for such men to be served by.

22

The Fire, the winde, the sea, the sunne, and moone,
The flitting Aire, and the swift-winged How'rs,
And all the watchmen, that so nimbly runne,
And centinel about the walled towers
Of the worlds citie, in their heav'nly bowr's.
    And, least their pleasant gods should want delight,
    Neptune spues out the Lady Aphrodite,
And but in heaven proude Junos peacocks skorne to lite.

23

The senselesse Earth, the Serpent, dog, and catte,
And woorse then all these, Man, and woorst of men
Usurping Jove, and swilling Bacchus fat,
And drunke with the vines purple blood, and then
The Fiend himselfe they conjure from his denne,
    Because he onely yet remain'd to be
    Woorse then the worst of men, they flie from thee,
And weare his altar-stones out with their pliant knee.

24

All that he speakes (and all he speakes are lies)
Are oracles, 'tis he (that wounded all)
Cures all their wounds, he (that put out their eyes)
That gives them light, he (that death first did call

22.3 watchmen: stars.

22.5 worlds citie: i.e., in comparison with God's. Cf. the contrast of the two cities in Augustine's *City of God*.

22.6 least: lest.

22.7 One of the legends about the origin of Venus is that she was born from the sea.

22.8 but: only. The peacock was sacred to Juno. The allusion suggests the southern constellation Pavo.

23.5 they: various pagan worshippers of "Earth, the Serpent, . . . The Fiend himselfe."

Into the world) that with his orizall,
    Inspirits earth: he heav'ns al-seeing eye,
    He earths great Prophet, he, whom rest doth flie,
That on salt billowes doth, as pillowes, sleeping lie.

25

How hopelesse any patronage of it.

But let him in his cabin restles rest,
The dungeon of darke flames, and freezing fire,
Justice in heav'n against man makes request
To God, and of his Angels doth require
Sinnes punishment: if what I did desire,
    Or who, or against whome, or why, or whear,
    Of, or before whom ignorant I wear,
Then should my speech their sands of sins to mountaines rear.

26

Wear not the heav'ns pure, in whose courts I sue,
The Judge, to whom I sue, just to requite him,
The cause for sinne, the punishment most due,
Justice her selfe the plaintiffe to endite him,
The Angells holy, before whom I cite him,
    He against whom, wicked, unjust, impure;
    Then might he sinnefull live, and die secure,
Or triall might escape, or triall might endure,

27

The Judge might partiall be, and over-pray'd,
The place appeald from, in whose courts he sues,
The fault excus'd, or punishment delayd,
The parties selfe accus'd, that did accuse,
Angels for pardon might their praiers use:
    But now no starre can shine, no hope be got.
    Most wretched creature, if he knewe his lot,
And yet more wretched farre, because he knowes it not.

24.5 orizall: orison, prayer (?).

25 gloss: it : At 1610.

25.5 I: Justice.

27.1 over-pray'd: over-ruled.

28

All the Creatures having disleagued themselves with him

What should I tell how barren earth is growne,
All for to sterve her children, didst not thou
Water with heav'nly showers her wombe unsowne,
And drop downe cloudes of flow'rs, didst not thou bowe
Thine easie eare unto the plowmans vowe,
    Long might he looke, and looke, and long in vaine
    Might load his harvest in an emptie wayne,
And beat the woods, to finde the poore okes hungrie graine.

29

The swelling sea seethes in his angrie waves,
And smites the earth, that dares the traytors nourish,
Yet oft his thunder their light corke outbraves,
Mowing the mountaines, on whose temples flourish
Whole woods of garlands, and, their pride to cherish,
    Plowe through the seaes greene fields, and nets display
    To catch the flying winds, and steale away,
Coozning the greedie sea, prisning their nimble prey.

30

How often have I seene the waving pine,
Tost on a watrie mountaine, knocke his head
At heav'ns too patient gates, and with salt brine
Quench the Moones burning hornes, and safely fled
From heav'ns revenge, her passengers, all dead
    With stiffe astonishment, tumble to hell?
    How oft the sea all earth would overswell,
Did not thy sandie girdle binde the mightie well?

31

Would not the aire be fill'd with steames of death,
To poyson the quicke rivers of their blood,

28.2 sterve: kill.

28.7 wayne: wagon.

29.6 nets: sails.

30.1 pine: ship's mast.

31.2 quicke: living.

Did not thy windes fan, with their panting breath,
The flitting region? would not the hastie flood
Emptie it selfe into the seas wide wood,
    Did'st not thou leade it wandring from his way,
    To give men drinke, and make his waters strey,
To fresh the flowrie medowes, through whose fields they play?

32

Who makes the sources of the silver fountaines
From the flints mouth, and rocky valleis slide,
Thickning the ayrie bowells of the mountaines?
Who hath the wilde heards of the forrest tide
In their cold denns, making them hungrie bide
    Till man to rest be laid? can beastly he,
    That should have most sense, onely senseles be,
And all things else, beside himselfe, so awefull see?

33

Wear he not wilder then the salvage beast,
Prowder then haughty hills, harder then rocks,
Colder then fountaines, from their springs releast,
Lighter then aire, blinder then senseles stocks,
More changing then the rivers curling locks,
    If reason would not, sense would soone reproove him,
    And unto shame, if not to sorrow, moove him,
To see cold floods, wild beasts, dul stocks, hard stones out-love him.

For his extreame ungratefulnes.

34

Under the weight of sinne the earth did fall,
And swallowed Dathan; and the raging winde,
And stormie sea, and gaping Whale, did call
For Jonas; and the aire did bullets finde,

31.4 flitting: shifting, unsubstantial.

31.5 wood: expanse, figuratively from "forest."

32.4 tide: tied.

34.2 Dathan: He, Korah, and Abiram, rebelling against the authority of Moses, were swallowed up by the earth in punishment. Num. 16:1–33.

34.4 Jonas: Jonah.

And shot from heav'n a stony showre, to grinde
 The five proud Kings, that for their idols fought,
 The Sunne it selfe stood still to fight it out,
And fire from heav'n flew downe, when sin to heav'n did shout.

35

Should any to himselfe for safety flie?
The way to save himselfe, if any were,
Wear to flie from himselfe: should he relie
Upon the promise of his wife? but there,
What can he see, but that he most may feare,
 A Syren, sweete to death: upon his friends?
 Who that he needs, or that he hath not lends?
Or wanting aide himselfe, ayde to another sends?

So that beeing destitute of all hope, or any remedie,

36

His strength? but dust: his pleasure? cause of paine:
His hope? false courtier: youth, or beawtie? brittle:
Intreatie? fond: repentance? late, and vaine:
Just recompence? the world wear all too little:
Thy love? he hath no title to a tittle:
 Hells force? in vaine her furies hell shall gather:
 His Servants, Kinsmen, or his children rather?
His child, if good, shall judge, if bad, shall curse his father.

37

His life? that brings him to his end, and leaves him:
His ende? that leaves him to beginne his woe:
His goods? what good in that, that so deceaves him?
His gods of wood? their feete, alas, are slowe
To goe to helpe, that must be help't to goe:
 Honour, great woorth? ah, little woorth they be
 Unto their owners: wit? that makes him see
He wanted wit, that thought he had it, wanting thee.

34.6 five proud Kings: defeated by Joshua when the sun stood still at his command; Josh. 10:3.

34.8 sin: of 250 followers of Korah (l. 2 above); Num. 16:35.

37.8 wanted: lacked.

38

The sea to drinke him quicke? that casts him dead:
Angells to spare? they punish: night to hide?
The world shall burne in light: the heav'ns to spread
Their wings to save him? heav'n it selfe shall slide,
And rowle away like melting starres, that glide
  Along their oylie threads: his minde pursues him:
  His house to shrowde, or hills to fall, and bruse him?
As Seargeants both attache, and witnesses accuse him:

39

He can look for nothing, but a fearful sentence.

What need I urge, what they must needs confesse?
Sentence on them, condemn'd by their owne lust;
I crave no more, and thou canst give no lesse,
Then death to dead men, justice to unjust;
Shame to most shamefull, and most shameles dust:
  But if thy Mercie needs will spare her friends,
  Let Mercie there begin, where Justice endes.
Tis cruell Mercie, that the wrong from right defends.

40

The effect of Justice her speech: the inflammation of the heavenly Powers,

She ended, and the heav'nly Hierarchies,
Burning in zeale, thickly imbranded weare:
Like to an armie, that allarum cries,
And every one shakes his ydraded speare,
And the Almighties selfe, as he would teare
  The earth, and her firme basis quite in sunder,
  Flam'd all in just revenge, and mightie thunder,
Heav'n stole it selfe from earth by clouds that moisterd under.

41

Appeased by Mercie, who is described by her cherfulnes to defend Man.

As when the cheerfull Sunne, elamping wide,
Glads all the world with his uprising raye,

38.1 quicke: alive. casts him : casts his 1610.

38.5 melting: shooting.

38.8 Seargeants: those who summon persons to appear before a court or arrest (attache) them.

40.2 imbranded: armed with brands or swords.

40.8 moisterd under: rained.

41.1 elamping: shining forth.

And wooes the widow'd earth afresh to pride,
And paints her bosome with the flowrie Maye,
His silent sister steales him quite away,
    Wrap't in a sable clowde, from mortall eyes,
    The hastie starres at noone begin to rise,
And headlong to his early roost the sparrowe flies.

42

But soone as he againe dishadowed is,
Restoring the blind world his blemish't sight,
As though another day wear newely ris,
The cooz'ned birds busily take their flight,
And wonder at the shortnesse of the night:
    So Mercie once againe her selfe displayes,
    Out from her sisters cloud, and open layes
Those sunshine lookes, whose beames would dim a thousand dayes.

43

Our inabilitie to describe her.

How may a worme, that crawles along the dust,
Clamber the azure mountaines, thrown so high,
And fetch from thence thy faire Idea just,
That in those sunny courts doth hidden lie,
Cloath'd with such light, as blinds the Angels eye;
    How may weake mortall ever hope to file
    His unsmooth tongue, and his deprostrate stile?
O raise thou from his corse, thy now entomb'd exile.

44

One touch would rouze me from my sluggish hearse,
One word would call me to my wished home,
One looke would polish my afflicted verse,
One thought would steale my soule from her thicke lome,
And force it wandring up to heav'n to come,
    Thear to importune, and to beg apace
    One happy favour of thy sacred grace,
To see, (what though it loose her eyes?) to see thy face.

41.4 paints : paint 1610.
41.5 silent sister: the moon, eclipsing the sun.
43.7 deprostrate: extremely prostrate.
44.8 loose: lose.

45

Her beautie, resembled by the creatures, which are all fraile shadows of her essentiall perfection.

If any aske why roses please the sight,
Because their leaves upon thy cheekes doe bowre;
If any aske why lillies are so white,
Because their blossoms in thy hand doe flowre:
Or why sweet plants so gratefull odours shoure;
It is because thy breath so like they be:
Or why the Orient Sunne so bright we see;
What reason can we give, but from thine eies, and thee?

46

Ros'd all in lively crimsin ar thy cheeks,
Whear beawties indeflourishing abide,
And, as to passe his fellowe either seekes,
Seemes both doe blush at one anothers pride:
And on thine eyelids, waiting thee beside,

Her Attendants.

Ten thousand Graces sit, and when they moove
To earth their amourous belgards from above,
They flie from heav'n, and on their wings convey thy love.

47

All of discolour'd plumes their wings ar made,
And with so wondrous art the quills ar wrought,
That whensoere they cut the ayrie glade,
The winde into their hollowe pipes is caught:
As seemes the spheres with them they down have brought:
Like to the seaven-fold reede of Arcadie,
Which Pan of Syrinx made, when she did flie
To Ladon sands, and at his sighs sung merily.

48

Her perswasive power.

As melting hony, dropping from the combe,
So still the words, that spring between thy lipps,

45.2 Because: it is because.

46.2 indeflourishing: not ceasing to flourish.

46.7 belgards: loving looks.

47.1 discolour'd: variegated.

47.7 Syrinx fled Pan and was changed into a reed bed from which he made his pipes. Her father was the river Ladon. The music is compared with the fabled music of the spheres (l. 5).

Thy lippes, whear smiling sweetnesse keepes her home,
And heav'nly Eloquence pure manna sipps,
He that his pen but in that fountaine dipps,
    How nimbly will the golden phrases flie,
    And shed forth streames of choycest rhetorie,
Welling celestiall torrents out of poësie?

49

Like as the thirstie land, in summers heat,
Calls to the cloudes, and gapes at everie showre,
As though her hungry clifts all heav'n would eat,
Which if high God into her bosome powre,
Though much refresht, yet more she could devoure:
    So hang the greedie ears of Angels sweete,
    And every breath a thousand cupids meete,
Some flying in, some out, and all about her fleet.

50

Upon her breast, Delight doth softly sleepe,
And of eternall joy is brought abed,
Those snowie mountelets, through which doe creepe
The milkie rivers, that ar inly bred
In silver cesternes, and themselves doe shed
    To wearie Travailers, in heat of day,
    To quench their fierie thirst, and to allay
With dropping nectar floods, the furie of their way.

51

Her kind offices to Man.

If any wander, thou doest call him backe,
If any be not forward, thou incit'st him,
Thou doest expect, if any should growe slacke,
If any seeme but willing, thou invit'st him,
Or if he doe offend thee, thou acquit'st him,
    Thou find'st the lost, and follow'st him that flies,
    Healing the sicke, and quickening him that dies,
Thou art the lame mans friendly staffe, the blind mans eyes.

49.3 clifts: clefts, fissures.
50.7 thirst : thrist 1610.

52

So faire thou art that all would thee behold,
But none can thee behold, thou art so faire,
Pardon, O pardon then thy Vassall bold,
That with poore shadowes strives thee to compare,
And match the things, which he knowes matchlesse are;
O thou vive mirrhour of celestiall grace,
How can fraile colours pourtraict out thy face,
Or paint in flesh thy beawtie, in such semblance base?

53

Her Garments, wrought by her owne hands, wherwith shee cloaths her selfe, composd of all the Creatures,

Her upper garment was a silken lawne,
With needle-woorke richly embroidered,
Which she her selfe with her owne hand had drawne,
And all the world therein had pourtrayed,
With threads, so fresh, and lively coloured,
That seem'd the world she newe created thear,
And the mistaken eye would rashly swear
The silken trees did growe, and the beasts living wear.

54

The Earth,

Low at her feet the Earth was cast alone,
(As though to kisse her foot it did aspire,
And gave it selfe for her to tread upon)
With so unlike, and different attire,
That every one that sawe it, did admire
What it might be, was of so various hewe;
For to it selfe it oft so diverse grewe,
That still it seem'd the same, and still it seem'd a newe.

55

And here, and there few men she scattered,
(That in their thought the world esteeme but small,
And themselves great) but she with one fine thread
So short, and small, and slender wove them all,
That like a sort of busie ants, that crawle
About some molehill, so they wandered:

52.6 vive: lifelike.

54.6 be: be, that.

And round about the waving Sea was shed,
But, for the silver sands, small pearls were sprinkled.

Sea,

56

So curiously the underworke did creepe,
And curling circlets so well shadowed lay,
That afar off the waters seem'd to sleepe,
But those that neere the margin pearle did play,
Hoarcely enwaved wear with hastie sway,
As though they meant to rocke the gentle eare,
And hush the former that enslumbred wear,
And here a dangerous rocke the flying ships did fear.

57

High in the ayrie element there hung
Another clowdy sea, that did disdaine
(As though his purer waves from heaven sprung)
To crawle on earth, as doth the sluggish maine:
But it the earth would water with his raine,
That eb'd, and flow'd, as winde, and season would,
And oft the Sun would cleave the limber mould
To alabaster rockes, that in the liquid rowl'd.

Ayre,

58

Beneath those sunny banks, a darker cloud,
Dropping with thicker deaw, did melt apace,
And bent it selfe into a hollowe shroude,
On which, if Mercy did but cast her face,
A thousand colours did the bowe enchace,
That wonder was to see the silke distain'd
With the resplendance from her beawtie gain'd,
And Iris paint her locks with beames, so lively feign'd.

59

About her head a cyprus heav'n she wore,
Spread like a veile, upheld with silver wire,

The celestiall bodies,

57.8 alabaster rockes: i.e., clouds.

58.6 distain'd: dyed.

59.1 cyprus: cypress, a light, transparent material.

In which the starres so burn't in golden ore,
As seem'd, the azure web was all on fire,
But hastily, to quench their sparkling ire,
   A flood of milke came rowling up the shore,
   That on his curded wave swift Argus bore,
And the immortall swan, that did her life deplore.

60

Yet strange it was, so many starres to see
Without a Sunne, to give their tapers light:
Yet strange it was not, that it so should be:
For, where the Sunne centers himselfe by right,
Her face, and locks did flame, that at the sight,
   The heavenly veile, that else should nimbly moove,
   Forgot his flight, and all incens'd with love,
With wonder, and amazement, did her beautie proove.

61

The third heaven.

Over her hung a canopie of state,
Not of rich tissew, nor of spangled gold,
But of a substance, though not animate,
Yet of a heav'nly, and spirituall mould,
That onely eyes of Spirits might behold:
   Such light as from maine rocks of diamound,
   Shooting their sparks at Phebus, would rebound,
And little Angels, holding hands, daunc't all around.

62

Seemed those little sprights, through nimbless bold,
The stately canopy bore on their wings,

59.6 the Milky Way.

59.7 Argus: the constellation.

59.8 swan: Cygnus, another constellation.

60.2 Sunne: thought to be the source of light in the stars. See *Paradise Lost*, 7. 364ff.

60.8 proove: commend.

61 gloss: mentioned by Paul in 2 Cor. 12:2 and usually interpreted (e.g., Geneva Bible margin note) as the highest heaven, invisible (l. 5) to men.

61.6 maine: large.

62.1 nimbless: nimbleness.

But them it selfe, as pendants, did uphold,
Besides the crownes of many famous kings,
Among the rest, thear David ever sings,
  And now, with yeares growne young, renewes his layes
  Unto his golden harpe, and ditties playes,
Psalming aloud in well tun'd songs his Makers prayse.

63

Thou self-Idea of all joyes to come,
Whose love is such, would make the rudest speake,
Whose love is such, would make the wisest dumbe,
O when wilt thou thy too long silence breake,
And overcome the strong to save the weake!
  If thou no weapons hast, thine eyes will wound
  Th' Almighties selfe, that now sticke on the ground,
As though some blessed object thear did them empound. Her Objects.

64

Ah miserable Abject of disgrace, Repentance.
What happines is in thy miserie?
I both must pittie, and envie thy case.
For she, that is the glorie of the skie,
Leaves heaven blind, to fix on thee her eye.
  Yet her (though Mercies selfe esteems not small)
  The world despis'd, they her Repentance call,
And she her selfe despises, and the world, and all.

65

Deepely, alas empassioned she stood,
To see a flaming brand, tost up from hell,
Boyling her heart in her owne lustfull blood,
That oft for torment she would loudely yell,
Now she would sighing sit, and nowe she fell
  Crouching upon the ground, in sackcloath trust,

63.1 self-Idea: representation.
63.2 such: such, as.
63.7 that: i.e., thine eyes.
63.8 empound: confine.
64.7 despis'd : despisd' 1610.
65.6 trust: trussed.

Early, and late she prayed, and fast she must,
And all her haire hung full of ashes, and of dust.

66

Of all most hated, yet hated most of all
Of her owne selfe she was; disconsolat
(As though her flesh did but infunerall
Her buried ghost) she in an arbour sat
Of thornie brier, weeping her cursed state,
And her before a hastie river fled,
Which her blind eyes with faithfull penance fed,
And all about, the grasse with tears hung downe his head.

67

Her eyes, though blind abroad, at home kept fast,
Inwards they turn'd, and look't into her head,
At which shee often started, as aghast,
To see so fearfull spectacles of dread,
And with one hand, her breast shee martyred,
Wounding her heart, the same to mortifie,
The other a faire damsell held her by,
Which if but once let goe, shee sunke immediatly.

Faith.

68

But Faith was quicke, and nimble as the heav'n,
As if of love, and life shee all had been,
And though of present sight her sense were reaven,
Yet shee could see the things could not be seen:
Beyond the starres, as nothing wear between,
She fixt her sight, disdeigning things belowe,
Into the sea she could a mountaine throwe,
And make the Sun to stande, and waters backewards flowe.

69

Such when as Mercie her beheld from high,
In a darke valley, drownd with her owne tears,
One of her graces she sent hastily,

66.7 blind: i.e., with tears.

68.4 things: things that.

Smiling Eirene, that a garland wears
Of guilded olive, on her fairer hears,
    To crowne the fainting soules true sacrifice,
    Whom when as sad Repentance comming spies,
The holy Desperado wip't her swollen eyes.

70

But Mercie felt a kinde remorse to runne
Through her soft vaines, and therefore, hying fast
To give an end to silence, thus begunne.
Aye-honour'd Father, if no joy thou hast
But to reward desert, reward at last
    The Devils voice, spoke with a serpents tongue,
    Fit to hisse out the words so deadly stung,
And let him die, deaths bitter charmes so sweetely sung.

Her deprecative speech for Man, in which

71

He was the father of that hopeles season,
That so serve other Gods, forgot their owne,
The reason was, thou wast above their reason:
They would have any Gods, rather then none,
A beastly serpent, or a senselesse stone:
    And these, as Justice hates, so I deplore:
    But the up-plowed heart, all rent, and tore,
Though wounded by it selfe, I gladly would restore.

She translates the principal fault unto the Devill.

72

He was but dust; Why fear'd he not to fall?
And beeing fall'n, how can he hope to live?
Cannot the hand destroy him, that made all?
Could he not take away, aswell as give?
Should man deprave, and should not God deprive?
    Was it not all the worlds deceiving spirit,
    (That, bladder'd up with pride of his owne merit,
Fell in his rise) that him of heav'n did disinherit?

And repeating Justice her aggravation of mans sinne,

69.4 Eirene: Peace.
69.5 hears: hairs.
70.8 die: die, who.
72 gloss: sinne, : sinne. 1610.
72.7 bladder'd: swelled.

73

Mittigates it
1. by a contrarie inference.

He was but dust: how could he stand before him?
And beeing fall'n, why should he feare to die?
Cannot the hand that made him first, restore him?
Deprav'd of sinne, should he deprived lie
Of grace? can he not hide infirmitie
That gave him strength? unworthy the forsaking,
He is, who ever weighs, without mistaking,
Or Maker of the man, or manner of his making.

74

Who shall thy temple incense any more;
Or to thy altar crowne the sacrifice;
Or strewe with idle flow'rs the hallow'd flore;
Or what should Prayer deck with hearbs, and spice,
Her vialls, breathing orisons of price?

2. By interessing her selfe in the cause, and Christ.

If all must paie that which all cannot paie?
O first begin with mee, and Mercie slaie,
And thy thrice-honour'd Sonne, that now beneath doth strey.

75

But if or he, or I may live, and speake,
And heav'n can joye to see a sinner weepe,
Oh let not Justice yron scepter breake
A heart alreadie broke, that lowe doth creep,
And with prone humblesse her feets dust doth sweep.
Must all goe by desert? is nothing free?
Ah, if but those that onely woorthy be,
None should thee ever see, none should thee ever see.

76

That is as sufficient to satisfie, as Man was impotent.

What hath man done, that man shall not undoe,
Since God to him is growne so neere a kin?
Did his foe slay him? he shall slay his foe:

74 gloss: interessing: concerning.

74.5 vialls: see Rev. 5:8: various heavenly beings have "harps, and golden vials full of odors, which are the prayers of saints."

74.8 strey: stray, wander.

Hath he lost all? he all againe shall win;
Is Sinne his Master? he shall master sinne:
    Too hardy soule, with sinne the field to trie:
    The onely way to conquer, was to flie,
But thus long death hath liv'd, and now deaths selfe shall die.

77

He is a path, if any be misled,
He is a robe, if any naked bee,
If any chaunce to hunger, he is bread,
If any be a bondman, he is free,
If any be but weake, howe strong is hee?
    To dead men life he is, to sicke men health,
    To blinde men sight, and to the needie wealth,
A pleasure without losse, a treasure without stealth.

78

Whom shee celebrates from the time of his nativitie.

Who can forget, never to be forgot,
The time, that all the world in slumber lies,
When, like the starres, the singing Angels shot
To earth, and heav'n awaked all his eyes,
To see another Sunne, at midnight rise,
    On earth? was never sight of pareil fame,
    For God before Man like himselfe did frame,
But God himselfe now like a mortall man became.

79

From the effects of it in himselfe.

A Child he was, and had not learn't to speake,
That with his word the world before did make,
His Mothers armes him bore, he was so weake,
That with one hand the vaults of heav'n could shake,
See how small roome my infant Lord doth take,
    Whom all the world is not enough to hold.
    Who of his yeares, or of his age hath told?
Never such age so young, never a child so old.

78.6 earth? : earrh? 1610. pareil: equal.

79.2 word: the creative Word of John 1, "without which not anything was made that was made."

80

And yet but newely he was infanted,
And yet alreadie he was sought to die,
Yet scarcely borne, alreadie banished,
Not able yet to goe, and forc't to flie,
But scarcely fled away, when by and by,
    The Tyrans sword with blood is all defil'd,
    And Rachel, for her sonnes with furie wild,
Cries, O thou cruell King, and O my sweetest child.

81

Egypt,

Egypt his Nource became, whear Nilus springs,
Who streit, to entertaine the rising sunne,
The hasty harvest in his bosome brings;
But now for drieth the fields wear all undone,
And now with waters all is overrunne,
    So fast the Cynthian mountaines powr'd their snowe,
    When once they felt the sunne so neere them glowe,
That Nilus Egypt lost, and to a sea did growe.

82

The Angels,

Men.

The Angells caroll'd lowd their song of peace,
The cursed Oracles wear strucken dumb,
To see their Sheapheard, the poore Sheapheards press,
To see their King, the Kingly Sophies come,
And them to guide unto his Masters home,
    A Starre comes dauncing up the orient,
    That springs for joye over the strawy tent,
Whear gold, to make their Prince a crowne, they all present.

80.4 flie: i.e., to Egypt to escape Herod. Matt. 2:13ff.

80.7 Rachel: a quotation in Matt. 2:18 explaining Herod's slaughter of the children as fulfillment of a prophecy.

81.4 But: until. drieth: drought.

81.6 Cynthian: i.e., Mountains of the Moon, the supposed source of the Nile.

82 Having completed the story of Jesus' birth as given in Matthew, Fletcher now turns to the account in Luke.

82.2 The cessation of the pagan oracles at the time of Jesus' birth was apparently verified by Plutarch's account, *Of the Cessation of the Oracles*, Prudentius' *Apotheosis*, and Athanasius' *On the Incarnation* 47.

82.4 Sophies: wise men, Matt. 2:1ff.

83

Young John, glad child, before he could be borne,
Leapt in the woombe, his joy to prophecie,
Old Anna though with age all spent, and worne,
Proclaimes her Saviour to posteritie,
And Simeon fast his dying notes doeth plie.
    Oh how the blessed soules about him trace.
    It is the fire of heav'n thou doest embrace,
Sing, Simeon, sing, sing Simeon, sing apace.

84

The effect of Mercies speech.

With that the mightie thunder dropt away
From Gods unwarie arme, now milder growne,
And melted into teares, as if to pray
For pardon, and for pittie, it had knowne,
That should have been for sacred vengeance throwne:
    Thereto the Armies Angelique devow'd
    Their former rage, and all to Mercie bow'd,
Their broken weapons at her feet they gladly strow'd.

85

A Transition to Christs second victorie.

Bring, bring ye Graces all your silver flaskets,
Painted with every choicest flowre that growes,
That I may soone unflow'r your fragrant baskets,
To strowe the fields with odours whear he goes,
Let what so e're he treads on be a rose.
    So downe shee let her eyelids fall, to shine
    Upon the rivers of bright Palestine,
Whose woods drop honie, and her rivers skip with wine.

83.1 John: i.e., the Baptist. The story is told in Luke 1:41ff.; that of Anna is in 2:36ff.; and that of Simeon in 2:25ff.

84.6 devow'd : devo'wed 1610: disavowed.

84.7 bow'd : bo'wd 1610.

How many riddlinge thoughts strangly appeare
Unfolded in this shadow: for first here
I see the Fountaine in the Streams. I see
the water wahd by washing in't. And wee urd
through nature black to pitch, and inck are sco
to snow, while water's on an other pour'd
I see againe. Ile not say all I can
least I turne Jordan to an Ocean
G:Y·sculp

Christs Victorie on Earth.

1

Thear all alone she spi'd, alas the while;
In shadie darknes a poore Desolate,
That now had measur'd many a wearie mile,
Through a wast desert, whither heav'nly fate,
And his owne will him brought; he praying sate,
    And him to prey, as he to pray began,
    The Citizens of the wilde forrest ran,
And all with open throat would swallowe whole the man.

Christ brought into the place of combat, the wildernes, among the wilde beasts. Mark 1. 13.

2

Soone did the Ladie to her Graces crie,
And on their wings her selfe did nimbly strowe,
After her coach a thousand Loves did flie,
So downe into the wildernesse they throwe,
Whear she, and all her trayne that with her flowe
    Thorough the ayrie wave, with sayles so gay,
    Sinking into his brest that wearie lay,
Made shipwracke of themselves, and vanish't quite away.

Described by his proper Attribute, The Mercie of God.

3

Seemed that Man had them devoured all,
Whome to devoure the beasts did make pretence,
But him their salvage thirst did nought appall,
Though weapons none he had for his defence:
What armes for Innocence, but Innocence?
    For when they saw their Lords bright cognizance
    Shine in his face, soone did they disadvaunce,
And some unto him kneele, and some about him daunce.

1 gloss: Mark I. 13. : Mark. 1610.

2 gloss: Attribute, : Attribute. 1610.

2.2 strowe: strew, spread out.

4

Whom the creatures cannot but adore.

Downe fell the Lordly Lions angrie mood,
And he himselfe fell downe, in congies lowe;
Bidding him welcome to his wastfull wood,
Sometime he kist the grasse whear he did goe,
And, as to wash his feete he well did knowe,
With fauning tongue he lickt away the dust,
And every one would neerest to him thrust,
And every one, with new, forgot his former lust.

5

Unmindfull of himselfe, to minde his Lord,
The Lamb stood gazing by the Tygers side,
As though betweene them they had made accord,
And on the Lions back the goate did ride,
Forgetfull of the roughnes of the hide,
If he stood still, their eyes upon him bayted,
If walk't, they all in order on him wayted,
And when he slep't, they as his watch themselves conceited.

6

By his unitie with the Godhead.

Wonder doeth call me up to see, O no,
I cannot see, and therefore sinke in woonder,
The man, that shines as bright as God, not so,
For God he is himselfe, that close lies under
That man, so close, that no time can dissunder
That band, yet not so close, but from him breake
Such beames, as mortall eyes are all too weake
Such sight to see, or it, if they should see, to speake.

7

His proper place.

Upon a grassie hillock he was laid,
With woodie primroses befreckeled,
Over his head the wanton shadowes plaid
Of a wilde olive, that her bowgh's so spread,
As with her leav's she seem'd to crowne his head,
And her greene armes to' embrace the Prince of peace,
The Sunne so neere, needs must the winter cease,
The Sunne so neere, another Spring seem'd to increase.

4.2 congies: bows.

8

His haire was blacke, and in small curls did twine,
As though it wear the shadowe of some light,
And underneath his face, as day, did shine,
But sure the day shined not halfe so bright,
Nor the Sunnes shadowe made so darke a night.
Under his lovely locks, her head to shroude,
Did make Humilitie her selfe growe proude,
Hither, to light their lamps, did all the Graces croude.

The beutie of his bodie.
Cant. 5. 11.
Psalm 45. 2.

9

One of ten thousand soules I am, and more,
That of his eyes, and their sweete wounds complaine,
Sweete are the wounds of love, never so sore,
Ah might he often slaie mee so againe.
He never lives, that thus is never slaine.
What boots it watch? those eyes, for all my art,
Mine owne eyes looking on, have stole my heart,
In them Love bends his bowe, and dips his burning dart.

10

As when the Sunne, caught in an adverse clowde,
Flies crosse the world, and thear a new begets,
The watry picture of his beautie proude,
Throwes all abroad his sparkling spangelets,
And the whole world in dire amazement sets,
To see two dayes abroad at once, and all
Doubt whither nowe he rise, or nowe will fall:
So flam'd the Godly flesh, proude of his heav'nly thrall.

11

His cheekes as snowie apples, sop't in wine,
Had their red roses quencht with lillies white,

Gen. 49. 12.
Cant. 5. 10.

8 gloss: Song of Songs so describes the bridegroom, often interpreted as Christ. Ps. 45:2 describes a "king" (also interpreted as Christ) as "fairer than the children of men" — authorities for the remarkably physical description that follows, conventionally Petrarchan if addressed to a woman.

Psalm 45 : Psalm. 45 1610.

9.6 What boots it watch?: What good does it do to be watchful or careful?

11 gloss: "his eyes shall be red with wine, and his teeth white with milk," Gen. 49:12; "My beloved is white and ruddy," Song of Songs 5:10; "he [inter-

And like to garden strawberries did shine,
Wash't in a bowle of milke, or rose-buds bright
Unbosoming their brests against the light:
    Here love-sicke soules did eat, thear dranke, and made
    Sweete-smelling posies, that could never fade,
But worldly eyes him thought more like some living shade.

Isa. 53. 2.

12

For laughter never look't upon his browe,
Though in his face all smiling joyes did bide,
No silken banners did about him flowe,
Fooles make their fetters ensignes of their pride:
He was best cloath'd when naked was his side,
    A Lambe he was, and wollen fleece he bore,
    Wove with one thread, his feete lowe sandalls wore,
But bared were his legges, so went the times of yore.

13

As two white marble pillars that uphold
Gods holy place whear he in glorie sets,
And rise with goodly grace and courage bold,
To beare his Temple on their ample jetts,
Vein'd every whear with azure rivulets,
    Whom all the people on some holy morne,
    With boughs and flowrie garlands doe adorne,
Of such, though fairer farre, this Temple was upborne.

14

By preparing himself to the combate

Twice had Diana bent her golden bowe,
And shot from heav'n her silver shafts, to rouse
The sluggish salvages, that den belowe,
And all the day in lazie covert drouze,
Since him the silent wildernesse did house,

preted as Christ] hath no form nor comeliness; and when we shall see him, there is no beauty that we should desire him," Isa. 53:2.

13.1 Cf. the two pillars (of brass) designed for Solomon's temple (1 Kings 7:15–22), developed by Paul (1 Cor. 6:19) to represent the body.

13.4 jetts: projections.

14.1 Twice: i.e., two new moons. Jesus was in the wilderness for forty days before being tempted.

The heav'n his roofe, and arbour harbour was,
The ground his bed, and his moist pillowe grasse.
But fruit thear none did growe, nor rivers none did passe.

15

At length an aged Syre farre off he sawe
Come slowely footing, everie step he guest
One of his feete he from the grave did drawe,
Three legges he had, the woodden was the best,
And all the waie he went, he ever blest
With benedicities, and prayers store,
But the bad ground was blessed ne'r the more,
And all his head with snowe of Age was waxen hore.

With his Adversarie, that seemd what he was not,

16

A good old Hermit he might seeme to be,
That for devotion had the world forsaken,
And now was travailing some Saint to see,
Since to his beads he had himselfe betaken,
Whear all his former sinnes he might awaken,
And them might wash away with dropping brine,
And almes, and fasts, and churches discipline,
And dead, might rest his bones under the holy shrine.

Some devout Essene.

17

But when he neerer came, he lowted lowe
With prone obeysance, and with curt'sie kinde,
That at his feete his head he seemd to throwe;
What needs him now another Saint to finde?
Affections are the sailes, and faith the wind,
That to this Saint a thousand soules conveigh
Each hour': O happy Pilgrims thither strey!
What caren they for beasts, or for the wearie way?

18

Soone the old Palmer his devotions sung,
Like pleasing anthems, moduled in time,

16 gloss: Essene: a Jewish sect of Jesus' time.
17.1 lowted: bowed.
18.2 moduled: modulated, musically.

For well that aged Syre could tip his tongue
With golden foyle of eloquence, and lime,
And licke his rugged speech with phrases prime.
    Ay me, quoth he, how many yeares have beene,
    Since these old eyes the Sunne of heav'n have seene!
Certes the Sonne of heav'n they now behold I weene.

19

Ah, mote my humble cell so blessed be
As heav'n to welcome in his lowely roofe,
And be the Temple for thy deitie!
Loe how my cottage worships thee aloofe,
That under ground hath hid his head, in proofe
    It doth adore thee with the feeling lowe,
    Here honie, milke, and chesnuts wild doe growe,
The boughs a bed of leaves upon thee shall bestowe.

20

(Closely tempting him to despaire of Gods providence, and provide for himselfe.)

But oh, he said, and therewith sigh't full deepe,
The heav'ns, alas, too envious are growne,
Because our fields thy presence from them keepe;
For stones doe growe, where corne was lately sowne:
(So stooping downe, he gather'd up a stone)
    But thou with corne canst make this stone to eare.
    What needen we the angrie heav'ns to feare?
Let them envie us still, so we enjoy thee here.

21

But was what he seemed not, Satan, & would faine have lead him

Thus on they wandred, but those holy weeds
A monstrous Serpent, and no man did cover.
So under greenest hearbs the Adder feeds:
And round about that stinking corps did hover
The dismall Prince of gloomie night, and over
    His ever-damned head the Shadowes err'd
    Of thousand peccant ghosts, unseene, unheard,
And all the Tyrant feares, and all the Tyrant fear'd.

18.4 lime: set to entrap, from birdlime.
20 gloss: Closely: secretly.
21.6 err'd: wandered.
21.7 peccant: evil.

22

He was the Sonne of blackest Acheron,
Whear many frozen soules doe chattring lie,
And rul'd the burning waves of Phlegethon,
Whear many more in flaming sulphur frie,
At once compel'd to live and forc't to die,
Whear nothing can be heard for the loud crie
Of oh, and ah, and out alas that I
Or once againe might live, or once at length might die.

23

Ere long they came neere to a balefull bowre,
Much like the mouth of that infernall cave,
That gaping stood all Commers to devoure,
Darke, dolefull, dreary, like a greedy grave,
That still for carrion carkasses doth crave.
The ground no hearbs, but venomous did beare,
Nor ragged trees did leave, but every whear
Dead bones, and skulls wear cast, and bodies hanged wear.

1. To Desperation, charac̃terd by his place,

24

Upon the roofe the bird of sorrowe sat
Elonging joyfull day with her sad note,
And through the shady aire, the fluttring bat
Did wave her leather sayles, and blindely flote,
While with her wings the fatall Shreechowle smote
Th' unblessed house, thear, on a craggy stone,
Celeno hung, and made his direfull mone,
And all about the murdered ghosts did shreek, and grone.

25

Like clowdie moonshine, in some shadowie grove,
Such was the light in which DESPAIRE did dwell,

22.1, 3 Acheron, Phlegethon: rivers of Hades.
23.2 cave: hell's mouth.
24.1 bird of sorrowe: the raven.
24.2 elonging: delaying.
24.7 Celeno: a harpy.
24.8 grone. : grone, 1610.

Countenance, Apparell, horrible apparitions, &c.

But he himselfe with night for darkenesse strove.
His blacke uncombed locks dishevell'd fell
About his face, through which, as brands of hell,
  Sunk in his skull, his staring eyes did glowe,
  That made him deadly looke, their glimpse did showe
Like Cockatrices eyes, that sparks of poyson throwe.

26

His cloaths wear ragged clouts, with thornes pind fast,
And as he musing lay, to stonie fright
A thousand wilde Chimera's would him cast:
As when a fearefull dreame, in mid'st of night,
Skips to the braine, and phansies to the sight
  Some winged furie, strait the hasty foot,
  Eger to flie, cannot plucke up his root,
The voyce dies in the tongue, and mouth gapes without boot.

27

Now he would dreame that he from heaven fell,
And then would snatch the ayre, afraid to fall;
And now he thought he sinking was to hell,
And then would grasp the earth, and now his stall
Him seemed hell, and then he out would crawle,
  And ever, as he crept, would squint aside,
  Lest him, perhaps, some Furie had espide,
And then, alas, he should in chaines for ever bide.

28

Therefore he softly shrunke, and stole away,
Ne ever durst to drawe his breath for feare,
Till to the doore he came, and thear he lay
Panting for breath, as though he dying were,
And still he thought, he felt their craples teare
  Him by the heels backe to his ougly denne,
  Out faine he would have leapt abroad, but then
The heav'n, as hell, he fear'd, that punish guilty men.

25.8 Cockatrices: basilisks, supposed to kill with a glance.
26.3 Chimera's: fantasies.
26.8 boot: avail, remedy.
28.5 craples: grapnels.

29

Within the gloomie hole of this pale wight
The Serpent woo'd him with his charmes to inne,
Thear he might baite the day, and rest the night,
But under that same baite a fearefull grin
Was readie to intangle him in sinne.
    But he upon ambrosia daily fed,
    That grew in Eden, thus he answered,
So both away wear caught, and to the Temple fled.

30

Well knewe our Saviour this the Serpent was,
And the old Serpent knewe our Saviour well,
Never did any this in falshood passe,
Never did any him in truth excell:
With him we fly to heav'n, from heav'n we fell
    With him: but nowe they both together met
    Upon the sacred pinnacles, that threat
With their aspiring tops, Astræas starrie seat.

31

Here did PRESUMPTION her pavillion spread,
Over the Temple, the bright starres among,
(Ah that her foot should trample on the head
Of that most reverend place!) and a lewd throng
Of wanton boyes sung her a pleasant song
    Of love, long life, of mercie, and of grace,
    And every one her deerely did embrace,
And she herselfe enamour'd was of her owne face.

2. To Presumption, characterd by her place,

Attendants, &c.

32

A painted face, belied with vermeyl store,
Which light Eüëlpis every day did trimme,

29.2 inne: enter.

29.3 Thear: where. baite: stay during.

29.8 moving to the second temptation, on the Temple.

30.8 Astræa: goddess of Justice, driven from earth by mankind to become the constellation Virgo.

32.2 Eüëlpis: a name coined from a Greek adjective meaning hopeful or cheerful.

That in one hand a guilded anchor wore,
Not fixed on the rocke, but on the brimme
Of the wide aire she let it loosely swimme:
  Her other hand a sprinkle carried,
  And ever, when her Ladie wavered,
Court-holy water all upon her sprinkeled.

33

Poore foole, she thought herselfe in wondrous price
With God, as if in Paradise she wear,
But, wear shee not in a fooles paradise,
She might have seene more reason to despere:
But him she, like some ghastly fiend, did feare,
  And therefore as that wretch hew'd out his cell
  Under the bowels, in the heart of hell,
So she above the Moone, amid the starres would dwell.

34

Her Tent with sunny cloudes was seel'd aloft,
And so exceeding shone with a false light,
That heav'n it selfe to her it seemed oft,
Heav'n without cloudes to her deluded sight,
But cloudes withouten heav'n it was aright,
  And as her house was built, so did her braine
  Build castles in the aire, with idle paine,
But heart she never had in all her body vaine.

35

Like as a ship, in which no ballance lies,
Without a Pilot, on the sleeping waves,
Fairely along with winde, and water flies,
And painted masts with silken sayles embraves,
That Neptune selfe the bragging vessell saves,
  To laugh a while at her so proud aray;
  Her waving streamers loosely shee lets play,
And flagging colours shine as bright as smiling day:

33.5 him: Desperation (of st. 23).

34.1 seel'd: canopied.

35.1 ballance: balance-reef, a sail used to steady a ship in stormy weather.

36

But all so soone as heav'n his browes doth bend,
Shee veils her banners, and pulls in her beames,
The emptie barke the raging billows send
Up to th' Olympique waves, and Argus seemes
Againe to ride upon our lower streames:
    Right so PRESUMPTION did her selfe behave,
    Tossed about with every stormie wave,
And in white lawne shee went, most like an Angel brave.

37

Gently our Saviour shee began to shrive,
Whither he wear the Sonne of God, or no;
For any other shee disdeign'd to wive:
And if he wear, shee bid him fearles throw
Himselfe to ground, and thearwithall did show
    A flight of little Angels, that did wait
    Upon their glittering wings, to latch him strait,
And longed on their backs to feele his glorious weight.

And by her Temptation.

38

But when she saw her speech prevailed nought,
Her selfe she tombled headlong to the flore:
But him the Angels on their feathers caught,
And to an ayrie mountaine nimbly bore,
Whose snowie shoulders, like some chaulkie shore,
    Restles Olympus seem'd to rest upon
    With all his swimming globes: so both are gone,
The Dragon with the Lamb. Ah, unmeet Paragon.

3. To Vaine-Glorie.

36.2 beames: spars.

36.4 Olympique: celestial. Argus: i.e., the Argo, fabled ship that carried Jason and his companions to Colchis.

36.8 brave: fine.

37.1 shrive: question.

37.7 latch: catch.

38.6 Olympus: the heavens with their turning spheres, "swimming globes."

38.8 unmeet Paragon: unsuitable companion.

Poetically described from the place where her court stood.
A garden.

39

All suddenly the hill his snowe devours,
In liew whereof a goodly garden grew,
As if the snow had melted into flow'rs,
Which their sweet breath in subtill vapours threw,
That all about perfumed spirits flew.
    For what so ever might aggrate the sense,
    In all the world, or please the appetence,
Heer it was powred out in lavish affluence.

40

Not lovely Ida might with this compare,
Though many streames his banks besilvered,
Though Xanthus with his golden sands he bare,
Nor Hibla, though his thyme depastured,
As fast againe with honie blossomed.
    Ne Rhodope, ne Tempes flowrie playne,
    Adonis garden was to this but vayne,
Though Plato on his beds a flood of praise did rayne.

41

For in all these, some one thing most did grow,
But in this one, grew all things els beside,
For sweet varietie herselfe did throw
To every banke, here all the ground she dide
In lillie white, there pinks eblazed wide;

39 The third temptation begins.

39.6 aggrate: please.

40.1 Ida: mountain near Troy, the source of many rivers, where Paris judged that Venus was the most beautiful goddess.

40.3 Xanthus: river at Troy, also called the Scamander.

40.4 Hibla: i.e., Hybla, Sicilian mountain famous for honey produced from its thyme and other flowers.

40.6 Rhodope: mountain in Thrace. Tempe: valley in Thessaly, described as the most beautiful place on earth.

40.7 Adonis garden: symbol of fertility in Greek legend and ceremony, described at length in *Faerie Queen*, 3.6. It is not clear where Plato praised it; Socrates briefly alludes to it near the end of the *Phædrus*.

41.4 dide: dyed.

41.5 eblazed: shone forth in bright colors.

And damask't all the earth, and here shee shed
Blew violets, and there came roses red,
And every sight the yeelding sense, as captive led.

42

The garden like a Ladie faire was cut,
That lay as if shee slumber'd in delight,
And to the open skies her eyes did shut;
The azure fields of heav'n wear sembled right
In a large round, set with the flowr's of light,
The flowr's-de-luce, and the round sparks of deaw,
That hung upon their azure leaves, did shew
Like twinkling starrs, that sparkle in the eav'ning blew.

43

Upon a hillie banke her head shee cast,
On which the bowre of Vaine-Delight was built,
White, and red roses for her face wear plac't,
And for her tresses Marigolds wear spilt:
Them broadly shee displaid, like flaming guilt,
Till in the ocean the glad day wear drown'd,
Then up againe her yellow locks she wound,
And with greene fillets in their prettie calls them bound.

44

What should I here depeint her lillie hand,
Her veines of violets, her ermine brest,
Which thear in orient colours living stand,
Or how her gowne with silken leaves is drest;
Or how her watchmen, arm'd with boughie crest,
A wall of prim hid in his bushes bears,
Shaking at every winde their leavie spears,
While she supinely sleeps, ne to be waked fears?

42.8 the : th' 1610.

43.8 calls: cauls, close-fitting netted caps.

44.6 prim: privet hedge.

45

Over the hedge depends the graping Elme,
Whose greener head, empurpuled in wine,
Seemed to wonder at his bloodie helme,
And halfe suspect the bunches of the vine,
Least they, perhaps, his wit should undermine.
  For well he knewe such fruit he never bore:
  But her weake armes embraced him the more,
And with her ruby grapes laught at her paramour.

46

Under the shadowe of these drunken elmes
A Fountaine rose, where Pangloretta uses,
(When her some flood of fancie overwhelms,
And one of all her favourites she chuses)
To bath herselfe, whom she in lust abuses,
  And from his wanton body sucks his soule,
  Which drown'd in pleasure, in that shaly bowle,
And swimming in delight, doth amorously rowle.

47

The font of silver was, and so his showrs
In silver fell, onely the guilded bowles
(Like to a fornace, that the min'rall powres)
Seem'd to have moul't in their shining holes:
And on the water, like to burning coles,
  On liquid silver, leaves of roses lay:
  But when PANGLORIE here did list to play,
Rose water then it ranne, and milke it rain'd they say.

48

The roofe thicke cloudes did paint, from which three boyes
Three gaping mermaides with their eawrs did feede,

45.1 graping: bearing grapes.

46.2 Pangloretta: Allglory, Vainglory. uses: is accustomed.

46.7 shaly: like a dish or goblet.

46.8 amorously : amarously 1610.

47.4 moul't: melted.

48.2 eawrs: ewers.

Whose brests let fall the streame, with sleepie noise,
To Lions mouths, from whence it leapt with speede,
And in the rosie laver seem'd to bleed.
    The naked boyes unto the waters fall,
    Their stonie nightingales had taught to call,
When Zephyr breath'd into their watry interall.

49

And all about, embayed in soft sleepe,
A heard of charmed beasts aground wear spread,
Which the faire Witch in goulden chaines did keepe,
And them in willing bondage fettered,
Once men they liv'd, but now the men were dead,
    And turn'd to beasts, so fabled Homer old,
    That Circe, with her potion, charm'd in gold,
Us'd manly soules in beastly bodies to immould.

50

From her Court, and Courtiers.
1. Pleasure in drinking.

Through this false Eden, to his Lemans bowre,
(Whome thousand soules devoutly idolize)
Our first destroyer led our Saviour.
Thear in the lower roome, in solemne wise,
They daunc't a round, and powr'd their sacrifice
    To plumpe Lyæus, and among the rest,
    The jolly Priest, in yvie garlands drest,
Chaunted wild Orgialls, in honour of the feast.

51

Others within their arbours swilling sat,
(For all the roome about was arboured)
With laughing Bacchus, that was growne so fat,
That stand he could not, but was carried,
And every evening freshly watered,
    To quench his fierie cheeks, and all about

48.8 interall: entrails; internal workings.

49.2 aground: on the ground.

50.1 Lemans: paramour's.

50.6 Lyæus: Bacchus.

50.8 Orgialls: songs sung at Bacchic orgies.

Small cocks broke through the wall, and sallied out
Flaggons of wine, to set on fire that spueing rout.

52

This their inhumed soules esteem'd their wealths,
To crowne the bouzing kan from day to night,
And sicke to drinke themselves with drinking healths,
Some vomiting, all drunken with delight.
Hence to a loft, carv'd all in yvorie white,
They came, whear whiter Ladies naked went,
Melted in pleasure, and soft languishment,
And sunke in beds of roses, amourous glaunces sent.

in Luxurie.

53

Flie, flie thou holy child that wanton roome,
And thou my chaster Muse those harlots shun,
And with him to a higher storie come,
Whear mounts of gold, and flouds of silver run,
The while the owners, with their wealth undone,
Starve in their store, and in their plentie pine,
Tumbling themselves upon their heaps of mine.
Glutting their famish't soules with the deceitfull shine.

2. Avarice.

54

Ah, who was he such pretious perills found?
How strongly Nature did her treasures hide;
And threw upon them mountains of thicke ground,
To darke their orie lustre; but queint Pride
Hath taught her Sonnes to wound their mothers side,
And gage the depth, to search for flaring shells,
In whose bright bosome spumie Bacchus swells,
That neither heav'n, nor earth henceforth in safetie dwells.

55

O sacred hunger of the greedie eye,
Whose neede hath end, but no end covetise,

51.7 cocks: petcocks. sallied out: emitted.

52.1 inhumed: buried.

53.7 mine: ore, especially gold.

Emptie in fulnes, rich in povertie,
That having all things, nothing can suffice,
How thou befanciest the men most wise?
    The poore man would be rich, the rich man great,
    The great man King, the King, in Gods owne seat
Enthron'd, with mortal arme dares flames, and thunder threat.

56

Therefore above the rest Ambition sat:
His Court with glitterant pearle was all enwall'd,
And round about the wall in chaires of State,
And most majestique splendor, wear enstall'd
A hundred Kings, whose temples wear impal'd
    In goulden diadems, set here, and thear
    With diamounds, and gemmed every whear,
And of their golden virges none disceptred wear.

3. Ambitious honour.

57

High over all, *Panglories* blazing throne,
In her bright turret, all of christall wrought,
Like Phœbus lampe in midst of heaven, shone:
Whose starry top, with pride infernall fraught,
Selfe-arching columns to uphold wear taught:
    In which, her Image still reflected was
    By the smooth christall, that most like her glasse,
In beauty, and in frailtie, did all others passe.

From her throne.

58

A Silver wande the sorceresse did sway,
And, for a crowne of gold, her haire she wore,
Onely a garland of rosebuds did play
About her locks, and in her hand, she bore
A hollowe globe of glasse, that long before,
    She full of emptinesse had bladdered,
    And all the world therein depictured,
Whose colours, like the rainebowe, ever vanished.

56.8 virges: rods of office.

57.3 Phœbus : Phæbus 1610.

59

Such watry orbicles young boyes doe blowe
Out from their sopy shells, and much admire
The swimming world, which tenderly they rowe
With easie breath, till it be waved higher,
But if they chaunce but roughly once aspire,
    The painted bubble instantly doth fall.
    Here when she came, she gan for musique call,
And sung this wooing song, to welcome him withall.

From her temptation.

Love is the blossome whear thear blowes
Every thing, that lives, or growes,
Love doth make the heav'ns to move,
And the Sun doth burne in love;
Love the strong, and weake doth yoke,
And makes the yvie climbe the oke,
Under whose shadowes Lions wilde,
Soft'ned by Love, growe tame, and mild;
Love no med'cine can appease,
He burnes the fishes in the seas, 10
Not all the skill his wounds can stench,
Not all the sea his fire can quench;
Love did make the bloody spear
Once a levie coat to wear,
While in his leaves thear shrouded lay
Sweete birds, for love, that sing, and play;
And of all loves joyfull flame,
I the bud, and blossome am.
    Onely bend thy knee to me,
    Thy wooeing, shall thy winning be. 20

See, see the flowers that belowe,
Now as fresh as morning blowe,
And of all, the virgin rose,
That as bright Aurora showes,

59.1 orbicles: bubbles.

59.3 rowe: move along.

59.5 aspire: exhale.

Song 14 levie: leafy.

How they all unleaved die,
Loosing their virginitie:
Like unto a summer-shade,
But now borne, and now they fade.
Every thing doth passe away,
Thear is danger in delay, 30
Come, come gather then the rose,
Gather it, or it you lose.
All the sande of Tagus shore
Into my bosome casts his ore;
All the valleys swimming corne
To my house is yeerely borne;
Every grape, of every vine
Is gladly bruis'd to make me wine,
While ten thousand kings, as proud,
To carry up my traine, have bow'd, 40
And a world of Ladies send me
In my chambers to attend me:
All the starres in heav'n that shine,
And ten thousand more, are mine:
Onely bend thy knee to mee,
Thy wooing shall thy winning bee.

60

Thus sought the dire Enchauntress in his minde
Her guilefull bayt to have embosomed,
But he her charmes dispersed into winde,
And her of insolence admonished,
And all her optique glasses shattered.
So with her Syre to hell shee tooke her flight,
(The starting ayre flew from the damned spright,)
Whear deeply both aggriev'd, plunged themselves in night.

The effect of this victorie in Satan.

61

But to their Lord, now musing in his thought,
A heavenly volie of light Angels flew,

The Angels.

25 unleaved: having lost their leaves.
33 Tagus: Spanish river fabled to have golden sand.
60.7 starting: disturbed.
61.2 volie: flying company.

And from his Father him a banquet brought,
Through the fine element, for well they knew,
After his lenten fast, he hungrie grew,
    And, as he fed, the holy quires combine
    To sing a hymne of the celestiall Trine;
All thought to passe, and each was past all thought divine.

62

The Creatures.

The birds sweet notes, to sonnet out their joyes,
Attemper'd to the layes Angelicall,
And to the birds, the winds attune their noyse,
And to the winds, the waters hoarcely call,
And Eccho back againe revoyced all,
    That the whole valley rung with victorie.
    But now our Lord to rest doth homewards flie:
See how the Night comes stealing from the mountains high.

INRI
LVK: 22:47
LVK: 7:37
LVK: 23:1
LVK: 22:21
Mat 27: 37
What you see here does but the picture show
of sorrowes picture. Miracle of woe.
Greefe was miscall'd till now, what plaints before
ere mou'd the bowells of the earth: or toare
the rocks: nay more: the heau'ns put out their the lig
and truc'd with darkness, to auoide that sight.
Blind Israell: this this your hardness shewes:
yee then turn'd stones, whilst thus those Jewes stones turn'd
G:Y: sculp:

Christs Triumph over and after Death.

Vincenti dabitur.

Christs Triumph over Death.

1

So downe the silver streames of Eridan,
On either side bank't with a lilly wall,
Whiter then both, rides the triumphant Swan,
And sings his dirge, and prophesies his fall,
Diving into his watrie funerall:
    But Eridan to Cedron must submit
    His flowry shore, nor can he envie it,
If when Apollo sings, his swans doe silent sit.

Christs Tryumph over death, on the crosse, exprest 1. in generall by his joy to undergoe it: singing before he went to the garden, Mat. 26. 30.

2

That heav'nly voice I more delight to heare,
Then gentle ayres to breath, or swelling waves
Against the sounding rocks their bosomes teare,
Or whistling reeds, that rutty Jordan laves,
And with their verdure his white head embraves,
    To chide the windes, or hiving bees, that flie
    About the laughing bloosms of sallowie,
Rocking asleepe the idle groomes that lazie lie.

3

And yet, how can I heare thee singing goe,
When men incens'd with hate, thy death foreset?
Or els, why doe I heare thee sighing so,
When thou, inflam'd with love, their life doest get?
That Love, and hate, and sighs, and songs are met;

Vincenti dabitur.: To the victor it shall be given.

1 gloss: "and when they had sung a hymn, they went out into the Mount of Olives," where the Garden of Gethsemane was. expre*s*t : expre*st.* 1610.

1.1 Eridan: the Po River in Italy.

1.6 Cedron: the brook Cedron, near Gethsemane (John 18:1).

2.2 breath: breathe.

2.7 sallowie: willows.

But thus, and onely thus thy love did crave,
To sende thee singing for us to thy grave,
While we sought thee to kill, and thou sought'st us to save.

4

By his griefe in the undergoing it.

When I remember Christ our burden beares,
I looke for glorie, but finde miserie;
I looke for joy, but finde a sea of teares;
I looke that we should live, and finde him die;
I looke for Angels songs, and heare him crie:
Thus what I looke, I cannot finde so well,
Or rather, what I finde, I cannot tell,
These bankes so narrowe are, those streames so highly swell.

5

Christ suffers, and in this, his teares begin,
Suffers for us, and our joy springs in this,
Suffers to death, here is his Manhood seen,
Suffers to rise, and here his Godhead is.
For Man, that could not by himselfe have ris,
Out of the grave doth by the Godhead rise,
And God, that could not die, in Manhood dies,
That we in both might live, by that sweete sacrifice.

6

Goe giddy braines, whose witts are thought so fresh,
Plucke all the flowr's that Nature forth doth throwe,
Goe sticke them on the cheekes of wanton flesh;
Poore idol, (forc't at once to fall and growe)
Of fading roses, and of melting snowe:
Your songs exceede your matter, this of mine,
The matter, which it sings, shall make divine,
As starres dull puddles guild, in which their beauties shine.

7

By the obscure fables of the Gentiles, typing it.

Who doth not see drown'd in Deucalions name,
(When earth his men, and sea had lost his shore)

7.1 Deucalion: son of Prometheus who ruled in Thessaly when Zeus decided to destroy the earth by a flood. With his son he built a ship, by which

Old Noah; and in Nisus lock, the fame
Of Sampson yet alive; and long before
In Phaethons, mine owne fall I deplore:
    But he that conquer'd hell, to fetch againe
    His virgin widowe, by a serpent slaine,
Another Orpheus was then dreaming poets feigne.

8

That taught the stones to melt for passion,
And dormant sea, to heare him, silent lie,
And at his voice, the watrie nation
To flocke, as if they deem'd it cheape, to buy
With their owne deaths his sacred harmonie:
    The while the waves stood still to heare his song,
    And steadie shore wav'd with the reeling throng
Of thirstie soules, that hung upon his fluent tongue.

9

What better friendship, then to cover shame?
What greater love, then for a friend to die?
Yet this is better to asself the blame,
And this is greater, for an enemie:
But more then this, to die, not suddenly,
    Not with some common death, or easie paine,
    But slowely, and with torments to be slaine,
O depth, without a depth, farre better seene, then saine!

By the cause of it in him, his Love.

they saved themselves and Deucalion's wife, permitting continuation of the human race. They are "types" (see gloss), pagan equivalents of the biblical story of Noah, who in turn is a type of Christ.

7.3 Nisus: king of Megara, attacked by Minos, who could not be successful as long as a lock of yellow hair remained on Nisus' head. His daughter Scylla cut it off and the town was quickly taken. Thus Nisus is a type of Samson, who also prefigures Christ.

7.5 Phaethon: Phaeton, killed for poorly guiding the horses of the Sun.

7.6 he: Orpheus (l. 8), who did the wonders recounted in stanza 8, again a type of Christ. His "virgin widowe" was Euridice.

9.3 asself: assume.

9.8 saine: said.

By the effect it should have in us.

10

And yet the Sonne is humbled for the Slave,
And yet the Slave is proude before the Sonne:
Yet the Creator for his creature gave
Himselfe, and yet the creature hasts to runne
From his Creator, and self-good doth shunne:
  And yet the Prince, and God himselfe doth crie
  To Man, his Traitour, pardon not to flie,
Yet Man his God, and Traytour doth his Prince defie.

11

Who is it sees not that he nothing is,
But he that nothing sees; what weaker brest,
Since Adams Armour fail'd, dares warrant his?
That made by God of all his creatures best,
Strait made himselfe the woorst of all the rest:
  "If any strength we have, it is to ill,
  "But all the good is Gods, both pow'r, and will:
The dead man cannot rise, though he himselfe may kill.

12

But let the thorny schools these punctualls
Of wills, all good, or bad, or neuter diss;
Such joy we gained by our parentalls,
That good, or bad, whither I cannot wiss,
To call it a mishap, or happy miss
  That fell from Eden, and to heav'n did rise:
  Albee the mitred Card'nall more did prize
His part in Paris, then his part in Paradise.

11.6-7 The quotation marks conventionally indicate a moralizing passage. Thus they are not closed in 1610.

12.1 punctualls: subtleties.

12.2 diss: discuss (?).

12.3 parentalls: parents: Adam and Eve.

12.4 whither: whether, i.e., which. wiss: know.

12.7 Card'nall: probably the Englishman William Allen (1532–94), founder of the English seminary at Douai and supporter of Phillip II, who urged the English to rebel against Elizabeth.

13

A Tree was first the instrument of strife,
Whear Eve to sinne her soule did prostitute,
A Tree is now the instrument of life,
Though ill that trunke, and this faire body suit:
Ah, cursed tree, and yet O blessed fruit!
 That death to him, this life to us doth give:
 Strange is the cure, when things past cure revive,
And the Physitian dies, to make his patient live.

By the instrument, the cursed Tree,

14

Sweete Eden was the arbour of delight,
Yet in his hony flowr's our poyson blew;
Sad Gethseman the bowre of balefull night,
Whear Christ a health of poison for us drewe,
Yet all our hony in that poyson grewe:
 So we from sweetest flowr's, could sucke our bane,
 And Christ from bitter venome, could againe
Extract life out of death, and pleasure out of paine.

2. exprest in particular, 1. by his fore-passion in the Garden.

15

A Man was first the author of our fall,
A Man is now the author of our rise,
A Garden was the place we perish all,
A Garden is the place he payes our price,
And the old Serpent with a newe devise,
 Hath found a way himselfe for to beguile,
 So he, that all men tangled in his wile,
Is now by one man caught, beguil'd with his owne guile.

16

The dewie night had with her frostie shade
Immant'led all the world, and the stiffe ground
Sparkled in yce, onely the Lord, that made
All for himselfe, himselfe dissolved found,
Sweat without heat, and bled without a wound:

16.4 dissolved: unfrozen (?).
16.5 Sweat: sweated.

Of heav'n, and earth, and God, and Man forlore,
Thrice begging helpe of those, whose sinnes he bore,
And thrice denied of those, not to denie had swore.

17

Yet had he beene alone of God forsaken,
Or had his bodie beene imbroyl'd alone
In fierce assault, he might, perhaps, have taken
Some joy in soule, when all joy els was gone,
But that with God, and God to heav'n is flow'n;
And Hell it selfe out from her grave doth rise,
Black as the starles night, and with them flies,
Yet blacker then they both, the Sonne of blasphemies.

18

As when the Planets, with unkind aspect,
Call from her caves the meager pestilence,
The sacred vapour, eager to infect,
Obeyes the voyce of the sad influence,
And vomits up a thousand noysome sents,
The well of life, flaming his golden flood
With the sicke ayre, fevers the boyling blood,
And poisons all the bodie with contagious food.

19

The bold Physitian, too incautelous,
By those he cures, himselfe is murdered,
Kindnes infects, pitie is dangerous,
And the poore infant, yet not fully bred,
Thear where he should be borne, lies buried:
So the darke Prince, from his infernall cell,
Casts up his griesly Torturers of hell,
And whets them to revenge, with this insulting spell.

16.6 forlore: abandoned.

16.7 Thrice: In Gethsemane, according to Matthew and Mark, Jesus asked his followers to stay awake while he prayed. They nevertheless went to sleep three times.

16.8 those: those, who.

19.1 incautelous: unwary.

20

See how the world smiles in eternall peace;
While we, the harmles brats, and rustie throng
Of Night, our snakes in curles doe pranke, and dresse:
Why sleepe our drouzie scorpions so long?
Whear is our wonted vertue to doe wrong?
    Are we our selves; or are we Graces growen?
    The Sonnes of hell, or heav'n? was never knowne
Our whips so over-moss't, and brands so deadly blowne.

21

O long desired, never hop't for howre,
When our Tormentour shall our torments feele!
Arme, arme your selves, sad Dires of my pow'r,
And make our Judge for pardon to us kneele,
Slise, launch, dig, teare him with your whips of steele:
    My selfe in honour of so noble prize,
    Will powre you reaking blood, shed with the cries
Of hastie heyres, who their owne fathers sacrifice.

22

With that a flood of poyson, blacke as hell,
Out from his filthy gorge, the beast did spue,
That all about his blessed bodie fell,
And thousand flaming serpents hissing flew
About his soule, from hellish sulphur threw,
    And every one brandisht his fierie tongue,
    And woorming all about his soule they clung,
But he their stings tore out, and to the ground them flung.

23

So have I seene a rocks heroique brest,
Against proud Neptune, that his ruin threats,
When all his waves he hath to battle prest,

20-21 spoken by Satan to his followers.

20.3 pranke: adorn.

20.8 deadly blowne: blooming lifelessly.

21.3 Dires: the Diræ or Furies.

22.3 his: Jesus'.

And with a thousand swelling billows beats
The stubborne stone, and foams, and chafes, and frets
  To heave him from his root, unmooved stand;
  And more in heapes the barking surges band,
The more in pieces beat, flie weeping to the strand.

24

So may wee oft a vent'rous father see,
To please his wanton sonne, his onely joy,
Coast all about, to catch the roving bee,
And stung himselfe, his busie hands employ
To save the honie, for the gamesome boy:
  Or from the snake her rank'rous teeth erace,
  Making his child the toothles Serpent chace,
Or, with his little hands, her tum'rous gorge embrace.

25

Thus Christ himselfe to watch, and sorrow gives,
While, deaw'd in easie sleepe, dead Peter lies:
Thus Man in his owne grave securely lives,
While Christ alive, with thousand horrours dies,
Yet more for theirs, then his owne pardon cries:
  No sinnes he had, yet all our sinnes he bare,
  So much doth God for others evills care,
And yet so careles men for their owne evills are.

26

2. By his passion itselfe, amplified,
1. from the general causes.

See drouzie Peter, see whear Judas wakes,
Whear Judas kisses him whom Peter flies:
O kisse more deadly then the sting of snakes!
False love more hurtfull then true injuries!
Aye me! how deerly God his Servant buies?
  For God his man, at his owne blood doth hold,
  And Man his God, for thirtie pence hath sold.
So tinne for silver goes, and dunghill drosse for gold.

23.7 barking: harsh-sounding.

24.3 Coast: search.

26 gloss: 2. is not in 1610.

26.5 buies: buys.

27

Yet was it not enough for Sinne to chuse
A Servant, to betray his Lord to them;
But that a Subject must his King accuse,
But that a Pagan must his God condemne,
But that a Father must his Sonne contemne,
    But that the Sonne must his owne death desire,
    That Prince, and People, Servant, and the Sire,
Gentil, and Jewe, and he against himselfe conspire?

28

Parts, and

Was this the oyle, to make thy Saints adore thee,
The froathy spittle of the rascall throng?
Ar these the virges, that ar borne before thee,
Base whipps of corde, and knotted all along?
Is this thy golden scepter, against wrong,
    A reedie cane? is that the crowne adornes
    Thy shining locks, a crowne of spiny thornes?
Ar theas the Angels himns, the Priests blasphemous scornes?

29

Effects of it.

Who ever sawe Honour before asham'd;
Afflicted Maiestie, debased height;
Innocence guiltie, Honestie defam'd;
Libertie bound, Health sick, the Sunne in night?
But since such wrong was offred unto right,
    Our night is day, our sicknes health is growne,
    Our shame is veild, this now remaines alone
For us, since he was ours, that wee bee not our owne.

30

2. From the particular causes.

Night was ordeyn'd for rest, and not for paine,
But they, to paine their Lord, their rest contemne,
Good lawes to save, what bad men would have slaine,
And not bad Judges, with one breath, by them

28.3 virges: rods signifying an office.

28.6 crowne: crown that.

30 gloss: 1. in 1610.

The innocent to pardon, and condemne:
    Death for revenge of murderers, not decaie
    Of guiltles blood, but now, all headlong sway
Mans Murderer to save, mans Saviour to slaie.

31

Fraile Multitude, whose giddy lawe is list,
And best applause is windy flattering,
Most like the breath of which it doth consist,
No sooner blowne, but as soone vanishing,
As much desir'd, as little profiting,
    That makes the men that have it oft as light,
    As those that give it, which the proud invite,
And feare: the bad mans friend, the good mans hypocrite.

32

Parts, and

It was but now their sounding clamours sung,
Blessed is he, that comes from the most high,
And all the mountaines with Hosanna rung,
And nowe, away with him, away they crie,
And nothing can be heard but crucifie:
    It was but now, the Crowne it selfe they save,
    And golden name of King unto him gave,
And nowe, no King, but onely Cæsar, they will have:

33

It was but now they gathered blooming May,
And of his armes disrob'd the branching tree,
To strowe with boughs, and blossomes all thy way,
And now, the branchlesse truncke a crosse for thee,
And May, dismai'd, thy coronet must be:
    It was but now they wear so kind, to throwe
    Their owne best garments, whear thy feet should goe,
And now, thy selfe they strip, and bleeding wounds they show.

31.1 list: pleasure.

32.4-8 paraphrased from the gospels, e.g., John 19:15; the mob had called him king.

33.1 gathered: i.e., to welcome Jesus to Jerusalem. See, e.g., John 12:13.

34

See whear the author of all life is dying:
O fearefull day! he dead, what hope of living?
See whear the hopes of all our lives are buying:
O chearfull day! they bought, what feare of grieving?
Love love for hate, and death for life is giving:
    Loe how his armes are stretch't abroad to grace thee,
    And, as they open stand, call to embrace thee,
Why stai'st thou then my soule; ô flie, flie thither hast thee.

35

His radious head, with shamefull thornes they teare,
His tender backe, with bloody whipps they rent,
His side and heart, they furrowe with a spear,
His hands, and feete, with riving nayles they tent,
And, as to disentrayle his soule they meant,
    They jolly at his griefe, and make their game,
    His naked body to expose to shame,
That all might come to see, and all might see, that came.

36

Whereat the heav'n put out his guiltie eye,
That durst behold so execrable sight,
And sabled all in blacke the shadie skie,
And the pale starres strucke with unwonted fright,
Quenched their everlasting lamps in night:
    And at his birth as all the starres heav'n had,
    Wear not enough, but a newe star was made,
So now both newe, and old, and all away did fade.

Effects of it in heaven.

37

The mazed Angels shooke their fierie wings,
Readie to lighten vengeance from Gods throne,

In the heavenly Spirits.

34.8 hast: haste.

35.1 radious: radiant.

35.4 tent: probe.

35.5 disentrayle: draw forth.

36 Darkness was over the land on the day of the Crucifixion from the sixth hour until the ninth.

37, 38 glosses: In : in 1610.

37.1 mazed: dazed.

One downe his eyes upon the Manhood flings,
Another gazes on the Godhead, none
But surely thought his wits wear not his owne:
  Some flew, to looke if it wear very hee,
  But, when Gods arme unarmed they did see,
Albee they sawe it was, they vow'd it could not bee.

38

In the Creatures subcœlestiall.

The sadded aire hung all in cheerelesse blacke,
Through which, the gentle windes soft sighing flewe,
And Jordan into such huge sorrowe brake,
(As if his holy streame no measure knewe,)
That all his narrowe bankes he overthrewe,
  The trembling earth with horrour inly shooke,
  And stubborne stones, such griefe unus'd to brooke,
Did burst, and ghosts awaking from their graves gan looke.

39

The wise Philosopher cried, all agast,
The God of nature surely languished,
The sad Centurion cried out as fast,
The Sonne of God, the Sonne of God was dead,

In the wicked Jews.

The headlong Jew hung downe his pensive head,
  And homewards far'd, and ever, as he went,
  He smote his brest, halfe desperately bent,
The verie woods, and beasts did seeme his death lament.

40

In Judas.

The gracelesse Traytour round about did looke,
(He lok't not long, the Devill quickely met him)

37.6 very: verily.

38.5 That the Jordan flooded at the time of the Crucifixion is not biblical; the earthquake of line 6 and the ghosts of line 8 are (e.g., Matt. 27:51ff.).

39.1 The Philosopher is not biblical.

39.2 languished : lanquished 1610.

39.3 Centurion: reported in the gospels, e.g., Matt. 27:54. The regret of the Jews at the end of this stanza is described in Luke 23:48.

40ff. Judas' suicide: according to Matt. 27 Judas, recognizing his crime, "went and hanged himself." According to Acts 1:18 he fell and "burst asunder in the midst, and all his bowels gushed out."

To finde a halter, which he found, and tooke,
Onely a gibbet nowe he needes must get him,
So on a wither'd tree he fairly set him,
    And helpt him fit the rope, and in his thought
    A thousand furies, with their whippes, he brought,
So thear he stands, readie to hell to make his vault.

41

For him a waking bloodhound, yelling loude,
That in his bosome long had sleeping layde,
A guiltie Conscience, barking after blood,
Pursued eagerly, ne ever stai'd,
Till the betrayers selfe it had betray'd.
    Oft chang'd he place, in hope away to winde,
    But change of place could never change his minde,
Himselfe he flies to loose, and followes for to finde.

42

Thear is but two wayes for this soule to have,
When parting from the body, forth it purges,
To flie to heav'n, or fall into the grave,
Where whippes of scorpions, with the stinging scourges,
Feed on the howling ghosts, and firie Surges
    Of brimstone rowle about the cave of night,
    Where flames doe burne, and yet no sparke of light,
And fire both fries, and freezes the blaspheming spright.

43

Thear lies the captive soule, aye-sighing sore,
Reck'ning a thousand yeares since her first bands,
Yet staies not thear, but addes a thousand more,
And at another thousand never stands,
But tells to them the starres, and heapes the sands,
    And now the starres are told, and sands are runne,
    And all those thousand thousand myriads done,
And yet but now, alas! but now all is begunne.

41.8 loose: lose.

43.5 tells: counts.

43.6 told: counted.

44

With that a flaming brand a Furie catch't,
And shooke, and tost it round in his wilde thought,
So from his heart all joy, all comfort snatch't,
With every starre of hope, and as he sought,
(With present feare, and future griefe distraught)
    To flie from his owne heart, and aide implore
    Of him, the more he gives, that hath the more,
Whose storehouse is the heavens, too little for his store.

45

Stay wretch on earth, cried Satan, restles rest,
Know'st thou not Justice lives in heav'n; or can
The worst of creatures live among the best;
Among the blessed Angels cursed man?
Will Judas now become a Christian?
    Whither will hopes long wings transport thy minde;
    Or canst thou not thy selfe a sinner finde;
Or cruell to thy selfe, wouldst thou have Mercie kinde?

46

He gave thee life: why shouldst thou seeke to slay him?
He lent thee wealth: to feed thy avarice?
He cal'd thee friend: what, that thou shouldst betray him?
He kist thee, though he knew his life the price:
He washt thy feet: should'st thou his sacrifice?
    He gave thee bread, and wine, his bodie, blood,
    And at thy heart to enter in he stood,
But then I entered in, and all my snakie brood.

47

As when wild Pentheus, growne madde with fear,
Whole troups of hellish haggs about him spies,
Two bloodie Sunnes stalking the duskie sphear,
And twofold Thebes runs rowling in his eyes:

47.1 Pentheus: king of Thebes who refused to honor Dionysus and as a consequence was torn apart by the female bacchantes. But first the god maddened him so that he dressed like a bacchant woman and saw two suns and two cities of Thebes (Euripides, *Bacchanals*, 918–19).

Or through the scene staring Orestes flies,
With eyes flung back upon his Mothers ghost,
That, with infernall serpents all embost,
And torches quencht in blood, doth her stern sonne accost.

48

Such horrid gorgons, and misformed formes
Of damned fiends, flew dauncing in his heart,
That now, unable to endure their stormes,
Flie, flie, he cries, thy selfe, what ere thou art,
Hell, hell alreadie burnes in every part.
So downe into his Torturers armes he fell,
That readie stood his funeralls to yell,
And in a clowd of night to waft him quick to hell.

49

Yet oft he snacht, and started as he hung:
So when the senses halfe enslumb'red lie,
The headlong bodie, readie to be flung,
By the deluding phansie, from some high,
And craggie rock, recovers greedily,
And clasps the yeelding pillow, halfe asleepe,
And, as from heav'n it tombled to the deepe,
Feeles a cold sweat through every trembling member creepe.

50

Thear let him hang, embowelled in blood,
Whear never any gentle Sheapheard feed
His blessed flocks, nor ever heav'nly flood
Fall on the cursed ground, nor holesome seed
That may the least delight or pleasure breed:
Let never Spring visit his habitation,
But nettles, kixe, and all the weedie nation,
With emptie elders grow, sad signes of desolation.

47.5 Orestes: son of Agamemnon who avenged his father's death by killing his mother, Clytemnestra. He is punished (in the plays by Æschylus and Euripides) by the snaky Erinyes.

47.7 embost: enveloped.

50.1 embowelled: encased in.

50.7 kixe: dry weed stem.

51

Thear let the Dragon keepe his habitance,
And stinking karcases be throwne avaunt,
Faunes, Sylvans, and deformed Satyrs daunce,
Wild-cats, wolves, toads, and shreechowles direly chaunt,
Thear ever let some restles spirit haunt,
  With hollow sound, and clashing cheynes, to scarr
  The passenger, and eyes like to the starr,
That sparkles in the crest of angrie Mars afarr.

52

But let the blessed deawes for ever showr
Upon that ground, in whose faire fields I spie
The bloodie ensigne of our Saviour:
Strange conquest, whear the Conquerour must die,
And he is slaine, that winns the victorie:
  But he, that living, had no house to owe it,
  Now had no grave, but Joseph must bestowe it,
O runne ye Saints apace, and with sweete flowr's bestrowe it.

In the blessed Joseph, &c.

53

And ye glad Spirits, that now sainted sit
On your cœlestiall thrones, in beawtie drest,
Though I your teares recoumpt, O let not it
With after-sorrowe wound your tender brest,
Or with new griefe unquiet your soft rest:
  Inough is me your plaints to sound againe,
  That never could inough my selfe complaine,
Sing then, O sing aloude thou Arimathean Swaine.

54

But long he stood, in his faint armes uphoulding
The fairest spoile heav'n ever forfeited,
With such a silent passion griefe unfoulding,
That, had the sheete but on himselfe beene spread,
He for the corse might have beene buried:

52.6 owe: own.

52.7 Joseph: of Arimathea (53.8), who helped bury Jesus.

53.3 recoumpt: recount.

And with him stood the happie theefe, that stole
By night his owne salvation, and a shole
Of Maries drowned, round about him, sat in dole.

55

At length (kissing his lipps before he spake,
As if from thence he fetcht againe his ghost)
To Mary thus, with teares, his silence brake.
Ah woefull soule! what joy in all our cost,
When him we hould, we have alreadie lost?
Once did'st thou loose thy Sonne, but found'st againe,
Now find'st thy Sonne, but find'st him lost, and slaine.
Ay mee! though he could death, how canst thou life sustaine?

56

Whear ere, deere Lord, thy Shadowe hovereth,
Blessing the place, wherein it deigns abide,
Looke how the earth darke horrour covereth,
Cloathing in mournfull black her naked side,
Willing her shadowe up to heav'n to glide,
To see and if it meet thee wandring thear,
That so, and if her selfe must misse thee hear,
At least her shadow may her dutie to thee bear.

57

See how the Sunne in daytime cloudes his face,
And lagging Vesper, loosing his late teame,
Forgets in heav'n to runne his nightly race,
But, sleeping on bright Œtas top, doeth dreame
The world a Chaos is, no joyfull beame
Looks from his starrie bowre, the heav'ns doe mone,

54.6 happy theefe: Nicodemus, Jewish ruler who sought salvation through Jesus at night, John 3:1–2.

54.7-8 shole/Of Maries: Mary Magdalene and Jesus' mother.

55.6 The account of the twelve-year-old Jesus questioning teachers while his mother sought him is in Luke 2:41–51.

56.6, 7 and if: i.e., if.

57.4 Œtas: high mountain between Thessaly and Macedonia from behind which the sun, moon, and stars were said to rise.

And Trees drop teares, least we should greeve alone,
The windes have learnt to sigh, and waters hoarcely grone.

58

And you sweete flow'rs, that in this garden growe,
Whose happie states a thousand soules envie,
Did you your owne felicities but knowe,
Your selves unpluckt would to his funerals hie,
You never could in better season die:
O that I might into your places slide,
The gate of heav'n stands gaping in his side,
Thear in my soule should steale, and all her faults should hide.

59

Are theas the eyes, that made all others blind;
Ah why ar they themselves now blemished?
Is this the face, in which all beawtie shin'd;
What blast hath thus his flowers debellished?
Ar these the feete, that on the watry head
Of the unfaithfull Ocean passage found;
Why goe they now so lowely under ground,
Wash't with our woorthles teares, and their owne precious wound?

60

One hem but of the garments that he wore,
Could medicine whole countries of their paine,
One touch of this pale hand could life restore,
One word of these cold lips revive the slaine:
Well the blinde man thy Godhead might maintaine,
What though the sullen Pharises repin'd?
He that should both compare, at length would finde
The blinde man onely sawe, the Seers all wear blinde.

61

Why should they thinke thee worthy to be slaine?
Was it because thou gav'st their blinde men eyes;

59.4 debellished: disfigured.

59.6 passage found: i.e., when he walked on the water.

60.5 blinde man: as recounted in John 9.

Or that thou mad'st their lame to walke againe;
Or for thou heal'dst their sick mens maladies;
Or mad'st their dumbe to speake; and dead to rise?
O could all these but any grace have woon,
What would they not to save thy life have done?
The dumb man would have spoke, and lame man would have runne.

62

Let mee, O let me neere some fountaine lie,
That through the rocke heaves up his sandie head,
Or let me dwell upon some mountaine high,
Whose hollowe root, and baser parts ar spread
On fleeting waters, in his bowells bred,
That I their streames, and they my teares may feed,
Or, cloathed in some Hermits ragged weed,
Spend all my daies, in weeping for this cursed deed.

63

The life, the which I once did love, I leave,
The love, in which I once did live, I loath,
I hate the light, that did my light bereave,
Both love, and life, I doe despise you both,
O that one grave might both our ashes cloath!
A Love, a Life, a Light I now obteine,
Able to make my Age growe young againe,
Able to save the sick, and to revive the slaine.

64

Thus spend we teares, that never can be spent,
On him, that sorrow now no more shall see:
Thus send we sighs, that never can be sent,
To him, that died to live, and would not be,
To be thear whear he would; here burie we
This heav'nly earth, here let it softly sleepe,
The fairest Sheapheard of the fairest sheepe.
So all the bodie kist, and homewards went to weepe.

63.2 which : whieh 1610.

65

So home their bodies went, to seeke repose,
But at the grave they left their soules behinde;
O who the force of love cœlestiall knowes!
That can the cheynes of natures selfe unbinde,
Sending the Bodie home, without the minde.
  Ah blessed Virgin, what high Angels art
  Can ever coumpt thy teares, or sing thy smart,
When every naile, that pierst his hand, did pierce thy heart?

66

So Philomel, perch't on an aspin sprig,
Weeps all the night her lost virginitie,
And sings her sad tale to the merrie twig,
That daunces at such joyfull miserie,
Ne ever lets sweet rest invade her eye:
  But leaning on a thorne her daintie chest,
  For feare soft sleepe should steale into her brest,
Expresses in her song greefe not to be exprest.

67

So when the Larke, poore birde, afarre espi'th
Her yet unfeather'd children (whom to save
She strives in vaine) slaine by the fatall sithe,
Which from the medowe her greene locks doeth shave,
That their warme nest is now become their grave;
  The woefull mother up to heaven springs,
  And all about her plaintive notes she flings,
And their untimely fate most pittifully sings.

65.7 coumpt: count.

65.8 See the prophecy by Simeon, Luke 2:35.

66.1 Philomel: girl raped by Tereus, who cut out her tongue so that she could not report the crime; later changed into a nightingale.

MAR: 8.9.
IOHN: 11.43:
MAT: 22.19
MAR.7: 26.
MAR. XVI
Forget those horrid stiles of death: see here
who died, and by his presence there
imbalm'd the graue. See here who rose. and so
left hell infeebled, and the powers below.
and death suppress'd. So that a child (no doubt)
may safly play wth it, now the Stings pluck'd out.
G.y: sculp

Christs Triumph after Death.

1

But now the second Morning, from her bowre,
Began to glister in her beames, and nowe
The roses of the day began to flowre
In th' easterne garden; for heav'ns smiling browe
Halfe insolent for joy begunne to showe:
    The early Sunne came lively dauncing out,
    And the bragge lambes ranne wantoning about,
That heav'n, and earth might seeme in tryumph both to shout.

Christs Triumph after death.

1. In his Resurrection, manifested by the effects of it in the Creatures.

2

Th' engladded Spring, forgetfull now to weepe,
Began t' eblazon from her leavie bed,
The waking swallowe broke her halfe-yeares sleepe,
And everie bush lay deepely purpured
With violets, the woods late-wintry head
    Wide flaming primroses set all on fire,
    And his bald trees put on their greene attire,
Among whose infant leaves the joyeous birds conspire.

3

And now the taller Sonnes (whom Titan warmes)
Of unshorne mountaines, blowne with easie windes,
Dandled the mornings childhood in their armes,
And, if they chaunc't to slip the prouder pines,
The under Corylets did catch the shines,
    To guild their leaves, sawe never happie yeare
    Such joyfull triumph, and triumphant cheare,
As though the aged world anew created wear.

1.7 bragge: mettlesome.

2.3 waking swallowe: Here and in stanzas 6 and 9 Fletcher employs a folk belief that swallows hibernate. Thus in Christian iconography the swallow came to represent the resurrection of Christ. See E. S. Whittlesey, *Symbols and Legends in Western Art* (New York: Charles Scribner, 1972). Even Samuel Johnson thought that "Swallows certainly sleep all the winter." *Boswell's Life of Johnson*, ed. George B. Hill (Oxford: Oxford University Press, 1934), 2:55.

2.4 purpured: purpled.

3.5 Corylets: hazel copses.

4

Say Earth, why hast thou got thee new attire,
And stick'st thy habit full of dazies red?
Seems that thou doest to some high thought aspire,
And some newe-found-out Bridegroome mean'st to wed:
Tell me ye Trees, so fresh apparelled,
    So never let the spitefull Canker wast you,
    So never let the heav'ns with lightening blast you,
Why goe you now so trimly drest, or whither hast you?

5

Answer me Jordan, why thy crooked tide
So often wanders from his neerest way,
As though some other way thy streame would slide,
And faine salute the place where something lay?
And you sweete birds, that shaded from the ray,
    Sit carolling, and piping griefe away,
    The while the lambs to heare you daunce, and play,
Tell me sweete birds, what is it you so faine would say?

6

And, thou faire Spouse of Earth, that everie yeare,
Gett'st such a numerous issue of thy bride,
How chance thou hotter shin'st, and draw'st more neere?
Sure thou somewhear some worthie sight hast spide,
That in one place for joy thou canst not bide:
    And you dead Swallowes, that so lively now
    Through the flit aire your winged passage rowe,
How could new life into your frozen ashes flowe?

7

Ye Primroses, and purple violets,
Tell me, why blaze ye from your leavie bed,
And wooe mens hands to rent you from your sets,
As though you would somewhear be carried,
With fresh perfumes, and velvets garnished?
    But ah, I neede not aske, t'is surely so,

6.1 Spouse of Earth: the sun.

6.7 flit: light.

You all would to your Saviours triumphs goe,
Thear would ye all awaite, and humble homage doe.

8

Thear should the Earth herselfe with garlands newe
And lovely flowr's embellished adore,
Such roses never in her garland grewe,
Such lillies never in her brest she wore,
Like beautie never yet did shine before:
Thear should the Sunne another Sunne behold,
From whence himselfe borrowes his locks of gold,
That kindle heav'n, and earth with beauties manifold.

In himselfe.

9

Thear might the violet, and primrose sweet
Beames of more lively, and more lovely grace,
Arising from their beds of incense meet;
Thear should the Swallowe see newe life embrace
Dead ashes, and the grave unheale his face,
To let the living from his bowels creepe,
Unable longer his owne dead to keepe:
Thear heav'n, and earth should see their Lord awake from sleepe.

10

Their Lord, before by other judg'd to die,
Nowe Judge of all himselfe, before forsaken
Of all the world, that from his aide did flie,
Now by the Saints into their armies taken,
Before for an unworthie man mistaken,
Nowe worthy to be God confest, before
With blasphemies by all the basest tore,
Now worshipped by Angels, that him lowe adore.

11

Whose garment was before indipt in blood,
But now, imbright'ned into heav'nly flame,
The Sun it selfe outglitters, though he should
Climbe to the toppe of the celestiall frame,

9.5 unheale: unhele, i.e., reveal, uncover.

And force the starres go hide themselves for shame:
    Before that under earth was buried,
    But nowe about the heav'ns is carried,
And thear for ever by the Angels heried.

12

So fairest Phosphor the bright Morning starre,
But neewely washt in the greene element,
Before the drouzie Night is halfe aware,
Shooting his flaming locks with deaw besprent,
Springs lively up into the orient,
    And the bright drove, fleec't all in gold, he chaces
    To drinke, that on the Olympique mountaine grazes,
The while the minor Planets forfeit all their faces.

13

2. In his Ascention to heaven, whose joyes are described,

So long he wandred in our lower spheare,
That heav'n began his cloudy starres despise,
Halfe envious, to see on earth appeare
A greater light, then flam'd in his owne skies:
At length it burst for spight, and out thear flies
    A globe of winged Angels, swift as thought,
    That, on their spotted feathers, lively caught
The sparkling Earth, and to their azure fields it brought.

14

The rest, that yet amazed stood belowe,
With eyes cast up, as greedie to be fed,
And hands upheld, themselves to ground did throwe,
So when the Trojan boy was ravished,
As through th' Idalian woods they saie he fled,
    His aged Gardians stood as dismai'd,

11.8 heried: honored.

12.1 Phosphor: i.e., Lucifer.

12.4 besprent: sprinkled.

13.7 caught: reflected.

14 The account of the Ascension is from Acts 1:9–11.

14.4 Trojan boy: Hector's son, Astyanax.

Some least he should have fallen back afraid,
And some their hasty vowes, and timely prayers said.

15

Tosse up your heads ye everlasting gates,
And let the Prince of glorie enter in:
At whose brave voly of sideriall States,
The Sunne to blush, and starres growe pale wear seene,
When, leaping first from earth, he did begin
To climbe his Angells wings; then open hang
Your christall doores, so all the chorus sang
Of heav'nly birds, as to the starres they nimbly sprang.

16

Hearke how the floods clap their applauding hands,
The pleasant valleyes singing for delight,
And wanton Mountaines daunce about the Lands,
The while the fieldes, struck with the heav'nly light,
Set all their flowr's a smiling at the sight,
The trees laugh with their blossoms, and the sound
Of the triumphant shout of praise, that crown'd
The flaming Lambe, breaking through heav'n, hath passage found.

17

Out leap the antique Patriarchs, all in hast,
To see the powr's of Hell in triumph lead,
And with small starres a garland interchast
Of olive leaves they bore, to crowne his head,
That was before with thornes degloried,
After them flewe the Prophets, brightly stol'd

1. By the accesse of all good, the blessed Societie of the Saints,

15.1-2 paraphrased from Ps. 24:9. Milton uses the same passage for the return of the Son to heaven after the creation (*PL*, 7. 565ff.).

15.3 voly: i.e., volley, flight.

16.3 paraphrased from Ps. 114.4.

17.1 Patriarchs: released from hell by Christ's visit there between his death and resurrection.

17.2 lead: led.

17.3 interchast: ornamented.

In shining lawne, and wimpled manifold,
Striking their yvorie harpes, strung all in chords of gold.

18

To which the Saints victorious carolls sung,
Ten thousand Saints at once, that with the sound,
The hollow vaults of heav'n for triumph rung:
The Cherubins their clamours did confound
With all the rest, and clapt their wings around:
Downe from their thrones the Dominations flowe,
And at his feet their crownes, and scepters throwe,
And all the princely Soules fell on their faces lowe.

Angels, &c.

19

Nor can the Martyrs wounds them stay behind,
But out they rush among the heav'nly crowd,
Seeking their heav'n out of their heav'n to find,
Sounding their silver trumpets out so loude,
That the shrill noise broke through the starrie cloude,
And all the virgin Soules, in pure araie,
Came dauncing forth, and making joyeous plaie;
So him they lead along into the courts of day.

20

So him they lead into the courts of day,
Whear never warre, nor wounds abide him more,
But in that house, eternall peace doth plaie,
Acquieting the soules, that newe before
Their way to heav'n through their owne blood did skore,
But now, estranged from all miserie,
As farre as heav'n, and earth discoasted lie,
Swelter in quiet waves of immortalitie.

The sweete quiet and peace, injoyed under God.

17.7 lawne: fine linen.
18.4 confound: intermingle.
20.4 newe: recently.
20.5 skore: mark.
20.7 discoasted: removed.

21

And if great things by smaller may be ghuest,
So, in the mid'st of Neptunes angrie tide,
Our Britan Island, like the weedie nest
Of true Halcyon, on the waves doth ride,
And softly sayling, skornes the waters pride:
While all the rest, drown'd on the continent,
And tost in bloodie waves, their wounds lament,
And stand, to see our peace, as struck with woonderment.

Shadowed by the peace we enjoy under our Soveraigne.

22

The Ship of France religious waves doe tosse,
And Greece it selfe is now growne barbarous,
Spains Children hardly dare the Ocean crosse,
And Belges field lies wast, and ruinous,
That unto those, the heav'ns ar invious,
And unto them, themselves ar strangers growne,
And unto these, the Seas ar faithles knowne,
And unto her, alas, her owne is not her owne.

23

Here onely shut we Janus yron gates,
And call the welcome Muses to our springs,
And ar but Pilgrims from our heav'nly states,
The while the trusty Earth sure plentie brings,
And Ships through Neptune safely spread their wings.
Goe blessed Island, wander whear thou please,
Unto thy God, or men, heav'n, lands, or seas,
Thou canst not loose thy way, thy King with all hath peace.

21 In 1610 this stanza is renumbered 20 and all of the rest of the poem follows this numbering, resulting in an apparent total of only fifty stanzas.

21.4 Halcyon: a bird which according to Ovid (*Metamorphoses* 11. 745–46) sits on floating nests in quiet spring weather.

22.2 Greece : Greec 1610.

22.5-8 Those, them, these, her: respectively, the French, Greeks, Spanish, and Belgium.

23.1 Janus: The gates of his temple in ancient Rome were closed only during times of peace.

24

Deere Prince, thy Subjects joy, hope of their heirs,
Picture of peace, or breathing Image rather,
The certaine argument of all our pray'rs,
Thy Harries, and thy Countries lovely Father,
Let Peace, in endles joyes, for ever bath her
    Within thy sacred brest, that at thy birth
    Brought'st her with thee from heav'n, to dwell on earth,
Making our earth a heav'n, and paradise of mirth.

25

Let not my Liege misdeem these humble laies,
As lick't with soft, and supple blandishment,
Or spoken to disparagon his praise;
For though pale Cynthia, neere her brothers tent,
Soone disappeares in the white firmament,
    And gives him back the beames, before wear his,
    Yet when he verges, or is hardly ris,
She the vive image of her absent brother is.

26

Nor let the Prince of peace his beadsman blame,
That with his Stewart dares his Lord compare,
And heav'nly peace with earthly quiet shame:
So Pines to lowely plants compared ar,
And lightning Phœbus to a little starre:
    And well I wot, my rime, albee unsmooth,
    Ne, saies but what it meanes, ne meanes but sooth,
Ne harmes the good, ne good to harmefull person doth.

24.4 Harries: Prince Henry, who died two years later and in whose memory Fletcher wrote a poem.

24.5 bath her: bathe herself.

25.4 Cynthia: the moon, near her brother, the sun.

25.6 beames: beams, that.

25.7 verges: begins to set.

25.8 vive: living.

26.2 Stewart: i.e., James Stuart, with pun.

27

Gaze but upon the house, whear Man embowr's:
With flowr's, and rushes paved is his way,
Whear all the Creatures ar his Servitours,
The windes doe sweepe his chambers every day,
And cloudes doe wash his rooms, the seeling gay,
    Starred aloft the guilded knobs embrave:
    If such a house God to another gave,
How shine those glittering courts, he for himselfe will have?

The beauty of the place

28

And if a sullen cloud, as sad as night,
In which the Sunne may seeme embodied,
Depur'd of all his drosse, we see so white,
Burning in melted gold his watrie head,
Or round with yvorie edges silvered,
    What lustre superexcellent will he
    Lighten on those, that shall his sunneshine see,
In that all-glorious court, in which all glories be?

The Claritie (as the schoole cals it) of the Saints bodies.

29

If but one Sunne, with his diffusive fires,
Can paint the starres, and the whole world with light,
And joy, and life into each heart inspires,
And every Saint shall shine in heav'n, as bright
As doth the Sunne in his transcendent might,
    (As faith may well beleeve, what Truth once sayes)
    What shall so many Sunnes united rayes
But dazle all the eyes, that nowe in heav'n we praise?

30

Here let my Lord hang up his conquering launce,
And bloody armour with late slaughter warme,
And looking downe on his weake Militants,

27.6 knobs: i.e., stars.

28 gloss: Claritie : Caritie 1610. The spiritual bodies of resurrected believers discussed by Paul in 1 Cor. 15:44 and by various later theologians.

28.3 Depur'd: cleansed.

28.8 court: i.e., heaven.

Behold his Saints, mid'st of their hot alarme,
Hang all their golden hopes upon his arme.
    And in this lower field dispacing wide,
    Through windie thoughts, that would their sayles misguide,
Anchor their fleshly ships fast in his wounded side.

31

Here may the Band, that now in Tryumph shines,
And that (before they wear invested thus)
In earthly bodies carried heavenly mindes,
Pitcht round about in order glorious,
Their sunny Tents, and houses luminous,
    All their eternall day in songs employing,
    Joying their ende, without ende of their joying,
While their almightie Prince Destruction is destroying.

32

The impletion of the Appetite.

Full, yet without satietie, of that
Which whetts, and quiets greedy Appetite,
Whear never Sunne did rise, nor ever sat,
But one eternall day, and endles light
Gives time to those, whose time is infinite,
    Speaking with thought, obtaining without fee,
    Beholding him, whom never eye could see,
And magnifying him, that cannot greater be.

33

How can such joy as this want words to speake?
And yet what words can speake such joy as this?
Far from the world, that might their quiet breake,
Here the glad Soules the face of beauty kisse,
Powr'd out in pleasure, on their beds of blisse.
    And drunke with nectar torrents, ever hold
    Their eyes on him, whose graces manifold,
The more they doe behold, the more they would behold.

30.6 dispacing: moving about.

30.7 their : theit 1610.

32 gloss: impletion: satisfaction, filling.

34

Their sight drinkes lovely fires in at their eyes,
Their braine sweete incense with fine breath accloyes,
That on Gods sweating altar burning lies,
Their hungrie eares feede on their heav'nly noyse,
That Angels sing, to tell their untould joyes;
   Their understanding naked Truth, their wills
   The all, and selfe-sufficient Goodnesse fills,
That nothing here is wanting, but the want of ills.

The joy of the senses, &c.

35

No Sorrowe nowe hangs clowding on their browe,
No bloodles Maladie empales their face,
No Age drops on their hayrs his silver snowe,
No Nakednesse their bodies doeth embase,
No Povertie themselves, and theirs disgrace,
   No feare of death the joy of life devours,
   No unchast sleepe their precious time deflowrs,
No losse, no griefe, no change waite on their winged hour's.

2. By the amotion of all evill.

36

But now their naked bodies skorne the cold,
And from their eyes joy lookes, and laughs at paine,
The Infant wonders how he came so old,
And old man how he came so young againe;
Still resting, though from sleepe they still refraine,
   Whear all are rich, and yet no gold they owe,
   And all are Kings, and yet no Subjects knowe,
All full, and yet no time on foode they doe bestowe.

37

For things that passe are past, and in this field,
The indeficient Spring no Winter feares,
The Trees together fruit, and blossome yeild,
Th' unfading Lilly leaves of silver beares,

34.2 accloyes: fills full.

35 gloss: amotion: removal.

36.5 still : stiil 1610.

37.1 passe: change.

And crimson rose a skarlet garment weares:
And all of these on the Saints bodies growe,
Not, as they woont, on baser earth belowe;
Three rivers heere of milke, and wine, and honie flowe.

By the accesse of all good againe

38

in the glorie of the Holy Cittie.

About the holy Cittie rowles a flood
Of moulten chrystall, like a sea of glasse,
On which weake streame a strong foundation stood,
Of living Diamounds the building was,
That all things else, besides it selfe, did passe.
Her streetes, in stead of stones, the starres did pave,
And little pearles, for dust, it seem'd to have,
On which soft-streaming Manna, like pure snowe, did wave.

39

In the beatificall vision of God.

In mid'st of this Citie cœlestiall,
Whear the eternall Temple should have rose,
Light'ned th' Idea Beatificall:
End, and beginning of each thing that growes,
Whose selfe no end, nor yet beginning knowes,
That hath no eyes to see, nor ears to heare,
Yet sees, and heares, and is all-eye, all-eare,
That no whear is contain'd, and yet is every whear.

40

Changer of all things, yet immutable,
Before, and after all, the first, and last,
That mooving all, is yet immoveable,
Great without quantitie, in whose forecast,

38 The details of this and the following stanza come from the description of the New Jerusalem, Revelation 4 and 21–22.

39 gloss: In : in 1610.

39.3 Light'ned: shone. th'Idea Beatificall: There is no temple in the Heavenly City because "the Lord God Almighty and the Lamb are the temple of it" (Rev. 21:22).

39.8 a traditional idea, represented, for instance, in *Pantagruel* 3. 13, where God is described as a being whose center is everywhere and whose circumference nowhere. Rabelais attributes the image to Hermes Trismegistus.

40.4 forecast: forethought.

Things past are present, things to come are past,
  Swift without motion, to whose open eye
  The hearts of wicked men unbrested lie,
At once absent, and present to them, farre, and nigh.

41

It is no flaming lustre, made of light,
No sweet concent, or well-tim'd harmonie,
Ambrosia, for to feast the Appetite,
Or flowrie odour, mixt with spicerie.
No soft embrace, or pleasure bodily,
  And yet it is a kinde of inward feast,
  A harmony, that sounds within the brest,
An odour, light, embrace, in which the soule doth rest.

42

A heav'nly feast, no hunger can consume,
A light unseene, yet shines in every place,
A sound, no time can steale, a sweet perfume,
No windes can scatter, an intire embrace,
That no satietie can ere unlace,
  Ingrac't into so high a favour, thear
  The Saints, with their Beaw-peers, whole worlds outwear,
And things unseene doe see, and things unheard doe hear.

43

And of Christ.

Ye blessed soules, growne richer by your spoile,
Whose losse, though great, is cause of greater gaines,
Here may your weary Spirits rest from toyle,
Spending your endlesse eav'ning, that remaines,
Among those white flocks, and celestiall traines,
  That feed upon their Sheapheards eyes, and frame
  That heav'nly musique of so woondrous fame,
Psalming aloude the holy honours of his name.

44

Had I a voice of steel to tune my song,
Wear every verse as smoothly fil'd as glasse,

42.7 Beaw-peers: compeers.

And every member turned to a tongue,
And every tongue wear made of sounding brasse,
Yet all that skill, and all this strength, alas,
    Should it presume to guild, wear misadvis'd,
    The place, whear David hath new songs devis'd,
As in his burning throne he sits emparadis'd.

45

Most happie Prince, whose eyes those starres behould,
Treading ours under feet, now maist thou powre
That overflowing skill, whearwith of ould
Thou woont'st to combe rough speech, now maist thou showr
Fresh streames of praise upon that holy bowre,
    Which well we heaven call, not that it rowles,
    But that it is the haven of our soules.
Most happie Prince, whose sight so heav'nly sight behoulds.

46

Ah foolish Sheapheards, that wear woont esteem,
Your God all rough, and shaggy-hair'd to bee;
And yet farre wiser Sheapheards then ye deeme,
For who so poore (though who so rich) as hee,
When, with us hermiting in lowe degree,
    He wash't his flocks in Jordans spotles tide,
    And, that his deere remembrance aie might bide,
Did to us come, and with us liv'd, and for us di'd?

47

But now so lively colours did embeame
His sparkling forehead, and so shiny rayes
Kindled his flaming locks; that downe did streame
In curles, along his necke, whear sweetly playes
(Singing his wounds of love in sacred layes)
    His deerest Spouse, Spouse of the deerest Lover,

44.6 guild: adorn.

46.2 God: Pan.

46.6 wash't: i.e., baptized.

47.6 Spouse: the Christian church, bride of Christ.

Knitting a thousand knots over, and over,
And dying still for love, but they her still recover.

48

Faire Egliset, that at his eyes doth dresse
Her glorious face, those eyes, from whence ar shed
Infinite belamours, whear to expresse
His love, high God all heav'n as captive leads,
And all the banners of his grace dispreads,
And in those windowes, doth his armes englaze,
And on those eyes, the Angels all doe gaze,
And from those eies, the lights of heav'n do gleane their blaze.

49

But let the Kentish lad, that lately taught
His oaten reed the trumpets silver sound,
Young Thyrsilis, and for his musique brought
The willing sphears from heav'n, to lead a round
Of dauncing Nymphs, and Heards, that sung, and crown'd
Eclectas hymen with ten thousand flowrs
Of choycest prayse, and hung her heav'nly bow'rs
With saffron garlands, drest for Nuptiall Paramours,

48.1 Egliset: church, from French *église*.

49.1 Kentish lad: Giles concludes with praise for his older brother Phineas who, as the pastoral Thyrsilis, has turned from the lower pastoral ("His oaten reed") to a higher subject ("the trumpets silver sound"). Giles is referring to the later part of *The Purple Island* as it moves from man's physiology to a religious conclusion. There Phineas asserts that he must change his "oaten Quill/For trumpet 'larms" (11. 2. 5–6) as he begins to write about the subject of man's moral and religious actions represented by Eclecta (11. 8), or Choice, the daughter of Intellect and Will (Voletta). After various difficulties Eclecta is finally saved from a great dragon, Satan, by a knight, Christ, whom she marries: "He still a Bridegroom, she a gladsome Bride" (12. 76. 3) — that is, Christ and his church — "While all the hills glad *Hymens* loudly vaunt" (12. 77. 4). The story closes, as Giles was evidently aware, with the appeal, "Come *Hymen, Hymen* come, come, drest in thy golden pall" (12. 87. 7). Thus Phineas' otherwise undatable poem at least in part antedates that of his younger brother, the "greene Muse, hiding her younger head/Under old Chamus flaggy banks" (50. 4–5) at Cambridge.

49.8 saffron: Hymen was traditionally so clothed.

50

Let his shrill trumpet, with her silver blast,
Of faire Electa, and her Spousall bed,
Be the sweet pipe, and smooth Encomiast:
But my greene Muse, hiding her younger head
Under old Chamus flaggy banks, that spread
    Their willough locks abroad, and all the day
    With their owne watry shadowes wanton play,
Dares not those high amours, and love-sick songs assay.

51

Impotent words, weake sides, that strive in vaine,
In vaine, alas, to tell so heav'nly sight,
So heav'nly sight, as none can greater feigne,
Feigne what he can, that seemes of greatest might,
    Might any yet compare with Infinite?
    Infinite sure those joyes, my words but light,
Light is the pallace whear she dwells. O blessed wight!

I GROW & WITHER BOTH TOGETHER
I G.W. ANº ÆTATIS SVÆ 21. 1611

George Wither

George Wither was born in 1588 in the village of Bentworth, east of Winchester in southern England. He grew up there, where his family was well established. After two years in Magdalen College, Oxford, he left without a degree and in time moved to London, where he studied law and became a friend of a group of young lawyer–poets which included William Browne, William Ferrar, and Christopher Brooke, the participants in his *Shepheards Hunting.* Undoubtedly he himself was already writing verse; as he says, his group

> at twice-ten have sung more,
> Then some will doe, at fourescore.
>
> *Shepheards Hunting* 4. 279–80.

He publicly mourned the death of Prince Henry on November 6, 1612, with *Obsequies* and celebrated the marriage of the Prince's sister Elizabeth to Frederick of Germany the following February fourteenth with *Epithalamion.*

But also published in 1613 was his *Abuses Stript and Whipt,* which he dedicated to himself. It is a generalized satire at which someone, probably the Earl of Northumberland, took offense. As a result, in the spring of 1614 Wither was jailed in the Marshalsea Prison, the first of several such experiences. He describes his reactions in the first three parts of the *Shepheards Hunting,* which he wrote while there. Released, apparently through royal intervention, he continued to write and helped his friend Browne with the publication of his *Shepheards Pipe* (1614), to which he contributed two pastorals which were reprinted as Eclogues 4 and 5 of his own *Shepheards Hunting.* They apparently were written before he was jailed.

In 1615 appeared *Fidelia,* another pastoral, to which was appended his most famous poem, "Shall I wasting in despair." He returned to satire with *Withers Motto* (1621), dedicated "To any body," and was jailed again. The next year he published an incomplete collection of his early work whose title, *Juvenilia,* indicates his opinion of it; but his real poetic career was over. During the rest of his long life he wrote a great deal of verse which is mostly forgotten today and which became, indeed, the synonym for bad poetry for the later seventeenth and eighteenth centuries — garrulous, pedantic, and dull. As he himself admitted, his reputation "withered." He fought ineffectually on the Parliamentary side in the Civil War and spent much of his later life trying to collect for damages done to him by the Royalists and particularly by the poet John Denham. He died in 1667 and was buried in London.

The Restoration and the eighteenth century ignored Wither, but Coleridge, Southey, and Lamb rediscovered his early writing, after Bishop Percy had printed "Shall I wasting" in his *Reliques*. Lamb especially wrote of him with sympathy and discernment. Except for this one lyric, however, Wither has been pretty much forgotten. His works were reprinted by the Spenser Society in 1871–82, Frank Sidgwick inadequately edited some of the early work in *The Poetry of George Wither* (London: A. H. Bullen, 1902), and the Scolar Press (Menston, England, 1970) has recently made the *Juvenilia* available again in a somewhat illegible facsimile.

Of the poets represented in this collection, Wither is in some ways the most readable today. Only rarely is he difficult, as when in the *Shepheards Hunting* (4. 113–38) he designates awards for achievements which are hard to identify. His writing is not so complex in its religious content as that of Giles or Phineas Fletcher nor in its philosophical reflections as that of More nor in its contemporary allusions as that of Drayton. Anyone can sense at once his genuine admiration for Princess Elizabeth in *Epithalamion*, his sense of outrage at his unmerited imprisonment for publishing his *Abuses*, and his exalted view of the poet's calling. "Shall I wasting" comes very near to the Cavalier poets at their best. His "Christmas Carroll" is as warmly evocative as Dickens'. The unfortunate later tendency to moralize and lecture appears here only once, when he unexpectedly devotes lines 205–58 of *Epithalamion* to a sentimental sermon on the vanity of the world. Apparently the Princess received it with good grace, but as Allan Pritchard has convincingly argued (*Studies in Philology*, 59 [1962]: 211–30), Wither's decline as a poet occurred because of his "grossly mistaken view of the nature and function of poetry" as narrow didacticism.

An interesting aspect of Wither's early poetry is its indication that someone outside James' court could aspire to poetic prominence. Wither tried at first to make his way by celebrating the affairs of court with the funeral poem for Prince Henry and the wedding poem for Elizabeth. One quickly recognizes, however, that this is an outsider speaking: he comes up from his home in the country to see the public display for the wedding, but he remains at a distance. To gain further recognition, in 1613 he also published *Abuses* and was jailed. Actually, *Abuses* is a generalized and unsubversive satire; one has the impression that Wither intended no harm but wanted to moralize upon and reform abuses widespread in his society. He is consequently very sorry for himself. As Lamb justly remarked, "He is for ever anticipating persecution and martyrdom; fingering, as it were, the flames, to try how he can bear them" ("On the Poetical Works of George Wither").

A statement in *Epithalamion*, lines 269–70, admits that the pastoral was not popular at court, though Wither later (ll. 527–42) pleads for its acceptance there. The pastoral indeed was not a popular court form, despite its famous model in Spenser (though Wither claims instead as his model the Psalms of David): such writers there as Jonson, Campion, Chapman, and Shakespeare were not employing this rather old-fashioned mode. Wither accordingly turned to a different audience. The many printings of his early poems show that he was successful, and they indicate some of the differences between the taste of the courtiers and that of the public. What some of the former thought of his writing can be inferred from Jonson's disparaging portrait of him as Chronomasti in the masque *Time Vindicated* (1623). Of Wither's later career the biographer Aubrey records the tradition that, when he was captured by Royalist forces in 1643, the poet John Denham successfully pleaded for his life, arguing that "whilest G. W. lived, he [Denham] should not be the worst poet in England."

Wither frames his *Epithalamion* in couplets (ll. 1–278 and 513–52) which objectively narrate the occasion, a feature not found in the various epithalamia of the early seventeenth century nor in their model by Spenser (see further C. G. Osgood, *MLN*, 76 [1961]: 205–8). The *Epithalamion* itself is written in six-line stanzas of four-foot trochees, a very simple pattern compared with any contemporary wedding poem. Its thirty-nine stanzas follow the wedding day from dawn into night as did Spenser's but lack the complexity of thought or structure of the more famous poem. One lacks any sense, too, of immediate participation on the poet's part. Only once (ll. 469–70) does he verge on the sensual, but he then quickly retreats. Without being actively of their party, Wither has Puritan leanings.

Another poem in the pastoral form is Wither's best, the *Shepheards Hunting*. Incarcerated, Wither bravely accepts the thesis of Edward Dyer's "My mind to me a kingdom is," later to be given definitive expression in Lovelace's "To Althea: from Prison." Accordingly the first three eclogues detail to his friends his woes: in the first to "Willy," William Browne of Tavistock, the best known of the group, friend of Drayton and author of the *Shepheards Pipe* (1614); in the second to "Willy" and "Cuddy," the latter being Christopher Brooke, the friend of Donne who was jailed for witnessing his marriage; and in the third to "Willy," "Cuddy," and "Alexis," who was William Ferrar, brother of the courtier Nicholas. Aside from his continuing complaints about being jailed, the eclogues are interesting on a number of accounts. They are written in easy couplets with a considerable variety of contrasting songs interwoven. The allegory of his *Abuses* as a pack of hunting hounds is vivid and authentic until the author forgets their literal meaning and has the entire pack chase through "Kitchin, Parlor, Hall, and Chamber" (3. 55). Likewise he occasionally forgets that Browne as Willy is one of the interlocutors and refers to him as an absent friend "Tavy," e.g., 3. 171. He defends the value of his satires, observing that their subjects will be valid "as long [as] mortality [will] last," 3. 103.

Except for the intrusive and repetitive lines about his jail experiences (5. 183–234), the last two eclogues deal with different material, a statement of Wither's high regard for the poetic calling. The fourth is in the same tetrameter couplets that Milton was to employ in "L'Allegro" and "Il Penseroso," an influence which E. M. Clark perhaps overestimates (*Studies in Philology*, 56 [1959]: 626–46). In this eclogue Wither observes that he draws his imagery from the "meanest objects":

> By the murmure of a spring,
> Or the least boughes rusteling.
> By a Dazie whose leaves spred,
> Shut when *Tytan* goes to bed;
> Or a shady bush or tree,
> She could more infuse in mee,
> Then all Natures beauties can,
> In some other wiser man.
>
> [4. 371–78]

Lines 71–140 of this eclogue depict in this way one of the loveliest Mayday celebrations in English literature. One can only wish that he had followed this bent more often.

In Eclogue 5 Wither raises the still difficult issue of how a poet can write and at the same time support himself (ll. 143–82). His answer is that, society being what it is and poets having the standing in it that they have, one must try to do both. As Philaster, Wither assures his friend that the poet–shepherd must not forsake his occupation–sheep nor need he

> neglect thy calling for thy *Muse*.
> But, let these two, so each of other borrow,
> That they may season mirth, and lessen sorrow.
> Thy Flocke will helpe thy charges to defray,
> Thy *Muse* to passe the long and teadious day.
> [5. 152–56]

Wither's address "To the Reader" of the *Shepheards Hunting* had promised that its author would go through the traditional literary development from pastoral to epic: he would follow the "sleight matter" of those pastorals with "a greater matter," the epic. He seems to have tried; at least *Britains Remembrancer* (1628), though not an epic, memorializes at length the plague year of 1625. But his real ability was the "sleight matter" of these pastorals, where "That slender *Muse* of mine" (*Shepheards Hunting*, 5. 209) had its natural expression.

The text of *Epithalamion* reprinted here is from the *Juvenilia* (London, 1622), which Wither seems to have considered the definitive printing of his early poetry. From the same collection comes the *Shepheards Hunting*, first printed in 1615. Its two final eclogues had been appended to William Browne's *Shepheards Pipe* of 1614. There Wither's pastoral name had been Thirsis, changed in 1615 to Roget and finally to Philarete (lover of virtue) with some consequent adaptation of the context. "Shall I wasting in despair" was omitted from the 1622 *Juvenilia*; the text here is from the 1633 edition, where it appears as a song in *Faire-Virtue*. The final two lyrics were printed at the end of that volume.

Epithalamion.

To the All-Vertuous and Thrice Excellent Princesse Elizabeth,
sole daughter to our dread Soveraigne, *James*
by the grace of *God, King of* Great Britaine,
France *and* Ireland, &c.

and Wife to the High and Mighty Prince,
Frederick the fifth, Count Palatine of the Rheine,
Duke of Bavier, &c. Elector, and Arch-sewer to
the sacred Roman Empire, during
the vacancy Vicar of the same, *and Knight of the*
most honorable Order of the Garter.

George Wither *wisheth all the Health; Joyes, Honours,*
and Felicities of this World, in this life, and the
perfections of eternity in the World to come.

To the Christian Readers.

Readers; for that in my booke of Satyricall Essayes, *I have been deemed over* Cynicall*; to shew, that I am not wholly inclined to that* Vaine*: But indeede especially, out of the love which in duty I owe to those incomparable* Princes, *I have in honour of their* Royall Solemnities, *published these short* Epithalamiæs. *By which you may perceive (how ever the world thinke of me) I am not of such a Churlish* Constitution, *but I can afford* Vertue *her deserved honour; and have as well an affable looke to encourage* Honesty*; as a sterne frowne to cast on* Villanie*; If the* Times *would suffer me, I could be as pleasing as* 10 *others; and perhaps ere long I will make you amends for my former rigor; Meane while I commit this unto your censures; and bid you farewell.*

G. W.

1 Satyricall Essayes: his *Abuses Stript, and Whipt* (1613).

Epithalamion.

Bright *Northerne* Starre, and great *Minervæs* peere,
Sweete *Lady* of this *Day*: *Great Britaines* deere.
Loe thy poore *Vassall*, that was erst so rude,
With his most *Rusticke Satyrs* to intrude,
Once more like a poore *Silvan* now drawes neare;
And in thy sacred *Presence* dares appeare.
Oh let not that sweete *Bowe* thy *Brow* be bent,
To scarre him with a *Shaft* of discontent:
One looke with *Anger*, nay thy gentlest *Frowne*,
10 Is twice enough to cast a *Greater* downe.
My *Will* is ever, never to offend,
These that are good; and what I here intend,
Your *Worth* compels me to. For lately greev'd,
More then can be exprest, or well beleev'd;
Minding for ever to abandon sport,
And live exilde from places of resort;
Carelesse of all, I yeelding to securitie,
Thought to shut up my *Muse* in darke obscuritie:
And in content, the better to repose,
20 A lonely *Grove* upon a *Mountaine* chose.
East from *Caer Winn*, mid-way twixt *Arle* and *Dis*,
True *Springs*, where *Britains* true *Arcadia* is.
But ere I entred my entended course,
Great Æolus began to offer force.
* The boisterous *King* was growne so mad with rage,
That all the Earth, was but his furies stage.

* He here remembers and describes the late Winter, which was so exceeding tempestuous and windy.

21-22 *Caer Winn* is the ancient name for the town of Winchester. A few miles east of it is New Alresford (*Arle*), and a little further is Bentworth, Wither's birthplace, "where *Britains* true *Arcadia* is." As for a literal spring, Drayton in *Poly-Olbion*, Song 2, line 237 gloss, mentions Alresford Pond, "yeelding an unusual abundance of water" to the River Itchen. It is not clear which neighboring town is *Dis*.

24 *Æolus*: god of the winds.

25 rage, : rage; 1622.

25 gloss: John Stowe reports in his *Annales* (London, 1631), p. 1002, that "In the moneths of October, November, and December, this yeere 1612. There happened many great Winds, violent Stormes, and Tempests, as well by land as Sea, which did exceeding great damage, with extreame shipwracke throughout the Ocean."

Fire, *Ayre*, *Earth*, *Sea*, were intermixt in one:
Yet *Fire*, through *Water*, *Earth* and *Ayre* shone.
The *Sea*, as if she ment to whelme them under,
Beat on the *Cliffes*, and rag'd more loud then thunder: 30
And whil'st the *vales* she with salt waves did fill,
The *Aire* showr'd *flouds*, that drencht our highest hill;
And the proud trees, that would no dutie know,
Lay over-turned, twenties in a Row.
Yea, every Man for feare, fell to *Devotion*;
Lest the whole *Ile* should have bin drencht in th'Ocean.
Which I perceiving, conjur'd up my *Muse*,
The *Spirit*, whose good helpe I sometime use:
And though I ment to breake her rest no more,
I was then faine her aide for to implore. 40
And by her helpe indeed, I came to know,
Why, both the *Ayre* and *Seas* were troubled so.
For having urg'd her, that she would unfold
What cause she knew: Thus much at last she told.
Of late (quoth she) *there is by powers Divine*
A match concluded, twixt Great Thame *and* Rhine.
Two famous Rivers, *equall both to* Nile*:*
The one, the pride of Europes *greatest Ile.*
Th'other disdaining to be closely pent;
Washes a great part of the Continent. 50
Yet with abundance, doth the Wants *supply,*
Of the still-thirsting Sea, *that's never dry.*
And now, these, *being not alone endear'd,*
To mightie Neptune, *and his watrie* Heard*:*
But also to the great and dreadfull Jove,
With all his sacred Companies above,
Both have assented by their Loves *inviting:*
To grace (with their owne presence) this Uniting.
Jove *call'd a* Summons *to the* Worlds *great wonder,*
'Twas that we heard of late, which we thought thunder. 60

The reason of the tempestuous Winter.

A thousand Legions *he intends to send them,*
Of Cherubins *and* Angels *to attend them:*
And those strong Windes, *that did such blustring keepe,*

33 know, : know; 1622.
45 *Divine* : *Divine:* 1622.

Were but the Tritons, *sounding in the* Deepe;
To warne each River, *petty* Streame *and* Spring,
Their aide unto their Soveraigne *to bring.*
The Floods *and* Showres *that came so plenteous downe,*
And lay entrencht in every Field *and* Towne,
Were but retainers to the Nobler sort,
70 *That owe their Homage at the* Watrie Court*:*
Or else the Streames *not pleas'd with their owne store,*
To grace the Thames, *their* Mistris, *borrowed more.*
Exacting from their neighbouring Dales *and* Hills,
But by consent all (nought against their wills.)
Yet now, since in this stirre are brought to ground
Many faire buildings, many hundreds drown'd,
And daily found of broken Ships great store,
That lie dismembred upon every shore:
With divers other mischiefes knowne to all,
80 *This is the cause that those great harmes befall.*
Whilst other, things in readinesse, did make,
Hells *hatefull* Hags *from out their prisons brake:*
And spighting at this hopefull match, began
To wreake their wrath on Ayre, Earth, Sea, *and* Man.
Some having shapes of Romish *shavelings got,*
Spew'd out their venome; and began to plot
Which way to thwart it: others made their way
With much distraction thorough Land *and* Sea
Extreamely raging. But Almightie Jove
90 *Perceives their* Hate *and* Envie *from above:*
He'le checke their furie, and in yrons chain'd,
Their libertie abus'd, shall be restrain'd:
Hee'le shut them up, from comming to molest
The Meriments of Hymens *holy feast.*
Where shall be knit that sacred Gordian *knot,*
Which in no age to come shall be forgot.
Which Policie *nor* Force *shall nere untie,*
But must continue to eternitie:
Which for the whole Worlds *good was fore-decree'd,*
100 *With* Hope *expected long; now come indeed.*

The cause of all such dangers as fall out during the distemperature of the ayre.

86 Some English Roman Catholics opposed the marriage. See, for instance, a contemporary statement in John Nichols, *Progresses . . . of King James*, 2:467.

And of whose future glory, worth, *and* merit
Much I could speake with a prophetike spirit.
Thus by my *Muses* deare assistance, finding
The cause of this disturbance, with more minding
My Countries welfare, then my owne content,
And longing to behold this *Tales* event:
My lonely life I suddenly forsooke,
And to the *Court* againe my Journey tooke.

He noteth the most admirable alteration of the weather a while before these Nuptials.

Meane-while I saw the furious *Windes* were laid;
The risings of the swelling *Waters* staid. 110
The *Winter* gan to change in every thing,
And seem'd to borrow mildnesse of the *Spring*.
The *Violet* and *Primrose* fresh did grow;
And as in *Aprill*, trim'd both *Cops* and *rowe*.
The *Citie*, that I left in mourning clad,
Drouping, as if it would have still beene sad,
I found deckt up in roabes so neat and trimme,
Faire *Iris* would have look't but stale and dimme
In her best colours, had she there appear'd;
The *Sorrowes* of the *Court* I found well cleer'd, 120
Their wofull habits quite cast off, and ty'rd
In such a glorious fashion: I admir'd.
All her chiefe *Peeres* and choisest *beauties* to,
In greater pompe, then *Mortals* use to doe,
Wait as attendants. *Juno*'s come to see;
Because she heares that this solemnitie
Exceeds faire *Hippodamia's* (where the strife
'Twixt *her*, *Minerva*, and lame *Vulcans* wife
Did first arise,) and with her leades along
A noble, stately, and a mighty throng. 130

The glorious preparation, of this solemnity, the state whereof is here allegorically described.

106 event: outcome.

115 mourning: for the death of Elizabeth's brother Henry the previous November. Probably it is the cause of the poet's sorrow above at line 13.

119 appear'd; : appear'd, 1622.

123 to: too.

127-29 Wither has confused the wedding of Pirithous and Hippodamia, where Mars sowed dissension, with that of Peleus and Thetis, where Discord did the same with a golden apple, leading ultimately to the judgment of Paris among Juno, Venus, and Minerva.

128 her: Juno.

Venus, (attended with her rarest features,
Sweet lovely-smiling, and heart-moving creatures,
The very fairest *Jewels* of her treasure,
Able to move the senceles stones to pleasure.)
Of all her sweetest *Saints*, hath robd their shrines;
And brings them for the Courtiers *Valentines*.
Nor doth Dame *Pallas*, from these triumphs lurke;
Her noblest wits, she freely sets on worke.
Of late she summond them unto this place,
140 To doe your maskes and *Revels* better grace.
Here* *Mars* himselfe to, clad in Armour bright,
Hath showne his furie in a bloudlesse fight;
And both on land and water, sternely drest,
Acted his bloudy *Stratagems* in jest:
Which (to the people, frighted by their error,)
With seeming wounds and death did ad more terror,
Besides, to give the greater cause of wonder,
Jove did vouchsafe a ratling peale of thunder:
Comets and *Meteors* by the starres exhald,
150 Were from the *Middle-Region* lately cald;
And to a place appointed made repaire,
To show their fierie Friscols in the aire,
People innumerable doe resort,
As if all *Europe* here would keepe one Court:
Yea, *Hymen* in his Safferon-coloured weed,
To celebrate his rites is full agreed.
All this I see: which seeing, makes me borrow
Some of their mirth a while, and lay downe sorrow.
And yet not this: but rather the delight
160 My heart doth take in the much hoped sight
Of these thy glories, long already due;
And this sweet comfort, that my eyes doe view
Thy happy Bridegroome, *Prince Count Palatine*,

* Meaning the Sea-fight, and the taking of the Castle on the water, which was most artificially performed.

The fier-workes he alludeth to those exhalations.

138 noblest wits: See the gloss below at line 442.

141ff. The fireworks, presented on the Thursday night before the wedding, and the sea fight (on the Thames) on the Saturday were expensive and successful shows. For contemporary reports, see Nicholls, *Progresses*, 2:527ff.

152 Friscols: friskings.

155 Hymen was traditionally attired in a saffron-colored robe.

Now thy best friend and truest *Valentine*.
Upon whose brow, my minde doth reade the storie
Of mightie *fame*, and a true future glorie.
Me thinkes I doe foresee already, how
Princes and *Monarchs* at his stirrop bow:
I see him shine in steele; the bloudy fields
Already won, and how his proud *foe* yeelds. 170
God hath ordaind him happinesse great store:
And yet in nothing is he happy more,
Then in thy love (faire *Princesse*:) For (unlesse
Heaven, like to *Man*, be prone to ficklenesse)
Thy *Fortunes* must be greater in effect,
Then *time* makes show of, or *men* can expect.
Yet, notwithstanding all those goods of *fate*,
Thy *Minde* shall ever be above thy *state*:
For over and beside thy proper merit,
Our last *Eliza* grants her Noble spirit 180
To be re-doubled on thee; and your *names*
Being both one, shall give you both one fames.
Oh blessed thou! and they to whom thou giv'st
The leave for to be attendants where thou liv'st:
And haplesse we, that must of force let goe,
The matchlesse treasure we esteeme of so.
But yet we trust 'tis for our good and thine;
Or else thou shouldst not change thy *Thame* for *Rhyne*.
We hope that this will the uniting prove
Of *Countries* and of *Nations* by your *love*: 190
And that from out your blessed loynes, shall come
Another terror to the *Whore of Rome*:
And such a stout *Achilles*, as shall make
Her tottering Walls and weake foundation shake:
For *Thetis*-like, thy fortunes doe require,
Thy *Issue* should be greater then his *sire*.
But (*Gracious Princesse*) now since thus it fares,

164 *Valentine*: The wedding took place on Sunday, February 14, 1613.

182 fames: The plural seems to be used only for the rhyme.

192 *Whore of Rome*: Protestants regularly interpreted the Whore of Babylon in Revelation as the Roman Catholic Church.

195 *Thetis*: the mother, by Peleus, of Achilles.

And God so well for you and us prepares:
Since he hath daign'd such honours for to doe you,
200 And showne himselfe so favourable to you:
Since he hath chang'd your sorrowes, and your sadnes,
Into such great and unexpected gladnesse:
Oh now remember you to be at leasure,
Sometime to thinke on him amidst your pleasure:
Let not these glories of the *world* deceave you,
Nor her vaine favours of your selfe bereave you.
Consider yet for all this Jollitie,
Y'are mortall, and must feele mortalitie:
And that God can in midst of all your Joyes,
210 Quite dash this pompe, and fill you with annoyes.
Triumphes are fit for *Princes*; yet we finde
They ought not wholly to take up the minde,
Nor yet to be let passe; as things in vaine:
For out of all things, wit will knowledge gaine.
Musique may teach of difference in degree,
The best tun'd *Common-Weales* will framed bee:
And that he moves, and lives with greatest grace,
That unto *Time* and *Measure* ties his pace.
Then let these things be [a] *Emblemes*, to present
220 Your minde with a more lasting true content.
When you behold the infinite resort,
The glory and the splendor of the Court;
What wondrous favours God doth here bequeath you,
How many hundred thousands are beneath you;
And view with admiration your great blisse,
Then with your selfe you may imagine this.
'Tis but a blast, or transitory shade,
Which in the turning of a hand may fade.
Honours, which you your selfe did never winne,
230 *And might (had God been pleas'd) anothers binne.*
And thinke, if shadowes have such majestie,
What are the glories of eternitie;
Then by this image of a *fight on Sea*,
Wherein you heard the thundring Canons plea;

a He declares what use is to be made of these showes and triumphes, and what meditations the minde may be occupied about, when we behold them.

201 Elizabeth's brother Henry had died the previous November.
215-16 That is, society is a harmony.

And saw flames breaking from their murthering throts,
Which in true skirmish, fling resistlesse shots;
Your wisedome may (and will no doubt) begin,
To cast what perill a poore *Souldiers* in:
You will conceave his miseries and cares,
How many dangers, deaths, and wounds he shares: 240
Then though the most pass't over, and neglect them,
That *Rethericke* will move you to respect them.
And if hereafter, you should hap to see
Such *Mimick Apes* (that Courts disgraces be:)
I meane such Chamber-combatants; who never
Weare other Helmet, then a Hat of *Bever*:
Or nere board *Pinnace* but in silken saile;
And in the steed of boysterous shirts of maile,
Goe arm'd in *Cambrick*: If that such a *Kite*
(I say) should scorne an *Eagle* in your sight; 250
Your *wisedome* judge (by this experience) can,
Which hath most worth, *Hermaphrodite*, or *Man*.
The *nights* strange * prospects, made to feed the eies, * Fire-workes.
With Artfull fiers, mounted in the skies:
Graced with horred claps of sulphury thunders
May make you minde th'Almighties greater wonders.
Nor is there any thing, but you may thence
Reape inward gaine; as well as please the *Sense*.
But pardon me (*oh fairest*) that am bold,
My heart thus freely, plainely, to unfold. 260
What though I know, you knew all this before:
My love *this* showes, and that is something more.
Doe not my honest service here disdaine,
I am a faithfull, though an humble Swaine.
I'me none of those that have the meanes or place,
With showes of cost to doe your *Nuptials* grace:
But onely master of mine owne desire,
Am hither come with others to admire.
I am not of those *Heliconian* wits,
Whose pleasing straines the *Courts* knowne humour fits. 270

254 skies, : skies: 1622.
255 thunders : thunders; 1622.
269 wits, : wits; 1622.

But a poore rurall *Shepheard*, that for need,
Can make sheepe Musique on an *Oaten* reed:
Yet for my *love* (Ile this be bold to boast)
It is as much to you, as his that's most.
Which, since I no way else can now explaine,
If you'l in midst of all these *glories* daigne
To lend your eares unto my *Muse* so long,
She shall declare it in a *Wedding song*.

Epithalamion

The Marriage being on S. *Valentines* day, the Author showes it by beginning with the salutation of a supposed Valentine.

Valentine, good morrow to thee,
280 Love and service both I owe thee:
And would waite upon thy pleasure;
But I cannot be at leasure:
For, I owe this *day* as debter,
To (a thousand times) thy better.

Hymen now will have effected
What hath been so long expected:
Thame thy *Mistris*, now unwedded;
Soone, must with a *Prince* be bedded.
If thou'lt see her *Virgin* ever,
290 Come, and doe it now, or never.

Where art thou, oh faire *Aurora*?
Call in *Ver* and Lady *Flora*:
And you daughters of the *Morning*,
In your neat'st, and feat'st adorning:
Cleare your fore-heads, and be sprightfull,
That this *day* may seeme delightfull.

All you *Nimphs* that use the Mountaines,
Or delight in groves and fountaines;
Sheapheardesses, you that dally,

276 daigne : daigne, 1622.

291-92 *Aurora . . . Ver . . . Flora*: goddesses of the dawn, spring, flowers.

Either upon Hill or Valley: 300
And you daughters of the *Bower*,
That acknowledge *Vestæs* power.

Oh you sleepe too long; awake yee,
See how *Time* doth overtake yee.
Harke, the *Larke* is up and singeth,
And the house with ecchoes ringeth.
Pretious howers, why neglect yee,
Whil'st affaires thus expect yee?

Come away upon my blessing,
The *Bride-chamber* lies to dressing: 310
Strow the wayes with leaves of *Roses*,
Some make *garlands*, some make *poses*:
'Tis a favour, and't may joy you,
That your *Mistris* will employ you.

Where's [a] *Sabrina*, with her daughters,
That doe sport about her waters:
Those that with their lockes of *Amber*,
Haunt the fruitfull hills of [b] Camber:
We must have to fill the number,
All the *Nimphs* of *Trent* and *Humber*. 320

a Severne.
b Wales.

Fie, your haste is scarce sufficing,
For the *Bride*'s awake and rising.
Enter beauties, and attend her;
All your helpes and service lend her:
With your quaint'st and new'st devises,
Trim your Lady, faire *Thamisis*.

See; shee's ready: with *Joyes* greet her,
Lads, goe bid the *Bride-groome* meet her:
But from rash approach advise him,
Lest a too much Joy surprize him, 330
None I ere knew yet, that dared,
View an *Angell* unprepared.

315-20 rivers to the west and north of England.

Now unto the *Church* she hies her;
Envie bursts, if she espies her:
In her gestures as she paces,
Are united all the *Graces*:
Which who sees and hath his senses,
Loves in spight of all defences.

O most true majestick creature!
340 *Nobles* did you note her feature?
Felt you not an inward motion,
Tempting *Love* to yeeld devotion;
And as you were even desiring,
Something check you for aspiring?

That's her *Vertue* which still tameth
Loose desires, and bad thoughts blameth:
For whil'st others were unruly,
She observ'd *Diana* truly:
And hath by that meanes obtained
350 Gifts of her that none have gained.

Yon's the *Bride-groome*, d'yee not spie him?
See how all the *Ladies* eye him.
Venus his perfection findeth,
And no more *Adonis* mindeth.
Much of him my heart divineth:
On whose brow all *Vertue* shineth.

Two such *Creatures Nature* would not
Let one place long keepe: she should not:
One shee'l have (she cares not whether,)
360 But our *Loves* can spare her neither.
Therefore ere we'le so be spighted,
They in one shall be united.

Natures selfe is well contented,
By that meanes to be prevented.
And behold they are retired,

359 whether: which.

So conjoyn'd, as we desired:
Hand in hand, not onely fixed,
But their hearts, are intermixed.

Happy they and we that see it,
For the good of *Europe* be it. 370
And heare *Heaven* my devotion,
Make this *Rhyne* and *Thame* an *Ocean*:
That it may with might and wonder,
Whelme the pride of [a] *Tyber* under.

a Tyber is the River which runneth by Rome.

Now yon [b] *Hall* their persons shroudeth,
Whither all this people croudeth:
There they feasted are with plenty,
Sweet *Ambrosia* is no deinty.
Groomes quaffe *Nectar*; for theres meeter,
Yea, more costly wines and sweeter. 380

b White-Hall.

Young men all, for joy goe ring yee,
And your merriest *Carols* sing yee.
Here's of *Damzels* many choices,
Let them tune their sweetest voyces.
Fet the *Muses* to, to cheare them;
They can ravish all that heare them.

Ladies, 'tis their *Highnesse* pleasures,
To behold you foot the *Measures*:
Lovely gestures addeth graces,
To your bright and *Angell* faces. 390
Give your active mindes the bridle:
Nothing worse then to be idle.

Worthies, your affaires forbeare yee,
For the *State* a while may spare yee:
Time was, that you loved sporting,
Have you quite forgot your Courting?

385 Fet: Fetch.

Joy the heart of *Cares* beguileth:
Once a yeere Apollo *smileth.*

Semel in anno ridet Apol.

Fellow Shepheards, how I pray you,
400 Can your *flocks* at this time stay you?
Let us also hie us thither,
Let's lay all our wits together,
And some *Pastorall* invent them,
That may show the *love* we ment them.

I my selfe though meanest stated,
And in *Court* now almost hated,
Will knit up my [a] *Scourge*, and venter
In the midst of them to enter;
For I know, there's no disdaining,
410 Where I looke for entertaining.

a Abuses stript and whipt. He noteth the mildnesse of the winter which, excepting that the beginning was very windy, was as temperate as the spring.

See, me thinkes the very *season*,
As if capable of Reason,
Hath laine by her native rigor,
The faire *Sun-beames* have more vigor.
They are *Æols* most endeared:
For the *Ayre*'s still'd and cleared.

Fawnes, and *Lambs* and *Kidds* doe play,
In the honour of this *day*:
The shrill *Black-Bird*, and the *Thrush*
420 Hops about in every bush:
And among the tender twigs,
Chaunt their sweet harmonious jigs.

Yea, and mov'd by this example,
They doe make each *Grove* a *temple*:
Where their *time* the best way using,
They their *Summer loves* are chusing,

Most men are of opinion, that this day every bird doth chuse her mate for that yeer.

398 The gloss is translated in this line. It is proverbial, meaning approval of reasonable recreation. See Tilley's *Dictionary of Proverbs,* Y 15.

407 The *Scourge* was appended to his *Abuses.*

422 jigs : ijgs 1622.

And unlesse some *Churle* do wrong them,
There's not an od bird among them.

Yet I heard as I was walking,
Groves and hills by *Ecchoes* talking: 430
Reeds unto the small brooks whistling,
Whil'st they danc't with pretty rushling.
Then for *us* to sleepe 'twere pitty;
Since *dumb creatures* are so witty.

But oh *Titan*, thou dost dally,
Hie thee to thy *Westerne Valley*:
Let this night one hower borrow:
She shall pay't againe to morrow:
And if thou'lt that favor do them,
Send thy sister *Phœbe* to them. 440

But shee's come her selfe unasked,
And brings [a] *Gods* and *Heroes* masked.
None yet saw, or heard in storie,
Such immortall, mortall glorie.
View not, without *preparation*;
Lest you faint in *admiration*.

a By these he means the two Masques, one of them being presented by the Lords, the other by the Gentry.

Say my *Lords*, and speake truth barely,
Mov'd they not exceeding rarely?
Did they not such praises merit,
As if *flesh* had all beene *spirit*? 450
True indeed, yet I must tell them,
There was *One* did farre excell them.

But (alas) this is ill dealing,
Night unawares away is stealing:
Their delay the poore *bed* wrongeth,
That for *Bride* with *Bride-groome* longeth:

442 gloss: The Lords' masque, by Thomas Campion, was presented on the wedding night; on Monday night the Middle Temple and Lincoln's Inn sponsored a masque by George Chapman. Finally, the Inner Temple and Gray's Inn presented one by Francis Beaumont on the following Saturday. See Nichols, *Progresses* 2, for details of the festivities.

And above all other places,
Must be blest with their embraces.

Revellers, then now forbeare yee,
460 And unto your rests prepare yee:
Let's a while your absence borrow,
Sleep to night, and *dance* to morrow.
We could well allow your Courting:
But 'twill hinder better sporting.

They are gone, and *Night* all lonely,
Leaves the *Bride* with *Bridegroome* onely.
Muse now tell; (for thou hast power
To flie thorough wall or tower:)
What contentments their hearts cheareth;
470 *And how lovely she appeareth.*

And yet doe not; tell it no man,
Rare conceits may so grow common:
Doe not to the *Vulgar* show them,
('Tis enough that *thou* dost know them.)
Their ill hearts are but the *Center*,
Where all misconceivings enter.

But thou *Luna* that dost lightly,
Haunt our downes and forrests nightly:
Thou that favour'st generation,
480 And art helpe to procreation:
See their *issue* thou so cherish,
I may live to see it flourish.

And you *Planets*, in whose power
Doth consist these lives of our;
You that teach us *Divinations*,
Helpe with all your *Constellations*,
How to frame in *Her*, a creature,
Blest in *Fortune*, *Wit*, and *Feature*.

484 our: The archaic form had not been entirely lost, and Wither needs it for the rhyme.

Lastly, oh you *Angels* ward them,
Set your sacred *Spels* to gard them; 490
Chase away such feares or terrors,
As not being, seeme through errors:
Yea, let not a *dreames* molesting,
Make them start when they are resting.

But THOU chiefly, most adored,
That shouldst onely be implored:
Thou to whom my meaning tendeth,
Whether er'e in show it bendeth:
Let them rest to night from sorrow,
And awake with joy to morrow. 500

Oh, to my *request* be heedfull,
Grant them *that*, and all things needfull.
Let not these my straines of *Folly*,
Make *true prayer* be unholy:
But if I have here offended:
Helpe, forgive, and see it mended.

Daigne me *this*. And if my *Muses*
Hastie issue she peruses,
Make it unto her seeme gratefull,
Though to all the *World* else hatefull. 510
But how er'e, yet *Soule* persever
Thus to wish her good for ever.

Thus ends the *Day*, together with my Song;
Oh may the Joyes thereof continue long!
Let *Heavens* just, all-seeing, sacred power
Favour this happy marriage day of your;
And blesse you in your chast embraces so,
We *Britains* may behold before you goe
The hopefull Issue we shall count so deare,
And whom (unborne) his foes already feare. 520

508 issue : issue; 1622. peruses, : peruses; 1622.
515 power : power, 1622.
516 your: as *our* at line 484.

Yea, I desire, that all your sorrowes may
Never be more, then they have been to day.
Which hoping; for acceptance now I sue,
And humbly bid your *Grace* and *Court* adue.
I saw the sight I came for; which I know
Was more then all the world beside could show.
But if amongst *Apollœs* Layes, you can
Be pleas'd to lend a gentle eare to *Pan*;
Or thinke your Country *Shepheard* loves as deare,
530 As if he were a *Courtier*, or a *Peere*:
Then I, that else must to my *Cell* of paine,
Will joyfull turne unto my *flocke* againe:
And there unto my fellow *shepheards* tell,
Why *you* are lov'd; wherein *you* doe excell.
And when we drive our *flocks* a field to graze them,
So chaunt your praises, that it shall amaze them:
And thinke that *Fate* hath new recald from death
Their still-lamented, sweete *Elizabeth*.
For though they see the *Court* but now and then,
540 They know *desert* as well as *Greater* men:
And honord *Fame* in them doth live or die,
As well as in the mouth of *Majestie*.
But taking granted what I here intreat,
At heaven for you my *devotions* beat:
And though I feare, *fate* will not suffer me
To doe you service, where your *Fortunes* be:
How ere my skill hath yet despised seem'd,
(And my unripened wit been misesteem'd:)
When all this costly *Showe* away shall flit,
550 And not one live that doth remember it;
If *Envies* trouble let not to persever;
I'le find a meanes to make it knowne for ever.

526 all : all, 1622.

543 intreat, : intreat: 1622.

551 let: restrain.

The Shepheards Hunting.

Being certaine Eglogues written during the time of the Authors Imprisonment in the Marshalsey.

To those Honoured, Noble, and right Vertuous Friends, my Visitants in the Marshalsey:

And to all other my unknowne Favourers, who either privately, or publikely wished me well in my imprisonment.

Noble Friends; you whose vertues made me first in love with Vertue; *and whose worths made mee be thought worthy of your loves: I have now at last (you see) by Gods assistance, and your encouragement, run through the* Purgatorie *of imprisonment; and by the worthy favour of a just* Prince, *stand free againe, without the least touch of dejected basenesse. Seeing therefore I was growne beyond my* Hope *so fortunate (after acknowledgement of my Creators love, together with the unequall'd Clemencie of so gracious a Soveraigne) I was troubled to thinke, by what meanes I might expresse my thankefulnes to so many well-deserving friends: No way I found to my desire,* 10 *neither yet ability to performe when I found it. But at length considering with my selfe what you were (that is) such, who favour honesty for no second reason, but because you yourselves are good; and ayme at no other reward, but the witnesse of a sound conscience that you doe well, I found, that thankfulnesse would prove the acceptablest present to sute with your dispositions; and that I imagined could be no way better expressed, then in manifesting your courtesies, and giving consent to your reasonable demaunds. For the first, I confesse (with thankes to the disposer of all things, and a true gratefull heart towards you) so many were the unexpected Visitations, and* 20 *unhoped kindnesses receyved, both from some among you of my Acquaintance, and many other unknowne Well-willers of my Cause, that I was perswaded to entertaine a much better conceit of the* Times, *then I lately conceyved, and assured my selfe, that* Vertue *had far more followers then I supposed.*

Somewhat it disturbed me to behold our ages Favourites, whilst they frowned on my honest enterprises, to take unto their protections the egregiousts fopperies: yet much more was my contentment, in that I was respected by so many of You, *amongst whom there are*

30 *some, who can and may as much dis-esteeme these, as they neglect me: nor could I feare their Malice or Contempt, whilst I enjoyed your favours, who (howsoever you are under-valued by Fooles for a time) shall leave unto your posterity so noble a memory, that your names shall be reverenced by Kings, when many of these who now flourish with a shew of usurped* Greatnesse, *shall eyther weare out of being, or dispoyled of all their patched reputation, grow contemptible in the eyes of their beloved Mistris the* World. *Your* Love *it is that (enabling me with patience to endure what is already past) hath made me also carefull better to prepare my selfe for all future misad-*
40 *ventures, by bringing to my consideration, what the passion of my just discontentments had almost quite banished from my remembrance.*

Further, to declare my thankefulnesse, in making apparant my willing minde to be commanded in any services of love, which you shal thinke fit (though I want abilitie to performe great matters) yet I have according to some of your requests, been contented to give way to the printing of these Eglogues*; which though it to many seeme a sleight matter, yet being well considered of, may prove a strong argument of my readinesse to give you content in a greater matter: for they being (as you well know) begotten with little care, and pre-*
50 *served with lesse respect, gave sufficient evidence, that I meant (rather then any way to deceive your trust) to give the world occasion of calling my discretion in question, as I now assure my selfe this will: and the sooner, because such expectations (I perceive) there are (of I know not what Inventions) as would have been frustrated, though I had employed the utmost and very best of my endeavours.*

Notwithstanding for your sakes, I have heere adventured once againe to make tryall of the Worlds censures: and what hath receyved beeing *from your Loves, I here re-dedicated to your Worths, which if your noble dispositions will like well of; or if you will but reasonably*
60 *respect what your selves drew mee unto, I shall be nothing displeased at others cavils, but resting my selfe contented with your good opinions, scorne all the rabble of uncharitable detractors: For none, I know, will maligne it, except those, who eyther particularly malice my person, or professe themselves enemies to my former Bookes; who (saving those that were incensed on others speeches) as divers of you (according to your protestations) have observed, are eyther open enemies of our Church; men notoriously guilty of some particular Abuses therein taxt, such malicious* Critickes *who have the repute of being judicious, by detracting from others; or at best, such Guls, as*

never approve any thing good, or learned, but eyther that which their shallow apprehensions can apply to the soothing of their owne opinions, or what (indeed rather) they understand not. 70

Trust me, how ill soever it hath been rewarded, my love to my Country is inviolate: my thankefulnesse to you unfained, my endeavour to doe every man good; all my ayme, content with honestie: and this my paines (if it may be so tearmed) more to avoid idlenesse, then for affectation of praise: and if notwithstanding all this, I must yet not onely rest my selfe content that my innocencie hath escaped with strict imprisonment (to the impayring of my state, and hinderance of my fortunes) but also be constrayned to see my guiltlesse lines, suffer the despight of ill tongues: yet for my further encouragement, let mee intreate the continuance of your first respect, wherein I shall find that comfort as will be sufficient to make mee set light, and so much contemne all the malice of my adversaries, that readie to burst with the venome of their owne hearts, they shall see 80

My Minde enamoured on faire *Vertues* light,
Transcends the limits of their bleared sight,
And plac'd above their *Envy* doth contemne,
Nay, sit and laugh at, their disdaine, and them.

But Noble Friends, *I make question neyther of yours, nor any honest mans respect, and therefore will no further urge it, nor trouble your patience: onely this Ile say, that you may not think me too well conceited of my selfe; though the* Time *were to blame, in ill requiting my honest endeavours, which in the eyes of the World deserved better; yet somewhat I am assured there was in me worthy that punishment, which when God shall give me grace to see and amend, I doubt not but to finde that regard as will be fitting for so much merit as my endeavors may justly challenge. Meane while, the better to hold my selfe in esteeme with you, and amend the world opinion of* Vertue, *I will study to amend my selfe, that I may be yet more worthy to be called* 90 100

Your Friend,
GEO: WITHER.

The Shepheards Hunting.

THE FIRST EGLOGUE.

The Argument.

Willy leaves his Flocke a while,
To lament his *Friends* exile;
Where, though prison'd, he doth finde,
Hee's still free that's free in Minde:
And that there is no defence
Halfe so firme as Innocence.

Philarete. Willie.

Philarete.

Willy, thou now full *jolly* tun'st thy *Reedes*,
Making the *Nymphs* enamor'd on thy strains,
And whilst thy harmles flock unscarred feeds,
Hast the contentment, of hils, groves, & plains:
Trust me, I *joy* thou and thy *Muse* so speedes
In such an Age, where so much mischiefe raignes:
And to my *Care* it some redresse will be,
Fortune hath so much *grace* to smile on thee.

Willy.

To smile on me? I nere yet knew her smile,
10 Unlesse 'twere when she purpos'd to deceive me;
Many a *Traine*, and many a *painted Wile*
She casts, in hope of *Freedome* to bereave me:
Yet now, because she sees I scorne her guile
To fawne on fooles, she for my *Muse* doth leave me.
And here of late, her wonted *Spite* doth tend,
To worke me *Care*, by frowning on my *friend*.

Philarete.

Why then I see her *Copper-coyne*'s no starling,
'Twill not be *currant* still, (for all the guilding)

17 starling: sterling.
18 (for : for 1622.

A *Knave*, or *Foole*, must ever be her *Darling*,
For they have minds to all occasions yeelding: 20
If we get any thing by all our parling.
It seemes an *Apple*, but it proves a *Weilding*:
But let that passe: sweet *Shepheard* tell me this,
For what beloved *Friend* thy sorrow is.

Willy.

Art thou, *Philarete*, in durance heere,
And dost thou aske me for what *Friend* I grieve?
Can I suppose thy love to me is deere,
Or this thy *joy* for my *content* believe?
When thou think'st thy *cares* touch not me as neere:
Or that I pinne thy *Sorrowes* at my sleeve? 30
I have in thee reposed so much trust,
I never thought, to find thee so unjust.

Philarete.

Why, *Willy*?

Willy.

Prethee doe not aske me why?
Doth it diminish any of thy *care*,
That I in freedome maken *melody*;
And think'st I cannot as well somewhat spare
From my *delight*, to mone thy *misery*?
'Tis time our *Loves* should these suspects forbeare:
Thou art that friend, which thou unnam'd shold'st know,
And not have drawne my love in question so. 40

Philarete.

Forgive me, and I'le pardon thy mistake,
And so let this thy *gentle-anger* cease,
(I never of thy love will question make)
Whilst that the number of our dayes encrease,
Yet to my selfe I much might seeme to take,

22 *Weilding*: wilding, a crab apple.

33 The 1622 text reads

Philarete.

Wil, why *Willy?* Prethee doe not ask me why?

And something neere unto presumption prease:
    To thinke me worthy *love* from such a *spirit*,
    But that I know thy kindnesse past my merit.

Besides; me thought thou spak'st now of a friend,
50 That seem'd more grievous discontents to beare,
Some things I find that doe in shew offend,
Which to my Patience little trouble are,
And they ere long I hope will have an end;
Or though they have not, much I doe not care:
    So this it was, made me that question move,
    And not suspect of honest *Willies* love.

Willie.

Alas, thou art exiled from thy Flocke,
And quite beyond the *Desarts* here confin'd,
Hast nothing to converse with but a *Rocke*;
60 Or at least *Out-lawes* in their *Caves* halfe pin'd:
And do'st thou at thy owne mis-fortune mocke,
Making thy selfe to, to thy selfe unkinde?
    When heretofore we talk't we did imbrace:
    But now I scarce can come to see thy face.

Philarete.

Yet all that *Willy*, is not worth thy sorrow,
For I have *Mirth* here thou would'st not beleeve,
From deepest *cares* the highest *joyes* I borrow.
If ought chance out this day, may make me grieve
I'le learne to mend, or scorne it by to morrow.
70 This barren place yeelds somewhat to relieve:
    For, I have found sufficient to content me,
    And more true blisse then ever freedome lent me.

Willie.

Are *Prisons* then growne places of delight?

Philarete.

'Tis as the *conscience* of the *Prisoner* is,
The very *Grates* are able to affright

46 prease: press.

The guilty Man, that knowes his deedes amisse;
All outward *Pleasures* are exiled quite,
And it is nothing (of it selfe) but this:
  Abhorred leanenesse, darkenesse, sadnesse, paines,
  Num'n-cold, sharpe-hunger, schorching thirst and chaines. 80

Willie.

And these are nothing?

Philarete.

Nothing yet to mee.
Onely my friends restraint is all my *paine.*
And since I truely find my *conscience* free
From that my *loanenesse* to, I reape some gaine.

Willie.

But grant in this no discontentment be:
It doth thy wished liberty restraine:
  And to thy *soule* I thinke there's nothing nearer,
  For I could never heare thee prize ought dearer.

Philarete.

True, I did ever set it at a Rate
Too deare for any *Mortals* worth to buy, 90
'Tis not our greatest *Shepheards* whole estate,
Shall purchase from me, my least *liberty*:
But I am subject to the powers of *Fate*,
And to obey them is no *slavery*:
  They may doe much, but when they have done all,
  Onely my *body* they may bring in *thrall.*

And 'tis not that (my *Willy*) 'tis my *mind*,
My *mind*'s more precious, freedome I so weigh
A thousand wayes they may my *body* bind,
In thousand *thrals*, but ne're my mind betray: 100
And thence it is that I *contentment* find,
And beare with *Patience* this my loade away:
  I'me still my selfe, and that I'de rather bee,
  Then to be Lord of all *these Downes* in fee.

104 in fee: absolutely.

Willie.

Nobly resolv'd, and I doe joy to hear't,
For 'tis the *minde* of *Man* indeed that's all.
There's nought so hard but a *brave* heart will bear't,
The *guiltlesse men* count great *afflictions* small,
They'le looke on *Death* and *Torment*, yet not fear't,
110 Because they know *'tis rising so to fall*:
Tyrants may boast they to much *power* are borne,
Yet he hath more that *Tyranies* can scorne.

Philarete.

'Tis right, but I no *Tyranies* endure,
Nor have I suffered ought worth name of care

Willie.

What e're thou'lt call't, thou may'st, but I am sure,
Many more pine that much lesse pained are:
Thy looke me thinkes doth say thy meaning's pure
And by this past I find what thou do'st dare:
But I could never yet the *reason* know,
120 Why thou art lodged in this house of wo.

Philarete.

Nor I by *Pan*, nor never hope to doe,
But thus it pleases some; and I doe guesse
Partly a *cause* that moves them thereunto,
Which neither will availe me to expresse,
Nor thee to heare, and therefore let it goe,
We must not say, they doe so that oppresse:
Yet I shall ne're to sooth *them* or *the times*,
Injure my selfe, by bearing others *crimes*.

Willie.

Then now thou maist speake freely, there's none heares,
130 But he, whom I doe hope thou do'st not doubt.

Philarete.

True: but if *doores* and *walles* have gotten *eares*,
And *Closet-whisperings* may be spread about:
Doe not blame him that in such *causes* feares

What in his *Passion* he may blunder out:
    In such a place, and such strict *times* as these,
    Where what we speake is tooke as *others* please.

But yet to morrow, if thou come this way,
I'le tell thee all my story to the end;
'Tis long, and now I feare thou canst not stay,
Because thy Flocke must watred be and pend, 140
And *Night* begins to muffle up the day,
Which to informe thee how alone I spend,
I'le onely sing a sorry *Prisoners Lay*,
    I fram'd this *Morne*, which though it suits no fields,
    Is such as fits me, and sad *Thraldome* yeelds.

Willie.

Well, I will fet my *Kit* another string,
And play unto it whil'st that thou do'st sing.

SONNET.

Philarete.

Now that my body dead-alive,
Bereav'd of comfort, lies in thrall.
Doe thou my soule begin to thrive, 150
And unto Hony, turne this Gall:
    So shall we both through outward wo,
    The way to inward comfort know.

As to the Flesh we food do give;
To keepe in us this Mortall breath:
So, Soules on Meditations live,
And shunne thereby immortall death:
    Nor art thou ever neerer rest,
    Then when thou find'st me most opprest.

First thinke my *Soule*; If I have Foes 160
That take a pleasure in my care,

138 end; : end, 1622.
146 fet my *Kit*: fetch my fiddle.

And to procure these outward woes,
Have thus entrapt me unaware:
    Thou should'st by much more carefull bee,
    Since greater foes lay waite for thee.

Then when Mew'd up in grates of steele,
Minding those joyes, mine eyes doe misse,
Thou find'st no torment thou do'st feele,
So grievous as Privation is:
170 Muse how the Damn'd in flames that glow,
    Pine in the losse of blisse they know.

Thou seest there's given so great might
To some that are but clay as I,
Their very anger can affright,
Which, if in any thou espie.
    Thus thinke; If Mortals frownes strike feare,
    How dreadfull will Gods wrath appeare?

By my late hopes that now are crost,
Consider those that firmer be:
180 And make the freedome I have lost,
A meanes that may remember thee:
    Had *Christ*, not thy Redeemer bin,
    What horrid thrall thou had'st been in.

These yron chaines, these bolts of steele,
Which other poore offenders grind,
The wants and cares which they doe feele,
May bring some greater thing to mind:
    For by their griefe thou shalt doe well,
    To thinke upon the paines of Hell.

190 Or, when through me thou seest a Man
Condemn'd unto a mortall death,
How sad he lookes, how pale, how wan,
Drawing with feare his panting breath:
    Thinke, if in that, such griefe thou see,
    How sad will, *Goe yee cursed be*.

195 quoted from Matt. 25:41.

Againe, when he that fear'd to Dye
(Past hope) doth see his Pardon brought,
Reade but the joy that's in his eye,
And then convey it to thy thought:
  There thinke, betwixt thy heart and thee, 200
  How sweet will, *Come yee blessed*, bee.

Thus if thou doe, though closed here,
My bondage I shall deeme the lesse,
I neither shall have cause to feare,
Nor yet bewaile my sad distresse:
  For whether live, or pine, or dye,
  We shall have blisse eternally.

* * *

Willy.

Trust me I see the *Cage* doth some *Birds* good,
And if they doe not suffer too much wrong,
Will teach them sweeter descants then the wood: 210
Beleeve't, I like the subject of thy *Song*,
It shewes thou art in no distempred mood:
But cause to heare the residue I long,
  My Sheepe to morrow I will neerer bring,
  And spend the day to heare thee talk and sing.

Yet e're we part, *Philarete*, areed,
Of whom thou learnd'st to make such songs as these,
I never yet heard any Shepheards reede
Tune in mishap, a straine that more could please;
Surely, *Thou* do'st invoke at this thy neede 220
Some power, that we neglect in other layes:
  For heer's a Name, and words, that but few swaines
  Have mention'd at their meeting on the Plaines.

201 quoted from Matt. 25:34.

202 closed: i.e., jailed.

213 cause: because.

216 areed: tell me.

222 Name, and words: i.e., religious doctrines.

Philarete.

Indeed 'tis true; and they are sore to blame,
They doe so much neglect it in their Songs,
For, thence proceedeth such a worthy fame,
As is not subject unto Envies wrongs:
That, is the most to be respected *name*
Of our true *Pan*, whose worth sits on all tongues:
230 And what the ancient Shepheards use to prayse
In sacred *Anthemes*, upon Holy-dayes.

Hee that first taught his Musicke such a straine
Was that sweet Shepheard, who (untill a King)
Kept Sheepe upon the hony-milky Plaine,
That is inrich't by *Jordans* watering;
He in his troubles eas'd the bodies paines,
By measures rais'd to the Soules ravishing:
And his sweet numbers onely most divine,
Gave first the being to this Song of mine.

Willy.

240 Let his good spirit ever with thee dwell,
That I might heare such Musicke every day.

Philarete.

Thankes, *Swaine*: but harke, thy *Weather* rings his Bell.
And *Swaines* to fold, or homeward drive away.

Willy.

And yon goes *Cuddy*, therefore fare thou well:
I'le make his Sheepe for mee a little stay;
And, if thou thinke it fit, I'le bring him to,
Next morning hither.

Philarete.

Prethee, *Willy*, do.

233 Shepheard: David. Wither remained deeply interested in the Psalms and later translated them all into verse.

THE SECOND EGLOGUE.

The Argument.

Cuddy here relates, how all
Pitty *Philarete's* thrall.
Who, requested, doth relate
The true cause of his estate;
Which broke off, because 'twas long,
They begin, a three-man-Song.

Willy. Cuddy. Philarete.

Willy.

Lo, *Philaret*, thy old friend heere, and I,
Are come to visit thee in these thy Bands,
Whil'st both our Flocks in an *Inclosure* by,
Doe picke the thin grasse from the fallowed lands.
He tels me thy restraint of liberty,
Each one throughout the Country understands:
  And there is not a gentle-natur'd *Lad*
  On all these *Downes*, but for thy sake is sad.

Cuddy.

Not thy acquaintance, and thy friends alone,
Pitty thy close restraint, as friends should doe: 10
But some that have but seene thee, for thee moane:
Yea, many that did never see thee to.
Some deeme thee in a fault, and most in none;
So divers wayes doe divers *Rumors* goe
  And at all meetings where our *Shepheards* bee,
  Now the maine Newes that's extant, is of thee.

Philarete.

Why, this is somewhat yet: had I but kept
Sheepe on the *Mountaines*, till the day of doome,
My *name* should in obscuritie have slept
In *Brakes*, in *Briars*, *shrubbed Furze* and *Broome*. 20

2 Bands: bonds, bondage.

12 to: too.

Into the Worlds wide eare it had not crept,
Nor in so many mens thoughts found a roome:
  But what cause of my sufferings doe they know?
  Good *Cuddy*, tell me, how doth *rumour* goe?

Cuddy.

Faith 'tis uncertaine; some speake this, some that:
Some dare say nought, yet seeme to thinke a cause,
And many a one prating he knowes not what
Comes out with *Proverbes* and *old ancient sawes*,
As if he thought thee guiltlesse, and yet not:
30 Then doth he speake halfe *Sentences*, then pawse:
  That what the most would say, we may suppose;
  But, what to say, the *Rumour* is, none knowes.

Philarete.

Nor care I greatly; for, it skils not much,
What the unsteady common-people deemes,
His *Conscience* doth not alwaies feele least touch,
That blamelesse in the sight of others seemes:
My cause is honest, and because 'tis such,
I hold it so, and not for mens esteemes:
  If they speake justly well of mee, I'me glad;
40 If falsely evill, it ne're makes me sad.

Willy.

I like that mind: but, *Shepheard*, you are quite
Beside the matter that I long to heare:
Remember what you promis'd yester-night,
Youl'd put us off with other talke, I feare;
Thou know'st that honest *Cuddies* heart's upright,
And none but he, except my selfe, is neere:
  Come therefore, and betwixt us two relate,
  The true occasion of thy present state.

Philarete.

My Friends I will; You know I am a *Swaine*,
50 That kept a poore Flocke on a barren *Plaine*:

27 what : what; 1622.

Who though it seemes, I could doe nothing lesse,
Can make a *Song*, and woe a *Shepheardesse*.
And not alone the fairest where I live,
Have heard me sing, and favours daign'd to give:
But, though I say't, the *noblest Nymph* of *Thame*,
Hath grac'd my *Verse*, unto my greater fame.
Yet, being young, and not much seeking prayse,
I was not noted out for *Shepheards layes*:
Nor feeding Flocks, as, you know, others be:
For the delight that most possessed me 60
Was hunting *Foxes*, *Wolves*, and *Beasts* of *Prey*:
That spoyle our *Foulds*, and beare our *Lambs* away.
For this, as also for the love I beare
Unto my *Country*, I laid-by all *care*
Of *gaine*, or of *preferment*, with *desire*
Onely to keepe that state I had entire.
And like a true growne *Huntsman* sought to speed
My selfe with *Hounds* of rare and choysest breed,
Whose *Names* and *Natures* ere I further goe,
Because you are my friends I'le let you know. 70
My first esteemed Dogge that I did finde,
Was by *descent* of olde *Acteons* kinde;
A *Brache*, which if I doe not aime amisse,
For all the world is just like one of his:
She's named *Love*, and scarce yet knowes her duty;
Her Damme's my Ladies pretty *Beagle*, *Beauty*.
I bred her up my selfe with wondrous charge,
Untill she grew to be exceeding large,
And waxt so wanton, that I did abhorre it,
And put her out amongst my neighbours for it. 80
The next is *Lust*, a Hound that's kept abroad
Mongst some of mine acquaintance, but a Toad
Is not more loathsome: 'tis a Curre will range

55 *noblest Nymph*: Elizabeth, daughter of James I. See *Epith.*

61 hunting: i.e., writing satires, for which Wither had been jailed.

68 *Hounds*: The "pack" which he details is composed of the titles of the various parts of his *Abuses*.

72 *Acteons*: a mythological hunter with a pack of fifty hounds.

73 *Brache*: bitch.

Extreamely, and is ever full of mange:
And cause it is infectious, she's not wunt
To come among the rest, but when they hunt.
Hate is the third, a Hound both deepe and long:
His *Sire* is *True*, or else supposed *Wrong*.
He'le have a snap at all that passe him by,
90 And yet pursues his game most eagerly.
With him goes *Envie* coupled, a leane Curre,
And yet she'le hold out, hunt we ne're so farre:
She pineth much, and feedeth little to,
Yet stands and snarleth at the rest that doe.
Then there's *Revenge*, a wondrous deep-mouth'd dog,
So fleet, I'me faine to hunt him with a clog,
Yet many times he'le much out-strip his bounds,
And hunts not closely with the other Hounds:
He'le venter on a *Lyon* in his *ire*;
100 Curst *Choller* was his *Damme*, and *Wrong* his *Sire*.
This *Choller*, is a *Brache*, that's very old,
And spends her mouth too-much to have it hold:
She's very teasty; an unpleasing Curre,
That bites the very Stones, if they but sturre:
Or when that ought but her displeasure moves,
She'le bite and snap at any one she loves.
But my quicke scented'st Dogge is *Jælousie*,
The truest of this breede's in *Italie*.
The *Damme* of mine would hardly fill a Glove,
110 It was a *Ladies* little Dogge, cal'd *Love*:
The *Sire* a poore deformed Curre, nam'd *Feare*;
As shagged and as rough as is a *Beare*:
And yet the Whelpe turn'd after neither kinde,
For he is very large, and nere-hand blinde.
Farre-off, hee seemeth of a pretty culler,
But doth not prove so, when you view him fuller.
A vile suspitious Beast; whose lookes are bad,
And I doe feare in time he will grow mad.
To him I couple *Avarice*, still poore;
120 Yet shee devoures as much as twenty more:

102 spends: uses.

114 nere-hand: almost.

A thousand Horse shee in her paunch can put,
Yet whine, as if she had an emptie gut;
And having gorg'd what might a Land have found,
Shee'le catch for more, and, hide it in the ground.
Ambition is a Hound as greedy full;
But hee for all the daintiest bits doth cull:
Hee scornes to licke up Crumbs beneath the Table,
Hee'le fetch't from boards and shelves, if he be able:
Nay, hee can climbe, if neede be; and for that
With him I hunt the *Martine*, and the *Cat*: 130
And yet sometimes in mounting, hee's so quicke,
Hee fetches falls, are like to breake his necke.
Feare is wel-mouth'd, but subject to *Distrust*;
A Stranger cannot make him take a Crust:
A little thing will soone his courage quaile,
And 'twixt his legges hee ever claps his Taile.
With him, *Despaire*, now, often coupled goes,
Which by his roring mouth each *hunts-man* knowes.
None hath a better minde unto the game;
But hee gives off, and alwaies seemeth lame. 140
My bloud-hound *Cruelty*, as swift as wind,
Hunts to the death, and never comes behind;
Who, but she's strapt, and musled to, withall,
Would eate her fellowes and the prey and all.
And yet, she cares not much for any food;
Unlesse it be the purest harmelesse blood.
    All these are kept abroad at charge of meny,
They doe not cost me in a yeare a penny.
But there's two couple of a midling size,
That seldome passe the sight of my owne eyes. 150
Hope, on whose head I've laid my life to pawne;
Compassion, that on every one will fawne.
This would, when 'twas a whelpe, with *Rabets* play
Or *Lambes*, and let them goe unhurt away:
Nay, now she is of growth, shee'le now and then
Catch you a *Hare*, and let her goe agen.

123 found: supported.
140 gives off: quits the field.

The two last, *Joy*, and *Sorrow*, make me wonder,
For they can ne're agree, nor bide asunder.
Joy's ever wanton, and no order knowes,
160 She'le run at *Larkes*, or stand and barke at *Crowes*.
Sorrow goes by her, and ne're moves his eye:
Yet both doe serve to helpe make up the cry:
Then comes behinde all these to beare the base,
Two couple more of a farre larger Race,
Such wide-mouth'd *Trollops*, that 'twould doe you good,
To heare their loud-loud *Ecchoes* teare the Wood:
There's *Vanity*, who by her gaudy *Hide*,
May farre away from all the rest be spide,
Though huge, yet quicke, for she's now here, now there;
170 Nay, looke about you, and she's every where:
Yet ever with the rest, and still in chace,
Right so, *Inconstancie* fils every place;
And yet so strange a fickle natur'd Hound,
Looke for her, and she's no where to be found.
Weakenesse is no faire Dogge unto the eye,
And yet she hath her proper qualitie.
But there's *Presumption*, when he heat hath got,
He drownes the *Thunder*, and the *Cannon-shot*:
And when at Start, he his full roaring makes,
180 The Earth doth tremble, and the Heaven shakes:
These were my Dogs, ten couple just in all,
Whom by the name of *Satyres* I doe call:
Mad Curs they be, and I can ne're come nigh them,
But I'me in danger to be bitten by them.
Much paines I tooke, and spent dayes not a few,
To make them keepe together, and hunt true:
Which yet I doe suppose had never bin,
But that I had a *Scourge* to keepe them in.
Now when that I this Kennell first had got,
190 Out of mine owne Demeanes I hunted not,
Save on these Downes, or among yonder *Rocks*,

157 *Sorrow,* : *Sorrow;* 1622.

164 Two couple more: the four satires in the second book of *Abuses*. They are much longer than the others.

188 *Scourge*: a supplementary satire to *Abuses*.

After those beasts that spoyl'd our Parish Flockes:
Nor during that time, was I ever wont,
With all my Kennell in one day to hunt:
Nor had done yet, but that this other yeere,
Some Beasts of *Prey* that haunt the *Deserts* heere,
Did not alone for many *Nights* together
Devoure, sometime a *Lambe,* sometime a *Weather*:
And so disquiet many a poore mans Heard,
But thereof loosing all were much afeard. 200
Yea, I among the rest, did fare as bad,
Or rather worse; for the best * *Ewes* I had, * *Hopes.*
(Whose breed should be my meanes of life and gaine,
Were in one Evening by these *Monsters* slaine:
Which mischiefe I resolved to repay,
Or else grow desperate and hunt all away.
For in a furie such as you shall see
Hunts-men, in missing of their sport will be)
I vow'd a *Monster* should not lurke about
In all this *Province*, but I'de finde him out. 210
And thereupon without respect or *care*,
How *lame*, how *full*, or how *unfit* they were,
In hast unkennell'd all my roaring crew,
Who were as mad, as if my mind they knew;
And e're they trail'd a flight-shot, the fierce Curres,
Had rous'd a *Hart*, and through *Brakes*, *Bryars*, and *Furres*
Follow'd at gaze so close, that *Love* and *Feare*
Got in together, and had surely, there
Quite overthrowne him, but that *Hope* thrust in
'Twixt both, and sav'd the pinching of his skin. 220
Whereby he scap't, till coursing overthwart,
Despaire came in, and grip't him to the hart.
I hallowed in the resdue to the fall,
And for an entrance, there I flesh't them all:
Which having done, I dip'd my staffe in blood

215 flight-shot: shot taken at a bird in flight.

217 at gaze: in view.

221 overthwart: transversely.

224 flesh't: rewarded with some of the game killed (so as to make them more excited in the chase).

And onward led my *Thunder* to the Wood;
Where what they did, I'le tell you out anon,
My keeper calles me, and I must be gon.
Goe, if you please a while, attend your Flocks,
230 And when the *Sunne* is over yonder Rocks,
Come to this *Cave* againe, where I will be,
If that my *Gardian* so much favour me.
Yet if you please, let us three sing a straine,
Before you turne your sheepe into the Plaine.

Willie.

I am content.

Cuddy.

As well content am I.

Philarete.

Then *Will* begin, and wee'le the rest supply.

SONG.

Willie.

Shepheard, would these Gates were ope,
Thou might'st take with us thy fortunes.

Philarete.

No, I'le make this narrow scope,
240 (Since my Fate doth so importune)
Meanes unto a wider Hope.

Cuddy.

Would thy Shepheardesse were here,
Who belov'd, loves so dearely?

Philarete.

Not for both your Flocks, I sweare,
And the gaine they yeeld you yeerely,
Would I so much wrong my Deare.

232 *Gardian* : *Gardian*, 1622.

Yet, to me, nor to this Place,
Would she now be long a stranger:
She would hold it in disgrace,
(If she fear'd not more my danger) 250
Where I am to shew her face.

Willie.

Shepheard, we would wish no harmes,
But something that might content thee.

Philarete.

Wish me then within her armes;
And that wish will ne're repent me,
If your wishes might prove charmes.

Willie.

Be thy Prison her embrace,
Be thy ayre her sweetest breathing.

Cuddy.

Be thy prospect her sweet Face,
For each looke a kisse bequeathing, 260
And appoint thy selfe the place.

* * *

Philarete.

Nay pray, hold there, for I should scantly then
Come meete you here this afternoone agen:
But fare you well, since wishes have no power,
Let us depart and keepe the pointed houre.

262-65 italics 1622.

262 scantly: scarcely.

THE THIRD EGLOGUE.

The Argument.

Philarete with his three Friends,
Heare his hunting storie ends.
Kinde *Alexis* with much ruth,
Wailes the banish't Shepheards youth:
But he slighteth Fortunes stings,
And in spight of Thraldome sings.

Philarete. Cuddy. Alexis. Willy.

Philarete.

So, now I see y'are *Shepheards* of your word;
Thus were you wont to promise, and to doe.

Cuddy.

More then our promise is, we can afford;
We come our selves, and bring another to:
Alexis, whom thou know'st well is no foe:
    Who loves thee much: and I doe know that he
    Would faine a hearer of thy Hunting be.

Philarete.

Alexis you are welcome, for you know
You cannot be but welcome where I am;
10 You ever were a friend of mine in show,
And I have found you are indeed the same:
Upon my first restraint you hither came,
    And proffered me more tokens of your love,
    Then it were fit my small deserts should prove.

Alexis.

'Tis still your use to underprise your merit;
Be not so coy to take my proffered love,
'Twill neither unbeseeme your *worth* nor *spirit*.

1 word; : word, 1622.
3 afford; : afford, 1622.

To offer court'sie doth thy friend behove:
And which are so, this is a place to prove.
  Then once againe I say, if *cause* there be. 20
  First make a *tryall*, if thou please, of me.

Philarete.

Thankes good *Alexis*; sit downe by me heere,
I have a taske, these *Shepheards* know, to doe;
A *Tale* already told this Morne well neere,
With which I very faine would forward goe,
And am as willing thou should'st heare it to:
  But thou canst never understand this last,
  Till I have also told thee what is past.

Willy.

It shall not neede, for I so much presum'd,
I on your mutuall friendships, might be bold, 30
That I a freedome to my selfe assum'd,
To make him know, what is already told.
If I have done amisse, then you may scold.
  But in my telling I prevised this,
  He knew not whose, nor to what end it is.

Philarete.

Well, now he may, for heere my Tale goes on:
My eager Dogges and I to Wood are gon.
Where, beating through the *Coverts*, every Hound
A severall *Game* had in a moment found:
I rated them, but they pursu'd their pray, 40
And as it fell (by hap) tooke all one way.
Then I began with quicker speed to follow,
And teaz'd them on, with a more chearefull hallow:
That soone we passed many weary miles,
Tracing the subtile game through all their wiles.
These doubl'd, those re-doubled on the scent,
Still keeping in full chase where ere they went.

34 prevised: foresaw.

38 *Coverts* : *Converts* 1622.

40 rated: berated.

Up *Hils*, downe *Cliffes*, through *Bogs*, and over *Plaines*,
Stretching their *Musicke* to the highest straines.
50 That when some Thicket hid them from mine eye,
My eare was ravish'd with their melodie.
Nor crost we onely Ditches, Hedges, Furrowes,
But Hamlets, Tithings, Parishes, and Burrowes:
They followed where so ev'r the game did go,
Through Kitchin, Parlor, Hall, and Chamber to.
And, as they pass'd the *City*, and the *Court*,
My *Prince* look'd out, and daign'd to view my sport.
Which then (although I suffer for it now)
(If some say true) he liking did allow;
60 And so much (had I had but wit to stay)
I might my selfe (perhaps) have heard him say.
But I, that time, as much as any daring,
More for my pleasure then my safetie caring;
Seeing fresh game from every covert rise,
(Crossing by thousands still before their eyes)
Rush'd in, and then following close my *Hounds*,
Some beasts I found lie dead, some full of wounds,
Among the willows, scarce with strength to move,
One I found heere, another there, whom *Love*
70 Had grip'd to death: and, in the selfe-same state,
Lay one devour'd by *Envy*, one by *Hate*;
Lust had bit some, but I soone past beside them,
Their festr'd wounds so stuncke, none could abide them.
Choller hurt divers, but *Revenge* kild more:
Feare frighted all, behinde him and before.
Despaire drave on a huge and mighty heape,
Forcing some downe from *Rocks* and *Hils* to leape:
Some into water, some into the fire,
So on themselves he made them wreake his *ire*.
80 But I remember, as I pass'd that way,
Where the great *King* and *Prince* of *Shepheards lay*,
About the wals were hid, some (once more knowne)
That my fell Curre *Ambition* had o'rethrowne:
Many I heard, pursu'd by *Pitty*, cry;

53 Tithings: rural divisions of land.

57 My *Prince*: i.e., James I.

And oft I saw my *Bloud-Hound*, *Cruelty*,
Eating her passage even to the hart,
Whither once gotten, she is loath to part.
All pli'd it well, and made so loud a cry,
'Twas heard beyond the Shores of *Britany*.
Some rated them, some storm'd, some lik'd the *game*, 90
Some thought *me worthy praise*, some *worthy blame*.
But I, not fearing th'one, mis-steeming t'other,
Both, in shrill hallowes and loud yernings smother.
Yea, the strong mettled, and my long-breath'd crew,
Seeing the *game* increasing in their view,
Grew the more frolicke, and the courses length
Gave better breath, and added to their strength.
Which *Jove* perceiving, for *Jove* heard their cries
Rumbling amongst the *Spheares concavities*:
Hee mark'd their *course*, and *courages* increase, 100
Saying, 'twere pitty such a chase should cease.
And therewith swore their mouthes should never wast,
But hunt as long's mortality did last.
Soone did they feele the power of his great gift,
And I began to finde their pace more swift:
I follow'd, and I rated, but in vaine
Striv'd to o'retake, or take them up againe.
They never stayed since, nor nights nor dayes,
But to and fro still run a thousand wayes:
Yea, often to this place where now I lie, 110
They'l wheele about to cheare me with their cry;
And one day in good time will vengeance take
On some offenders, for their Masters sake:
For know, my Friends, my freedome in this sort
For them I lose, and making my selfe sport.

Willy.

Why? was there any harme at all in this?

89 Wither's claim of widespread interest in his satires does not seem greatly exaggerated.

92 mis-steeming: mis-esteeming, undervaluing.

93 yernings: cries of hounds.

Philarete.

No, *Willy*, and I hope yet none there is.

Willy.

How comes it then?

Philarete.

Note, and I'le tell thee how.
Thou know'st that *Truth* and *Innocency* now,
120 If plac'd with meannesse, suffers more despight
Then *Villainies*, accompan'ed with might.
But thus it fell, while that my *Hounds* pursu'd
Their noysome prey, and every field laid strew'd
With *Monsters*, hurt and slaine; upon a beast,
More subtile, and more noysome then the rest,
My leane-flanckt Bitch, cald *Envy*, hapt to light:
And, as her wont is, did so surely bite,
That, though shee left behinde small outward smart,
The wounds were deepe, and rankled to the hart.
130 This, joyning to some other, that of late,
Were very eagerly pursu'd by *Hate*,
(To fit their purpose having taken leasure)
Did thus conspire to worke me a displeasure.
For imitation, farre surpassing *Apes*,
They laide aside their *Foxe* and *Wolvish shapes*,
And shrowded in the skinnes of harmlesse Sheepe
Into by-wayes, and open paths did creepe;
Where, they (as hardly drawing breath) did ly,
Shewing their wounds to every passer by;
140 To make them thinke that they were sheepe so foyl'd,
And by my Dogges, in their late hunting, spoyl'd.
Beside, some other that envy'd my game,
And, for their pastime, kept such *Monsters* tame:
As, you doe know, there's many for their pleasure

118 thee how. : the how? 1622.

124 beast: Allen Pritchard in *Review of English Studies* 14 (1963): 337–45, argues convincingly that Wither was jailed in the spring of 1614 for the implications in his *Abuses* directed at Henry Howard, Earl of Northampton, a Catholic sympathizer.

Keepe Foxes, Beares, & Wolves, as some great treasure:
Yea, many get their living by them to,
And so did store of these, I speake of, do.
Who, seeing that my *Kennell* had affrighted,
Or hurt some *Vermine* wherein they delighted;
And finding their owne power by much to weake, 150
Their *Malice* on my *Innocence* to wreake,
Swolne with the deepest rancour of despight,
Some of our greatest *Shepheards* Folds by night
They closely entred; and there having stain'd
Their hands in *villany*, of mee they plain'd,
Affirming, (without *shame*, or *honesty*,)
I, and my Dogges, had done it purposely.
Whereat they storm'd, and cald mee to a *tryall*,
Where *Innocence* prevailes not, nor *denyall*:
But for that *cause*, heere in this place I lie, 160
Where none so merry as my dogges, and I.

Cuddy.

Beleeve it, heere's a *Tale* will suten well,
For *Shepheards* in another *Age* to tell.

Willy.

And thou shalt be remembred with delight,
By this, hereafter, many a *Winters night.*
For, of this sport another *Age* will ring;
Yea, *Nymphes* that are unborne thereof shall sing,
And not a *Beauty* on our Greenes shall play,
That hath not heard of this thy hunting day.

Philarete.

It may be so, for if that gentle *Swaine*, 170
Who wonnes by *Tavy*, on the *Westerne plaine*,
Would make the *Song*, such life his *Verse* can give,
Then I doe know my *Name* might ever live.

154 closely: secretly.

170 *Swaine*: William Browne of Tavistock (Tavy).

171 wonnes: dwells.

Alexis.

But tell me; are our *Plaines* and *Nymphs* forgot,
And canst thou frolicke in thy trouble be?

Philarete.

Can I, *Alexis*, sayst thou? Can I not,
That am resolv'd to scorne more misery?

Alexis.

Oh, but that youth's yet greene, and young bloud hot,
And *liberty* must needs be sweet to thee.
180 But, now most sweet whil'st every bushy *Vale*,
And *Grove*, and *Hill*, rings of the *Nightingale*.

Me thinkes, when thou remembrest those *sweet layes*
Which thou would'st leade thy *Sheppeardesse* to heare,
Each Evening tyde among the *Leavy sprayes*,
The thought of that should make thy freedome deare:
For now, whil'st every *Nymph* on *Holy-dayes*
Sports with some *jolly Lad*, and maketh cheere,
Thine sighes for thee, and mew'd up from resort,
Will neither play her selfe, nor see their sport.

190 Those *Shepheards* that were many a Morning wont,
Unto their Boyes to leave the tender *Heard*
And beare thee company when thou didst hunt;
Me thinkes the sport thou hast so gladly shar'd
Among those *Swaynes* should make thee thinke upon't,
For't seemes all vaine, now, that was once indear'd.
It cannot be: since I could make relation,
How for lesse *cause* thou hast beene deepe in *passion*.

Philarete.

'Tis true: my tender heart was ever yet
Too capable of such conceits as these;
200 I never saw that *Object*, but from it,
The *Passions* of my *Love* I could encrease.

188 Thine : Thine, 1622.
191 *Heard* : *Heard*; 1622.

Those things which move not other men a whit,
I can, and doe make use of, if I please:
    When I am sad, to sadnesse I apply
    Each *Bird*, and *Tree*, and *Flowre* that I passe by.

So, when I will be merry, I aswell
Something for mirth from every thing can draw,
From *Miserie*, from *Prisons*, nay from *Hell*:
And as when to my *minde*, *griefe* gives a flaw,
Best comforts doe but make my woes more fell: 210
So when I'me bent to *Mirth*, from mischiefes paw,
    (Though ceas'd upon me) I would something cull,
    That spight of *care*, should make my *joyes* more full.

I feele those wants, *Alexis*, thou doest name,
Which spight of youths affections I sustaine;
Or else, for what is't I have gotten *Fame*,
And am more knowne then many an *elder Swaine*?
If such desires I had not learn'd to tame,
(Since many pipe much better on this *Plaine*:)
    But tune your *Reedes*, and I will in a *Song*, 220
    Expresse my *Care*, and how I take this *Wrong*.

SONNET.

I that ere'st-while the worlds sweet Ayre did draw,
(Grac'd by the fairest ever Mortall saw;)
Now closely pent, with walles of Ruth-lesse stone,
Consume my Dayes, and Nights and all alone.

When I was wont to sing of Shepheards loves,
My walkes were Fields, and Downes, and Hils, and Groves:
But now (alas) so strict is my hard doome,
Fields, Downes, Hils, Groves, and al's but one poore roome.

Each Morne, as soone as Day-light did appeare, 230
With Natures Musicke Birds would charme mine eare:

204 apply : apply, 1622.
211 paw, : paw. 1622.

Which now (instead) of their melodious straines,
Heare, ratling Shackles, Gyves, and Boults, and Chaines.

But, though that all the world's delight forsake me,
I have a *Muse*, and she shall Musicke make me:
Whose ayrie Notes, in spight of closest cages,
Shall give content to me, and after ages.

Nor doe I passe for all this outward ill,
My hearts the same, and undejected still;
240 And which is more then some in freedome winne,
I have true rest, and peace, and joy within.

And then my Mind, that spight of prison's free,
When ere she pleases any where can be;
Shee's in an houre, in *France*, *Rome*, *Turky*, *Spaine*,
In Earth, in Hell, in Heaven, and here againe.

Yet there's another comfort in my woe,
My cause is spread, and all the world may know,
My fault's no more, but speaking Truth, and Reason;
No Debt, nor Theft, nor Murther, Rape, or Treason.

250 Nor shall my foes with all their Might and Power
Wipe out their shame, nor yet this fame of our:
Which when they finde, they shall my fate envie,
Till they grow leane, and sicke, and mad, and die.

Then though my Body here in Prison rot,
And my wrong'd *Satyres* seeme a while forgot:
Yet, when both Fame, and life hath left those men,
My Verse and I'le revive, and live agen.

So thus enclos'd, I beare afflictions load,
But with more true content then some abroad;
260 For whilst their thoughts doe feele my Scourges sting,
In bands I'le leape, and dance, and laugh, and sing.

* * *

250 Power : Power, 1622.
260 thoughts : thoughts, 1622.

Alexis.

Why now I see thou droup'st not with thy care,
Neither exclaim'st thou on thy hunting day;
But dost with unchang'd resolution beare
The heavy burthen of exile away.
All that did truely know thee, did conceave,
Thy actions with thy spirit still agree'd;
Their good conceit thou doest no whit bereave,
But shewest that thou art still thy selfe indeed.
If that thy mind to basenesse now descends, 270
Thou'lt injure *Vertue*, and deceive thy friends.

Willie.

Alexis, he will injure *Vertue* much,
But more his friends, and most of all himselfe,
If on that common barre his minde but touch,
It wrackes his fame upon disgraces shelfe.
Whereas if thou steere on that happy course,
Which in thy just adventure is begun,
No thwarting Tide, nor adverse blast shall force
Thy *Barke* without the *Channels* bounds to run.
Thou art the same thou wert, for ought I see, 280
When thou didst freely on the Mountaines hunt,
In nothing changed yet, unlesse it be
More merrily dispos'd then thou wert wont.
Still keepe thee thus, so other men shall know,
Vertue can give content in midst of woe.
And see (though *mightines* with frownes doth threat)
That, to be *Innocent*, is to be *great*,
Thrive and farewell.

Alexis.

In this thy trouble flourish.

Cuddy.

While those that wish thee ill, fret, pine, and perish.

264 beare : beare, 1622.
277 begun, : begun; 1622.
279 without: outside.
284 other men : other 1622; correction from 1615.
286 see : she 1622; correction from 1615.

THE FOURTH EGLOGUE.

The Argument.

Philaret on *Willy* calls,
To sing out his Pastorals:
Warrants *Fame* shall grace his Rimes,
Spight of *Envy* and the Times;
And shewes how in care he uses,
To take comfort from his Muses.

Philarete. Willie.

Philarete.

Prethee, *Willy* tell me this,
What new accident there is,
That thou (once the blythest Lad)
Art become so wondrous sad?
And so carelesse of thy quill,
As if thou had'st lost thy skill?
Thou wert wont to charme thy flocks,
And among the massy rocks
Hast so chear'd me with thy Song,
10 That I have forgot my wrong.
Something hath thee surely crost,
That thy old want thou hast lost.
Tell me: Have I ought mis-said
That hath made thee ill-apaid?
Hath some Churle done thee a spight?
Dost thou misse a Lambe to night?
Frowns thy fairest *Shepheards* Lasse?
Or how comes this ill to passe?
Is there any discontent
20 Worse then this my banishment?

Willie.

Why, doth that so evill seeme
That thou nothing worst dost deeme?
Shepheards, there full many be,

10 my wrong: his being jailed.
12 want: wont, customary manner.

That will change *Contents* with thee.
Those that choose their Walkes at will,
On the Valley or the Hill.
Or those pleasures boast of can,
Groves or Fields may yeeld to man:
Never come to know the rest,
Wherewithall thy minde is blest. 30
Many a one that oft resorts
To make up the troope at sports
And in company some while,
Happens to straine forth a smile,
Feeles more want, and outward smart,
And more inward griefe of hart
Then this place can bring to thee,
While thy mind remaineth free.
Thou bewail'st my want of mirth,
But what find'st thou in this earth, 40
Wherein ought may be beleev'd
Worth to make me Joy'd; or griev'd?
And yet feele I (naithelesse)
Part of both I must confesse.
Sometime, I of mirth doe borrow,
Otherwhile as much of sorrow;
But, my present state is such,
As, nor Joy, nor grieve I much.

Philarete.

Why, hath *Willy* then so long
Thus forborne his wonted Song? 50
Wherefore doth he now let fall,
His well-tuned *Pastorall*?
And my eares that musike barre,
Which I more long after farre,
Then the liberty I want.

Willy.

That, were very much to grant,
But, doth this hold alway lad,

32 sports : sports. 1622.
34 smile, : smile. 1622.

Those that sing not, must be sad?
Did'st thou ever that Bird heare
60 Sing well, that sings all the yeare?
Tom the *Piper* doth not play
Till he weares his Pipe away:
There's a time to slacke the string,
And a time to leave to sing.

Philarete.

Yea; but no man now is still,
That can sing, or tune a quill.
Now to chant it, were but reason;
Song and *Musicke* are in season.
Now in this sweet jolly tide,
70 Is the earth in all her pride:
The faire Lady of the *May*
Trim'd up in her best array;
Hath invited all the Swaines,
With the Lasses of the Plaines,
To attend upon her sport
At the places of resort.
Coridon (with his bould Rout)
Hath alredy been about
For the elder Shepheards dole,
80 And fetch'd in the *Summer-Pole*:
Whil'st the rest have built a *Bower*,
To defend them from a shower;
Seil'd so close, with boughes all greene,
Tytan cannot pry betweene.
Now the *Dayrie-Wenches* dreame
Of their Strawberries and Creame:
And each doth her selfe advance
To be taken in, to dance:
Every one that knowes to sing,
90 Fits him for his Carrolling:
So do those that hope for meede,

60 well, : well; 1622.
74 Plaines, : Plaines. 1622.
80 *Summer-Pole*: May pole.

Either by the Pipe or Reede:
And though I am kept away,
I doe heare (this very day)
Many learned Groomes doe wend,
For the Garlands to contend.
Which a Nimph that hight *Desart*,
(Long a stranger in this part)
With her own faire hand hath wrought
A rare worke (they say) past thought, 100
As appeareth by the name,
For she cals them *Wreathes of Fame*.
She hath set in their due place
Ev'ry flowre that may grace;
And among a thousand moe,
(Whereof some but serve for shew)
She hath wove in *Daphnes* tree,
That they may not blasted be.
Which with *Time* she edg'd about,
Least the worke should ravell out. 110
And that it might wither never,
I intermixt it with *Live-ever*.
These are to be shar'd among
Those that doe excell for song:
Or their passions can rehearse
In the smooth'st and sweetest verse.
Then, for those among the rest,
That can play and pipe the best,
There's a Kidling with the Damme,
A fat Weather, and a Lambe. 120

95 learned Groomes: i.e., people of various accomplishments whom Wither will recognize in pastoral terms.

107 *Daphnes* tree: the laurel.

108 blasted: withered.

109 *Time*: punning on the flower.

112 *Live-ever*: a plant whose leaves stay green long after being picked.

113-16 First to be recognized are the poets.

113 among : among, 1622.

118 best, : best. 1622.

And for those that leapen far,
Wrastle, Runne, and throw the Barre,
There's appointed guerdons to.
He, that best, the first can doe,
Shall, for his reward, be paid,
With a *Sheep-hooke*, faire in-laid
With fine Bone, of a strange Beast
That men bring out of the West.
For the next, a *Scrip* of red,
130 Tassel'd with fine coloured Thred;
There's prepared for their meed,
That in running make most speede,
(Or the cunning Measures foote)
Cups of turned *Maple-roote*:
Whereupon the skilfull man
Hath ingrav'd the *Loves* of *Pan*:
And the last hath for his due,
A fine Napkin wrought with blew.
Then, my *Willy*, why art thou
140 Carelesse of thy merit now?
What dost thou heere, with a wight
That is shut up from delight,
In a solitary den,
As not fit to live with men?
Goe, my *Willy*, get thee gone,
Leave mee in exile alone.
Hye thee to that merry throng,
And amaze them with thy *Song*.
Thou art young, yet such a *Lay*
150 Never grac'd the month of May,
As (if they provoke thy skill)
Thou canst fit unto thy *Quill*.

121-38 It is not clear what accomplishments these four activities and their rewards represent.

122 Barre: an early javelin.

129 *Scrip*: a bag or wallet.

130 Thred; : Thred, 1622.

152 *Quill*. : *Quill*, 1622.

I with wonder heard thee sing,
At our last yeeres Revelling.
Then I with the rest was free,
When unknowne I noted thee:
And perceiv'd the ruder Swaines,
Envy thy farre sweeter straines.
Yea, I saw the *Lasses* cling
Round about thee in a Ring: 160
As if each one jealous were,
Any but her selfe should heare.
And I know they yet do long
For the res'due of thy song.
Haste thee then to sing it forth;
Take the benefit of worth.
And *Desert* will sure bequeath
Fames faire Garland for thy wreath,
Hye thee, *Willy*, hye away.

Willy.

Phila, rather let mee stay, 170
And be desolate with thee,
Then at those their *Revels* bee.
Nought such is my skill I wis,
As indeed thou deem'st it is.
But what ere it be, I must
Be content, and shall I trust.
For a Song I doe not passe,
Mong'st my friends, but what (alas)
Should I have to doe with them
That my Musicke doe contemne? 180
Some there are, as well I wot,
That the same yet favour not:
Yet I cannot well avow,
They my Carrols disalow:
But such malice I have spid,
'Tis as much as if they did.

165 Haste : Hast 1622.
172 bee. : bee, 1622.

Philarete.

Willy, What may those men be,
Are so ill, to malice thee?

Willy.

Some are worthy-well esteem'd,
190 Some without worth are so deem'd.
Others of so base a spirit,
They have nor esteeme, nor merit.

Philarete.

What's the wrong?

Willy.

A slight offence,
Wherewithall I can dispence;
But hereafter for their sake
To my selfe I'le musicke make.

Philarete.

What, because some Clowne offends,
Wilt thou punish all thy friends?

Willy.

Do not, *Phill*, mis-understand mee,
200 Those that love mee may command mee,
But, thou know'st, I am but yong,
And the *Pastorall* I sung,
Is by some suppos'd to be,
(By a straine) too high for me:
So they kindly let me gaine,
Not my labour for my paine.
Trust me, I doe wonder why
They should me my owne deny.
Though I'me young, I scorne to flit
210 On the wings of borrowed wit.
I'le make my owne feathers reare me,
Whither others cannot beare me.

195 sake : sake. 1622.

Yet I'le keepe my skill in store,
Till I've seene some Winters more.

Philarete.

But, in earnest, mean'st thou so?
Then thou art not wise, I trow:
Better shall advise thee *Pan*,
For thou dost not rightly than:
That's the ready way to blot
All the credit thou hast got. 220
Rather in thy Ages prime,
Get another start of Time:
And make those that so fond be,
(Spight of their owne dulnesse) see,
That the sacred *Muses* can
Make a childe in yeeres, a man.
It is knowne what thou canst doe,
For it is not long agoe,
When that *Cuddy*, *Thou*, and *I*,
Each the others skill to try, 230
At Saint *Dunstanes* charmed well,
(As some present there can tell)
Sang upon a sudden Theame,
Sitting by the Crimson streame,
Where, if thou didst well or no,
Yet remaines the Song to show.
Much experience more I've had,
Of thy skill (thou happy Lad)
And would make the world to know it;
But that time will further show it. 240
Envy makes their tongues now runne
More then doubt of what is done.
For that needs must be thy owne,

215 *Philarete.* : *Pillarete.* 1622.

231 Charles Lamb identified this as the Devil Tavern — more accurately, the Devil and St. Dunstan Tavern. Its Apollo Room was later celebrated by Jonson and by Drayton in his Ode, "Sacrifice to Apollo."

234 streame, : streame. 1622.

236 show. : show, 1622.

Or to be some others knowne:
But how then wil't suit unto
What thou shalt hereafter do?
Or I wonder where is hee,
Would with that song part to thee.
Nay, were there so mad a Swaine,
250 Could such glory sell for gaine,
Phœbus would not have combin'd,
That gift with so base a minde.
Never did the *Nine* impart
The sweet secrets of their Art,
Unto any that did scorne,
We should see their favours worne.
Therefore unto those that say,
Where they pleas'd to sing a Lay,
They could doo't, and will not tho;
260 This I speake, for this I know:
None ere drunke the *Thespian spring*,
And knew how, but he did sing.
For, that once infus'd in man,
Makes him shew't, doe what he can.
Nay, those that doe onely sip,
Or, but ev'n their fingers dip
In that sacred *Fount* (poore Elves)
Of that brood will shew themselves.
Yea, in hope to get them fame,
270 They will speake, though to their shame.
Let those then at thee repine,
That by their wits measure thine;
Needs those Songs must be thine owne,
And that one day will be knowne.
That poore imputation to,
I my selfe do undergoe:
But it will appeare ere long,

250 gaine, : gaine; 1622.

253 *Nine*: the Muses.

259 tho: then.

261 *Thespian spring*: the Hippocrene, sacred to the nine Muses.

264 shew't, : shew't 1622.

That 'twas Envy sought our wrong.
Who at twice-ten have sung more,
Then some will doe, at fourescore. 280
Cheere thee (honest *Willy*) then,
And begin thy Song agen.

Willy.

Faine I would, but I doe feare
When againe my Lines they heare,
If they yeeld they are my Rimes,
They will faine some other Crimes;
And 'tis no safe ventring-by
Where we see *Detraction* ly.
For doe what I can, I doubt,
She will picke some quarrell out; 290
And I oft have heard defended,
Little said, is soone amended.

Philarete.

See'st thou not in clearest dayes,
Oft thicke fogs cloud Heav'ns rayes.
And that vapours which doe breath
From the earths grosse wombe beneath,
Seeme not to us with black steames,
To pollute the Sunnes bright beames,
And yet vanish into ayre,
Leaving it (unblemisht) faire? 300
So (my *Willy*) shall it bee
With *Detractions* breath on thee.
It shall never rise so hie,
As to staine thy Poesie.
As that Sunne doth oft exhale
Vapours from each rotten Vale;
Poesie so sometime draines,
Grosse conceits from muddy braines;
Mists of Envy, fogs of spight,
Twixt mens judgements and her light: 310
But so much her power may do,

297 i.e., Seem they not to us to pollute, etc.

That shee can dissolve them to.
If thy Verse doe bravely tower,
As shee makes wing, she gets power:
Yet the higher she doth sore,
Shee's affronted still the more:
Till shee to the high'st hath past,
Then she rests with fame at last,
Let nought therefore, thee affright:
320 But make forward in thy flight:
For if I could match thy Rime,
To the very Starres I'de clime.
There begin again, and flye,
Till I reach'd Æternity.
But (alasse) my Muse is slow:
For thy place shee flags too low:
Yea, the more's her haplesse fate,
Her short wings were clipt of late.
And poore I, her fortune ruing,
330 Am my selfe put up a muing.
But if I my Cage can rid,
I'le flye where I never did.
And though for her sake I'me crost,
Though my best hopes I have lost,
And knew she would make my trouble
Ten times more then ten times double:
I should love and keepe her to,
Spight of all the world could doe.
For though banish't from my flockes,
340 And confin'd within these rockes,
Here I waste away the light,
And consume the sullen Night;
She doth for my comfort stay,
And keepes many cares away.
Though I misse the flowry Fields,
With those sweets the Spring-tyde yeelds,
Though I may not see those Groves,
Where the Shepheards chant their Loves,

330 a muing: encaged.
342 Night; : Night, 1622.

(And the Lasses more excell,
Then the sweet voyc'd *Philomel*) 350
Though of all those pleasures past,
Nothing now remaines at last,
But *Remembrance* (poore reliefe)
That more makes, then mends my griefe:
Shee's my mindes companion still,
Maugre Envies evill will.
(Whence she should be driven to,
Wer't in mortals power to do.)
She doth tell me where to borrow
Comfort in the midst of sorrow: 360
Makes the desolatest place
To her presence be a grace;
And the blackest discontents
To be pleasing ornaments.
In my former dayes of blisse,
Her divine skill taught me this,
That from every thing I saw,
I could some invention draw:
And raise pleasure to her height,
Through the meanest objects sight. 370
By the murmure of a spring,
Or the least boughes rusteling.
By a Dazie whose leaves spred,
Shut when *Tytan* goes to bed;
Or a shady bush or tree,
She could more infuse in mee,
Then all Natures beauties can,
In some other wiser man.
By her helpe I also now,
Make this churlish place allow 380
Some things that may sweeten gladnes,
In the very gall of sadnes.
The dull loannesse, the blacke shade,
That these hanging vaults have made,
The strange Musicke of the waves,
Beating on these hollow Caves,
This blacke Den which Rocks embosse
Over-growne with eldest Mosse.

The rude Portals that give light,
390 More to *Terror* then *Delight.*
This my Chamber of *Neglect*,
Wall'd about with *Disrespect*,
From all these and this dull ayre,
A fit object for *Despaire*,
She hath taught me by her might
To draw comfort and delight.
Therefore *thou best earthly blisse*,
I will cherish thee for this.
Poesie; thou sweetest content
400 That e're Heav'n to mortals lent:
Though they as a trifle leave thee
Whose dull thoughts cannot conceive thee,
Though thou be to them a scorne,
That to nought but earth are borne:
Let my life no longer be
Then I am in love with thee.
Though our wise ones call thee madnesse
Let me never taste of gladnesse
If I love not thy mad'st fits,
410 More then all their greatest wits.
And though some too seeming holy,
Doe account thy raptures folly:
Thou dost teach me to contemne,
What make *Knaves* and *Fooles* of them.
Oh high power! that oft doth carry
Men above.

Willie.

Good *Philarete* tarry,
I doe feare thou wilt be gon,
Quite above my reach anon.
The kinde flames of Poesie
420 Have now borne thy thoughts so high,
That they up in Heaven be,
And have quite forgotten me.
Call thy selfe to minde againe,

408 gladnesse : gladnesse. 1622.

Are these Raptures for a Swaine,
That attends on lowly Sheepe,
And with simple Heards doth keepe?

Philarete.

Thankes my *Willie*; I had runne
Till that Time had lodg'd the Sunne,
If thou had'st not made me stay;
But thy pardon here I pray. 430
Lov'd *Apolo's* sacred fire
Had rais'd up my spirits higher
Through the love of Poesie,
Then indeed they use to flye.
But as I said, I say still,
If that I had *Willi's* skill,
Envie nor Detractions tongue,
Should ere make me leave my song:
But I'de sing it every day
Till they pin'd themselves away. 440
Be thou then advis'd in this,
Which both just and fitting is:
Finish what thou hast begun,
Or at least still forward run.
Haile and Thunder ill hee'l beare
That a blast of winde doth feare:
And if words will thus afray thee,
Prethee how will deeds dismay thee?
Doe not thinke so rathe a *Song*
Can passe through the vulgar throng, 450
And escape without a touch,
Or that they can hurt it much:
Frosts we see doe nip that thing
Which is forward'st in the Spring:
Yet at last for all such lets
Somewhat of the rest it gets,

428 lodg'd the Sunne: sunset.
449 rathe: early, immature.
455 lets: hindrances.
456 gets, : gets. 1622.

And I'me sure that so maist thou.
Therefore my kind *Willie* now,
Since thy folding time drawes on
460 And I see thou must be gon,
Thee I earnestly beseech
To remember this my speech
And some little counsell take,
For *Philarete* his sake:
And I more of this will say,
If thou come next Holy-day.

THE FIFTH EGLOGUE.

The Argument.

Philaret Alexis moves,
To embrace the *Muses* loves;
Bids him never carefull seeme,
Of anothers dis-esteeme:
Since to them it may suffice,
They themselves can justly prize.

Philarete. Alexis.

Philarete.

Alexis, if thy worth doe not disdaine
The humble friendship of a meaner Swaine,
Or some more needfull businesse of the day,
Urge thee to be too hasty on thy way;
Come (gentle Shepheard) rest thee here by mee,
Beneath the shadow of this broad leav'd tree:
For though I seeme a stranger, yet mine eye
Observes in thee the markes of courtesie:
And if my judgement erre not, noted to,
10 More then in those that more would seeme to doe.
Such *Vertues* thy rare modesty doth hide.
Which by their proper luster I espy'd;

457 thou. : thou, 1622.
458 now, : now. 1622.

And though long maskt in silence they have beene,
I have a Wisedome through that silence seene,
Yea, I have learned knowledge from thy tongue,
And heard when thou hast in concealement sung.
Which me the bolder and more willing made
Thus to invite thee to this homely shade.
And though (it may be) thou couldst never spie,
Such worth in me, I might be knowne thereby: 20
In thee I doe; for here my neighbouring Sheepe
Upon the border of these Downes I keepe:
Where often thou at Pastorals and Playes,
Hast grac'd our Wakes on Summer Holy-dayes:
And many a time with thee at this cold spring
Met I, to heare your learned shepheards sing,
Saw them disporting in the shady Groves,
And in chaste Sonnets wooe their chaster Loves:
When I, endued with the meanest skill,
Mongst others have been urg'd to tune my quill. 30
But, (cause but little cunning I had got)
Perhaps thou saw'st me, though thou knew'st me not.

Alexis.

Yes *Philaret*, I know thee, and thy name.
Nor is my knowledge grounded all on fame:
Art thou not he, that but this other yeere,
Scard'st all the Wolves and Foxes in the Sheere?
And in a match at Foot-ball lately tride
(Having scarce twenty Satyrs on thy side)
Held'st play: and though assailed kept'st thy stand
Gainst all the best-tride Ruffians in the Land? 40
Did'st thou not then in dolefull Sonnets mone,
When the beloved of great *Pan* was gone?
And at the wedding of faire *Thame* and *Rhine*,

36 Scard'st all the Wolves and Foxes: by his *Abuses Whipt and Stript*; see Eclogue 2, line 61.

38 twenty Satyrs: again referring to the *Abuses*.

42 beloved of great *Pan*: Prince Henry, son of James I, who died in November 1612. Wither was among those who published memorial verses.

43 wedding: of James' daughter Elizabeth and Frederick of Germany. See *Epith.*

Sing of their glories to thy Valentine?
I know it, and I must confesse that long
In one thing I did doe thy nature wrong:
For, till I mark'd the ayme thy Satyrs had,
I thought them over-bold, and thee halfe mad.
But, since I did more neerely on thee looke,
50 I soone perceiv'd that I all had mistooke;
I saw that of a *Cynicke* thou mad'st show,
Where since, I finde, that thou wert nothing so;
And that of many thou much blame had'st got,
When as thy *Innocency* deserv'd it not.
But that too good opinion thou hast seem'd
To have of me (not so to be esteem'd,)
Prevailes not ought to stay him who doth feare,
He rather should reproofes then prayses heare.
'Tis true, I found thee plaine and honest to,
60 Which made mee like, then love, as now I do;
And, *Phila*, though a stranger, this to thee Ile say,
Where I doe love, I am not coy to stay.

Philarete.

Thankes, gentle Swaine, that dost so soone unfold
What I to thee as gladly would have told:
And thus thy wonted curtesie exprest
In kindly entertaining this request.
Sure, I should injure much my owne content,
Or wrong thy love to stand on complement:
Who hast acquaintance in one word begun,
70 As well as I could in an age have done.
Or by an over-weaning slownesse marre
What thy more wisdome hath brought on so farre.
Then sit thou downe, and Ile my minde declare,
As freely, as if we familiars were:
And if thou wilt but daigne to give me eare,
Something thou mayst for thy more profit heare.

Alexis.

Philarete, I willingly obey.

62 coy: hesitant.

Philarete.

Then know, *Alexis*, from that very day,
When as I saw thee at thy Shepheards Coate,
Where each (I thinke) of other tooke first note; 80
I meane that Pastor who by *Tavies* springs,
Chaste Shepheards loves in sweetest numbers sings,
And with his Musicke (to his greater fame)
Hath late made proud the fairest *Nymphs* of Thame.
E'ne then (me thought) I did espy in thee
Some unperceiv'd and hidden worth to bee:
Which, in thy more apparant vertues, shin'd;
And, among many, I (in thought) devin'd,
By something my conceit had understood,
That thou wert markt one of the *Muses* brood. 90
That, made me love thee: and that Love I beare
Begat a Pitty, and that Pitty, Care:
Pitty I had to see good parts conceal'd,
Care I had how to have that good reveal'd,
Since 'tis a fault admitteth no excuse,
To possesse much, and yet put nought in use.
Hereon I vow'd (if wee two ever met)
The first request that I would strive to get,
Should be but this, that thou would'st shew thy skill,
How thou could'st tune thy Verses to thy quill: 100
And teach thy *Muse* in some well-framed Song,
To shew the *Art* thou hast supprest so long:
Which if my new-acquaintance may obtaine,
I will for ever honour this daies gaine.

Alexis.

Alas! my small experience scarce can tell,
So much as where those *Nymphs*, the *Muses*, dwell;
Nor (though my slow conceit still travels on)
Shall I ere reach to drinke of *Hellicon*.
Or, if I might so favour'd be to taste

81 Pastor: William Browne of Tavistock ("*Tavies* springs"). His poetry about the "fairest *Nymphs* of Thame" is *The Shepherd's Pipe*, to which this eclogue was appended.

90 brood. : brood, 1622.

110 What those sweet streames but over-flow in waste,
And touch *Parnassus*, where it low'st doth lie,
I feare my skill would hardly flag so hie.

Philarete.

Despaire not Man, the Gods have prized nought
So deere, that may not be with labour bought:
Nor need thy paine be great, since *Fate* and *Heaven*,
That (as a blessing) at thy birth have given.

Alexis.

Why, say they had?

Philarete.

Then use their gifts thou must.
Or be ungratefull, and so be unjust:
For if it cannot truely be deni'd,
120 Ingratitude mens benefits doe hide;
Then more ungratefull must he be by ods,
Who doth conceale the bounty of the Gods.

Alexis.

That's true indeed, but *Envy* haunteth those
Who seeking Fame, their hidden skill disclose:
Where else they might (obscur'd) from her espying,
Escape the blasts and danger of envying:
Cryticks will censure our best straines of Wit,
And pur-blind *Ignorance* misconster it.
And which is bad, (yet worse then this doth follow)
130 Most hate the *Muses*, and contemne *Apollo*.

Philarete.

So let them: why should wee their hate esteeme?
Is't not enough we of our selves can deeme?
'Tis more to their disgrace that we scorne them,
Then unto us that they our Art contemne.
Can we have better pastime then to see
Their grosse heads may so much deceived bee,
As to allow those doings best, where wholly
We scoffe them to their face, and flout their folly?

Or to behold blacke *Envy* in her prime,
Die selfe-consum'd, whilst we vie lives with time: 140
And, in despight of her, more fame attaine,
Then all her malice can wipe out againe?

Alexis.

Yea, but if I appli'd mee to those straines,
Who should drive forth my Flocks unto the plaines,
Which, whil'st the *Muses* rest, and leasure crave,
Must watering, folding, and attendance have?
For if I leave with wonted care to cherish
Those tender *heards*, both I and they should perish.

Philarete.

Alexis, now I see thou dost mistake,
There is no meaning thou thy Charge forsake; 150
Nor would I wish thee so thy selfe abuse,
As to neglect thy calling for thy *Muse*.
But, let these two, so each of other borrow,
That they may season mirth, and lessen sorrow.
Thy Flocke will helpe thy charges to defray,
Thy *Muse* to passe the long and teadious day:
Or whilst thou tun'st sweet measures to thy *Reed*,
Thy Sheepe, to listen, will more neere thee feed;
The Wolves will shun them, birds above thee sing,
And Lamkins dance about thee in a Ring. 160
Nay, which is more; in this thy low estate,
Thou in contentment shalt with Monarks mate:
For mighty *Pan*, and *Ceres*, to us grants,
Our Fields and Flocks shall helpe our outward wants:
The *Muses* teach us Songs to put off cares,
Grac'd with as rare and sweet conceits as theirs:
And we can thinke our Lasses on the Greenes
As faire, or fairer, then the fairest Queenes:
Or, what is more then most of them shall doe,
Wee'le make their juster fames last longer to, 170
And have our Lines by greatest Princes grac'd
When both their name and memori's defac'd.
Therefore, *Alexis*, though that some disdaine
The heavenly Musicke of the Rurall plaine,

What is't to us, if they (o'reseene) contemne
The dainties which were nere ordain'd for them?
And though that there be other-some envy
The prayses due to sacred Poesie,
Let them disdaine, and fret till they are weary,
180 Wee in our selves have that shall make us merry:
Which, he that wants, and had the power to know it,
Would give his life that he might die a Poet.

Alexis.

A brave perswasion.

Philarete.

Here thou see'st mee pent
Within the jawes of strict imprisonment;
A fore-lorne *Shepheard*, voyd of all the meanes,
Whereon Mans common hope in danger leanes:
Weake in my selfe, exposed to the *Hate*
Of those whose *Envies* are insatiate:
Shut from my friends, banish'd from all delights;
190 Nay worse, excluded from the sacred *Rites*.
Here I doe live mongst out-lawes markt for death,
As one unfit to draw the common breath,
Where those who to be good did never know,
Are barred from the meanes should make them so.
I suffer, cause I wish'd my Country well,
And what I more must beare I cannot tell.
I'me sure they give my Body little scope,
And would allow my *Minde* as little *Hope*:
I waste my Meanes, which of it selfe is slender,
200 Consume my Time (perhaps my fortunes hinder)
And many Crosses have, which those that can
Conceive no wrong that hurts another man,

183-84 Wither evidently was in the Marshalsea Prison when he wrote these lines, as he was during the composition of Eclogues 1–3. Lines 183-234 were not printed in *The Shepherd's Pipe* with Eclogue 4 and the rest of Eclogue 5. Yet the opening lines of this eclogue indicate that he had not yet been jailed; Eclogue 4 and the first 182 lines of Eclogue 5 therefore must have been written before the spring of 1614 and lines 183-234 added later.

190 sacred *Rites*: church services.

Will not take note of; though if halfe so much
Should light on them, or their owne person touch,
Some that themselves (I feare) most worthy thinke,
With all their helpes would into basenesse shrinke.
But, spight of *Hate*, and all that Spight can do,
I can be patient yet, and merry to.
That slender *Muse* of mine, by which my *Name*,
Though scarse deserv'd, hath gain'd a little fame, 210
Hath made mee unto such a Fortune borne,
That all misfortunes I know how to scorne;
Yea, midst these bands can sleight the *Great'st* that bee,
As much as their disdaine misteemes of mee.
This Cave, whose very presence some affrights,
I have oft made to Eccho forth delights,
And hope to turne, if any Justice be,
Both shame and care on those that wish'd it me.
For while the World rancke villanies affords,
I will not spare to paint them out in words; 220
Although I still should into troubles runne,
I knew what man could act, ere I begun;
And I'le fulfill what my *Muse* drawes mee to,
Maugre all *Jayles*, and *Purgatories* to.
For whil'st shee sets mee honest task's about,
Vertue, or shee, (I know) will beare mee out:
And if, by *Fate*, th'abused power of some
Must, in the worlds-eye, leave mee overcome,
They shall find one Fort yet, so fenc'd I trow,
It cannot feare a Mortals over-throw. 230
This *Hope*, and *Trust*, that great power did infuse,
That first inspir'd into my brest a *Muse*,
By whom I doe, and ever will contemne
All those ill haps, my foes despight, and them.

Alexis.

Th'hast so well (yong *Philaret*) plaid thy part,
I am almost in love with that sweet Art:
And if some power will but inspire my song,
Alexis will not be obscured long.

213 bands: bonds.

Philarete.

Enough kinde Pastor: But oh! yonder see
240 Two honest Shepheards walking hither, bee
Cuddy and *Willy*, that so dearely love,
Who are repairing unto yonder Grove:
Let's follow them: for never braver Swaines
Made musicke to their flocks upon these Plaines.
They are more worthy, and can better tell
What rare contents doe with a Poet dwell.
Then whiles our sheepe the short sweet grasse do sheare
And till the long shade of the hils appeare,
Wee'le heare them sing: for though the one be young,
250 Never was any that more sweetly sung.

A Postscript to the Reader.

If you have read this, and received any content, I am glad, (though it bee not so much as I could wish you); if you thinke it idle, why then I see wee are not likely to fall out; for I am just of your minds; yet weigh it well before you runne too farre in your censures, lest this prove less barren of Wit, then you of courtesie. It is very true (I know not by what chance) that I have of late been so highly beholding to Opinion, *that I wonder how I crept so much into her favour, and (if I did thinke it worthie the fearing) I should be afraid that she having so undeservedly befriended mee beyond my Hope or expectation, will,*
10 *upon as little cause, ere long, againe picke some quarrell against mee; and it may bee, meanes to make use of* this, *which I know must needes come farre short of their expectation, who by their earnest desire of it, seem'd to be fore-possest with a farre better conceite, then I can beleeve it prooves worthy of. So much at least I doubted, and therefore loth to deceive the world (though it often beguile me) I kept it to my selfe, indeed, not dreaming ever to see it published: But now, by the overmuch perswasion of some friends, I have been constrained to expose it to the generall view. Which seeing I have done, some things I desire thee to take notice of. First, that I am* Hee, *who to*

243 braver: finer.
1 *content*: i.e., contentment.
2 *you);* : *you)* 1622.
7 (if : if 1622.
18-19 *some things* : *somethings* 1622.

pleasure my friend, have fram'd my selfe a content out of that which would otherwise discontent mee. Secondly, that I have coveted more to effect what I thinke truely honest in it selfe, then by a seeming shew of Art, to catch the vaine blastes of uncertaine Opinion. *This that I have here written, was no part of my studie, but onely a recreation in imprisonment: and a trifle, neither in my conceit fitting, nor by me intended to bee made common; yet some, who it should seeme esteemed it worthy more respect then I did, tooke paines to coppy it out, unknowne to mee, and in my absence got it both Authorized and prepared for the Presse; so that if I had not hindred it, last* Michaelmas-Tearme *had beene troubled with it. I was much blamed by some Friends for withstanding it, to whose request I should more easily have consented, but that I thought (as indeed I yet doe) I should thereby more disparage my selfe, then content them. For I doubt I shall bee supposed one of those, who out of their arrogant desire of a little preposterous* Fame, *thrust into the world every unseasoned trifle that drops out of their unsetled braines; whose basenesse how much I hate, those that know mee can witnesse, for if I were so affected, I might perhaps present the World with as many severall* Poems, *as I have seene yeeres; and justly make my selfe appeare to bee the Author of some things that others have shamefully usurped and made use of as their owne. But I will be content other men should owne some of those Issues of the* Braine, *for I would be loath to confesse all that might in that kinde call me Father. Neither shall any more of them, by my consent, in haste againe trouble the world, unlesse I know which way to benefit it with lesse prejudice to my owne estate. And therefore if any of those lesse serious* Poems *which are already disperst into my friends hands come amongst you, let not their publication be imputed to me, nor their lightnesse be any disparagement to what hath been since more serious written, seeing it is but such stuffe as riper judgements have in their farre elder yeeres been much more guilty of.*

I know an indifferent Crittick *may finde many faults, as well in the slightnesse of this present* Subject, *as in the erring from the true*

28 *Authorized*: i.e., received an official license to print it.

30 Michaelmas-Tearme: the quarter of the year beginning on September twenty-ninth.

44 *haste* : *hast* 1622.

47 *hands* : *hands,* 1622.

nature of an Eglogue*: moreover, it altogether concernes my self, which divers may dislike. But neither can bee done on just cause: The first hath bin answered already: The last might consider that I was there where my owne estate was chiefly to bee looked unto, and all the comfort I could minister unto my selfe, little enough.*

If any man deeme it worthy his reading I shall bee glad: if hee 60 *thinke his paines ill bestow'd, let him blame himselfe for medling with that concerned him not: I neither commended it to him, neither cared whether he read it or no; because I know those that were desirous of it, will esteeme the same as much as I expeƈt they should.*

But it is not unlikely, some wil thinke I have in divers places been more wanton (as they take it) then befitting a Satirist*; yet their severity I feare not, because I am assured all that I ever yet did, was free from* Obscænity*: neyther am I so* Cynical*, but that I thinke a modest expression of such amorous conceits as sute with Reason, will yet very well become my yeeres; in which not to have feeling of the* 70 *power of* Love*, were as great an argument of much stupidity, as an oversottish affeƈtion were of extreame folly. Lastly, if you thinke it hath not well answered the Title of the* Shepheards Hunting*, goe quarrell with the* Stationer*, who bid himselfe God-Father, and imposed the* Name *according to his owne liking; and if you, or hee, finde any faults, pray mend them.*

Valete.

FINIS.

65 Satirist : Satiriƈt 1622.
76 *Valete*: Good-bye.

[Shall I wasting.]

Shall I wasting in Dispaire,
Dye because a *Womans* faire?
Or make pale my cheekes with care,
Cause anothers Rosie are?
Be shee fairer then the Day,
Or the Flowry Meads in May;
    If shee be not so to me,
    What care I how faire shee be.

Should my heart be grievd or pin'd,
Cause I see a *Woman* kind? 10
Or a well disposed Nature,
Joyned with a lovely Feature?
Be shee meeker, kinder, than
Turtle-Dove, or *Pelican*:
    If shee be not so to me,
    What care I, how kind she be.

Shall a *Womans* Virtues move,
Me, to perish for her love?
Or, her well-deserving knowne,
Make me quite forget mine owne? 20
Be shee with that Goodnesse blest,
Which may gaine her, name of *Best*:
    If she be not such to me,
    What care I, how good she be.

Cause her Fortune seemes too high,
Shall I play the foole, and dye?
Those that beare a Noble minde,
Where they want of Riches find,
Thinke, what with them, they would doe,
That without them, dare to wooe. 30
    And, unlesse that mind I see,
    What care I, though Great she be.

14 *Pelican*: traditionally thought to feed its young with its own blood.
15 so to me : so me 1633.

Great, or *Good*, or *Kind*, or *Faire*,
I will ne're the more dispaire,
If She love me, this beleeve;
I will die, er'e she shall grieve.
If she slight me, when I wooe;
I can scorne, and let her goe.
For, if shee be not for me,
40 What care I, for whom she be.

An Epitaph upon a Woman, and her Child, buried together in the same Grave.

Beneath this Marble Stone doth lye,
The Subject of Deaths Tyranny.
A Mother: who in this close Tombe,
Sleepes with the issue of her wombe.
Though cruelly enclinde was he
And with the fruit shooke downe the Tree,
Yet was his cruelty in vaine,
For, Tree, and Fruit, shall spring againe.

A Christmas Carroll.

So, now is come our joyfulst *Feast*;
Let every man be jolly.
Each Roome, with Yvie leaves is drest,
And every Post, with Holly.
Though some Churles at our mirth repine,
Round your forheads Garlands twine,
Drowne sorrow in a Cup of Wine,
And let us all be merry.

Now, all our Neighbours Chimneys smoke,
10 And *Christmas* blocks are burning;

5 he : he; 1633.
6 Tree, : Tree. 1633.
7 Wine, : Wine. 1633.

Their Ovens, they with bakt-meats choke,
And all their Spits are turning.
    Without the doore, let sorrow lie:
    And, if for cold, it hap to die,
    Weele bury't in a *Christmas* Pye.
And evermore be merry.

Now, every *Lad* is wondrous trimm,
And no man minds his Labour.
Our *Lasses* have provided them,
A Bag-pipe, and a Tabor. 20
    Young men, and Mayds, and Girles & Boyes,
    Give life, to one anothers Joyes:
    And, you anon shall by their noyse,
Perceive that they are merry.

Ranke Misers now, doe sparing shun:
Their Hall of Musicke soundeth:
And, Dogs, thence with whole shoulders run,
So, all things there aboundeth.
    The Countrey-folke, themselves advance;
    For *Crowdy-Mutton's* come out of *France*: 30
    And *Jack* shall pipe, and *Jyll* shall daunce,
And all the Towne be merry.

Ned Swash hath fetcht his Bands from pawne,
And all his best Apparell.
Brisk *Nell* hath bought a Ruffe of Lawne,
With droppings of the Barrell.
    And those that hardly all the yeare
    Had Bread to eat, or Raggs to weare,
    Will have both Clothes, and daintie fare:
And all the day be merry. 40

Now poore men to the *Justices*,
With Capons make their arrants,

30 The meaning is not clear. Crowdy-Mutton may be a mutton pie.

33 Bands: ornamental ruffs.

42 arrants: errands.

And if they hap to faile of these,
They plague them with their Warrants.
    But now they feed them with good cheere,
    And what they want, they take in Beere:
    For, Christmas *comes but once a yeare*:
And then they shall be merry.

Good *Farmours*, in the Countrey, nurse
50 The poore, that else were undone.
Some *Land lords*, spend their money worse
On Lust, and Pride at *London*.
    There, the Roysters they doe play;
    Drabb and Dice their Lands away,
    Which may be ours, another day:
And therefore lets be merry.

The Clyent now his suit forbeares,
The Prisoners heart is eased,
The Debtor drinks away his cares,
60 And, for the time is pleased.
    Though others Purses be more fat,
    Why should we pine or grieve at that?
    Hang sorrow, care will kill a Cat.
And therefore lets be merry.

Harke, how the *Wagges*, abrode doe call
Each other foorth to rambling.
Anon, youle see them in the Hall,
For Nutts, and Apples scambling.
    Harke, how the Roofes with laughters sound!
70 Annon they'l thinke the house goes round:
    For, they the Sellars depth have found.
And, there they will be merry.

51 worse : worse, 1633.
54 Lands : Landt 1633.
62 that?: punctuation inverted in 1633.
68 scambling: scrambling.

The *Wenches* with their *Wassell-Bowles*,
About the Streets are singing:
The *Boyes* are come to catch the *Owles*,
The *Wild-mare*, in is bringing.
    Our *Kitchin-Boy* hath broke his *Boxe*,
    And, to the dealing of the *Oxe*,
    Our honest neighbours come by flocks,
And, here, they will be merry. 80

Now *Kings* and *Queenes*, poore Sheep-cotes have,
And mate with every body:
The honest, now, may play the *knave*,
And wise men play at *Noddy*.
    Some Youths will now a *Mumming* goe;
    Some others play at *Rowland-hoe*,
    And, twenty other Gameboyes moe:
Because they will be merry.

Then wherefore in these merry daies,
Should we I pray, be duller? 90
No; let us sing some *Roundelayes*,
To make our mirth the fuller.
    And, whilest thus inspir'd we sing,
    Let all the Streets with ecchoes ring:
    Woods, and Hills, and every thing,
Beare witnesse we are merry.

75-76 Owles and Wild-mare seem to have been games.

84 *Noddy*: a card game similar to cribbage.

86 *Rowland-hoe*: another game.

87 Gameboyes: games.

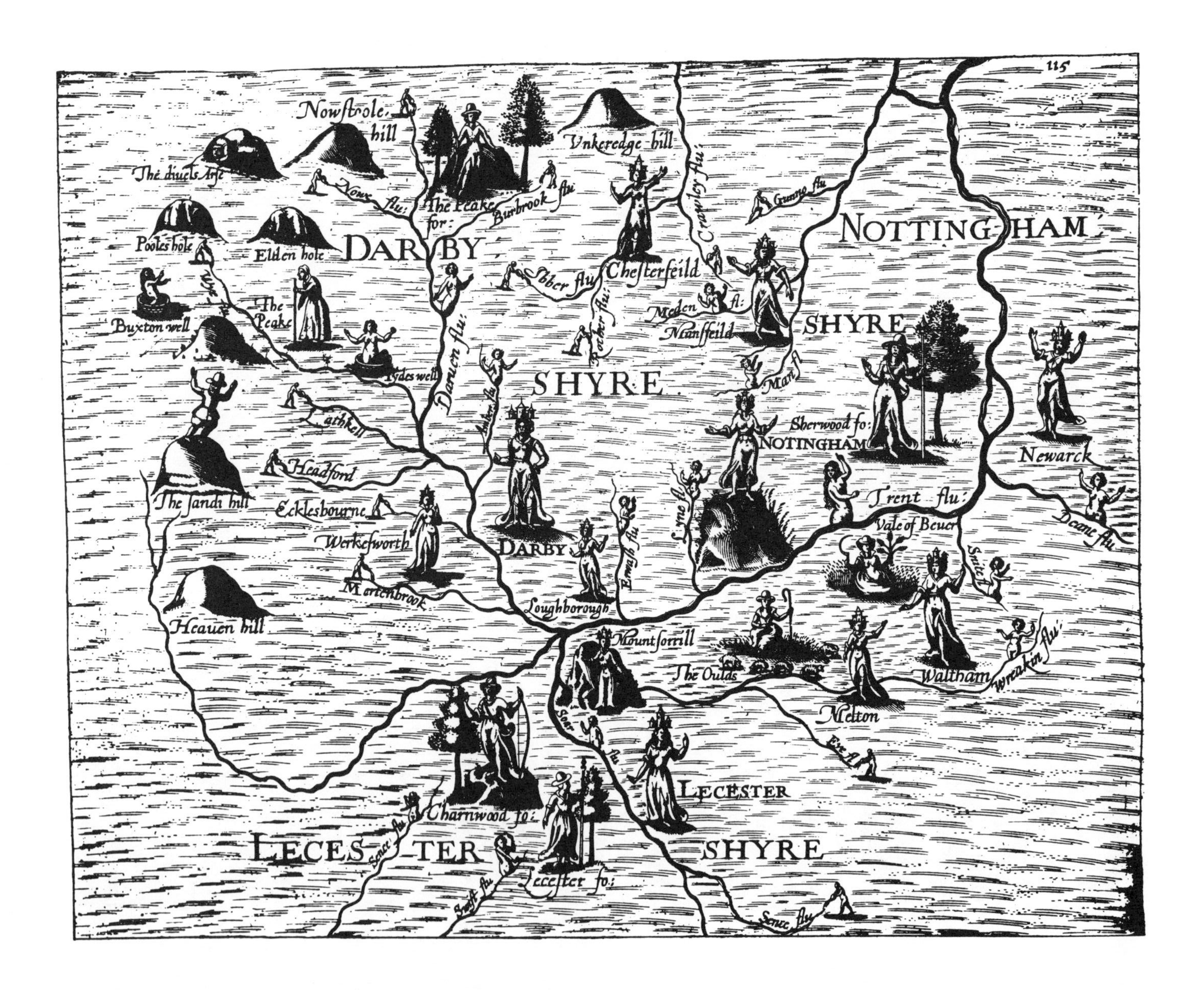
115
Nowstrole hill
The diuels Arse
Vnkeredge hill
Vowx flu:
The Peake for:
Burbrook flu
Crawley flu:
Gunne flu
NOTTINGHAM
Pooles hole
Elden hole
DARBY
Chesterfeild
Sober flu
Wye flu
Buxton well
The Peake
Darwen flu:
Meden fl:
Manffeild
SHYRE
Tydes well
SHYRE
Man fl:
Lathkell
Sherwood fo:
NOTINGHAM
Newarck
Headford
The Sandi hill
Trent flu:
Ecklesbourne
Werkesworth
Vale of Beuer
Deane flu
DARBY
Erwash flu
Smite fl:
Mertenbrook
Heauen hill
Loughborough
Mountsorrill
The Oulds
Waltham
Wreakin flu:
Melton
Soar flu
Eye fl:
LECESTER
Charnwood fo:
LECESTER
SHYRE
Leicester fo:
Sence flu

Michael Drayton

Michael Drayton was born in the village of Hartshill in Warwickshire in 1563, and so is the oldest writer represented in this volume. He seems to have grown up in that area but attended neither university. Instead, he became attached as a page to the household of Sir Henry Goodere in Polesworth, who encouraged his interest in writing (for testimony see the dedication to the *Odes*). Drayton fell in love with Sir Henry's younger daughter, Anne, for whom he retained deep affection and friendship for the rest of his life despite her marriage to Sir Henry Rainsford. Her birthplace is celebrated in the "Hymne to His Ladies Birth-Place," included among the odes, and she herself was his Idea, to whom in 1593 he addressed his first original work, *Idea. The Shepheards Garland*, a pastoral imitation of Spenser. She is more widely known as the Idea to whom he addressed many of his sonnets. There is no hint of jealousy in his fine elegy for the death of her husband, Sir Henry, early in 1622, but Drayton seems never to have married.

In the 1590s he began his career in London as a professional writer, turning first to English history with a series of long fictional "Epistles" supposedly exchanged between important people of the past. Modeled on Ovid's *Heroides*, they appeared in 1597 as *Englands Heroicall Epistles*. The *Barrons Wars* of 1603 continues his patriotic interest in England's past, a concern which was to find ultimate expression in his longest work, the *Poly-Olbion*. Organized by geography, this topographical poem was published in eighteen "Songs" in 1613 with copious annotations by John Selden; Drayton expanded it in 1622 by the addition of twelve more parts. For a while during 1597 to 1602 he wrote for the stage, mostly in collaboration. The surviving *Sir John Oldcastle*, written with Wilson, Hathaway, and Munday, again evinces his concern for English history.

There is a tradition that Drayton was a friend of Shakespeare — indeed that Shakespeare died at Stratford as a result of a drinking bout there with Ben Jonson and him. But firm evidence is lacking; the allusion to Shakespeare in the Elegy to Reynolds does not suggest intimacy. For many years Drayton and Jonson were certainly not friends, but in the 1620s they came at least to respect one another, as the praise of Jonson's plays in the same elegy shows, coupled with Jonson's reciprocation in the Ode prefixed to the volume in which the elegy appeared.

When his own feelings surface, as they occasionally do in the elegies, it is clear that Drayton suffered disappointments in his career, beginning perhaps with the indifference or hostility of King James himself from early in his English reign. The relatively poor reception given his major work, *Poly-Olbion*, must have reinforced the natural moroseness which finds expression in works like *The Owle* (1604), a very obscure allegory of contemporary society modeled to some degree upon Spenser's *Mother Hubberds Tale* (for a thorough consideration of the relationships of Drayton to Spenser and to contemporary Spenserians, see the Ph.D. dissertation by Richard John, "In the Field of the Muses," Rutgers University, 1970). The marked bitterness of many of the elegies reminds us of the moral decay of James' court, centering around the murder of Sir Thomas Overbury and a subsequent cover-up in which the king himself may have been implicated. The glory of Elizabeth's reign had been frittered away, and Drayton views the corruption of the 1620s with a clear-seeing eye. Jonson similarly castigates these faults in poems like "A Speach According to Horace" and "Epistle to a Friend" which must have been written about the same time. James' last years were ones of bitter disillusion for many.

No one ever impugned Drayton's high moral character. Testimony to the esteem in which he was held is his burial in 1631 in Westminster Abbey, the inscription for his tomb written, according to tradition, by Jonson. His fame, however, languished in the Restoration and the eighteenth century; he returned to recognition with Coleridge and Lamb. There is an outstanding scholarly biography by Bernard H. Newdigate, *Michael Drayton and His Circle* (Oxford: Shakespeare Head Press, 1961). A more popular treatment is by J. A. Berthelot, *Michael Drayton* (New York: Twayne, 1967), based in part on his Ph.D. dissertation, "A Handbook of the Poetical Works of Michael Drayton with Critical Interpretations" (University of Denver, 1962).

Drayton must be recognized as having written the first successful odes in English, although Jonson has somewhat competitive claims (for a comparison of their originality, see D. S. J. Parsons, *Queens Quarterly*, 75 [1968]: 675–84). His "To the Reader" is evidence of this self-consciousness of innovation, and the first ode, "To Himselfe," outlines the history of the form, primarily a classical one which had been practiced during the previous century in France and then introduced to England by the otherwise negligible George Sowthorne. Drayton overlooks odes by Barnabe Barnes in his *Parthenophil and Parthenophe* (1593); for a full history of the form see Robert Shafer, *The English Ode to 1660* (Princeton: Princeton University Press, 1918), and Carol Maddison, *Apollo and the Nine* (Baltimore: Johns Hopkins Press, 1960). As he writes it, the ode is a lyric which may utter almost any personal feeling and accordingly is not clearly distinguishable from other lyric forms except that in his hands it almost always consists of very short rhyming lines. Indeed, the last one, memorializing Agincourt, Drayton called a ballad, but it is evident from "To the Reader" that he is thinking of the Chaucerian ballade, with which his poem has really very little connection. Much harder to evaluate is the influence which he claims for Welsh bardic poetry upon these pieces, the explanation lying perhaps in the fact that bardic poetry was an oral tradition (see his dedicatory poem with its mention of John Hughes) that may have employed vigorous rhyming short lines. Like other folk poetry, it probably was based on stress, which is a factor in Drayton's imitations and may underlie his identification of it with the poetry of John Skelton.

Within these strongly rhythmic poems he packs a surprising variety of subject matter. Some odes, like "The Heart" or "The Cryer," suggest comparison with poems by John Donne, and the complexity of "Loves Conquest" is remarkable. "To His Rivall" anticipates Suckling. Some are metrical experiments which failed, like the "Anacreontic" with its adjacent rhymes pushed apart by terminal punctuation; the scansion of his "Skeltoniad" seems merely uncertain, probably reflecting the way he read its namesake. The "Ode Written in the Peake" with its gray, wintry scene should be compared with Jonson's on the same subject. Two of the odes are deservedly famous: those to the Virginian Voyage and to Agincourt. Michael West has argued that the former is not entirely successful, inconsistently combining as it does the pastoral and the heroic (*Renaissance Quarterly*, 24 [1971]: 501–6), a critical issue upon which each reader must make up his own mind. "Agincourt" seldom fails to please, and its animated meter inspired Tennyson's "Charge of the Light Brigade" and Longfellow's "Skeleton in Armor."

The elegies are so named because of their couplet form, considered then the English equivalent of classical elegiac meter. Except for the first one, an extraordinarily interesting personal statement (to Anne, or to someone else?), their contents divide almost equally between funeral poems and social satires, the latter comparable to those of Donne and Jonson with much of the same bitterness about the degeneracy of contemporary life (see especially those addressed to Sandys, to Browne, and to Jeffreys). Everything in society is "arsey-varsey." Drayton's best advice is that of stoicism, which offered thoughtful people a way to live with such difficulties: "arm thy soul with patience." Especially interesting is the autobiographical material included in the elegy addressed to his friend Reynolds, followed by his evaluations of contemporary writers in imitation of similar evaluations which "Grave morall Spenser" had made in *Colin Clout*. Shakespeare is seen only as a writer of comedy. The low state in which Drayton finds literature in the 1620s appears also in his elegies to Sandys and to Jeffreys.

The last selection, *Nimphidia*, is a perennial favorite. Its stanza form is reminiscent of the short, frequently rhymed lines of the odes as well as of Chaucer's "Tale of Sir Thopas," which is its closest literary model. Like Drayton, Chaucer was satirizing romances; as the earlier poet mocks the quest of the chivalric knight, so the later parodies the extra-marital love affair. At its end, because of Proserpina's intervention, the men have completely forgotten about the love affairs, but the women all remember and "Among themselves do closely smile." One wonders whether Drayton is recalling some actual episode or whether in its inconclusive outcome the fight between Oberon and Pigwiggen allegorizes some social issue. If so, there does not appear to be sufficient evidence for identification and one may best be satisfied with the piece as a whimsical fairy tale. It provides the closest literary analogue to Mercutio's Queen Mab speech in the first act of *Romeo and Juliet*; diminutive fairies participate in both and much of the pleasure lies in their Lilliputian details. Because of staging the fairies in *A Midsummer Night's Dream* are full-sized human beings, but the similarities of the play and the poem are otherwise extensive: Oberon is jealous in each (though Titania's Indian boy is scarcely represented by the bumptious Pigwiggen), and Puck faithfully executes his king's orders.

The only difficult feature of Drayton's poem is the occasional grammatical eccentricity of placing conjunctions within the clauses which they introduce, as "Each circumstance and having scand," for "And having scand each circumstance"; or "Your greevous thirst and to asswage," for "And to asswage your greevous thirst." (The structure is occasionally found elsewhere in his poetry, e.g., Elegy to

Sandys, l. 97.) But the narrative is direct and uncomplicated, the responses of the men convincingly juvenile, the fairy details authentic folklore. It remains one of the most immediately pleasing poems of its day.

Alone among the authors represented in this book, Drayton has enjoyed an excellent modern edition, that by J. William Hebel, *The Works of Michael Drayton* (Oxford: Shakespeare Head Press, 1931–41) in five volumes, the last, which consists of notes and bibliography of early editions, being completed by Kathleen Tillotson and Bernard H. Newdigate. When the set was reprinted in 1961 some corrections and additions were made, especially by Bent Juel-Jensen in the bibliography. One must, however, remark that like Shakespeare's first folio Drayton's poems were sometimes corrected during the press run with the result that copies differ from one another, a fact which can be seen in the present text. For example, line 73 in the Elegy upon the Three Sons is quite different from Hebel's recorded variants, and his "*Prosperpyna*" in *Nimphidia*, line 405, is corrected in the Widener copy at Harvard (formerly the property of Charles II), the basic text in this edition for the *Elegies* and *Nimphidia* as they appear in *The Battaile of Agincourt* (1627). The elegies on the three sons and that on Lady Penelope Clifton had appeared earlier in Henry Fitzgeffrey's *Certaine Elegies* (1618, reissued in 1620) with a number of variants which Hebel lists (5: 218). The *Odes* are reprinted from *Poems* (1619), Drayton's first collected edition of his works. Of the *Odes*, those to his Valentine, the Heart, the Sacrifice to Apollo, to his Rival, the Cryer, to his Coy Love, and to his Ladies Birth-Place appear for the first time in 1619. The rest had been printed in *Poems Lyrick and Pastorall* (1606); Hebel prints variants in 5: 148–49.

Mention should also be made of the selection, with some notes, by John Buxton, *Poems of Michael Drayton* (Cambridge: Harvard University Press, 1953). A facsimile of the 1619 *Poems* appeared from the Scolar Press (Menston, England) in 1969 and one of the 1627 *Battaile of Agincourt* in 1972.

Odes.

To the Worthy Knight, and My Noble Friend, Sir Henry Goodere, a Gentleman of His Majesties Privie *Chamber*.

These *Lyrick* Pieces, short, and few,
Most worthy Sir, I send to you,
To reade them, be not wearie:
They may become JOHN HEWES his Lyre,
Which oft at *Powlsworth* by the fire
Hath made us gravely merry.

Beleeve it, he must have the Trick
Of Ryming; with Invention quick,
That should doe *Lyricks* well:
But now I have done in this kind, 10
Though in my selfe I cannot find,
Your Judgement best can tell.

Th'old *British* BARDS, upon their Harpes,
For falling Flatts, and rising Sharpes,
That curiously were strung;
To stirre their Youth to Warlike Rage,
Or their wyld Furie to asswage,
In these loose Numbers sung.

No more I for Fooles Censures passe,
Then for the braying of an Asse, 20
Nor once mine Eare will lend them:

Dedication: In 1606 the volume of Odes had been addressed to Drayton's patron, Sir Walter Aston. Sir Henry Goodere was a minor poet and good friend of John Donne. He married his cousin, his uncle Henry's daughter; her sister was Drayton's Idea, later wife of Sir Henry Rainsford. Sir Henry Goodere (or Goodyer or Goodier) inherited the family estate at Polesworth, in Warwickshire.

4 HEWES: (or Hughes), perhaps a Welsh folk singer of Polesworth; otherwise unidentified.

13 *British*: more precisely Welsh, like the singer Taliesin. The Welsh bards are contrasted with English singers in *Poly-Olbion*, Song 4; see also Song 6.

15 curiously: Drayton refers to the fact that folk music often employs unusual scales.

If you but please to take in gree
These *Odes*, sufficient 'tis to mee;
Your liking can commend them.

Yours,
MICH. DRAYTON.

To the Reader.

Odes *I have called these my few Poems; which how happie soever they prove, yet Criticisme it selfe cannot say, that the Name is wrongfully usurped: For (not to begin with Definitions against the Rule of Oratorie, nor* ab ovo, *against the prescript Rule of Poetrie in a Poeticall Argument, but somewhat only to season thy Pallat with a slight description) an Ode is knowne to have been properly a Song, moduled to the ancient Harpe, and neither too short-breathed, as hasting to the end, nor composed of the longest Verses, as unfit for the sudden Turnes and loftie Tricks with which* Apollo *used to* 10 *manage it. They are (as the Learned say) divers: Some transcendently loftie, and farre more high then the Epick (commonly called the Heroique Poeme) witnesse those of the inimitable* Pindarus, *consecrated to the glorie and renowne of such as returned in triumph from* Olympus, Elis, Isthmus, *or the like: Others, among the Greekes, are amorous, soft, and made for Chambers, as other for Theaters; as were* Anacreon's, *the very Delicacies of the Grecian* Erato, *which Muse seemed to have beene the Minion of that Teian old Man, which composed them: Of a mixed kinde were* Horaces, *and may truely there-*

22 in gree: with goodwill.

3 *Definitions*: Rhetorical theory stated that one should not begin a discourse with definitions.

4 ab ovo: from its ultimate origin. Narrative, says Horace in *Ars Poetica* 147, should not go all the way back to ultimate beginnings.

7 *too short-breathed*: composed in very short lines.

12 Pindar wrote odes celebrating the victors in the battles named.

15 *Chambers*: private rooms.

16 Erato: Muse of love poetry.

17 *Teian*: Anacreon was born in Teos, in Asia Minor.

fore be called his mixed; whatsoever else are mine, little partaking of the high Dialect of the first: 20

Though we be all to seeke
Of *Pindar*, that great Greeke.

Nor altogether of Anacreon, *the Arguments being Amorous, Morall, or what else the Muse pleaseth. To write much in this kind, neither know I how it will rellish, nor in so doing, can I but injuriously presuppose Ignorance or Slouth in thee, or draw censure upon my selfe, for sinning against the* Decorum *of a Preface, by reading a Lecture, where it is inough to summe the Points: New they are, and the worke of playing Houres; but what other commendation is theirs, and whether inherent in the subject, must be thine to judge. But to act* 30 *the goe-betweene of my Poems and thy Applause, is neither my Modestie nor Confidence, that oftner then once have acknowledged thee kind, and doe not doubt hereafter to doe somewhat, in which I shall not feare thee just: And would at this time also gladly let thee understand, what I thinke above the rest, of the last Ode of this Number, or if thou wilt, Ballad in my Booke: for both the great Master of Italian Rymes,* Petrarch, *and our* Chaucer, *and other of the upper House of the Muses, have thought their Canzons honoured in the Title of a Ballad; which, for that I labour to meet truely therein with the old English Garbe, I hope as able to justifie, as the learned* 40 Colin Clout *his Roundelay. Thus requesting thee, in thy better Judgement, to correct such Faults as have escaped in the Printing, I bid thee farewell.*

M. DRAYTON.

39 Drayton does not distinguish between the ballad and the ballade forms.

41 In the Epistle to Gabriel Harvey, prefixed to the *Shepherd's Calendar*, "E.K." explains and defends the new poetry found in the book. Drayton seems here to identify E.K. with Spenser (who called himself Colin Clout).

Odes.

To Himselfe, And The Harpe.

And why not I, as hee
That's greatest, if as free,
    (In sundry strains that strive,
Since there so many be)
    Th'old *Lyrick* kind revive?

I will, yea, and I may;
Who shall oppose my way?
    For what is he alone,
That of himselfe can say,
10   Hee's Heire of *Helicon*?

Apollo, and the Nine,
Forbid no Man their Shrine,
    That commeth with hands pure;
Else they be so divine,
    They will him not indure.

For they be such coy Things,
That they care not for Kings,
    And dare let them know it;
Nor may he touch their Springs,
20   That is not borne a Poet.

Pyreneus, *King of* Phocis, *attempting to ravish the Muses.*

The *Phocean* it did prove,
Whom when foule Lust did move,
    Those Mayds unchaste to make,
Fell, as with them he strove,
    His Neck and justly brake.

1 hee: Horace, who also had revived the ode, which originated in Greece.

10 *Helicon*: spring sacred to the nine Muses.

11-15 Milton frequently echoes this idea, e.g. "he who would not be frustrate of his hope to write well hereafter in laudable things, ought him selfe to bee a true Poem," *Apology for Smectymnuus* in Yale Prose Works, 1:890. The idea has been traced to Plato, particularly the *Laws* 7.

21 gloss: The story outlined here is told in Ovid, *Metamorphoses* 5. 274ff.

That instrument ne'r heard,
Strooke by the skilfull Bard,
It strongly to awake;
But it th'infernalls skard,
And made *Olympus* quake. 30

As those Prophetike strings
Whose sounds with fiery Wings,
Drave Fiends from their abode,
Touch'd by the best of Kings,
That sang the holy Ode.

Sam. lib. 1. cap. 16.

So his, which Women slue,
And it int' *Hebrus* threw,
Such sounds yet forth it sent,
The Bankes to weepe that drue,
As downe the Streame it went. 40

Orpheus *the* Thracian Poet. Caput Hebre lyramque Exip. &c. Ovid. lib. 11. Metam.

That by the Tortoyse shell,
To MAYAS Sonne it fell,
The most thereof not doubt
But sure some Power did dwell,
In Him who found it out.

Mercury *inventor of the Harpe, as* Horace Ode 10. lib. 7 curvæque lyræ parentem.

The Wildest of the field,
And Ayre, with Rivers t'yeeld,
Which mov'd; that sturdy Glebes,
And massie Oakes could weeld,
To rayse the pyles of *Thebes*. 50

Thebes *fayned to have been raysed by Musicke.*

And diversly though Strung,
So anciently We sung
To it, that Now scarce knowne,

34 best of Kings: David, identified in the gloss for having driven fiends (madness) from Saul by his playing.

36 gloss: the story of the murder of Orpheus, again from Ovid.

41 gloss: Horace, *Odes* 1. 10 (Drayton's reference is wrong), identifies Mercury as inventor of the lyre.

48 gloss: The story is told about Amphion, a legendary musician.

If first it did belong
    To *Greece*, or if our Owne.

The ancient British *Priests, so called of their abode in woods.*

The *Druydes* imbrew'd,
With Gore, on Altars rude
    With Sacrifices crown'd,
In hollow Woods bedew'd,
60   Ador'd the Trembling sound.

Pindar *Prince of the* Greeke lyricks, *of whom* Horace: Pindarum quisquis studet, &c. Ode 2. lib. 4.

Though wee be All to seeke,
Of PINDAR that Great *Greeke*,
    To Finger it aright,
The Soule with power to strike,
    His hand retayn'd such Might.

Horace *first of the* Romans *in that kind.*

Or him that *Rome* did grace,
Whose Ayres we all imbrace,
    That scarcely found his Peere,
Nor giveth PHŒBUS place,
70   For Strokes divinely cleere.

The Irish *Harpe.*

The *Irish* I admire,
And still cleave to that Lyre,
    As our Musike's Mother,
And thinke, till I expire,
    APOLLO's such another.

As *Britons*, that so long
Have held this Antike Song,
    And let all our Carpers
Forbeare their fame to wrong,
80   Th'are right skilfull Harpers.

56 *Druydes*: Drayton gives further details in *Poly-Olbion*, Song 9, lines 415ff.

61 gloss: quoting the opening of Horace's *Odes* 4. 2: "Whoever attempts to rival Pindar . . ."

65 His: Pindar's.

76 *Britons*: again, Welsh.

Southerne, I long thee spare,
Yet wish thee well to fare,
    Who me pleased'st greatly,
As first, therefore more rare,
    Handling thy Harpe neatly.

Southerne, *an* English *Lyrick.*

To those that with despight
Shall terme these Numbers slight,
    Tell them their Judgement's blind,
Much erring from the right,
    It is a Noble kind. 90

Nor is't the Verse doth make,
That giveth, or doth take,
    'Tis possible to clyme,
To kindle, or to slake,
    Although in SKELTON's Ryme.

An old English *Rymer.*

To The New Yeere.

Rich Statue, double-faced,
With Marble Temples graced,
    To rayse thy God-head hyer,
In flames where Altars shining,
Before thy Priests divining,
    Doe od'rous Fumes expire.

Great JANUS, I thy pleasure,
With all the *Thespian* Treasure,
    Doe seriously pursue;

81 *Southerne*: John Southern or Soowthern, who in 1584 published a volume of sonnets, odes, and other verse forms. Heavily indebted to Ronsard, they are not very well done. Drayton is correct, however, in recognizing him as probably the first to use these forms in English.

95 SKELTON: John Skelton (c. 1460–1529), a poet no longer in favor in Stuart times who claimed that "Though my rime be ragged, Tatter'd and jagged . . . It hath in it some pith."

1 Statue: of Janus. Ovid, *Fasti* 1, details the tradition of his worship.

8 *Thespian*: perhaps, dramatic. Thespis traditionally originated tragedy.

10 To th' passed yeere returning,
As though the old adjourning,
    Yet bringing in the new.

Thy ancient Vigils yeerely,
I have observed cleerely,
    Thy Feasts yet smoaking bee;
Since all thy store abroad is,
Give something to my Goddesse,
    As hath been us'd by thee.

Give her th'*Eoan* brightnesse,
20 Wing'd with that subtill lightnesse,
    That doth trans-pierce the Ayre;
The Roses of the Morning
The rising Heav'n adorning,
    To mesh with flames of Hayre.

Those ceaselesse Sounds, above all,
Made by those Orbes that move all,
    And ever swelling there,
Wrap'd up in Numbers flowing,
Them actually bestowing,
30   For Jewels at her Eare.

O Rapture great and holy,
Doe thou transport me wholly,
    So well her forme to vary,
That I aloft may beare her,
Whereas I will insphere her
    In Regions high and starry.

And in my choise Composures,
The soft and easie Closures,
    So amorously shall meet;

17 Goddesse: Idea, finally named in line 81.

18 As: which.

19 *Eoan*: morning or eastern.

37 Composures: poems.

That ev'ry lively Ceasure 40
Shall tread a perfect Measure,
    Set on so equall feet.

That Spray to fame so fertle,
The Lover-crowning Mirtle,
    In Wreaths of mixed Bowes,
Within whose shades are dwelling
Those Beauties most excelling,
    Inthron'd upon her Browes.

Those Paralels so even,
Drawne on the face of Heaven, 50
    That curious Art supposes,
Direct those Gems, whose cleerenesse
Farre off amaze by neerenesse,
    Each Globe such fire incloses.

Her Bosome full of Blisses,
By nature made for Kisses,
    So pure and wond'rous cleere,
Whereas a thousand Graces
Behold their lovely Faces,
    As they are bathing there. 60

O, thou selfe-little blindnesse,
The kindnesse of unkindnesse,
    Yet one of those divine;
Thy Brands to me were lever,
Thy Fascia, and thy Quiver,
    And thou this Quill of mine.

40 Ceasure: cæsura; pause.

49 Paralels: of latitude and longitude imposed upon maps by the heavens, in astronomy ("That curious Art").

61 thou: Cupid.

63 Yet : yet 1619.

64 lever: preferable.

65 Fascia: band.

66 And thou this: and thou shouldst have this.

This Heart so freshly bleeding,
Upon it owne selfe feeding,
　　Whose wounds still dropping be;
70　O Love, thy selfe confounding,
Her coldnesse so abounding,
　　And yet such heat in me.

Yet if I be inspired,
Ile leave thee so admired,
　　To all that shall succeed,
That were they more then many,
'Mongst all, there is not any,
　　That Time so oft shall reed.

Nor Adamant ingraved,
80　That hath been choisely'st saved,
　　IDEA's Name out-weares;
So large a Dower as this is,
The greatest often misses,
　　The Diadem that beares.

To His Valentine.

Muse, bid the Morne awake,
　　Sad Winter now declines,
Each Bird doth chuse a Make,
　　This day's Saint VALENTINES;
For that good Bishops sake
Get up, and let us see,
What Beautie it shall bee,
　　That Fortune us assignes.

But lo, in happy How'r,
10　　The place wherein she lyes,
In yonder climbing Tow'r,
　　Gilt by the glitt'ring Rise;

3 Each Bird: as in Chaucer's *Parliament of Fowls.*

O JOVE! that in a Show'r,
As once that Thund'rer did,
When he in drops lay hid,
    That I could her surprize.

Her Canopie Ile draw,
    With spangled Plumes bedight,
No Mortall ever saw
    So ravishing a sight; 20
That it the Gods might awe,
And pow'rfully trans-pierce
The Globie Universe,
    Out-shooting ev'ry Light.

My Lips Ile softly lay
    Upon her heav'nly Cheeke,
Dy'd like the dawning Day,
    As polish'd Ivorie sleeke:
And in her Eare Ile say;
O, thou bright Morning-Starre, 30
'Tis I that come so farre,
    My Valentine to seeke.

Each little Bird, this Tyde,
    Doth chuse her loved Pheere,
Which constantly abide
    In Wedlock all the yeere,
As Nature is their Guide:
So may we two be true,
This yeere, nor change for new,
    As Turtles coupled were. 40

The Sparrow, Swan, the Dove,
    Though VENUS Birds they be,
Yet are they not for Love
    So absolute as we:

13 JOVE: As a shower of gold the god seduced Danaë and fathered Perseus.

34 Pheere: fere, companion.

For Reason us doth move;
They but by billing woo:
Then try what we can doo,
    To whom each sense is free.

Which we have more then they,
50   By livelyer Organs sway'd,
Our Appetite each way
    More by our Sense obay'd:
Our Passions to display,
This Season us doth fit;
Then let us follow it,
    As Nature us doth lead.

One Kisse in two let's breake,
    Confounded with the touch,
But halfe words let us speake,
60   Our Lip's imploy'd so much;
Untill we both grow weake,
With sweetnesse of thy breath;
O smother me to death:
    Long let our Joyes be such.

Let's laugh at them that chuse
    Their Valentines by lot,
To weare their Names that use,
    Whom idly they have got:
Such poore choise we refuse,
70 Saint VALENTINE befriend;
We thus this Morne may spend,
    Else Muse, awake her not.

58 Confounded: intermingled.

The Heart.

If thus we needs must goe,
What shall our one Heart doe,
This One made of our Two?

Madame, two Hearts we brake,
And from them both did take
The best, one Heart to make.

Halfe this is of your Heart,
Mine in the other part,
Joyn'd by our equall Art.

Were it cymented, or sowne, 10
By Shreds or Pieces knowne,
We each might find our owne.

But 'tis dissolv'd, and fix'd,
And with such cunning mix'd,
No diff'rence that betwixt.

But how shall we agree,
By whom it kept shall be,
Whether by you, or me?

It cannot two Brests fill,
One must be heartlesse still, 20
Untill the other will.

It came to me to day,
When I will'd it to say,
With whether it would stay?

It told me, In your Brest,
Where it might hope to rest:
For if it were my Ghest,

10-15 Drayton is differentiating between a true union of two different things (in which they cannot be distinguished) and a mixture (in which they can be).

For certainety it knew,
That I would still anew
30 Be sending it to you.

Never, I thinke, had two
Such worke, so much to doo,
A Unitie to woo.

Yours was so cold and chaste,
Whilst mine with zeale did waste,
Like Fire with Water plac'd.

How did my Heart intreat,
How pant, how did it beat,
Till it could give yours heat!

40 Till to that temper brought,
Through our perfection wrought,
That blessing eythers Thought.

In such a Height it lyes,
From this base Worlds dull Eyes,
That Heaven it not envyes.

All that this Earth can show,
Our Heart shall not once know,
For it too vile and low.

The Sacrifice To Apollo.

Priests of APOLLO, sacred be the Roome,
For this learn'd Meeting: Let no barbarous Groome,
How brave soe'r he bee,
Attempt to enter;

1 Ben Jonson's *Leges Convivales*: "Over the Door at the Entrance into the Apollo," comes to mind at once, but P. Simpson in *Modern Language Review* 34 (1939): 367ff shows that the room at the Devil Tavern was not built until 1624.

But of the Muses free,
None here may venter;
This for the *Delphian* Prophets is prepar'd:
The prophane Vulgar are from hence debar'd.

And since the Feast so happily begins,
Call up those faire Nine, with their Violins; 10
They are begot by JOVE,
Then let us place them,
Where no Clowne in may shove,
That may disgrace them:
But let them neere to young APOLLO sit;
So shall his Foot-pace over-flow with Wit.

Where be the Graces, where be those fayre Three?
In any hand They may not absent bee:
They to the Gods are deare,
And they can humbly 20
Teach us, our Selves to beare,
And doe things comely:
They, and the Muses, rise both from one Stem,
They grace the Muses, and the Muses them.

Bring forth your Flaggons (fill'd with sparkling Wine)
Whereon swolne BACCHUS, crowned with a Vine,
Is graven; and fill out,
It well bestowing,
To ev'ry Man about,
In Goblets flowing: 30
Let not a Man drinke, but in Draughts profound;
To our God PHŒBUS let the Health goe Round.

Let your Jests flye at large; yet therewithall
See they be Salt, but yet not mix'd with Gall:
Not tending to disgrace,

5 But of . . . free: unless admitted by.
10 Nine: the Muses.
16 Foot-pace: dais.
23 one Stem: Both groups were fathered by Jove.

But fayrely given,
Becomming well the place,
Modest, and even;
That they with tickling Pleasure may provoke
40 Laughter in him, on whom the Jest is broke.

Or if the deeds of HEROES ye rehearse,
Let them be sung in so well-ord'red Verse,
That each word have his weight,
Yet runne with pleasure;
Holding one stately height,
In so brave measure,
That they may make the stiffest Storme seeme weake,
And dampe JOVES Thunder, when it lowd'st doth speake.

And if yee list to exercise your Vayne,
50 Or in the Sock, or in the Buskin'd Strayne,
Let Art and Nature goe
One with the other;
Yet so, that Art may show
Nature her Mother;
The thick-brayn'd Audience lively to awake,
Till with shrill Claps the Theater doe shake.

Sing Hymnes to BACCHUS then, with hands uprear'd,
Offer to JOVE, who most is to be fear'd:
From him the Muse we have,
60 From him proceedeth
More then we dare to crave;
'Tis he that feedeth
Them, whom the World would starve; then let the Lyre
Sound, whilst his Altars endlesse flames expire.

50 i.e., in comedy or tragedy.

63 Them: poets.

To Cupid.

Maydens, why spare ye?
Or whether not dare ye
    Correct the blind Shooter?
Because wanton VENUS,
So oft that doth paine us,
    Is her Sonnes Tutor.

Now in the Spring,
He proveth his Wing,
    The Field is his Bower,
And as the small Bee, 10
About flyeth hee,
    From Flower to Flower.

And wantonly roves,
Abroad in the Groves,
    And in the Ayre hovers,
Which when it him deweth,
His Fethers he meweth,
    In sighes of true Lovers.

And since doom'd by Fate,
(That well knew his Hate) 20
    That Hee should be blinde;
For very despite,
Our Eyes be his White,
    So wayward his kinde.

If his Shafts loosing,
(Ill his Marke choosing)
    Or his Bow broken;
The Moane VENUS maketh,
And care that she taketh,
    Cannot be spoken. 30

17 meweth: covers.
23 White: target.
25 loosing: losing.

To VULCAN commending
Her love, and straight sending
    Her Doves and her Sparrowes,
With Kisses unto him,
And all but to woo him,
    To make her Sonne Arrowes.

Telling what he hath done,
(Sayth she, Right mine owne Sonne)
    In her Armes she him closes,
40 Sweetes on him fans,
Layd in Downe of her Swans,
    His Sheets, Leaves of Roses.

And feeds him with Kisses;
Which oft when he misses,
    He ever is froward:
The Mothers o'r-joying,
Makes by much coying
    The Child so untoward.

Yet in a fine Net,
50 That a Spider set,
    The Maydens had caught him;
Had she not been neere him,
And chanced to heare him,
    More good they had taught him.

An Amouret Anacreontick.

Most good, most faire.
Or Thing as rare,
To call you's lost;

48 untoward: unruly.

51 Maydens: those of line 1.

Title: As his "To the Reader" shows, Drayton attempted to imitate Anacreon's love poetry, but this piece reads far more like the rhyming of John Skelton. The punctuation separating many of the closely rhymed lines is clearly deliberate.

For all the cost
Words can bestow,
So poorely show
Upon your prayse,
That all the wayes
Sense hath, come short:
Whereby Report 10
Falls them under;
That when Wonder
More hath seyzed,
Yet not pleased,
That it in kinde
Nothing can finde,
You to expresse:
Neverthelesse,
As by Globes small,
This Mightie ALL 20
Is shew'd, though farre
From Life, each Starre
A World being:
So wee seeing
You, like as that,
Onely trust what
Art doth us teach;
And when I reach
At Morall Things,
And that my Strings 30
Gravely should strike,
Straight some mislike
Blotteth mine ODE.
As with the Loade,
The Steele we touch,
Forc'd ne'r so much,
Yet still removes

11 them under: short of them.
15 kinde: nature.
25 that: the star as a world.
32 mislike: dissatisfaction.
34 Loade: loadstone, magnet.

To that it loves,
Till there it stayes;
40 So to your prayse
I turne ever,
And though never
From you moving,
Happie so loving.

Loves Conquest.

Wer't granted me to choose,
How I would end my dayes;
Since I this Life must loose,
It should be in Your praise;
For there is no *Bayes*
Can be set above you.

S'impossibly I love You
And for You sit so hie,
Whence none may remove You
10 In my cleere Poesie,
That I oft deny
You so ample Merit.

The freedome of my Spirit
Maintayning (still) my Cause,
Your Sex not to inherit,
Urging the *Salique* Lawes;
But your Vertue drawes
From Me every due.

Thus still You me pursue,
20 That no where I can dwell,
By Feare made just to You,

5 *Bayes*: poetic honors.

8 for: it is because.

16 *Salique*: French laws whereby inheritance derived only through the male line.

Who Naturally rebell,
Of You that excell
    That should I still Endyte,

    Yet will You want some Ryte.
That lost in Your high praise
    I wander to and fro,
As seeing sundry Waies:
Yet which the right not know
    To get out of this Maze. 30

To The Virginian Voyage.

You brave Heroique Minds,
Worthy your Countries Name,
    That Honour still pursue,
    Goe, and subdue,
Whilst loyt'ring Hinds
Lurke here at home, with shame.

Britans, you stay too long,
Quickly aboord bestow you,
    And with a merry Gale
    Swell your stretch'd Sayle, 10
With Vowes as strong,
As the Winds that blow you.

Your Course securely steere,
West and by South forth keepe,
    Rocks, Lee-shores, nor Sholes,

22 Who: I who.

23 and 24 reveal the meaning when reversed.

25 want: lack.

28 seeing: perhaps to be emended to seeking.

29 right: sc. way.

Title: Approval for the Virginia expedition was granted on April 6, 1606; in December three ships sailed with 140 people aboard. Drayton's interest in the Virginia plantation continued throughout his life.

When EOLUS scowles,
You need not feare,
So absolute the Deepe.

And cheerefully at Sea,
20 Successe you still intice,
To get the Pearle and Gold,
And ours to hold,
VIRGINIA,
Earth's onely Paradise.

Where Nature hath in store
Fowle, Venison, and Fish,
And the fruitfull'st Soyle,
Without your Toyle,
Three Harvests more,
30 All greater then your Wish.

And the ambitious Vine
Crownes with his purple Masse,
The Cedar reaching hie
To kisse the Sky,
The Cypresse, Pine
And use-full Sassafras.

To whose, the golden Age
Still Natures lawes doth give,
No other Cares that tend,
40 But Them to defend
From Winters rage,
That long there doth not live.

16 EOLUS: god of the winds.

25-48 Hakluyt in his *Principal Navigations* provided this information, reporting voyages of the 1580s. See J. Q. Adams, *Modern Language Notes* 33 (1918): 405ff, and Gerhard Friedrich, *Modern Language Notes* 72 (1957): 401ff.

36 use-full: as a medicine.

37 whose: sc. possessors.

41 rage 1606 : age 1619.

When as the Lushious smell
Of that delicious Land,
    Above the Seas that flowes,
    The cleere Wind throwes,
Your Hearts to swell
Approching the deare Strand.

In kenning of the Shore
(Thanks to God first given,) 50
    O you the happy'st men,
    Be Frolike then,
Let Cannons roare,
Frighting the wide Heaven.

And in Regions farre
Such *Heroes* bring yee foorth,
    As those from whom We came,
    And plant Our name,
Under that Starre
Not knowne unto our North. 60

And as there Plenty growes
Of Lawrell every where,
    APOLLO's Sacred tree,
    You it may see,
A Poets Browes
To crowne, that may sing there.

Thy Voyages attend,
Industrious HACKLUIT,
    Whose Reading shall inflame
    Men to seeke Fame, 70
And much commend
To after-Times thy Wit.

59 Starre: Drayton does not seem to have any particular one in mind. If it is Canopus it is not visible from the Virginia plantations.

68 Besides compiling his famous collection of accounts of voyages, Hakluyt was also one of the patentees of the Virginia group.

An Ode Written In The Peake.

This while we are abroad,
    Shall we not touch our Lyre?
Shall we not sing an ODE?
    Shall that holy Fire,
In us that strongly glow'd,
    In this cold Ayre expire?

Long since the Summer layd
    Her lustie Brav'rie downe,
The Autumne halfe is way'd,
10   And BOREAS 'gins to frowne,
Since now I did behold
    Great BRUTES first builded Towne.

Though in the utmost *Peake*,
    A while we doe remaine,
Amongst the Mountaines bleake
    Expos'd to Sleet and Raine,
No Sport our Houres shall breake,
    To exercise our Vaine.

What though bright PHŒBUS Beames
20   Refresh the Southerne Ground,
And though the Princely *Thames*
    With beautious Nymphs abound,
And by old *Camber's* Streames
    Be many Wonders found;

Title: The Peak is a hilly area between Manchester and Sheffield in Derbyshire. See also the Elegy on Lady Stanhope and *Poly-Olbion*, Song 26, lines 378ff. and its accompanying map, reproduced here on p. 196.

8 Brav'rie: finery.

9 way'd: gone.

10 BOREAS: the north wind.

11 now: when (?).

12 Towne: traditionally New Troy, i.e., London.

17 breake: interrupt, distract.

18 Vaine: vein, the writing of poetry.

20 Refresh : refresh 1619.

23 *Camber's*: Cambria's, i.e., Wales'.

Yet many Rivers cleare
    Here glide in Silver Swathes,
And what of all most deare,
    Buckston's delicious Bathes,
Strong Ale and Noble Cheare,
    T'asswage breeme Winters scathes. 30

Those grim and horrid Caves,
    Whose Lookes affright the day,
Wherein nice Nature saves,
    What she would not bewray,
Our better leasure craves,
    And doth invite our Lay.

In places farre or neere,
    Or famous, or obscure,
Where wholesome is the Ayre,
    Or where the most impure, 40
All times, and every-where,
    The Muse is still in ure.

His Defence Against The Idle Critick.

The Ryme nor marres, nor makes,
Nor addeth it, nor takes,
    From that which we propose;
Things imaginarie
Doe so strangely varie,
    That quickly we them lose.

And what's quickly begot,
As soone againe is not,
    This doe I truely know:

28 *Buckston*: a village in the southern part of the Peak District. In *Poly-Olbion* Drayton favorably compares its hot baths with those at Bath.

30 breeme: rough, stormy.

42 ure: use.

10 Yea, and what's borne with paine,
That Sense doth long'st retaine,
  Gone with a greater Flow.

Yet this Critick so sterne,
But whom, none must discerne,
  Nor perfectly have seeing,
Strangely layes about him,
As nothing without him
  Were worthy of being.

That I my selfe betray
20 To that most publique way,
  Where the Worlds old Bawd,
Custome, that doth humor,
And by idle rumor,
  Her Dotages applaud.

That whilst she still prefers
Those that be wholly hers,
  Madnesse and Ignorance,
I creepe behind the Time,
From spertling with their Crime,
30 And glad too with my Chance.

O wretched World the while,
When the evill most vile
  Beareth the fayrest face,
And inconstant lightnesse,
With a scornefull slightnesse,
  The best Things doth disgrace.

12 perhaps, to be overcome only by stronger sensations.

17 As: as though.

19, 25 That: perhaps, It is true that . . .

24 Her: that of Custome, the antecedent also of *she* in the next line.

29 From spertling with: to keep from splashing in. Crime: that of madness and ignorance.

30 Chance: fortune, lot.

Whilst this strange knowing Beast,
Man, of himselfe the least,
  His Envie declaring,
Makes Vertue to descend, 40
Her Title to defend,
  Against him, much preparing.

Yet these me not delude,
Nor from my place extrude,
  By their resolved Hate;
Their vilenesse that doe know,
Which to my selfe I show,
  To keepe above my Fate.

To His Rivall.

  Her lov'd I most,
  By thee that's lost,
Though she were wonne with leasure;
  She was my gaine,
  But to my paine,
Thou spoyl'st me of my Treasure.

  The Ship full fraught
  With Gold, farre sought,
Though ne'r so wisely helmed,
  May suffer wracke 10
  In sayling backe,
By Tempest over-whelmed.

  But shee, good Sir,
  Did not preferre
You, for that I was ranging;

38 Man, of: Man, knowing about.
41-42 much preparing to defend her title against him.
46 i.e., I who know their vileness.
15 for that: because.

But for that shee
Found faith in mee,
And she lov'd to be changing.

Therefore boast not
20 Your happy Lot,
Be silent now you have her;
The time I knew
She slighted you,
When I was in her favour.

None stands so fast,
But may be cast
By Fortune, and disgraced:
Once did I weare
Her Garter there,
30 Where you her Glove have placed.

I had the Vow
That thou hast now,
And Glances to discover
Her Love to mee,
And she to thee
Reades but old Lessons over.

She hath no Smile
That can beguile,
But as my Thought I know it;
40 Yea, to a Hayre,
Both when and where,
And how she will bestow it.

What now is thine,
Was onely mine,
And first to me was given;
Thou laugh'st at mee,
I laugh at thee,
And thus we two are even.

But Ile not mourne,
But stay my Turne, 50
The Wind may come about, Sir,
And once againe
May bring me in,
And helpe to beare you out, Sir.

A Skeltoniad.

The Muse should be sprightly,
Yet not handling lightly
Things grave; as much loath,
Things that be slight, to cloath
Curiously: To retayne
The Comelinesse in meane,
Is true Knowledge and Wit.
Nor me forc'd Rage doth fit,
That I thereto should lacke
Tabacco, or need Sacke, 10
Which to the colder Braine
Is the true *Hyppocrene*;
Nor did I ever care
For great Fooles, nor them spare.
Vertue, though neglected,
Is not so dejected,
As vilely to descend
To low Basenesse their end;
Neyther each ryming Slave
Deserves the Name to have 20
Of Poet: so the Rabble
Of Fooles, for the Table,
That have their Jests by Heart,
As an Actor his Part,
Might assume them Chayres

Title: See the note to line 95 of the Ode to Himselfe.

6 meane: demeanor.

10 Tabacco: as a stimulant.

12 *Hyppocrene*: fountain sacred to the Muses near Mount Helicon.

Amongst the Muses Heyres.
Parnassus is not clome
By every such Mome;
Up whose steepe side who swerves,
30 It behoves t'have strong Nerves:
My Resolution such,
How well, and not how much
To write, thus doe I fare,
Like some few good that care
(The evill sort among)
How well to live, and not how long.

The Cryer.

Good Folke, for Gold or Hyre,
But helpe me to a Cryer;
For my poore Heart is runne astray
After two Eyes, that pass'd this way.
O yes, O yes, O yes,
If there be any Man,
In Towne or Countrey, can
Bring me my Heart againe,
Ile please him for his paine;
10 And by these Marks I will you show,
That onely I this Heart doe owe.
It is a wounded Heart,
Wherein yet sticks the Dart,
Ev'ry piece sore hurt throughout it,
Faith, and Troth, writ round about it:
It was a tame Heart, and a deare,
And never us'd to roame;
But having got this Haunt, I feare
'Twill hardly stay at home.

27 clome: climbed.
28 Mome: blockhead.
34 some : some, 1619.
5 O yes: oyez, the call of a public crier: hear ye!
11 owe: own.

For Gods sake, walking by the way, 20
If you my Heart doe see,
Either impound it for a Stray,
Or send it backe to me.

To His Coy Love,

A CANZONET.

I pray thee leave, love me no more,
Call home the Heart you gave me,
I but in vaine that Saint adore,
That can, but will not save me:
These poore halfe Kisses kill me quite;
Was ever Man thus served?
Amidst an Ocean of Delight,
For Pleasure to be sterved.

Shew me no more those Snowie Brests,
With Azure Riverets branched, 10
Where whilst mine Eye with Plentie feasts,
Yet is my Thirst not stanched.
O TANTALUS, thy Paines ne'r tell,
By me thou art prevented;
'Tis nothing to be plagu'd in Hell,
But thus in Heaven tormented.
Clip me no more in those deare Armes,
Nor thy Life's Comfort call me;
O, these are but too pow'rfull Charmes,
And doe but more inthrall me. 20
But see how patient I am growne,
In all this coyle about thee;
Come nice Thing, let thy Heart alone,
I cannot live without thee.

8 sterved: killed.

14 prevented: anticipated.

A Hymne To His Ladies Birth-Place.

Coventry, that do'st adorne
The Countrey wherein I was borne,
Yet therein lyes not thy prayse,
Why I should crowne thy Tow'rs with Bayes:
'Tis not thy Wall, me to thee weds,
Thy Ports, nor thy proud Pyrameds,
Nor thy Trophies of the Bore,
But that Shee which I adore,
Which scarce Goodnesse selfe can payre,
10 First their breathing blest thy Ayre;
IDEA, in which Name I hide
Her, in my heart Deifi'd,
For what good, Man's mind can see,
Onely Her IDEAS be;
She, in whom the Vertues came
In Womans shape, and tooke her Name,
She so farre past Imitation,
As but Nature our Creation
Could not alter, she had aymed,
20 More then Woman to have framed:
She, whose truely written Story,
To thy poore Name shall adde more glory,
Then if it should have beene thy Chance,
T'have bred our Kings that Conquer'd *France*.
Had She beene borne the former Age,
That house had beene a Pilgrimage,

Coventry finely walled.

The Shoulderbone of a Bore of mighty bignesse.

Title: Further information about the area appears in *Poly-Olbion*, Song 13, lines 253–326, especially 280–300.

2 Countrey: Drayton was born in the village of Hartshill in Warwickshire, not far from Coventry.

6 Pyrameds: buildings.

7 gloss: Camden in his *Brittania* also notes this famous bone of a wild bore.

8 Shee: Drayton's Idea, Anne Goodere (1571–1633?), daughter of his early patron Sir Henry Goodere, who owned a house on Much Park Street in Coventry.

9 payre: equal.

22 thy: Coventry's.

And reputed more Divine,
Then *Walsingham* or BECKETS Shrine.
That Princesse, to whom thou do'st owe
Thy Freedome, whose Cleere blushing snow, 30
The envious Sunne saw, when as she
Naked rode to make Thee free,
Was but her Type, as to foretell,
Thou should'st bring forth one, should excell
Her Bounty, by whom thou should'st have
More Honour, then she Freedome gave;
And that great Queene, which but of late
Ru'ld this Land in Peace and State,
Had not beene, but Heaven had sworne,
A Maide should raigne, when she was borne. 40
Of thy Streets, which thou hold'st best,
And most frequent of the rest,
Happy *Mich-Parke* ev'ry yeere,
On the fourth of *August* there,
Let thy Maides from FLORA's bowers,
With their Choyce and daintiest flowers
Decke Thee up, and from their store,
With brave Garlands crowne that dore.
The old Man passing by that way,
To his Sonne in Time shall say, 50
There was that Lady borne, which long
To after-Ages shall be sung;
Who unawares being passed by,
Back to that House shall cast his Eye,
Speaking my Verses as he goes,
And with a Sigh shut ev'ry Close.
Deare Citie, travelling by thee,
When thy rising Spyres I see,
Destined her place of Birth;

Two famous Pilgrimages, the one in Norfolk, *the other in* Kent.

Godiva, *Duke* Leofricks *wife, who obtained the Freedome of the City, of her husband, by riding thorow it naked.*

Queene Elizabeth.

A noted Streete in Coventry.

His Mistresse birth-day.

28 gloss: At Walsingham was a celebrated shrine dedicated to the Virgin Mary, which had been the object of many pilgrimages as had been that of St. Thomas à Becket at Canterbury.

29 This famous story is also told at greater length in *Poly-Olbion*, Song 13. There Drayton fancifully derives *Good*-ere from *God*-iva, who is thus Anne's "Type" (l. 33) or model.

53 unawares: unnoticed.

60 Yet me thinkes the very Earth
Hallowed is, so farre as I
Can thee possibly descry:
Then thou dwelling in this place,
Hearing some rude Hinde disgrace
Thy Citie with some scurvy thing,
Which some Jester forth did bring,
Speake these Lines where thou do'st come,
And strike the Slave for ever dumbe.

To The Cambro-Britans, and their Harpe, his Ballad of AGINCOURT.

Faire stood the Wind for *France*,
When we our Sayles advance,
Nor now to prove our chance,
  Longer will tarry;
But putting to the Mayne,
At *Kaux*, the Mouth of *Sene*,
With all his Martiall Trayne,
  Landed King HARRY.

And taking many a Fort,
10 Furnish'd in Warlike sort,
Marcheth tow'rds *Agincourt*,
  In happy howre;
Skirmishing day by day,
With those that stop'd his way,
Where the *French* Gen'rall lay,
  With all his Power.

Title: The Cambro-Britons were the Welsh British. Drayton was also to write a much longer poem about the great victory of Henry V, *The Battaile of Agincourt*. Details here are taken mostly from Holinshed's *History*, which was also Shakespeare's main source. Much was made of Henry's birth in the Welsh town of Monmouth.

Which in his Hight of Pride,
King Henry to deride,
His Ransome to provide
  To the King sending. 20
Which he neglects the while,
As from a Nation vile,
Yet with an angry smile,
  Their fall portending.

And turning to his Men,
Quoth our brave Henry then,
Though they to one be ten,
  Be not amazed.
Yet have we well begunne,
Battels so bravely wonne, 30
Have ever to the Sonne,
  By Fame beene raysed.

And for my Selfe (quoth he)
This my full rest shall be,
England ne'r mourne for Me,
  Nor more esteeme me.
Victor I will remaine,
Or on this Earth lie slaine,
Never shall Shee sustaine,
  Losse to redeeme me. 40

Poiters and *Cressy* tell,
When most their Pride did swell,
Under our Swords they fell,
  No lesse our skill is,
Then when our Grandsire Great,
Clayming the Regall Seate,
By many a Warlike feate,
  Lop'd the *French* Lillies.

33 he) : he, 1619.

45 Grandsire: Henry's great-grandfather, Edward III, who won important victories over the French in the battles named in line 41.

The Duke of *Yorke* so dread,
50 The eager Vaward led;
With the maine, HENRY sped,
Among'st his Hench-men.
EXCESTER had the Rere,
A Braver man not there,
O Lord, how hot they were,
On the false *French-men*!

They now to fight are gone,
Armour on Armour shone,
Drumme now to Drumme did grone,
60 To heare, was wonder;
That with Cryes they make,
The very Earth did shake,
Trumpet to Trumpet spake,
Thunder to Thunder.

Well it thine Age became,
O Noble ERPINGHAM,
Which didst the Signall ayme,
To our hid Forces;
When from a Medow by,
70 Like a Storme suddenly,
The *English* Archery
Stuck the *French* Horses,

With *Spanish* Ewgh so strong,
Arrowes a Cloth-yard long,
That like to Serpents stung,
Piercing the Weather;
None from his fellow starts,
But playing Manly parts,
And like true *English* hearts,
80 Stuck close together.

77 starts: runs away.

When downe their Bowes they threw,
And forth their Bilbowes drew,
And on the *French* they flew,
    Not one was tardie;
Armes were from shoulders sent,
Scalpes to the Teeth were rent,
Downe the *French* Pesants went,
    Our Men were hardie.

This while our Noble King,
His broad Sword brandishing, 90
Downe the *French* Hoast did ding,
    As to o'r-whelme it;
And many a deepe Wound lent,
His Armes with Bloud besprent,
And many a cruell Dent
    Bruised his Helmet.

Gloster, that Duke so good,
Next of the Royall Blood,
For famous *England* stood,
    With his brave Brother; 100
Clarence, in Steele so bright,
Though but a Maiden Knight,
Yet in that furious Fight,
    Scarce such another.

Warwick in Bloud did wade,
Oxford the Foe invade,
And cruell slaughter made,
    Still as they ran up;
Suffolke his Axe did ply,
Beaumont and Willoughby 110
Bare them right doughtily,
    Ferrers and Fanhope.

82 Bilbowes: finely tempered swords.
91 ding: throw.

Upon Saint CRISPIN's day
Fought was this Noble Fray,
Which Fame did not delay,
    To *England* to carry;
O, when shall *English* Men
With such Acts fill a Pen,
Or *England* breed againe,
120   Such a King HARRY?

FINIS.

Elegies upon Sundry Occasions.

Of his Ladies not Comming to London.

That ten-yeares-travell'd *Greeke* return'd from Sea
Ne'r joyd so much to see his *Ithaca*,
As I should you, who are alone to me,
More then wide *Greece* could to that wanderer be.
The winter windes still Easterly doe keepe,
And with keene Frosts have chained up the deepe;
The Sunne's to us a niggard of his Rayes,
But revelleth with our *Antipodes*;
And seldome to us when he shewes his head,
Muffled in vapours, he straight hies to bed. 10
In those bleake mountaines can you live where snowe
Maketh the vales up to the hilles to growe;
Whereas mens breathes doe instantly congeale,
And attom'd mists turne instantly to hayle;
Belike you thinke, from this more temperate cost,
My sighes may have the power to thawe the frost,
Which I from hence should swiftly send you thither,
Yet not so swift, as you come slowly hither.
How many a time, hath *Phebe* from her wayne,
With *Phœbus* fires fill'd up her hornes againe; 20
Shee through her Orbe, still on her course doth range,
But you keepe yours still, nor for me will change.
The Sunne that mounted the sterne Lions back,
Shall with the Fishes shortly dive the Brack,
But still you keepe your station, which confines

Title: The lady has not been identified.

1 *Greeke*: Odysseus.

4 be. : be, 1627.

6 Frosts: Drayton evidently was writing during a very cold winter. Stowe, *Annales* (1631), p. 1023, records them in 1614–15 and 1621–22.

10 bed. : bed, 1627.

15 cost: coast.

23-24 The sun that had been in Leo in August is about to enter Pisces on February 11.

24 Brack: the sea.

25 station: the position of sun or planets. His lady "stays fixed."

You, nor regard him travelling the signes.
Those ships which when you went, put out to Sea,
Both to our *Groenland*, and *Virginia*,
Are now return'd, and Custom'd have their fraught,
30 Yet you arrive not, nor returne me ought.
The *Thames* was not so frozen yet this yeare,
As is my bosome, with the chilly feare
Of your not comming, which on me doth light,
As on those Climes, where halfe the world is night.
Of every tedious houre you have made two,
All this long Winter here, by missing you:
Minutes are monthes, and when the houre is past,
A yeare is ended since the Clocke strooke last,
When your remembrance puts me on the Racke,
40 And I should Swound to see an *Almanacke*,
To reade what silent weekes away are slid,
Since the dire Fates you from my sight have hid.
I hate him who the first Devisor was
Of this same foolish thing, the Hower-glasse,
And of the Watch, whose dribbling sands and Wheele,
With their slow stroakes, make mee too much to feele
Your slackenesse hither. O how I doe ban,
Him that these Dialls against walles began,
Whose Snayly motion of the mooving hand,
50 (Although it goe) yet seeme to me to stand;
As though at *Adam* it had first set out,
And had been stealing all this while about,
And when it backe to the first point should come,
It shall be then just at the generall Doome.

27-28 Although these voyages have been uncertainly identified with fleets which sailed to Greenland and America in 1621, Drayton is alluding to a "Discovery of Greenland" as Stowe calls it (p. 1017) by a fleet of the Virginia Company which sailed in the spring of 1614 and returned in September. That fall Captain John Smith returned from his exploration of America as reported at the beginning of his *Description of New England* (1616), an adventure which had begun the previous spring. Together with the evidence above in line 6 and lines 23–24 it is clear that Drayton's lady had left him in London in the spring of 1614 and that in the cold of the following February he wrote his protest over her failure to return. See *Notes and Queries* 220 (1975): 306.

47 hither. : hither, 1627.

The Seas into themselves retract their flowes,
The changing Winde from every quarter blowes,
Declining Winter in the Spring doth call,
The Starrs rise to us, as from us they fall;
Those Birdes we see, that leave us in the Prime,
Againe in Autumne re-salute our Clime. 60
Sure, either Nature you from kinde hath made,
Or you delight else to be Retrograde.
But I perceive by your attractive powers,
Like an Inchantresse you have charm'd the howers
Into short minutes, and have drawne them back,
So that of us at *London*, you doe lack
Almost a yeare. The Spring is scarse begonne
There where you live, and Autumne almost done
With us more Eastward. Surely you devise,
By your strong Magicke, that the Sunne shall rise 70
Where now it setts, and that in some few yeares
You'l alter quite the Motion of the Spheares.
Yes, and you meane, I shall complaine my love
To gravell'd Walkes, or to a stupid Grove,
Now your companions; and that you the while
(As you are cruell) will sit by and smile,
To make me write to these, while Passers by
Sleightly looke in your lovely face, where I
See Beauties heaven, whilst silly blockheads, they
Like laden Asses, plod upon their way, 80
And wonder not, as you should point a Clowne
Up to the *Guards*, or *Ariadnes* Crowne;
Of Constellations, and his dulnesse tell,

59 Prime: spring.

61 from kinde: i.e., unnatural.

67 yeare. The : yeare, the 1627. The meaning may be that she has been gone almost a year.

68 done : done. 1627.

69 Eastward. Surely : Eastward, surely 1627.

77 by : by, 1627.

78 Sleightly: indifferently.

82 *Guards*: the two "pointer stars" of the Big Dipper. *Ariadnes* Crowne: the constellation Corona Borealis.

Hee'd thinke your words were certainly a Spell;
Or him some peice from *Creet*, or *Marcus* show,
In all his life which till that time ne'r saw
Painting: except in Alehouse or old Hall
Done by some Druzzler, of the Prodigall.
Nay doe, stay still, whilst time away shall steale
90 Your youth, and beautie, and your selfe conceale
From me I pray you, you have now inur'd
Me to your absence, and I have endur'd
Your want this long, whilst I have starved bine
For your short Letters, as you helde it sinne
To write to me, that to appease my woe,
I reade ore those, you writ a yeare agoe,
Which are to me, as though they had bin made,
Long time before the first *Olympiad*.
For thankes and curt'sies sell your presence then
100 To tatling Women, and to things like men,
And be more foolish then the *Indians* are
For Bells, for Knives, for Glasses, and such ware,
That sell their Pearle and Gold, but here I stay,
So would I not have you but come away.

85 *Marcus*: Probably Friar Marco de Niça, who according to Hakluyt discovered in 1539 "new islands of California rich in pearles." This Spanish explorer reported the existence of seven cities of extraordinary wealth in the New World. He conquered Cevola, whose people "have Emralds and other jewels. . . . They use vessels of gold and silver." *Principal Navigations* (Glasgow, 1904), 9:142.

88 Druzzler: apparently a slang term for a journeyman sign painter. Prodigall: Falstaff also alludes to this biblical subject for tavern wall paintings in *2 Henry IV* 2. 1. 143.

98 first *Olympiad*: 776 B.C., from which ancient Greeks computed their calendar.

100 things like men: eunuchs.

104 So . . . you: sc. stay there.

To Master George Sandys Treasurer for the English Colony in Virginia.

Friend, if you thinke my Papers may supplie
You, with some strange omitted Noveltie,
Which others Letters yet have left untould,
You take me off, before I can take hould
Of you at all; I put not thus to Sea,
For two monthes Voyage to *Virginia*,
With newes which now, a little something here,
But will be nothing ere it can come there.
I feare, as I doe Stabbing, this word, State;
I dare not speake of the *Palatinate*, 10
Although some men make it their hourely theame,
And talke what's done in *Austria*, and in *Beame*,
I may not so; what *Spinola* intends,
Nor with his *Dutch*, which way Prince *Maurice* bends;
To other men, although these things be free,
Yet (GEORGE) they must be misteries to mee.
I scarce dare praise a vertuous friend that's dead,
Lest for my lines he should be censured;
It was my hap before all other men

Title: Sandys: poet and friend of Drayton. He was elected treasurer of the Virginia Colony on May 2, 1621; on July 27 he sailed for America but news of his safe arrival was not brought back until February 1622. He remained there as treasurer until 1624 and probably for some time later.

4 take me off: distract me.

7 now: now is.

9 Stabbing, : Stabbing; 1627. State; : State, 1627. In 1620 a proclamation was issued forbidding public discussion of affairs of state.

10-14 Frederick IV, Elector of the Protestant German state, the Palatinate, claimed Bohemia and was crowned its king in 1619. He was quickly driven out as the Thirty Years War began. The next year Ambrose Spinola led the forces of the Empire (*Austria*) against him in the Palatinate, forcing him to flee to Holland. *Beame* is Drayton's phonetic spelling of Germanic Böhm(en), Bohemia.

14 *Dutch . . . Maurice*: In 1621 a twelve-year peace between Holland and Spain expired. Maurice, Prince of Orange, quickly resumed the war.

20 To suffer shipwrack by my forward pen
When King JAMES entred; at which joyfull time
I taught his title to this Ile in rime:
And to my part did all the Muses win,
With high-pitch *Pæans* to applaud him in:
When cowardise had tyed up every tongue,
And all stood silent, yet for him I sung;
And when before by danger I was dar'd,
I kick'd her from me, nor a jot I spar'd.
Yet had not my cleere spirit in Fortunes scorne,
30 Me above earth and her afflictions borne,
He next my God on whom I built my trust,
Had left me troden lower then the dust:
But let this passe; in the extreamest ill,
Apollo's brood must be couragious still,
Let Pies, and Dawes, sit dumb before their death,
Onely the Swan sings at the parting breath.
And (worthy GEORGE) by industry and use,
Let's see what lines *Virginia* will produce;
Goe on with OVID, as you have begunne,
40 With the first five Bookes; let your numbers run
Glib as the former, so shall it live long,
And doe much honour to the *English* tongue:
Intice the Muses thither to repaire,
Intreat them gently, trayne them to that ayre,
For they from hence may thither hap to fly,
T'wards the sad time which but to fast doth hie,
For Poesie is followed with such spight,
By groveling drones that never raught her height,
That she must hence, she may no longer staye:
50 The driery fates prefixed have the day,
Of her departure, which is now come on,

20 shipwrack: Upon James' accession Drayton wrote "To the Majestie of King James" in which, unlike other poetic celebrations of the occasion, he did not also memorialize the dead Elizabeth. Failing to win the new king's favor, it was a disaster. pen : pen: 1627.

30 borne, : borne; 1627.

39 OVID: Sandys was translating the *Metamorphoses* and evidently had completed five books before he left. The whole appeared in 1626.

46 to: too.

And they command her straight wayes to be gon;
That bestiall heard so hotly her pursue,
And to her succour, there be very few,
Nay none at all, her wrongs that will redresse,
But she must wander in the wildernesse,
Like to the woman, which that holy JOHN
Beheld in *Pathmos* in his vision.
As th' *English* now, so did the stiff-neckt *Jewes*,
Their noble Prophets utterly refuse, 60
And of those men such poore opinions had,
They counted *Esay* and *Ezechiel* mad;
When *Jeremy* his Lamentations writ,
They thought the Wizard quite out of his wit,
Such sots they were, as worthily to ly,
Lock't in the chaines of their captivity,
Knowledge hath still her Eddy in her Flow,
So it hath beene, and it will still be so.
That famous *Greece* where learning flowrisht most,
Hath of her muses long since left to boast, 70
Th'unletter'd *Turke*, and rude *Barbarian* trades,
Where HOMER sang his lofty *Iliads*;
And this vaste volume of the world hath taught,
Much may to passe in little time be brought.
As if to *Symptoms* we may credit give,
This very time, wherein we two now live,
Shall in the compasse, wound the Muses more,
Then all the old *English* ignorance before;
Base Balatry is so belov'd and sought,
And those brave numbers are put by for naught, 80
Which rarely read, were able to awake
Bodyes from graves, and to the ground to shake
The wandring clouds, and to our men at armes,
'Gainst pikes and muskets were most powerfull charmes.
That, but I know, insuing ages shall
Raise her againe, who now is in her fall;
And out of dust reduce our scattered rimes,

57-58 The episode is described in Rev. 12:4–6.

81 awake : awake, 1627.

85 shall : shall, 1627.

Th'rejected jewels of these slothfull times,
Who with the Muses would mispend an hower,
90 But let blind Gothish Barbarisme devoure
These feverous Dogdays, blest by no record,
But to be everlastingly abhord.
If you vouchsafe rescription, stuffe your quill
With naturall bountyes, and impart your skill,
In the description of the place, that I
May become learned in the soyle thereby;
Of noble *Wyats* health, and let me heare,
The Governour; and how our people there,
Increase and labour, what supplyes are sent,
100 Which I confesse shall give me much content;
But you may save your labour if you please,
To write to me ought of your Savages.
As savage slaves be in great *Britaine* here,
As any one that you can shew me there.
And though for this, Ile say I doe not thirst,
Yet I should like it well to be the first,
Whose numbers hence into *Virginia* flew,
So (noble *Sandis*) for this time adue.

93 rescription: reply.

95 I : I, 1627.

96 become : be come 1627.

97 *Wyat*: Francis Wyat (1575–1644), governor of Virginia and husband of Sandys' niece Margaret.

104 there. : there 1627.

To my noble friend Master William Browne, of the evill time.

Deare friend, be silent and with patience see
What this mad times Catastrophe will be;
The worlds first Wisemen certainely mistooke
Themselves, and spoke things quite beside the booke,
And that which they have said of God, untrue,
Or else expect strange judgement to insue.
This Isle is a meere Bedlam, and therein,
We all lye raving, mad in every sinne,
And him the wisest most men use to call,
Who doth (alone) the maddest thing of all; 10
He whom the master of all wisedome found,
For a marckt foole, and so did him propound,
The time we live in, to that passe is brought,
That only he a Censor now is thought;
And that base villaine, (not an age yet gone,)
Which a good man would not have look'd upon;
Now like a God, with divine worship follow'd,
And all his actions are accounted hollow'd.
This world of ours, thus runneth upon wheeles,
Set on the head, bolt upright with her heeles; 20
Which makes me thinke of what the *Ethnicks* told,
Th'opinion, the *Pythagorists* uphold,

Title: William Browne of Tavistock was a close friend of Drayton and author of various poems imitating Spenser, especially *Britannia's Pastorals* (1613, for which edition Drayton wrote a dedicatory poem, and 1616). In it Browne calls Drayton "our second Ovid." He also published the *Shepherd's Pipe* in 1614 in collaboration with George Wither. This epistle may have been occasioned by these publications.

1 see : see, 1627.

9-10 i.e., Today people call wisest the man who does the maddest actions.

11 He: Cato, Roman symbol of law and stern morality, censor (see l. 14) in 184 B.C. during a period of great moral decadence.

15 villaine: perhaps Robert Carr, a Scot who supported James in dissolving Parliament in 1611 and was made the first Scottish member of the House of Lords for his devotion to the king. See below, line 76. He was at the peak of his power in 1614.

18 hollow'd: hallowed.

21 *Ethnicks*: pagans, i.e., ancient Greeks. told, : told 1627.

Wander from body to body.

That the immortall soule doth transmigrate;
Then I suppose by the strong power of fate,
That those which at confused *Babel* were,
And since that time now many a lingering yeare,
Through fools, and beasts, and lunatiques have past,
Are heere imbodyed in this age at last,
And though so long we from that time be gone,
30 Yet taste we still of that confusion.
For certainely there's scarse one found that now
Knowes what t'approove, or what to disallow,
All arsey varsey, nothing is it's owne,
But to our proverbe, all turnd upside downe;
To doe in time, is to doe out of season,
And that speeds best, thats done the farth'st from reason,
Hee's high'st that's low'st, hee's surest in that's out,
He hits the next way that goes farth'st about,
He getteth up unlike to rise at all,
40 He slips to ground as much unlike to fall;
Which doth inforce me partly to prefer,
The opinion of that mad Philosopher,
Who taught, that those all-framing powers above, *Zeno.*
(As tis suppos'd) made man not out of love
To him at all, but only as a thing,
To make them sport with, which they use to bring
As men doe munkeys, puppets, and such tooles
Of laughter: so men are but the Gods fooles.
Such are by titles lifted to the sky,
50 As wherefore no man knowes, God scarcely why;
The vertuous man depressed like a stone
For that dull Sot to raise himselfe upon;
He who ne're thing yet worthy man durst doe,

31 now : now, 1627.

43 gloss: None of the three philosophers named Zeno seem to have held this cynical view of the human condition. The Epicurean poet-philosopher Lucretius was reported to have been driven mad by a love philter, but his gods are indifferent to mankind, not sadistic.

52-58 Sot . . . Drone: again Carr? A commoner, he had been knighted in December 1607. In 1613 he was involved in the infamous scandal involving Lady Essex and Sir Thomas Overbury. In November 1613 he was created Earl of Somerset; he married the lady the next month.

Never durst looke upon his countreys foe,
Nor durst attempt that action which might get
Him fame with men: or higher might him set
Then the base begger (rightly if compar'd;)
This Drone yet never brave attempt that dar'd,
Yet dares be knighted, and from thence dares grow
To any title Empire can bestow; 60
For this beleeve, that Impudence is now
A Cardinall vertue, and men it allow
Reverence, nay more, men study and invent
New wayes, nay, glory to be impudent.
Into the clouds the Devill lately got,
And by the moisture doubting much the rot,
A medicine tooke to make him purge and cast;
Which in short time began to worke so fast,
That he fell too't, and from his backeside flew,
A rout of rascall, a rude ribauld crew 70
Of base Plebeians, which no sooner light
Upon the earth, but with a suddaine flight,
They spread this Ile, and as *Deucalion* once
Over his shoulder backe, by throwing stones
They became men, even so these beasts became,
Owners of titles from an obscure name.
He that by riot, of a mighty rent,
Hath his late goodly Patrimony spent,
And into base and wilfull beggery run
This man as he some glorious act had done, 80
With some great pension, or rich guift releev'd,
When he that hath by industry atchiev'd
Some noble thing, contemned and disgrac'd,
In the forlorne hope of the times is plac'd,

66 doubting: fearing. rot: a disease thought to be caused by dampness. The following lines suggest details of the cure.

70 rascall, : rascall 1627. The word is now obsolete as a collective noun.

71 light : light, 1627.

77 James' favoritism for certain followers, especially Scots, was notorious. See above, line 15 and note.

81 In February 1611 James had granted £ 34,000 to six favorites, of whom four were Scots.

As though that God had carelessly left all
That being hath on this terrestiall ball,
To fortunes guiding, nor would have to doe
With man, nor ought that doth belong him to,
Or at the least God having given more
90 Power to the Devill, then he did of yore,
Over this world: the feind as he doth hate
The vertuous man; maligning his estate,
All noble things, and would have by his will,
To be damn'd with him, using all his skill,
By his blacke hellish ministers to vexe
All worthy men, and strangely to perplexe
Their constancie, there by them so to fright,
That they should yeeld them wholely to his might.
But of these things I vainely doe but tell,
100 Where hell is heaven, and heav'n is now turn'd hell;
Where that which lately blasphemy hath bin,
Now godlinesse, much lesse accounted sin;
And a long while I greatly mervail'd why
Buffoons and Bawdes should hourely multiply,
Till that of late I construed it, that they
To present thrift had got the perfect way,
When I concluded by their odious crimes,
It was for us no thriving in these times.
As men oft laugh at little Babes, when they
110 Hap to behold some strange thing in their play,
To see them on the suddaine strucken sad,
As in their fancie some strange formes they had,
Which they by pointing with their fingers showe,
Angry at our capacities so slowe,
That by their countenance we no sooner learne
To see the wonder which they so discerne:
So the celestiall powers doe sit and smile
At innocent and vertuous men the while,
They stand amazed at the world ore-gone,
120 So farre beyond imagination,
With slavish basenesse, that they silent sit
Pointing like children in describing it.

121 they : the 1627.

Then noble friend the next way to controule
These worldly crosses, is to arme thy soule
With constant patience: and with thoughts as high
As these belowe, and poore, winged to flye
To that exalted stand, whether yet they
Are got with paine, that sit out of the way
Of this ignoble age, which raiseth none
But such as thinke their black damnation 130
To be a trifle; such, so ill, that when
They are advanc'd, those fewe poore honest men
That yet are living, into search doe runne
To finde what mischiefe they have lately done,
Which so preferres them; say thou he doth rise,
That maketh vertue his chiefe excercise.
And in this base world come what ever shall,
Hees worth lamenting, that for her doth fall.

Upon the three Sonnes of the Lord Sheffield, drowned in Humber.

Light Sonnets hence, and to loose Lovers flie,
And mournfull Maydens sing an Elegie
On those three SHEFFIELDS, over-whelm'd with waves,
Whose losse the teares of all the Muses craves;
A thing so full of pitty as this was,
Me thinkes for nothing should not slightly passe.
Treble this losse was, why should it not borrowe,
Through this Iles treble parts, a treble sorrowe:
But Fate did this, to let the world to knowe,
That sorrowes which from common causes growe, 10
Are not worth mourning for, the losse to beare,
But of one onely sonne, 's not worth one teare.
Some tender hearted man, as I, may spend

127 whether : whethet 1627.

Title: Lord Sheffield (1564–1641) lived in Butterworth, in Lincoln County. In December 1614 three of his six sons, John, Edmund, and Philip, were drowned at Whitgift Ferry on the Humber (Tillotson). No connection with Drayton has been traced, though Tillotson notes that Sheffield was connected with the Virginia Company. The elegy was first printed in 1618.

Some drops (perhaps) for a deceased friend.
Some men (perhaps) their Wifes late death may rue;
Or Wifes their Husbands, but such be but fewe.
Cares that have us'd the hearts of men to tuch
So oft, and deepely, will not now be such;
Who'll care for losse of maintenance, or place,
20 Fame, liberty, or of the Princes grace;
Or sutes in law, by base corruption crost,
When he shall finde, that this which he hath lost,
Alas, is nothing to his, which did lose
Three sonnes at once so excellent as those:
Nay, it is feard that this in time may breed
Hard hearts in men to their owne naturall seed;
That in respect of this great losse of theirs,
Men will scarce mourne the death of their owne heires.
Through all this Ile their losse so publique is,
30 That every man doth take them to be his,
And as a plague which had beginning there,
So catching is, and raigning every where,
That those the farthest off as much doe rue them,
As those the most familiarly that knew them;
Children with this disaster are wext sage,
And like to men that strucken are in age;
Talke what it is, three children at one time
Thus to have drown'd, and in their very prime;
Yea, and doe learne to act the same so well,
40 That then olde folke, they better can it tell.
Invention, oft that Passion us'd to faine,
In sorrowes of themselves but slight, and meane,
To make them seeme great, here it shall not need,
For that this Subject doth so farre exceed
All forc'd Expression, that what Poesie shall
Happily thinke to grace it selfe withall,
Falls so belowe it, that it rather borrowes
Grace from their griefe, then addeth to their sorrowes,
For sad mischance thus in the losse of three,

22 lost, : lost; 1627.

23 lose : lose, 1627.

48 sorrowes,: *-es,* did not print in the Houghton copy.

To shewe it selfe the utmost it could bee: 50
Exacting also by the selfe same lawe,
The utmost teares that sorrowe had to drawe,
All future times hath utterly prevented
Of a more losse, or more to be lamented.
Whilst in faire youth they lively flourish'd here,
To their kinde Parents they were onely deere:
But being dead, now every one doth take
Them for their owne, and doe like sorrowe make:
As for their owne begot, as they pretended
Hope in the issue, which should have discended 60
From them againe; nor here doth end our sorrow,
But those of us, that shall be borne to morrowe
Still shall lament them, and when time shall count,
To what vast number passed yeares shall mount,
They from their death shall duly reckon so,
As from the Deluge, former us'd to doe.
O cruell *Humber* guilty of their gore,
I now beleeve more then I did before
The *Brittish* Story, whence thy name begun
Of Kingly *Humber*, an invading *Hun*, 70
By thee devoured, for't is likely thou
With bloud wert Christned, bloud-thirsty till now.
The *Ouse*, the *Done*, and thou farre clearer *Trent*,
To drowne these SHEFFIELDS as you gave consent,
Shall curse the time, that ere you were infus'd,
Which have your waters basely thus abus'd.
The groveling Boore yee hinder not to goe,
And at his pleasure Ferry to and fro,

52 drawe, : drawe 1627.

56 onely: That is, none was married.

66 Deluge: dating of the human race from Deucalion's or Noah's flood.

68 before : before. 1627.

70 Drayton used this legend again in *Poly-Olbion*, Song 28.

72 now. : now 1627.

73 The Trent and Ouse unite to form the Humber which the Don (*Done*) joins near its mouth. *Done*, and : *Done*. And 1627.

75 "Time" is the subject of "Shall curse."

78 fro, : fro. 1627.

The very best part of whose soule, and bloud,
80 Compared with theirs, is viler then your mud.
But wherefore paper, doe I idely spend,
On those deafe waters to so little end,
And up to starry heaven doe I not looke,
In which, as in an everlasting booke,
Our ends are written. O let times rehearse
Their fatall losse, in their sad Aniverse.

To the noble lady, the Lady I.S. of worldly crosses.

Madame, to shew the smoothnesse of my vaine,
Neither that I would have you entertaine
The time in reading me, which you would spend
In faire discourse with some knowne honest friend,
I write not to you. Nay, and which is more,
My powerfull verses strive not to restore
What time and sicknesse have in you impair'd;
To other ends my Elegie is squar'd.
Your beauty, sweetnesse, and your gracefull parts
10 That have drawne many eyes, wonne many hearts,
Of me get little. I am so much man,
That let them doe their utmost that they can,
I will resist their forces: and they be
Though great to others, yet not so to me.
The first time I beheld you, I then sawe

84 booke, : booke. 1627.

85 written. : written, 1627.

Title: The lady has not been certainly identified. Tillotson suggests Jane, Countess of Shrewsbury, whose husband died in February 1618. R. L. Heffner (*Notes and Queries*, n.s. 5 [1958]: 376–81) argues that she is Isabella Rich, wife of Sir John Smith and sister of Penelope Clifton, the subject of the next elegy. In 1618 Isabella had been the object of much malicious gossip about her marriage.

6 restore : restore, 1627.

7 impair'd; : impair'd 1627.

10 hearts, : hearts. 1627.

11 little. : little, 1627.

That (in it selfe) which had the power to drawe
My stay'd affection, and thought to allowe
You some deale of my heart; but you have now
Got farre into it, and you have the skill
(For ought I see) to winne upon me still. 20
When I doe thinke how bravely you have borne
Your many crosses, as in Fortunes scorne,
And how neglectfull you have seem'd to be,
Of that which hath seem'd terrible to me,
I thought you stupid, nor that you had felt
Those griefes which (often) I have seene to melt
Another woman into sighes and teares,
A thing but seldome in your sexe and yeares;
But when in you I have perceiv'd agen,
(Noted by me, more then by other men) 30
How feeling and how sensible you are
Of your friends sorrowes, and with how much care
You seeke to cure them, then my selfe I blame,
That I your patience should so much misname,
Which to my understanding maketh knowne
"Who feeles anothers griefe, can feele their owne.
When straight me thinkes, I heare your patience say,
Are you the man that studied *Seneca*:
Plinies most learned letters; and must I
Read you a Lecture in Philosophie, 40
T'avoid the afflictions that have us'd to reach you;
I'le learne you more, Sir, then your bookes can teach you.
Of all your sex, yet never did I knowe
Any that yet so actually could showe
Such rules for patience, such an easie way,
That who so sees it shall be forc'd to say,
Loe what before seem'd hard to be discern'd,
Is of this Lady, in an instant learn'd.

24 me, : me. 1627.
26 melt : melt. 1627.
28 yeares; : yeares, 1627.
36 The opening quotation marks indicate a pithy or proverbial saying.
38-39 *Seneca*: *Plinies*: two noted Stoics.
43 knowe : knowe, 1627.

It is heavens will that you should wronged be
50 By the malicious, that the world might see
Your Dove-like meekenesse; for had the base scumme,
The spawne of Fiends, beene in your slander dumbe,
Your vertue then had perish'd, never priz'd,
For that the same you had not exercis'd;
And you had lost the Crowne you have, and glory,
Nor had you beene the subject of my Story.
Whilst they feele Hell, being damned in their hate,
Their thoughts, like Devils them excruciate,
Which by your noble suffrings doe torment
60 Them with new paines, and gives you this content
To see your soule an Innocent, hath suffred,
And up to heaven before your eyes be offred:
Your like we in a burning Glasse may see,
When the Sunnes rayes therein contracted be
Bent on some object, which is purely white,
We finde that colour doth dispierce the light,
And stands untainted: but if it hath got
Some little sully; or the least small spot,
Then it soone fiers it; so you still remaine
70 Free, because in you they can finde no staine.
God doth not love them least, on whom he layes
The great'st afflictions; but that he will praise
Himselfe most in them, and will make them fit,
Near'st to himselfe who is the Lambe to sit:
For by that touch, like perfect gold he tries them,
Who are not his, untill the world denies them.
And your example may worke such effect,
That it may be the beginning of a Sect
Of patient women; and that many a day
80 All Husbands may for you their Founder pray.
Nor is to me your Innocence the lesse,
In that I see you strive not to suppresse

57 hate, : hate 1627.

66 dispierce: disperse. The illustration is, of course, not true.

74 Lambe: the Son of God. In Rev. 3:21, "To him that overcometh will I grant to sit with me on my throne," where the Lamb, the Son of God, dwells.

75 touch: touchstone, used to test gold and silver.

Their barbarous malice; but your noble heart
Prepar'd to act so difficult a part,
With unremoved constancie is still
The same it was, that of your proper ill,
The effect proceeds from your owne selfe the cause,
Like some just Prince, who to establish lawes,
Suffers the breach at his best lov'd to strike,
To learne the vulgar to endure the like. 90
You are a Martir thus, nor can you be
Lesse to the world so valued by me:
If as you have begun, you still persever,
Be ever good, that I may love you ever.

An Elegie upon the death of the Lady Penelope Clifton.

Must I needes write, who's he that can refuse,
He wants a minde, for her that hath no Muse,
The thought of her doth heav'nly rage inspire,
Next powerfull, to those cloven tongues of fire.
Since I knew ought time never did allowe
Me stuffe fit for an Elegie, till now;
When *France* and *England's* HENRIE's dy'd, my quill,
Why, I know not, but it that time lay still.
'Tis more then greatnesse that my spirit must raise,
To observe custome I use not to praise; 10

89 breach: i.e., of the laws.

Title: Lady Penelope was the second daughter of Lord Rich and Penelope Devereux, Sidney's Stella. She married Sir Gervase Clifton in 1608 and was survived by one son at her death on October 26, 1613, aged twenty-three. Drayton's friends John and Francis Beaumont also wrote elegies for her. His was first printed in 1618.

4 tongues of fire: According to Acts 2:3 they appeared at Pentecost upon each of the assembled apostles.

6 That is, this is Drayton's first elegy, though he printed it sixth in 1627.

7 HENRIE's: Henry IV of France, murdered in 1610, and Prince Henry, son of King James, who died in 1612. Although many English poets lamented the latter, Drayton published nothing about it.

Nor the least thought of mine yet ere depended,
On any one from whom she was descended;
That for their favour I this way should wooe,
As some poore wretched things (perhaps) may doe;
I gaine the end, whereat I onely ayme,
If by my freedome I may give her fame.
  Walking then forth being newly up from bed,
O Sir (quoth one) the Lady CLIFTON's dead.
When, but that reason my sterne rage withstood,
20 My hand had sure beene guilty of his blood.
If shee be so, must thy rude tongue confesse it
(Quoth I) and com'st so coldly to expresse it.
Thou shouldst have given a shreeke, to make me feare thee;
That might have slaine what ever had beene neere thee.
Thou shouldst have com'n like Time with thy scalpe bare,
And in thy hands thou shouldst have brought thy haire,
Casting upon me such a dreadfull looke,
As seene a spirit, or th'adst beene thunder strooke,
And gazing on me so a little space,
30 Thou shouldst have shot thine eye balls in my face,
Then falling at my feet, thou shouldst have said,
O she is gone, and Nature with her dead.
  With this ill newes amaz'd by chance I past,
By that neere Grove, whereas both first and last,
I saw her, not three moneths before shee di'd.
When (though full Summer gan to vaile her pride,
And that I sawe men leade home ripened Corne,
Besides advis'd me well,) I durst have sworne
The lingring yeare, the Autumne had adjourn'd,
40 And the fresh Spring had beene againe return'd,
Her delicacie, lovelinesse, and grace,
With such a Summer bravery deckt the place:

11-12 Drayton disclaims any influence upon him from her father, who in any case was not an important patron of writers.

25 com'n: come in. Time is so depicted in emblem books.

34 neere Grove: Tillotson identifies this as an avenue of elms at the Clifton estate and observes that the accuracy of his description implies Drayton's presence there in Nottinghamshire in the late summer or fall of 1613.

38 advis'd : adnis'd 1627. well, : well. 1627.

But now alas, it lookt forlorne and dead;
And where she stood, the fading leaves were shed,
Presenting onely sorrowe to my sight,
O God (thought I) this is her Embleme right.
    And sure I thinke it cannot but be thought,
That I to her by providence was brought.
For that the Fates fore-dooming, shee should die,
Shewed me this wondrous Master peece, that I 50
Should sing her Funerall, that the world should know it,
That heaven did thinke her worthy of a Poet;
My hand is fatall, nor doth fortune doubt,
For what it writes, not fire shall ere race out.
A thousand silken Puppets should have died,
And in their fulsome Coffins putrified,
Ere in my lines, you of their names should heare
To tell the world that such there ever were,
Whose memory shall from the earth decay,
Before those Rags be worne they gave away. 60
Had I her god-like features never seene,
Poore sleight Report had tolde me she had beene
A hansome Lady, comely, very well,
And so might I have died an Infidell,
As many doe which never did her see,
Or cannot credit, what she was, by mee.
    Nature, her selfe, that before Art prefers
To goe beyond all our Cosmographers,
By Charts and Maps exactly that have showne,
All of this earth that ever can be knowne, 70
For that she would beyond them all descrie
What Art could not, by any mortall eye;
A Map of heaven in her rare features drue,
And that she did so lively and so true,
That any soule but seeing it, might sweare
That all was perfect heavenly that was there.
If ever any Painter were so blest,
To drawe that face, which so much heav'n exprest,
If in his best of skill he did her right,
I wish it never may come in my sight, 80

53 fatall: fated.

I greatly doubt my faith (weake man) lest I
Should to that face commit Idolatry.
    Death might have tyth'd her sex, but for this one,
Nay, have ta'n halfe to have let her alone;
Such as their wrinkled temples to supply,
Cyment them up with sluttish *Mercury*,
Such as undrest were able to affright,
A valiant man approching him by night;
Death might have taken such, her end deferd,
90 Untill the time she had beene climaterd,
When she would have bin at threescore yeares and three,
Such as our best at three and twenty be;
With envie then, he might have overthrowne her,
When age nor time had power to sease upon her.
    But when the unpittying Fates her end decreed,
They to the same did instantly proceed,
For well they knew (if she had languish'd so)
As those which hence by naturall causes goe,
So many prayers, and teares for her had spoken,
100 As certainly their Iron lawes had broken,
And had wak'd heav'n, who clearely would have show'd
That change of Kingdomes to her death it ow'd;
And that the world still of her end might thinke,
It would have let some Neighbouring mountaine sinke,
Or the vast Sea it in on us to cast,
As *Severne* did about some five yeares past:
Or some sterne Comet his curld top to reare,
Whose length should measure halfe our Hemisphere.
Holding this height, to say some will not sticke,
110 That now I rave, and am growne lunatique:
You of what sexe so ere you be, you lye,
'Tis thou thy selfe is lunatique, not I.

83 tyth'd: i.e., taken a tenth of all women.

86 *Mercury*: its compounds used as cosmetics.

90 climaterd, : climaterd; 1627. An especially critical period of life was thought to be the sixty-third or climacteric year.

92 be; : be, 1627.

104 sinke, : sinke. 1627.

106 Stowe notes in the *Annales* (1614) a flood of the Severn in January 1607.

I charge you in her name that now is gone,
That may conjure you, if you be not stone,
That you no harsh, nor shallow rimes decline,
Upon that day wherein you shall read mine.
Such as indeed are falsely termed verse,
And will but sit like mothes upon her herse;
Nor that no child, nor chambermaide, nor page,
Disturbe the room, the whilst my sacred rage, 120
In reading is; but whilst you heare it read,
Suppose, before you, that you see her dead,
The walls about you hung with mournfull blacke,
And nothing of her funerall to lacke,
And when this period gives you leave to pause,
Cast up your eyes, and sigh for my applause.

Upon the noble Lady Astons departure for Spaine.

I many a time have greatly marveil'd, why
Men say, their friends depart when as they die,
How well that word, a dying, doth expresse,
I did not know (I truely must confesse,)
Till her departure, for whose missed sight,
I am enforc'd this Elegy to write:
But since resistlesse fate will have it so,
That she from hence must to *Iberia* goe,
And my weake wishes can her not detaine,
I will of heaven in policy complaine, 10
That it so long her travell should adjourne,
Hoping thereby to hasten her returne.
Can those of *Norway* for their wage procure,
By their blacke spells a winde that shall endure

The witches of the Northerly regions sell windes to passengers.

115 decline: recite formally.

120 room : Rome 1627.

Title: Lady Aston was the wife of Drayton's patron, Sir Walter, who was ambassador to Spain from 1620 to 1625. Tillotson cites evidence from the *Tixall Letters* (London, 1815) that she was in Spain before 1621; line 58 then dates her departure in the autumn of 1620.

13 gloss: regions : legions 1627.

Till from aboard the wished land men see,
And fetch the harbour, where they long to be,
Can they by charmes doe this, and cannot I
Who am the Priest of *Phœbus*, and so hie
Sit in his favour, winne the Poets god,
20 To send swift *Hermes* with his snaky rod,
To *Æolus* Cave, commanding him with care,
His prosperous winds, that he for her prepare,
And from that howre, wherein she takes the seas,
Nature bring on the quiet *Halcion* dayes,
And in that hower that bird begin her nest,
Nay at that very instant, that long rest
May seize on *Neptune*, who may still repose,
And let that bird nere till that hower disclose,
Wherein she landeth, and for all that space
30 Be not a wrinkle seene on *Thetis* face,
Onely so much breath with a gentle gale,
As by the easy swelling of her saile,
May at *Sebastians* safely set her downe
Where, with her goodnes she may blesse the towne.

The nearest Harbour of *Spaine*.

If heaven in justice would have plagu'd by thee
Some Pirate, and grimme *Neptune* thou should'st be
His Executioner, or what is his worse,
The gripple Merchant, borne to be the curse
Of this brave Iland; let them for her sake,
40 Who to thy safeguard doth her selfe betake,
Escape undrown'd, unwrackt, nay rather let
Them be at ease in some safe harbour set,
Where with much profit they may vent their wealth
That they have got by villany and stealth,
Rather great *Neptune*, then when thou dost rave,
Thou once shouldst wet her saile but with a wave.

18 hie : hie, 1627.

19 Sit : sit 1627.

24 *Halcion* dayes: The halcyons are birds which supposedly nest in the ocean, keeping it calm during their brooding season.

30 *Thetis*: a sea deity.

34 towne. : towne 1627.

38 gripple: grasping.

Or if some proling Rover shall but dare,
To seize the ship wherein she is to fare,
Let the fell fishes of the Maine appeare,
And tell those Sea-thiefes, that once such they were 50
As they are now, till they assaid to rape
Grape-crowned *Bacchus* in a striplings shape,
That came aboard them, and would faine have saild,
To vine-spread * *Naxus*, but that him they faild,
Which he perceiving, them so monstrous made,
And warne them how, they passengers invade.

An Ile for the abundance of wine supposed to be the habitation of *Bachus*

Ye South and Westerne winds now cease to blow;
Autumne is come, there be no flowers to grow,
Yea from that place respire, to which she goes,
And to her sailes should show your selfe but foes, 60
But *Boreas* and yee Esterne windes arise,
To send her soon to *Spaine*, but be precise,
That in your aide you seeme not still so sterne,
As we a Summer should no more discerne,
For till that here againe, I may her see,
It will be winter all the yeare with me.

Yee swanne-begotten lovely brother stars,
So oft auspicious to poore Mariners,
Yee twin-bred lights of lovely *Leda's* brood,
Joves egge-borne issue smile upon the flood, 70
And in your mild'st aspect doe ye appeare
To be her warrant from all future feare.

Castor and Polox begot by *Jove* on *Leda* in the forme of a Swanne. A constellation ominous to Mariners.

And if thou ship that bear'st her, doe prove good,
May never time by wormes, consume thy wood
Nor rust thy iron, may thy tacklings last,
Till they for reliques be in temples plac't:
Maist thou be ranged with that mighty Arke,
Wherein just *Noah* did all the world imbarque,
With that which after *Troyes* so famous wracke,

47 proling: prowling.

51 rape : rape; 1627. The story comes from Ovid, *Met.* 3. 650–91. Milton alludes to it in *Comus*, lines 46–48.

54 *Naxus*: Naxos, an island in the Ægean Sea.

57 blow; : blow 1627.

61 *Boreas*: the North Wind.

80 From ten yeares travell brought *Ulisses* backe,
That Argo which to *Colchos* went from *Greece*,
And in her botome brought the goulden fleece
Under brave *Jason*; or that same of *Drake*,
Wherein he did his famous voyage make
About the world; or *Candishes* that went
As far as his, about the Continent.
And yee milde winds that now I doe implore,
Not once to raise the least sand on the shore,
Nor once on forfeit of your selves respire:
90 When once the time is come of her retire,
If then it please you, but to doe your due,
What for those windes I did, Ile doe for you;
Ile wooe you then, and if that not suffice,
My pen shall proove you to have dietyes,
Ile sing your loves in veines that shall flow,
And tell the storyes of your weale and woe,
Ile proove what profit to the earth you bring,
And how t'is you that welcome in the spring;
Ile raise up altars to you, as to show,
100 The time shall be kept holy, when you blow.
O blessed winds! your will that it may be,
To send health to her, and her home to me.

To my most dearely-loved friend Henery Reynolds Esquire, of Poets and Poesie.

My dearely loved friend how oft have we,
In winter evenings (meaning to be free,)
To some well chosen place us'd to retire;
And there with moderate meate, and wine, and fire,

85 *Candish*: Thomas Cavendish, who circumnavigated the globe in 1586–88.

90 retire: return, driven by winds from the south.

Title: Reynolds translated Tasso's *Aminta* (1628) and wrote an essay on poetry, *Mythomystes* (1632), preferring classical to modern authors. Some of his verses are set to music in Henry Lawes' *Ayres and Dialogues* of 1653 and 1655.

Have past the howres contentedly with chat,
Now talk'd of this, and then discours'd of that,
Spoke our owne verses 'twixt our selves, if not
Other mens lines, which we by chance had got,
Or some Stage pieces famous long before,
Of which your happy memory had store; 10
And I remember you much pleased were,
Of those who lived long agoe to heare,
As well as of those, of these latter times,
Who have inricht our language with their rimes,
And in succession, how still up they grew,
Which is the subject, that I now pursue;
For from my cradle (you must know that) I
Was still inclin'd to noble Poesie,
And when that once *Pueriles* I had read,
And newly had my *Cato* construed, 20
In my small selfe I greatly marveil'd then,
Amongst all other, what strange kinde of men
These Poets were; And pleased with the name,
To my milde Tutor merrily I came,
(For I was then a proper goodly page,
Much like a Pigmy, scarse ten yeares of age)
Clasping my slender armes about his thigh.
O my deare master! cannot you (quoth I)
Make me a Poet; doe it, if you can,
And you shall see, Ile quickly be a man. 30
Who me thus answered smiling, boy quoth he,
If you'le not play the wag, but I may see
You ply your learning, I will shortly read
Some Poets to you; *Phœbus* be my speed,
Too't hard went I, when shortly he began,

17 I : I, 1627.

19 *Pueriles*: the *Sententiæ Pueriles*, a frequently printed compilation of sentences from Latin writers collected by Leonard Culmann and designed for elementary schools.

22 Amongst : Amonst 1627.

29 Poet; doe it, : Poet, doe it; 1627.

30 man. : man, 1627.

And first read to me honest *Mantuan*,
Then *Virgils Eglogues*; being entred thus,
Me thought I straight had mounted *Pegasus*,
And in his full Careere could make him stop,
40 And bound upon *Parnassus* by-clift top.
I scornd your ballet then though it were done
And had for Finis, *William Elderton*.
But soft, in sporting with this childish jest,
I from my subject have too long digrest,
Then to the matter that we tooke in hand,
Jove and *Apollo* for the *Muses* stand.
That noble *Chaucer*, in those former times,
The first inrich'd our *English* with his rimes,
And was the first of ours, that ever brake,
50 Into the *Muses* treasure, and first spake
In weighty numbers, delving in the Mine
Of perfect knowledge, which he could refine,
And coyne for currant, and asmuch as then
The *English* language could expresse to men,
He made it doe; and by his wondrous skill,
Gave us much light from his abundant quill.
And honest *Gower*, who in respect of him,
Had only sipt at *Aganippas* brimme,
And though in yeares this last was him before,
60 Yet fell he far short of the others store.
When after those, foure ages very neare,
They with the Muses which conversed, were
That Princely *Surrey*, early in the time
Of the Eight *Henry*, who was then the prime
Of *Englands* noble youth; with him there came

36 *Mantuan*: Italian writer of Latin pastorals; a favorite writer of Shakespeare's pedant Holofernes in *Love's Labour's Lost*.

37 *Eglogues*; : *Eglogues*, 1627.

39 i.e., control him.

40 by-clift: with two peaks.

42 *Elderton*: a fluent writer of ballads (d. about 1592); at the end of his broadsides he frequently printed, "Finis Quod Elderton."

58 *Aganippas* brimme: fountain on Mount Helicon sacred to the Muses.

61 ages: generations, of about thirty years each.

Wyat; with reverence whom we still doe name
Amongst our Poets, *Brian* had a share
With the two former, which accompted are
That times best makers, and the authors were
Of those small poems, which the title beare, 70
Of songs and sonnets, wherein oft they hit
On many dainty passages of wit.
Gascoine and *Churchyard* after them againe
In the beginning of *Eliza's* raine,
Accoumpted were great Meterers many a day,
But not inspired with brave fier; had they
Liv'd but a little longer, they had seene
Their workes before them to have buried beene.
Grave morrall *Spencer* after these came on
Then whom I am perswaded there was none 80
Since the blind *Bard* his *Iliads* up did make,
Fitter a taske like that to undertake,
To set downe boldly, bravely to invent,
In all high knowledge, surely excellent.
The noble *Sidney*, with this last arose,
That *Heroe* for numbers, and for Prose.
That throughly pac'd our language as to show,
The plenteous *English* hand in hand might goe
With *Greeke* and *Latine*, and did first reduce
Our tongue from *Lillies* writing then in use; 90
Talking of Stones, Stars, Plants, of fishes, Flyes,
Playing with words, and idle Similies,
As th' *English*, Apes and very Zanies be

67 *Brian*: Sir Francis Bryan (d. 1550), soldier and close friend of Henry VIII. His poetic contributions to the *Songes and Sonettes* (1557) printed by Tottel cannot now be identified.

73 *Gascoine*: George Gascoigne (1525?–77), who printed his *Posies* in 1575; he is also important in the history of English drama, criticism, and satire. *Churchyard*: Thomas Churchyard (1520?–1604), author of narrative and historical poems. In *Colin Clout* Spenser calls him "Old Palæmon."

76 fier; : fier, 1627.

77 seene : seene, 1627.

86 *Heroe* for numbers: i.e., man distinguished for poetry.

90 *Lillies*: William Lily authored the most popular Latin grammar published in England in the sixteenth century.

Of every thing, that they doe heare and see,
So imitating his ridiculous tricks,
They spake and writ, all like meere lunatiques.
    Then *Warner* though his lines were not so trim'd,
Nor yet his Poem so exactly lim'd
And neatly joynted, but the Criticke may
100 Easily reproove him, yet thus let me say,
For my old friend, some passages there be
In him, which I protest have taken me,
With almost wonder, so fine, cleere, and new
As yet they have bin equalled by few.
    Neat *Marlow* bathed in the *Thespian* springs
Had in him those brave translunary things,
That the first Poets had, his raptures were
All ayre, and fire, which made his verses cleere,
For that fine madnes still he did retaine,
110 Which rightly should possesse a Poets braine.
    And surely *Nashe*, though he a Proser were
A branch of Lawrell yet deserves to beare,
Sharply *Satirick* was he, and that way
He went, since that his being, to this day
Few have attempted, and I surely thinke
Those words shall hardly be set downe with inke;
Shall scorch and blast, so as his could, where he,
Would inflict vengeance, and be it said of thee,
Shakespeare thou hadst as smooth a Comicke vaine,
120 Fitting the socke, and in thy naturall braine,
As strong conception, and as Cleere a rage,
As any one that trafiqu'd with the stage.
    Amongst these *Samuel Daniel*, whom if I
May spake of, but to sensure doe denie,
Onely have heard some wisemen him rehearse,

97 *Warner*: His *Albion's England* (1586–1606) is an important source for *Poly-Olbion*.

100 say, : say; 1627.

105 *Neat* is perplexing; perhaps to be emended to *Next*.

107 were : were, 1627.

113 Nashe's most famous (prose) satire is *Pierce Pennilesse* (1592).

120 and : aud 1627.

To be too much *Historian* in verse;
His rimes were smooth, his meeters well did close,
But yet his maner better fitted prose:
Next these, learn'd *Johnson*, in this List I bring,
Who had drunke deepe of the *Pierian* spring, 130
Whose knowledge did him worthily prefer,
And long was Lord here of the Theater,
Who in opinion made our learn'st to sticke,
Whether in Poems rightly dramatique,
Strong *Seneca* or *Plautus*, he or they,
Should beare the Buskin, or the Socke away.
Others againe here lived in my dayes,
That have of us deserved no lesse praise
For their translations, then the daintiest wit
That on *Parnassus* thinks, he highst doth sit, 140
And for a chaire may mongst the Muses call,
As the most curious maker of them all;
As reverent *Chapman*, who hath brought to us,
Musæus, *Homer*, and *Hesiodus*
Out of the Greeke; and by his skill hath reard
Them to that height, and to our tongue endear'd,
That were those Poets at this day alive,
To see their bookes thus with us to survive,
They would think, having neglected them so long,
They had bin written in the *English* tongue. 150
 And *Silvester* who from the *French* more weake,
Made *Bartas* of his sixe dayes labour speake

126 *Historian*: His *Civil Wars*, describing the struggles between the houses of York and Lancaster (1595–1609), is a long historical poem.

127 close, : close 1627.

129 *Johnson*: This is Drayton's first praise of the dramatist–poet. William Drummond (see below, l. 171) reported in his *Conversations* of 1619 that Jonson had told him that he and Drayton were not friends. But Jonson wrote a long adulatory poem prefixed to the collection in which these Epistles first appeared.

130 *Pierian*: reputed home of the Muses in Thessaly.

131 prefer: advance.

143 *Chapman*: recognized here as translator rather than as dramatist or poet.

151 *Silvester*: Joshua Sylvester's translation of Guillaume du Bartas' poetic expansion of Genesis 1 as the *Divine Weekes* (which Drayton suggests that he

In naturall *English*, who, had he there stayd,
He had done well, and never had bewraid,
His owne invention, to have bin so poore
Who still wrote lesse, in striving to write more.
Then dainty *Sands* that hath to *English* done,
Smooth sliding *Ovid*, and hath made him run
With so much sweetnesse and unusuall grace,
160 As though the neatnesse of the *English* pace,
Should tell the Jetting *Lattine* that it came
But slowly after, as though stiffe and lame.
So *Scotland* sent us hither, for our owne
That man, whose name I ever would have knowne,
To stand by mine, that most ingenious knight,
My *Alexander*, to whom in his right,
I want extreamely, yet in speaking thus
I doe but shew the love, that was twixt us,
And not his numbers which were brave and hie,
170 So like his mind was his cleare Poesie,
And my deare *Drummond* to whom much I owe
For his much love, and proud I was to know,
His poesie, for which two worthy men,
I *Menstry* still shall love, and *Hauthorne-den*,
Then the two *Beamounts* and my *Browne* arose,

has read in the original French) was one of the most popular and influential poems of the first quarter of the seventeenth century. Sylvester's original compositions in English, though extensive, were not so widely admired.

157 *Sands*: friend of Drayton to whom the second elegy is addressed. His translation of Ovid's *Metamorphoses* was published in 1626.

161 Jetting: strutting.

166 *Alexander*: Sir William, of Menstry, friend of Drayton who published a collection of sonnets and a long poem, *Doomsday*.

170 mind : mind, 1627.

171 *Drummond*: William Drummond of Hawthornden, friend also of Ben Jonson, who visited him in Scotland; author of minor poems and a history of Scotland.

175 two *Beamounts*: Sir John Beaumont (1583–1627), minor poet and author of *Metamorphosis of Tobacco*, for which Drayton wrote a dedicatory poem. A posthumous publication, *Bosworth Field* (1628), also has a commendatory piece by Drayton. Francis (1584–1616), brother of John and the dramatist who collaborated with John Fletcher. *Browne*: William Browne, another of the group of Spenserian poets, best known for his pastorals and the lyric on the death of the Countess of Pembroke.

My deare companions whom I freely chose
My bosome friends; and in their severall wayes,
Rightly borne Poets, and in these last dayes,
Men of much note, and no lesse nobler parts,
Such as have freely tould to me their hearts, 180
As I have mine to them; but if you shall
Say in your knowledge, that these be not all
Have writ in numbers, be inform'd that I
Only my selfe, to these few men doe tye,
Whose workes oft printed, set on every post,
To publique censure subject have bin most;
For such whose poems, be they nere so rare,
In private chambers, that incloistered are,
And by transcription daintyly must goe,
As though the world unworthy were to know 190
Their rich composures, let those men that keepe
These wonderous reliques in their judgement deepe,
And cry them up so, let such Peeces bee
Spoke of by those that shall come after me,
I passe not for them: nor doe meane to run,
In quest of these, that them applause have wonne
Upon our Stages in these latter dayes,
That are so many; let them have ther bayes
That doe deserve it; let those wits that haunt
Those publique circuits, let them freely chaunt 200
Their fine Composures, and their praise pursue,
And so my deare friend, for this time adue.

189 transcription: Many poems circulated only in manuscript collections. goe, : goe; 1627.

190 know : know, 1627.

196 worme : worme, 1627.

198 many; : many, 1627.

201 pursue, : pursue 1627.

Upon the death of his incomparable friend, Sir Henry Raynsford of Clifford.

Could there be words found to expresse my losse,
There were some hope, that this my heavy crosse
Might be sustained, and that wretched I
Might once finde comfort: but to have him die
Past all degrees that was so deare to me;
As but comparing him with others, hee
Was such a thing, as if some Power should say
I'le take Man on me, to shew men the way
What a friend should be. But words come so short
10 Of him, that when I thus would him report,
I am undone, and having nought to say,
Mad at my selfe, I throwe my penne away,
And beate my breast, that there should be a woe
So high, that words cannot attaine thereto.
T'is strange that I from my abundant breast,
Who others sorrowes have so well exprest:
Yet I by this in little time am growne
So poore, that I want to expresse my owne.
I thinke the Fates perceiving me to beare
20 My worldly crosses without wit or feare:
Nay, with what scorne I ever have derided,
Those plagues that for me they have oft provided,
Drew them to counsaile; nay, conspired rather,
And in this businesse laid their heads together
To finde some one plague, that might me subvert,
And at an instant breake my stubborne heart;
They did indeede, and onely to this end
They tooke from me this more then man, or friend.
Hard-hearted Fates, your worst thus have you done,
30 Then let us see what lastly you have wonne
By this your rigour, in a course so strict,

Title: Sir Henry married Anne Goodere (Drayton's "Idea"). According to Tillotson he was buried on January 30, 1622; Drayton seems to have visited him the previous summer.

7-8 The daring hyperbole suggests the Incarnation of the Son of God.

Why see, I beare all that you can inflict:
And hee from heaven your poore revenge to view,
Laments my losse of him, but laughes at you,
Whilst I against you execrations breath;
Thus are you scorn'd above, and curst beneath.
    Me thinks that man (unhappy though he be)
Is now thrice happy in respect of me,
Who hath no friend; for that in having none
He is not stirr'd as I am, to bemone   40
My miserable losse, who but in vaine,
May ever looke to finde the like againe.
This more then mine owne selfe; that who had seene
His care of me where ever I have beene,
And had not knowne his active spirit before,
Upon some brave thing working evermore:
He would have sworne that to no other end
He had beene borne: but onely for my friend.
    I had beene happy, if nice Nature had
(Since now my lucke falls out to be so bad)   50
Made me unperfect, either of so soft
And yeelding temper, that lamenting oft,
I into teares my mournefull selfe might melt;
Or else so dull, my losse not to have felt.
I have by my too deere experience bought,
That fooles and mad men, whom I ever thought
The most unhappy, are in deede not so:
And therefore I lesse pittie can bestowe
(Since that my sence, my sorrowe so can sound)
On those I see in Bedlam that are bound,   60
And scarce feele scourging; and when as I meete
A foole by Children followed in the Streete,
Thinke I (poore wretch) thou from my griefe art free,
Nor couldst thou feele it, should it light on thee;
But that I am a *Christian*, and am taught
By him who with his precious bloud me bought,

33 view, : view; 1627.
45 knowne : kuowne 1627.
60 Bedlam: London hospital for the insane.
62 Streete, : Streete. 1627.

Meekly like him my crosses to endure,
Else would they please me well, that for their cure,
When as they feele their conscience doth them brand,
70 Upon themselves dare lay a violent hand;
Not suffering Fortune with her murdering knife,
Stand like a Surgeon working on the life,
Desecting this part, that joynt off to cut,
Shewing that Artire, ripping then that gut,
Whilst the dull beastly World with her squint eye,
Is to behold the strange Anatomie.
I am perswaded that those which we read
To be man-haters, were not so indeed,
The Athenian *Timon*, and beside him more
80 Of which the *Latines*, as the *Greekes* have store;
Nor not they did all humane manners hate,
Nor yet maligne mans dignity and state.
But finding our fraile life how every day,
It like a bubble vanisheth away:
For this condition did mankinde detest,
Farre more incertaine then that of the beast.
Sure heaven doth hate this world and deadly too,
Else as it hath done it would never doe,
For if it did not, it would ne're permit
90 A man of so much vertue, knowledge, wit,
Of naturall goodnesse, supernaturall grace,
Whose courses when considerately I trace
Into their ends, and diligently looke,
They serve me for an Œconomike booke,
By which this rough world I not onely stemme,
In goodnesse but growe learn'd by reading them.
O pardon me, it my much sorrow is,
Which makes me use this long Parenthesis;
Had heaven this world not hated as I say,
100 In height of life it had not tane away
A spirit so brave, so active, and so free,
That such a one who would not wish to bee,

79 *Timon*: Athenian misanthrope; subject of a play by Shakespeare.
94 for an : for 1627.
100 not : not, 1627.

Rather then weare a Crowne, by Armes though got,
So fast a friend, so true a Patriot.
In things concerning both the worlds so wise,
Besides so liberall of his faculties,
That where he would his industrie bestowe,
He would have done, e're one could think to doe.
No more talke of the working of the Starres,
For plenty, scarcenesse, or for peace, or Warres. 110
They are impostures, therefore get you hence
With all your Planets, and their influence.
No more doe I care into them to looke,
Then in some idle Chiromantick booke,
Shewing the line of life, and *Venus* mount,
Nor yet no more would I of them account,
Then what that tells me, since that what so ere
Might promise man long life: of care and feare,
By nature freed, a conscience cleere, and quiet,
His health, his constitution, and his diet; 120
Counting a hundred, fourescore at the least,
Propt up by prayers, yet more to be encreast,
All these should faile, and in his fiftieth yeare
He should expire; henceforth let none be deare
To me at all, lest for my haplesse sake,
Before their time heaven from the world them take,
And leave me wretched to lament their ends
As I doe his, who was a thousand friends.

114 Chiromantick: pertaining to palmistry.

117 that . . . that: the life line.

123 Tillotson points out that his funeral monument shows him to have been forty-six when he died.

124 expire; : expire, 1627. deare : deare, 1627.

Upon the death of the Lady Olive Stanhope.

Canst thou depart and be forgotten so?
STANHOPE thou canst not, no deare STANHOPE, no:
But in despight of death the world shall see,
That Muse which so much graced was by thee
Can black Oblivion utterly out-brave,
And set thee up above thy silent Grave.
I mervail'd much the *Derbian* Nimphes were dumbe,
Or of those Muses, what should be become,
That of all those, the mountaines there among,
10 Not one this while thy *Epicedium* sung;
But so it is, when they of thee were reft,
They all those hills, and all those Rivers left,
And sullen growne, their former seates remove,
Both from cleare *Darwin*, and from silver *Dove*,
And for thy losse, they greeved are so sore,
That they have vow'd they will come there no more;
But leave thy losse to me, that I should rue thee,
Unhappy man, and yet I never knew thee:
Me thou didst love unseene, so did I thee,
20 It was our spirits that lov'd then and not wee;
Therefore without profanenesse I may call
The love betwixt us, love spirituall:
But that which thou affectedst was so true,
As that thereby thee perfectly I knew;
And now that spirit, which thou so lov'dst, still mine,
Shall offer this a Sacrifice to thine,
And reare this Trophe, which for thee shall last,
When this most beastly Iron age is past;
I am perswaded, whilst we two have slept,
30 Our soules have met, and to each other wept;

Title: Tillotson identifies Lady Olive as Olivia Beresford, b. 1591, md. John Stanhope 1608. The date of her death is not known. She lived in the area of Derby.

1 so? : so, 1627.

4 thee : thee; 1627.

10 *Epicedium*: funeral ode.

14 *Darwin*: the River Derwent.

That destenie so strongly should forbid,
Our bodies to converse as oft they did:
For certainly refined spirits doe know,
As doe the Angels, and doe here belowe
Take the fruition of that endlesse blisse,
As those above doe, and what each one is,
They see divinely, and as those there doe,
They know each others wills, so soules can too.
  About that dismall time, thy spirit hence flew,
Mine much was troubled, but why, I not knew, 40
In dull and sleepy sounds, it often left me,
As of it selfe it ment to have bereft me,
I ask'd it what the cause was, of such woe,
Or what it might be, that might vexe it so,
But it was deafe, nor my demand would here,
But when that ill newes came, to touch mine eare,
I straight wayes found this watchfull sperit of mine,
Troubled had bin to take its leave of thine,
For when fate found, what nature late had done,
How much from heaven, she for the earth had won 50
By thy deare birth; said, that it could not be
In so yong yeares, what it perceiv'd in thee,
But nature sure, had fram'd thee long before;
And as Rich Misers of their mighty store,
Keepe the most precious longst, so from times past,
She onely had reservd thee till the last;
So did thy wisedome, not thy youth behold,
And tooke thee hence, in thinking thou wast old.
Thy shape and beauty often have to me
Bin highly praysed, which I thought might be 60
Truely reported, for a spirit so brave,
Which heaven to thee so bountifully gave;
Nature could not in recompence againe,
In some rich lodging but to entertaine.

36 is, : is. 1627.
48 its : it 1627.
52 perceiv'd : percein'd 1627.
60 be : be, 1627.

Let not the world report then, that the Peake,
Is but a rude place only vast and bleake,
And nothing hath to boast of but her Lead,
When she can say that happily she bred
Thee, and when she shall of her wonders tell
70 Wherein she doth all other Tracts excell,
Let her account thee greatst, and still to time
Of all the rest, record thee for the prime.

To Master William Jeffreys, Chaplaine to the Lord Ambassadour in Spaine.

My noble friend, you challenge me to write
To you in verse, and often you recite,
My promise to you, and to send you newes;
As 'tis a thing I very seldome use,
And I must write of State, if to *Madrid*,
A thing our Proclamations here forbid,
And that word State such Latitude doth beare,
As it may make me very well to feare
To write, nay speake at all, these let you know
10 Your power on me, yet not that I will showe
The love I beare you, in that lofty height,
So cleere expression, or such words of weight,
As into *Spanish* if they were translated,
Might make the Poets of that Realme amated;
Yet these my least were, but that you extort
These numbers from me, when I should report
In home-spunne prose, in good plaine honest words

65 Peake: a hilly section in northwest Derbyshire, formerly mined. See Drayton's Ode on the area.

Title: The ambassador from 1620 to 1625 was Drayton's friend and patron Sir Walter Aston. See also the Elegy to Lady Aston. Little or nothing is known of Sir Walter's chaplain. Chaplaine : Chapliane 1627.

6 Proclamations: In December 1620 and again in July 1621 James tried to forbid public discussion of state matters by a proclamation; see the Elegy to Sandys, line 9. This poem must be dated no earlier than 1621.

9 these: sc. lines.

14 amated: cast down.

The newes our wofull *England* us affords.
    The Muses here sit sad, and mute the while;
A sort of swine unseasonably defile   20
Those sacred springs, which from the by-clift hill
Dropt their pure *Nectar* into every quill;
In this with State, I hope I doe not deale,
This onely tends the Muses common-weale.
    What canst thou hope, or looke for from his pen,
Who lives with beasts, though in the shapes of men,
And what a poore few are we honest still,
And dare be so, when all the world is ill.
    I finde this age of ours markt with this fate,
That honest men are still precipitate   30
Under base villaines, which till th'earth can vent
This her last brood, and wholly hath them spent,
Shall be so; then in revolution shall
Vertue againe arise by vices fall;
But that shall I not see, neither will I
Maintaine this, as one doth a Prophesie,
That our King *James* to *Rome* shall surely goe,
And from his chaire the *Pope* shall overthrow.
But ô this world is so given up to hell,
That as the old Giants, which did once rebell,   40
Against the Gods, so this now-living race
Dare sin, yet stand, and Jeere heaven in the face.
    But soft my Muse, and make a little stay,
Surely thou art not rightly in thy way.
To my good *Jeffrayes* was not I about
To write, and see, I suddainely am out;
This is pure *Satire*, that thou speak'st, and I

19 while; : while 1627.

21 by-clift hill: Parnassus.

28 dare be : dare to be 1627.

29 ours : oure 1627.

33 so; : so, 1627. shall : shall; 1627.

40 Giants: sons of Heaven and Earth who fought unsuccessfully against Jupiter and the other gods.

44 way. : way, 1627.

46 out; : out, 1627.

Was first in hand to write an Elegie.
To tell my countreys shame I not delight,
50 But doe bemoane't I am no *Democrite*:
O God, though Vertue mightily doe grieve
For all this world, yet will I not beleeve
But that shees faire and lovely, and that she
So to the period of the world shall be;
Else had she beene forsaken (sure) of all,
For that so many sundry mischiefes fall
Upon her dayly, and so many take
Armes up against her, as it well might make
Her to forsake her nature, and behind,
60 To leave no step for future time to find,
As she had never beene, for he that now
Can doe her most disgrace, him they alow
The times chiefe Champion, and he is the man,
The prize, and Palme that absolutely wanne,
For where Kings Clossets her free seat hath bin
She neere the Lodge, not suffered is to Inne,
For ignorance against her stands in state,
Like some great porter at a Pallace gate;
So dull and barbarous lately are we growne,
70 And there are some this slavery that have sowne,
That for mans knowledge it enough doth make,
If he can learne, to read an Almanacke;
By whom that trash of *Amadis de Gaule*,
Is held an author most authenticall,
And things we have, like Noblemen that be
In little time, which I have hope to see
Upon their foot-clothes, as the streets they ride

50 *Democrite*: Democritus, an Epicurean who believed that the gods are indifferent to mankind.

61 he: perhaps the rapidly rising George Villiers, Duke of Buckingham, created earl in 1617 and marquis in 1619.

73 *Amadis de Gaule*: a popular prose romance translated by Anthony Munday in 1589–90 and reprinted in 1618–19.

75-76 i.e., only recently raised to the peerage. See the Elegy to Browne, line 76.

77 foot-clothes: large and ornamental cloths placed upon horses. They hung to the ground on either side.

To have their hornebookes at their girdles ti'd,
But all their superfluity of spight
On vertues handmaid Poesy doth light, 80
And to extirpe her all their plots they lay,
But to her ruine they shall misse the way,
For tis alone the Monuments of wit,
Above the rage of Tyrants that doe sit,
And from their strength, not one himselfe can save,
But they shall tryumph o'r his hated grave.
In my conceipt, friend, thou didst never see
A righter Madman then thou hast of me,
For now as *Elegiack* I bewaile
These poore base times; then suddainely I raile 90
And am *Satirick*, not that I inforce
My selfe to be so, but even as remorse,
Or hate, in the proud fulnesse of their hight
Master my fancy, just so doe I write.
But gentle friend as soone shall I behold
That stone of which so many have us tould,
(Yet never any to this day could make)
The great *Elixar*, or to undertake
The *Rose-crosse* knowledge, which is much like that
A Tarrying-iron for fooles to labour at, 100
As ever after I may hope to see,
(A plague upon this beastly world for me,)
Wit so respected as it was of yore,
And if hereafter any it restore,
It must be those that yet for many a yeare,
Shall be unborne that must inhabit here,
And such in vertue as shall be asham'd
Almost to heare their ignorant Grandsires nam'd,
With whom so many noble spirits then liv'd,
That were by them of all reward depriv'd. 110

78 hornebookes: i.e., primers.

96 stone: the touchstone of the alchemists.

99 *Rose-crosse*: The secret society of the Rosicrucians claimed to have magic and supernatural knowledge.

100 Tarrying-iron: Tarrying irons or tiring irons were an early form of puzzle, the problem being to remove a set of iron rings from two loops on which they were mounted.

My noble friend, I would I might have quit
This age of these, and that I might have writ,
Before all other, how much the brave pen,
Had here bin honoured of the *English* men;
Goodnesse and knowledge, held by them in prise,
How hatefull to them Ignorance and vice,
But it falls out the contrary is true,
And so my *Jeffreyes* for this time adue.

Upon the death of Mistris Elianor Fallowfield.

Accursed Death, what neede was there at all
Of thee, or who to councell did thee call;
The subject whereupon these lines I spend
For thee was most unfit, her timelesse end
Too soone thou wroughtst, too neere her thou didst stand;
Thou shouldst have lent thy leane and meager hand
To those who oft the help thereof beseech,
And can be cured by no other Leech.
In this wide world how many thousands be,
10 That having past fourescore, doe call for thee.
The wretched debtor in the Jayle that lies,
Yet cannot this his Creditor suffice,
Doth woe thee oft with many a sigh and teare,
Yet thou art coy, and him thou wilt not heare.
The Captive slave that tuggeth at the Oares,
And underneath the Bulls tough sinewes rores,
Begs at thy hand, in lieu of all his paines,
That thou wouldst but release him of his chaines;
Yet thou a niggard listenest not thereto,
20 With one short gaspe which thou mightst easily do,
But thou couldst come to her ere there was neede,
And even at once destroy both flowre and seede.
But cruell Death if thou so barbarous be,
To those so goodly, and so young as shee;
That in their teeming thou wilt shew thy spight,

Title: The lady has not been identified.
16 Bulls tough sinewes: i.e., of the lash.
22 That is, she was pregnant.
25 spight, : spight; 1627.

Either from marriage thou wilt Maides affright,
Or in their wedlock, Widowes lives to chuse,
Their Husbands bed, and utterly refuse,
Fearing conception; so shalt thou thereby
Extirpate mankinde by thy cruelty. 30
 If after direfull Tragedy thou thirst,
Extinguish *Himens* Torches at the first;
Build Funerall pyles, and the sad pavement strewe,
With mournfull Cypresse, & the pale-leav'd Yewe.
Away with Roses, Myrtle, and with Bayes;
Ensignes of mirth, and jollity, as these,
Never at Nuptials used be againe,
But from the Church the new Bride entertaine
With weeping *Nenias*, ever and among,
As at departings be sad *Requiems* song. 40
 Lucina by th'olde Poets that wert sayd,
Women in Childe-birth evermore to ayde,
Because thine Altars long have layne neglected:
Nor as they should, thy holy fiers reflected
Upon thy Temples, therefore thou doest flye,
And wilt not helpe them in necessitie.
 Thinking upon thee, I doe often muse,
Whether for thy deare sake I should accuse
Nature or Fortune, Fortune then I blame,
And doe impute it as her greatest shame, 50
To hast thy timelesse end, and soone agen
I vexe at Nature, nay I curse her then,
That at the time of need she was no stronger,
That we by her might have enjoy'd thee longer.
 But whilst of these I with my selfe debate,
I call to minde how flinty-hearted Fate
Seaseth the olde, the young, the faire, the foule,
No thing of earth can Destinie controule:
But yet that Fate which hath of life bereft thee,
Still to eternall memory hath left thee, 60
Which thou enjoy'st by the deserved breath,
That many a great one hath not after death.

39 *Nenias*: funeral dirges.
41 *Lucina*: goddess of childbirth.
43 Altars : Altars, 1627.

Nimphidia, the Court of Fayrie.

Olde CHAUCER doth of *Topas* tell,
Mad RABLAIS of *Pantagruell*,
A latter third of *Dowsabell*,
With such poore trifles playing:
Others the like have laboured at
Some of this thing, and some of that,
And many of they know not what,
But that they must be saying.

Another sort there bee, that will
Be talking of the Fayries still, 10
Nor never can they have their fill,
As they were wedded to them;
No Tales of them their thirst can slake,
So much delight therein they take,
And some strange thing they faine would make,
Knew they the way to doe them.

Then since no Muse hath bin so bold,
Or of the Later, or the ould,
Those Elvish secrets to unfold,
Which lye from others reeding, 20
My active Muse to light shall bring,
The court of that proud Fayry King,
And tell there, of the Revelling,
Jove prosper my proceeding.

And thou NIMPHIDIA gentle *Fay*,
Which meeting me upon the way,
These secrets didst to me bewray,
Which now I am in telling:

3 *Dowsabell*: described by, among others, Drayton himself in his fourth Pastoral.

20 reeding: reading; instruction or comment.

24 *Jove* : *Jone* 1627.

25 NIMPHIDIA: Tillotson traces to a Greek adjective meaning bridal.

My pretty light fantastick mayde,
30 I here invoke thee to my ayde,
That I may speake what thou hast sayd,
  In numbers smoothly swelling.

This Pallace standeth in the Ayre,
By Nigromancie placed there,
That it no Tempests needs to feare,
  Which way so ere it blow it.
And somewhat Southward tow'rd the Noone,
Whence lyes a way up to the Moone,
And thence the *Fayrie* can as soone
40 Passe to the earth below it.

The Walls of Spiders legs are made,
Well mortized and finely layd,
He was the master of his Trade,
  It curiously that builded:
The Windowes of the eyes of Cats,
And for the Roofe, instead of Slats,
Is cover'd with the skinns of Batts,
  With Mooneshine that are guilded.

Hence *Oberon* him sport to make,
50 (Their rest when weary mortalls take)
And none but onely *Fayries* wake,
  Desendeth for his pleasure.
And *Mab* his merry Queene by night
Bestrids young Folks that lye upright,
(In elder Times the *Mare* that hight)
  Which plagues them out of measure.

Hence Shaddowes, seeming Idle shapes,
Of little frisking Elves and Apes,
To Earth doe make their wanton skapes,
60 As hope of pastime hasts them:

37 Noone: i.e., the ecliptic.

53 merry : meerry 1627.

54 upright: stretched out, face up.

55 *Mare*: nightmare, an incubus.

Which maydes think on the Hearth they see,
When Fyers well nere consumed be,
Their daunsing Hayes by two and three,
    Just as their Fancy casts them.

These make our Girles their sluttery rue,
By pinching them both blacke and blew,
And put a penny in their shue,
    The house for cleanely sweeping:
And in their courses make that Round,
In Meadowes, and in Marshes found, 70
Of them so call'd the *Fayrie* ground,
    Of which they have the keeping.

These when a Childe haps to be gott,
Which after prooves an Ideott,
When Folke perceive it thriveth not,
    The fault therein to smother:
Some silly doting brainelesse Calfe,
That understands things by the halfe,
Say that the *Fayrie* left this Aulfe,
    And tooke away the other. 80

But listen and I shall you tell,
A chance in *Fayrie* that befell,
Which certainely may please some well;
    In Love and Armes delighting:
Of *Oberon* that Jealous grewe,
Of one of his owne *Fayrie* crue,
Too well (he fear'd) his Queene that knew,
    His love but ill requiting.

Pigwiggen was this *Fayrie* knight,
One wondrous gratious in the sight 90

63 Hayes: dances with serpentine movements.

70 Marshes: ignis fatuus, supposedly caused by elves.

79 Aulfe: oaf. The idea of fairy exchanges of babies is widespread in folklore.

89 *Pigwiggen*: Pigwidgin, a proper name used before Drayton by Greene and Nashe but according to the NED of obscure meaning and origin.

Of faire Queene *Mab*, which day and night,
    He amorously observed;
Which made king *Oberon* suspect,
His Service tooke too good effect,
His saucinesse, and often checkt,
    And could have wisht him starved.

Pigwiggen gladly would commend,
Some token to queene *Mab* to send,
If Sea, or Land, him ought could lend,
100   Were worthy of her wearing:
At length this Lover doth devise,
A Bracelett made of Emmotts eyes,
A thing he thought that shee would prize,
    No whitt her state impayring.

And to the Queene a Letter writes,
Which he most curiously endites,
Conjuring her by all the rites
    Of love, she would be pleased,
To meete him her true Servant, where
110 They might without suspect or feare,
Themselves to one another cleare,
    And have their poore hearts eased.

At mid-night the appointed hower,
And for the Queene a fitting Bower,
(Quoth he) is that faire Cowslip flower,
    On *Hipcut* hill that groweth,
In all your Trayne there's not a *Fay*,
That ever went to gather May,
But she hath made it in her way,
120   The tallest there that groweth.

96 starved: dead.

102 Emmotts: ant's.

111 cleare: perhaps clare: declare.

116 *Hipcut*: Tillotson suggests two English villages named Hidcote, located near a hill.

119 made . . . way: gone that way.

When by *Tom Thum* a *Fayrie* Page,
He sent it, and doth him engage,
By promise of a mighty wage,
    It secretly to carrie:
Which done, the Queene her Maydes doth call,
And bids them to be ready all,
She would goe see her Summer Hall,
    She could no longer tarrie.

Her Chariot ready straight is made,
Each thing therein is fitting layde, 130
That she by nothing might be stayde,
    For naught must her be letting,
Foure nimble Gnats the Horses were,
Their Harnasses of Gossamere,
Flye Cranion her Chariottere,
    Upon the Coach-box getting.

Her Chariot of a Snayles fine shell,
Which for the colours did excell:
The faire Queene *Mab*, becomming well,
    So lively was the limming: 140
The seate the soft wooll of the Bee;
The cover (gallantly to see)
The wing of a pyde Butterflee,
    I trowe t'was simple trimming.

The wheeles compos'd of Crickets bones,
And daintily made for the nonce,
For feare of ratling on the stones,
    With Thistle-downe they shod it;
For all her Maydens much did feare,
If *Oberon* had chanc'd to heare, 150

132 letting: hindering.

135 Cranion: Tillotson suggests a crane fly — a daddy-long-legs — or perhaps a large spider.

140 limming: coloring.

148 downe : dowue 1627.

That *Mab* his Queene should have bin there,
    He would not have aboad it.

She mounts her Chariot with a trice,
Nor would she stay for no advice,
Untill her Maydes that were so nice,
    To wayte on her were fitted,
But ranne her selfe away alone;
Which when they heard there was not one,
But hasted after to be gone,
160   As she had beene diswitted.

Hop, and *Mop*, and *Drop* so cleare,
Pip, and *Trip*, and *Skip* that were,
To *Mab* their Soveraigne ever deare:
    Her speciall Maydes of Honour;
Fib, and *Tib*, and *Pinck*, and *Pin*,
Tick, and *Quick*, and *Jill*, and *Jin*,
Tit, and *Nit*, and *Wap*, and *Win*,
    The Trayne that wayte upon her.

Upon a Grashopper they got,
170 And what with Amble, and with Trot,
For hedge nor ditch they spared not,
    But after her they hie them.
A Cobweb over them they throw,
To shield the winde if it should blowe,
Themselves they wisely could bestowe,
    Lest any should espie them.

But let us leave Queene *Mab* a while,
Through many a gate, o'r many a stile,
That now had gotten by this wile,
180   Her deare *Pigwiggen* kissing,

152 aboad: put up with.

167 *Wap*, and *Win*: Tillotson suggests slang meanings: to wap for a win: to copulate for a penny.

180 *Pigwiggen* : *Pigwiggin* 1627.

And tell how *Oberon* doth fare,
Who grewe as mad as any Hare,
When he had sought each place with care,
And found his Queene was missing.

By grisly *Pluto* he doth sweare,
He rent his cloths, and tore his haire,
And as he runneth, here and there,
An Acorne cup he greeteth;
Which soone he taketh by the stalke
About his head he lets it walke, 190
Nor doth he any creature balke,
But layes on all he meeteth.

The *Thuskan* Poet doth advance,
The franticke *Paladine* of France,
And those more ancient doe inhaunce,
Alcides in his fury.
And others *Ajax Telamon*,
But to this time there hath bin non,
So Bedlam as our *Oberon*,
Of which I dare assure you. 200

And first encountring with a waspe,
He in his armes the Fly doth claspe
As though his breath he forth would graspe,
Him for *Pigwiggen* taking:
Where is my wife thou Rogue, quoth he,
Pigwiggen, she is come to thee,
Restore her, or thou dy'st by me,
Whereat the poore waspe quaking,

182 The idea of mad hares derives from their behavior during the breeding season.

183 care, : care. 1627.

185 grisly : grislly 1627.

187 runneth : rnnneth 1627.

190 walke: be placed.

193-200 heroes who went mad. The "*Thuskan* Poet" is Ariosto, author of *Orlando Furioso*. Stories of mad Hercules (*Alcides*) and Ajax are dramatized by Sophocles and Seneca.

Cryes, *Oberon*, great *Fayrie* King,
210 Content thee I am no such thing,
I am a Waspe behold my sting,
At which the *Fayrie* started:
When soone away the Waspe doth goe,
Poore wretch was never frighted so,
He thought his wings were much to slow,
O'rjoyd, they so were parted.

He next upon a Glow-worme light,
(You must suppose it now was night)
Which for her hinder part was bright,
220 He tooke to be a Devill.
And furiously doth her assaile,
For carrying fier in her taile,
He thrasht her rough coat with his flayle,
The mad King fea'rd no evill.

O quoth the *Gloworme*, hold thy hand,
Thou puisant King of *Fayrie* land,
Thy mighty stroaks who may withstand,
Hould, or of life despaire I:
Together then her selfe doth roule,
230 And tumbling downe into a hole,
She seem'd as black as any Cole,
Which vext away the *Fayrie*.

From thence he ran into a Hive,
Amongst the Bees hee letteth drive
And downe their Coombes begins to rive,
All likely to have spoyled:
Which with their Waxe his face besmeard,
And with their Honey daub'd his Beard,
It would have made a man afeard,
240 To see how he was moyled.

218 night : night, 1627.
222 taile, : taile 1627.
225 *Gloworme,* : *Gloworme* 1627.
238 Beard, : Beard 1627.
240 moyled: dirtied.

A new Adventure him betides,
He mett an Ant, which he bestrides,
And post thereon away he rides,
    Which with his haste doth stumble;
And came full over on her snowte,
Her heels so threw the durt about,
For she by no meanes could get out,
    But over him doth tumble,

And being in this piteous case,
And all be-slurried head and face, 250
On runs he in this Wild-goose chase,
    As here, and there, he rambles,
Halfe blinde, against a molehill hit,
And for a Mountaine taking it,
For all he was out of his wit,
    Yet to the top he scrambles.

And being gotten to the top,
Yet there himselfe he could not stop,
But downe on th'other side doth chop,
    And to the foot came rumbling: 260
So that the Grubs therein that bred,
Hearing such turmoyle over head,
Thought surely they had all bin dead,
    So fearefull was the Jumbling.

And falling downe into a Lake,
Which him up to the neck doth take,
His fury somewhat it doth slake,
    He calleth for a Ferry;
Where you may some recovery note,
What was his Club he made his Boate, 270
And in his Oaken Cup doth float,
    As safe as in a Wherry.

248 tumble, : tumble 1627.
251 chase, : chase 1627.
252 rambles, : rambles 1627.
260 rumbling: Buxton emends to tumbling.
272 Wherry: boat.

Men talke of the Adventures strange,
Of *Don Quishott*, and of their change,
Through which he Armed oft did range,
    Of *Sancha Panchas* travell:
But should a man tell every thing,
Done by this franticke *Fayrie* King,
And them in lofty Numbers sing
280   It well his wits might gravell.

Scarse set on shore, but therewithall,
He meeteth *Pucke*, which most men call
Hobgoblin, and on him doth fall,
    With words from frenzy spoken;
Hoh, hoh, quoth *Hob*, God save thy grace,
Who drest thee in this pitteous case,
He thus that spoild my soveraignes face,
    I would his necke were broken.

This *Puck* seemes but a dreaming dolt,
290 Still walking like a ragged Colt,
And oft out of a Bush doth bolt,
    Of purpose to deceive us.
And leading us makes us to stray,
Long Winters nights out of the way,
And when we stick in mire and clay,
    Hob doth with laughter leave us.

Deare *Puck* (quoth he) my wife is gone,
As ere thou lov'st King *Oberon*,
Let every thing but this alone,
300   With vengeance, and pursue her;
Bring her to me alive or dead,
Or that vilde thiefe, *Pigwiggens* head,
That villaine hath defil'd my bed,
    He to this folly drew her.

278 King, : King. 1627.
297 gone, : gone 1627.
302 *Pigwiggen* : *Pigwiggin* 1627.
303 bed, : bed 1627.

Quoth *Puck*, My Liege Ile never lin,
But I will thorough thicke and thinne,
Untill at length I bring her in,
    My dearest Lord nere doubt it:
Thorough Brake, thorough Brier,
Thorough Muck, thorough Mier, 310
Thorough Water, thorough Fier,
    And thus goes *Puck* about it.

This thing NIMPHIDIA over hard,
That on this mad King had a guard,
Not doubting of a great reward,
    For first this businesse broching;
And through the ayre away doth goe
Swift as an Arrow from the Bowe,
To let her Soveraigne *Mab* to know,
    What perill was approching. 320

The Queene bound with Loves powerfulst charme
Sate with *Pigwiggen* arme in arme,
Her merry Maydes that thought no harme,
    About the roome were skipping:
A Humble-Bee their Minstrell, playde
Upon his Hoboy; ev'ry Mayde
Fit for this Revells was arayde,
    The Hornepype neatly tripping.

In comes *Nimphidia*, and doth crie,
My Soveraigne for your safety flie, 330
For there is danger but too nie,
    I posted to forewarne you:
The King hath sent *Hobgoblin* out,
To seeke you all the Fields about,
And of your safety you may doubt,
    If he but once discerne you.

305 lin: desist.
313 over hard: i.e., overheard.
314 guard, : guard 1627.
326 Hoboy: oboe.

When like an uprore in a Towne,
Before them every thing went downe,
Some tore a Ruffe, and some a Gowne,
340 Gainst one another justling:
They flewe about like Chaffe i'th winde,
For hast some left their Maskes behinde;
Some could not stay their Gloves to finde,
There never was such bustling.

Forth ranne they by a secret way,
Into a brake that neere them lay;
Yet much they doubted there to stay,
Lest *Hob* should hap to finde them:
He had a sharpe and piercing sight,
350 All one to him the day and night,
And therefore were resolv'd by flight,
To leave this place behinde them.

At length one chanc'd to finde a Nut,
In th'end of which a hole was cut,
Which lay upon a Hazell roote,
There scattred by a Squirill:
Which out the kernell gotten had;
When quoth this *Fay* deare Queene be glad,
Let *Oberon* be ne'r so mad,
360 Ile set you safe from perill.

Come all into this Nut (quoth she)
Come closely in, be rul'd by me,
Each one may here a chuser be,
For roome yee neede not wrastle:
Nor neede yee be together heapt;
So one by one therein they crept,
And lying downe they soundly slept,
As safe as in a Castle.

Nimphidia that this while doth watch,
370 Perceiv'd if *Puck* the Queene should catch,

368 As safe [Buxton] : And safe 1627.

That he would be her over-match,
    Of which she well bethought her;
Found it must be some powerfull Charme,
The Queene against him that must arme,
Or surely he would doe her harme,
    For throughly he had sought her.

And listning if she ought could heare
That her might hinder, or might feare:
But finding still the coast was cleare,
    Nor creature had discride her; 380
Each circumstance and having scand,
She came thereby to understand,
Puck would be with them out of hand,
    When to her Charmes she hide her:

And first her Ferne seede doth bestowe,
The kernell of the Missletowe:
And here and there as *Puck* should goe,
    With terrour to affright him:
She Night-shade strawes to work him ill,
Therewith her Vervayne and her Dill, 390
That hindreth Witches of their will,
    Of purpose to dispight him.

Then sprinkles she the juice of Rue,
That groweth underneath the Yeu:
With nine drops of the midnight dewe,
    From Lunarie distilling:

383 out of hand: at once.

385 Ferne seede: supposedly invisible, with the power of conferring invisibility.

386 kernell of the Missletowe: used to make birdlime, a sticky substance.

387 should: Buxton emends to doth.

389 Night-shade: Red nightshade supposedly made one temporarily mad.

390 Vervayne: verbena, held sacred by the Romans and used in religious ceremonies and in medicine. The applications of these various drugs represent, of course, the folk medicine of the time.

396 As this entire passage reflects some of the traditions of the witch scenes in *Macbeth*, the "Lunarie distilling" suggests Hecate's "Upon the corner of the moon/There hangs a vaporous drop profound" (3. 5. 23–24).

The Molewarps braine mixt therewithall,
And with the same the Pismyres gall,
For she in nothing short would fall;
400 The *Fayrie* was so willing.

Then thrice under a Bryer doth creepe,
Which at both ends was rooted deepe,
And over it three times shee leepe;
Her Magicke much avayling:
Then on *Proserpyna* doth call,
And so upon her Spell doth fall,
Which here to you repeate I shall,
Not in one tittle fayling.

By the croking of the Frogge;
410 By the howling of the Dogge;
By the crying of the Hogge,
Against the storme arising;
By the Evening Curphewe bell,
By the dolefull dying knell,
O let this my direfull Spell,
Hob, hinder thy surprising.

By the Mandrakes dreadfull groanes;
By the Lubricans sad moanes;
By the noyse of dead mens bones,
420 In Charnell houses ratling:
By the hissing of the Snake,
The rustling of the fire-Drake,
I charge thee thou this place forsake,
Nor of Queene *Mab* be pratling.

397 Molewarps: mole's.

398 Pismyres: ant's.

405 *Proserpyna*: As Tillotson observes, she was sometimes equated with the Fairy Queen in medieval poetry.

417 Mandrakes: a narcotic plant which supposedly shrieked when pulled from the ground.

418 Lubricans: leprechaun's.

422 fire-Drake: fiery dragon.

By the Whirlewindes hollow sound,
By the Thunders dreadfull stound,
Yells of Spirits under ground,
    I chardge thee not to feare us:
By the Shreech-owles dismall note,
By the Blacke Night-Ravens throate, 430
I charge thee *Hob* to teare thy Coate
    With thornes if thou come neere us.

Her Spell thus spoke she stept aside,
And in a Chincke her selfe doth hide,
To see there of what would betyde,
    For shee doth onely minde him:
When presently shee *Puck* espies,
And well she markt his gloating eyes,
How under every leafe he pries,
    In seeking still to finde them. 440

But once the Circle got within,
The Charmes to worke doe straight begin,
And he was caught as in a Gin;
    For as he thus was busie,
A paine he in his Head-peece feeles,
Against a stubbed Tree he reeles,
And up went poore *Hobgoblins* heeles,
    Alas his braine was dizzie.

At length upon his feet he gets,
Hobgoblin fumes, *Hobgoblin* frets, 450
And as againe he forward sets,
    And through the Bushes scrambles,
A Stump doth trip him in his pace,
Downe comes poore *Hob* upon his face,
And lamentably tore his case,
    Amongst the Bryers and Brambles.

432 us. : us, 1627.
438 gloating: glancing.
452 scrambles, : scrambles.; 1627.
455 case: clothes.

A plague upon Queene *Mab*, quoth hee,
And all her Maydes where ere they be,
I thinke the Devill guided me,
460 To seeke her so provoked:
Where stumbling at a piece of Wood,
He fell into a dich of mudd,
Where to the very Chin he stood,
In danger to be choked.

Now worse then e're he was before:
Poore *Puck* doth yell, poore *Puck* doth rore;
That wak'd Queene *Mab* who doubted sore
Some Treason had beene wrought her:
Untill *Nimphidia* told the Queene
470 What she had done, what she had seene,
Who then had well-neere crack'd her spleene
With very extreame laughter.

But leave we *Hob* to clamber out,
Queene *Mab* and all her *Fayrie* rout,
And come againe to have a bout
With *Oberon* yet madding:
And with *Pigwiggen* now distrought,
Who much was troubled in his thought,
That he so long the Queene had sought,
480 And through the Fields was gadding.

And as he runnes he still doth crie,
King *Oberon* I thee defie,
And dare thee here in Armes to trie,
For my deare Ladies honour:
For that she is a Queene right good,
In whose defence Ile shed my blood,
And that thou in this jealous mood
Hast lay'd this slander on her.

473 out, : out: 1627.
475 a bout : about 1627.

And quickly Armes him for the Field,
A little Cockle-shell his Shield, 490
Which he could very bravely wield:
    Yet could it not be pierced:
His Speare a Bent both stiffe and strong,
And well-neere of two Inches long;
The Pyle was of a Horse-flyes tongue,
    Whose sharpnesse naught reversed.

And puts him on a coate of Male,
Which was of a Fishes scale,
That when his Foe should him assaile,
    No poynt should be prevayling: 500
His Rapier was a Hornets sting,
It was a very dangerous thing:
For if he chanc'd to hurt the King,
    It would be long in healing.

His Helmet was a Bettles head,
Most horrible and full of dread,
That able was to strike one dead,
    Yet did it well become him:
And for a plume, a horses hayre,
Which being tossed with the ayre, 510
Had force to strike his Foe with feare,
    And turne his weapon from him.

Himselfe he on an Earewig set,
Yet scarce he on his back could get,
So oft and high he did corvet,
    Ere he himselfe could settle:
He made him turne, and stop, and bound,
To gallop, and to trot the Round,
He scarce could stand on any ground,
    He was so full of mettle. 520

493 Bent: blade of grass.
495 Pyle: pointed metal head.

When soone he met with *Tomalin*,
One that a valiant Knight had bin,
And to King *Oberon* of Kin;
  Quoth he thou manly *Fayrie*:
Tell *Oberon* I come prepar'd,
Then bid him stand upon his Guard;
This hand his basenesse shall reward,
  Let him be ne'r so wary.

Say to him thus, that I defie,
530 His slanders, and his infamie,
And as a mortall enemie,
  Doe publickly proclaime him:
Withall, that if I had mine owne,
He should not weare the *Fayrie* Crowne,
But with a vengeance should come downe:
  Nor we a King should name him.

This *Tomalin* could not abide,
To heare his Soveraigne vilefide:
But to the *Fayrie* Court him hide;
540   Full furiously he posted,
With ev'ry thing *Pigwiggen* sayd:
How title to the Crowne he layd,
And in what Armes he was aray'd,
  And how himselfe he boasted.

Twixt head and foot, from point to point,
He told th'arming of each joynt,
In every piece, how neate, and quaint,
  For *Tomalin* could doe it:
How fayre he sat, how sure he rid,
550 As of the courser he bestrid,
How Mannag'd, and how well he did;
  The King which listened to it,

521 *Tomalin*: Tom of Lincoln, in balladry a knight stolen by fairies.

536 him. : him, 1627.

539 hide: hied.

544 And : As 1627.

552 it, : it. 1627.

Quoth he, goe *Tomalin* with speede,
Provide me Armes, provide my Steed,
And every thing that I shall neede,
    By thee I will be guided;
To strait account, call thou thy witt,
See there be wanting not a whitt,
In every thing see thou mee fitt,
    Just as my foes provided. 560

Soone flew this newes through *Fayrie* land,
Which gave Queene *Mab* to understand,
The combate that was then in hand,
    Betwixt those men so mighty:
Which greatly she began to rew,
Perceiving that all Fayrie knew,
The first occasion from her grew,
    Of these affaires so weighty.

Wherefore attended with her maides,
Through fogs, and mists, and dampes she wades, 570
To *Proserpine* the Queene of shades
    To treat, that it would please her,
The cause into her hands to take,
For ancient love and friendships sake,
And soone thereof an end to make,
    Which of much care would ease her.

A while, there let we *Mab* alone,
And come we to King *Oberon*,
Who arm'd to meete his foe is gone,
    For proud *Pigwiggen* crying: 580
Who sought the *Fayrie* King as fast,
And had so well his journeys cast,
That he arrived at the last,
    His puisant foe espying:

Stout *Tomalin*, came with the King,
Tom Thum doth on *Pigwiggen* bring,
That perfect were in every thing,
    To single fights belonging:

And therefore they themselves ingage,
590 To see them excercise their rage,
With faire and comly equipage,
Not one the other wronging.

So like in armes, these champions were,
As they had bin, a very paire,
So that a man would almost sweare,
That either, had bin either;
Their furious steedes began to naye
That they were heard a mighty way,
Their staves upon their rests they lay,
600 Yet e'r they flew together

Their Seconds minister an oath,
Which was indifferent to them both,
That on their Knightly faith, and troth,
No magicke them supplyed;
And sought them that they had no charmes,
Wherewith to worke each others harmes,
But came with simple open armes,
To have their causes tryed.

Together furiously they ran,
610 That to the ground came horse and man,
The blood out of their Helmets span,
So sharpe were their incounters;
And though they to the earth were throwne,
Yet quickly they regain'd their owne,
Such nimblenesse was never showne,
They were two Gallant Mounters.

When in a second Course againe,
They forward came with might and mayne,
Yet which had better of the twaine,
620 The Seconds could not judge yet;

600 together : together; 1627.
606 worke : worke, 1627.
609 furiously : furionsly 1627.

Their shields were into pieces cleft,
Their helmets from their heads were reft,
And to defend them nothing left,
    These Champions would not budge yet.

Away from them their Staves they threw,
Their cruell Swords they quickly drew,
And freshly they the fight renew;
    They every stroke redoubled:
Which made *Proserpina* take heed,
And make to them the greater speed, 630
For feare lest they too much should bleed,
    Which wondrously her troubled.

When to th'infernall *Stix* she goes,
She takes the Fogs from thence that rose,
And in a Bagge doth them enclose;
    When well she had them blended:
She hyes her then to *Lethe* spring,
A Bottell and thereof doth bring,
Wherewith she meant to worke the thing,
    Which onely she intended. 640

Now *Proserpine* with *Mab* is gone
Unto the place where *Oberon*
And proud *Pigwiggen*, one to one,
    Both to be slaine were likely:
And there themselves they closely hide,
Because they would not be espide;
For *Proserpine* meant to decide
    The matter very quickly.

And suddainly untyes the Poke,
Which out of it sent such a smoke, 650
As ready was them all to choke,
    So greevous was the pother;
So that the Knights each other lost,
And stood as still as any post,

649 Poke: bag.

Tom Thum, nor *Tomalin* could boast
    Themselves of any other.

But when the mist gan somewhat cease,
Proserpina commandeth peace:
And that a while they should release
660   Each other of their perill:
Which here (quoth she) I doe proclaime
To all in dreadfull *Plutos* name,
That as yee will eschewe his blame,
    You let me heare the quarrell,

But here your selves you must engage,
Somewhat to coole your spleenish rage:
Your greevous thirst and to asswage,
    That first you drinke this liquor:
Which shall your understanding cleare,
670 As plainely shall to you appeare,
Those things from me that you shall heare,
    Conceiving much the quicker.

This *Lethe* water you must knowe,
The memory destroyeth so,
That of our weale, or of our woe,
    It all remembrance blotted;
Of it nor can you ever thinke:
For they no sooner tooke this drinke;
But nought into their braines could sinke,
680   Of what had them besotted.

King *Oberon* forgotten had,
That he for jealousie ranne mad:
But of his Queene was wondrous glad,
    And ask'd how they came thither:
Pigwiggen likewise doth forget,
That he Queene *Mab* had ever met;
Or that they were so hard beset,
    When they were found together.

659 release : release, 1627.
670 appeare, : appeare; 1627.

Nor neither of them both had thought,
That e'r they had each other sought; 690
Much lesse that they a Combat fought,
  But such a dreame were lothing:
Tom Thum had got a little sup,
And *Tomalin* scarce kist the Cup,
Yet had their braines so sure lockt up,
  That they remembred nothing.

Queene *Mab* and her light Maydes the while,
Amongst themselves doe closely smile,
To see the King caught with this wile,
  With one another jesting: 700
And to the *Fayrie* Court they went,
With mickle joy and merriment,
Which thing was done with good intent,
  And thus I left them feasting.

FINIS.

698 closely: secretly.

VOLVETVR
TERNVM

Phineas Fletcher

Although Giles Fletcher published first, Phineas was the older of the brothers. He was born at Cranbrook, in Kent, in 1582. After attending Eton he matriculated at King's College, Cambridge, where he was awarded the M.A. in 1608 and was ordained. In 1611 he became a Fellow and happily settled into the life of a Cambridge don, writing poetry and a play, *Sicelides* (1614). Something happened, however, in 1615 which made him resign his position — with resentment at some "froward spites," according to his *Piscatory Eclogues* (1633). Thereafter he became a minister, serving a small parsonage in Norfolk until his death in 1650.

Before 1610 Fletcher had begun his longest poem, *The Purple Island* (not published until 1633; for its early composition see *Christs Victorie, and Triumph*, 4. 49n.), a topographical allegory of the human body which amplifies the model by Spenser in the Castle of Alma episode of book 2 of the *Faerie Queene*. It is the most elaborate literary expansion of the equation of the little world of man with the big world of nature. For an appreciation see R. G. Baldwin, *Philological Quarterly*, 40 (1961): 462–75. In 1627 Fletcher published a rather sensual *Brittains Ida*, ascribed to Spenser on its title page, which details the affair between Venus and Anchises, Æneas' father. Finally, in 1670 appeared his posthumous *A Father's Testament*; it includes some metrical translations from Boethius and a few original devotional poems. The standard discussion of his life and work is by A. B. Langdale, *Phineas Fletcher* (New York: Columbia University Press, 1937).

The period during which Fletcher wrote *The Apollyonists*, which he published in 1627, is remarkably hard to determine. Its final three stanzas certainly were written after the death of James in 1625. Stanzas referring to events in 1622 (4. 29) and 1623 (4. 2) must postdate those times. The Latin translation of Paolo Sarpi's Venetian history, which is glossed in 4. 14 (see also note to 4. 3) was not published (at Cambridge) until 1626; it had appeared in Italian (two editions) in 1624 and in French in 1625. Philippe de Mornay's *Mysterie of Iniquity* (1612), on which much of canto 3 is based, had first been printed (in French and Latin editions) in 1611. On the other hand, the narrative of Russian history in 3. 5ff., leading to the assassination of Boris Godunov in 1605, seems contemporary rather than retrospective, as does that of the history of the Venetian Republic from 1605 to 1607 (4. 3ff.); and the warm appreciation of Cambridge (5. 14) surely was written before 1615. Internal evidence, that is, suggests that Fletcher worked over his poem at different intervals during the course of almost two decades, with the bulk of it completed before 1615 and with final revision in the mid-1620s. Manuscript evidence for its companion Latin poem on the same subject, *Locustæ*, supports this long gestation period as Boas has demonstrated (*Poems*, 1: xiv–xv), but it is difficult to determine whether Fletcher conceived the work simultaneously in both languages or translated into English and at the same time greatly enlarged an earlier Latin composition. Recognition of this gap between conception and publication explains the curious feeling of anachronism which one may experience in reading the poem, as all of its historic events from the Armada to Charles I's accession seem to occur in a simultaneous present. Perhaps because he was not in London Fletcher shows none of the disillusion with James which affected so many writers, like Drayton, in the 1620s; that king remains his hero, as he was for the undergraduate Milton in his "Gunpowder Plot" epigrams and *In Quintum Novembris*.

After one has made allowance for its blatant Protestant and patriotic fervor, *The Apollyonists* is a remarkably interesting poem. In it Fletcher proves his ability to maintain coherence in a big pattern which is embellished with noteworthy details like the similes which close the first two cantos or the praise of Cambridge at 5. 14. It is hard to forget his description of Time (5. 8):

> Slow Time, which every houre grow'st old and young,
> Which every minute dy'st, and liv'st againe;
> Which mak'st the strong man weak, the weak man strong:
> Sad time which fly'st in joy, but creep'st in paine,
> Thy steppes uneven are still too short or long:
> Devouring Time, who bear'st a fruitfull traine,
> And eat'st what er'e thou bear'st.

The work is written in an original nine-line stanza combining the Spenserian with the popular ottava rima, rhyming *a b a b a b c c c*, the last line being an alexandrine. Fletcher's deliberate rhetorical interruption of his lines (the first stanza of the poem is a good example) is unpleasing to a modern ear, as is his occasional straining at parallelism (e.g., "Straight hate, pride, strife, warres, and seditions breed,/Get up, grow ripe." 3. 4). Except for the third, each canto has forty stanzas, suggesting the biblical period of preparation: the forty years spent by the Israelites in the wilderness or the forty days spent there by Jesus before he began his ministry. It is not clear whether the middle canto lacks one stanza by design or by accident; if the former, the reason is difficult to discover.

Like Spenser are the occasional archaisms, the moral earnestness, the lineal narrative, and to some degree the allegory. The allegory of *The Apollyonists* resembles more that of the Cantos of Mutability of the *Faerie Queene* than the symbolic knights and events which occupy for the most part the antecedent six books (and it must be remembered that these two cantos were first published in 1609, shortly before Fletcher may first have begun work on *The Apollyonists*). J. S. Dees has observed, however, that Fletcher's narrator functions differently from Spenser's ("The Narrator's Voice in *The Faerie Queene*, *Christs Victorie, and Triumph*, and *The Locusts, or Apollyonists*," Ph.D. dissertation, University of Illinois, 1968). Noteworthy are Fletcher's depictions of Satan and Sin (daughter of the Serpent and Eve), who seem analogous to the corresponding characters in *Paradise Lost* (see J. M. Patrick, *Notes and Queries*, n.s. 3 [1956]: 384–86). Equivocus, on the other hand, is quite different, representing as he does the Jesuits in general, Bellarmine more precisely, and Henry Garnet in particular (see note to 2. 5). Milton's "great Consult" in Hell is foreshadowed in Fletcher's "deepe Conclave" (1. 17), a statement of positions which runs through the second canto with the founding of the Inquisition and of the Jesuit order. The Satans of the two poems have much in common, and, of course, they derive from a common Protestant tradition. Early studies that point out these and other similarities are by H. E. Cory, *California Publications in Modern Philology*, 2 (1912): 362–67, and by E. G. Baldwin, *Journal of English and German Philology*, 33 (1934): 544–46.

The third canto begins a unique literary treatment of continental history as an educated Englishman viewed it in the early seventeenth century. Dominated, of course, by the patriotic fervor elicited by the discovery of the Gunpowder Plot in November 1605, toward which the whole story is moving, the poem pauses to review disturbances in Russia, for which the Jesuits are blamed. Fletcher must have learned this material at first hand, for his father had been an emissary there and had witnessed the beginning of the rise to power of Boris

Godunov. Upon his return he published a book detailing his experiences (see note to 3. 5). After an application of apocalyptic material from Daniel, the poem turns to a Protestant diatribe against the papacy, taken directly from the Huguenot propaganda of Philippe de Mornay (see note to 3. 33). Canto 4 picks up continental developments which followed the assassination of Henry IV in 1610 and then considers the attempts of the Venetians from 1605 to 1607 to free themselves from papal domination.

After the speeches and historical digressions which deliberately slow the movement of the plot, the poem achieves a well-realized climax with the uncovering of the nefarious Guy Fawkes, a happy outcome achieved only through the direct intervention of God. The frightened conspirators hiding amid their casks of gunpowder beneath the Houses of Parliament are well imagined (5. 4–7). At the final revelation of the plot Fletcher introduces an unexpected but artistically satisfying ode in praise of God (5. 21–28), who is depicted as the source of order and stability throughout the universe which he has created and who has maintained that order despite all efforts to overthrow it. Milton seems to imitate the spirit and some of the detail of *The Apollyonists* in his undergraduate Latin poem on the same subject, *In Quintum Novembris*, which may have been penned shortly after Fletcher's poem appeared in Cambridge in 1627, although he dates its composition the previous year. As W. R. Parker notes in *Milton: A Biography* (Oxford: Oxford University Press, 1968), 2: 732–33, if such influence is real, either Milton saw the manuscript, an unlikely possibility, or the poem "belongs one year later than Milton dated it."

The shorter poems which follow *The Apollyonists* here show a different side of Fletcher. The first, written while he was still in residence in Cambridge, is a fine poem for cold weather, gracefully developed in mythological terms. The second, addressed to Tomalin, is unique in that it elaborates within a pastoral framework a purely metaphysical treatment of "nothing" as entity and as non-entity. Here too his hostility against Cambridge after his departure in 1615 surfaces: "spitefull *Chame* of all ha's quite bereft me."

Again unique for his day is the witty response directed to "M.S." Her name means "bitter sweetnesse," as the second line explains. Whoever she was (Langdale, p. 43, thinks it was a friend, Lady Colepeper), she had blamed him for criticizing levity in women in a poem entitled "On womens lightnesse." His response, again in metaphysical fashion, is that he cannot praise women, for then he would be a liar and poets are liars. He told the truth and thus is no poet. Women, indeed, are like apples (and a "bitter-sweet" was a kind of apple), rotten to the core! Fletcher has an out, of course, though he does not express it: because he is writing a poem this too may be a lie. It is a remarkably witty piece.

Last are two untitled religious poems which rank with the best of this genre in a period noted for the excellence of this kind of writing. "Vast Ocean of light," in a complex and interesting ten-line stanza, is a remarkable attempt to describe the indescribable, an infinite God. Like Herbert, Fletcher has sought God everywhere, only to learn at last that he is hidden in such blinding brightness that he can be experienced only "on his cross: there, then, thus Love stands nail'd with love." The second details the beauties which vision may discover in nature; put into proper perspective (and Fletcher puns on the word), such beauties lead toward perception of God, where the sight again is blinded: "when thy sight that radiant beauty blears,/And dazels thy weak eyes; see with thine ears" — a powerful paradox.

The edition by Frederick S. Boas in *Giles and Phineas Fletcher: Poetical Works* (Cambridge: At the University Press, 1908), 2 vols., is excellent but has only textual notes. The texts printed here represent the only early edition of *The Apollyonists* (1627). The short poems with titles come from *Poeticall Miscellanies*, appended to *The Purple Island* (1633), and the final two are from *A Fathers Testament* (1670).

The Locusts, or Apollyonists.

To the right noble Lady Townshend.

Excellent Lady, as the Roote from which you sprang, those ever by me honoured, and truly honourable Parents; so the Stocke into which you are newly grafted (my most noble friend) challenge at my hand more honour, then I can, not more then I would give you. It may perhaps seeme strange, that I have consecrated these uncombed verses to your hands, yet unknowne; unknowne I confesse, if knowledge were by sight onely. But how should he not know the Branch, who knowes the Tree? How should I but see your ingenuous nature in their noble Genius? Who can be ignorant of the Science, who knowes as well the Roote that bare, and nourisht it, as the Stocke into which 10 *it is grafted? Marvell not then, that in the dedication of this little Pamphlet, I durst not separate you, who are so neere by Gods owne hand united. And not for mine (who cannot aspire to deserve any respect from you) but his sake, who is (my heart) your head, accept this poore service. So may you still enjoy on earth the joyes and fruites of a chaste, and loving bed; and at length the most glorious embraces of that most excellent Spouse in heaven.*

Your unknowne servant in all Christian love,
P. F.

The Locusts, or Apollyonists.

CANTO I.

1

Of Men, nay Beasts: worse, Monsters: worst of all,
Incarnate Fiends, English Italianat,
Of Priests, O no, Masse-Priests, Priests-Cannibal,
Who make their Maker, chewe, grinde, feede, grow fat

Dedication: Lady Townshend was Mary, daughter of Horatio de Vere, baron Vere of Tilbury, and wife of Sir Roger Townshend (1588–1637), to whom the accompanying Latin version of this poem, *Locustæ*, was dedicated. He had been patron of Phineas' brother Giles.

1.3-4 Priests-Cannibal,/Who make their Maker: referring to the Roman Catholic doctrine of transubstantiation.

With flesh divine: of that great Cities fall,
Which borne, nurs't, growne with blood, th' Earth's Empresse sat,
Clens'd, spous'd to Christ, yet backe to whoordome fel,
None can enough, something I faine would tell.
How black are quenched lights! Faln'e Heaven's a double hell.

2

Great Lord, who grasp'st all creatures in thy hand,
Who in thy lap lay'st downe proud Thetis head,
And bind'st her white curl'd locks in caules of sand,
Who gather'st in thy fist, and lay'st in bed
The sturdy winds; who ground'st the floting land
On fleeting seas, and over all hast spread
Heaven's brooding wings, to foster all below;
Who mak'st the Sun without all fire to glow,
The spring of heat and light, the Moone to ebbe and flow:

3

Thou world's sole Pilot, who in this poore Isle
(So small a bottome) hast embark't thy light,
And glorious selfe: and stear'st it safe, the while
Hoarse drumming seas, and winds lowd trumpets fight,
Who causest stormy heavens here onely smile:
Steare me poore Ship-boy, steare my course aright;
Breath gracious Spirit, breath gently on these layes,
Be thou my Compasse, Needle to my wayes,
Thy glorious work's my Fraught, my Haven is thy prayse.

4

Revel. 17. 2. 3. 4. 6.

Thou purple Whore, mounted on scarlet beast,
Gorg'd with the flesh, drunk with the blood of Saints,

1.5 great Cities: Rome's.

1.7 spous'd to Christ: the Church as the bride of Christ. Cf. Rev. 21:9 whoordome: the Catholic Church, interpreted by Protestants as the Whore of Babylon depicted in Rev. 17. See also stanza 4 below.

2.2 Thetis: a sea nymph; hence the sea personified.

2.3 caules: networks.

2.8 The question of whether the sun is hot was often decided in the negative.

3.9 Fraught: cargo.

Whose amorous golden Cup, and charmed feast
All earthly Kings, all earthly men attaints;
See thy live pictures, see thine owne, thy best,
Thy dearest sonnes, and cheere thy heart, that faints.
  Harke thou sav'd Island, harke, and never cease
  To prayse that hand which held thy head in peace.
Else had'st thou swumme as deep in blood, as now in seas.

5

The cloudy Night came whirling up the skie,
And scatt'ring round the dewes, which first shee drew
From milky poppies, loads the drousie eie:
The watry Moone, cold Vesper, and his crew
Light up their tapers: to the Sunne they fly,
And at his blazing flame their sparks renew.
  Oh why should earthly lights then scorne to tine
  Their lamps alone at that first Sunne divine?
Hence as false falling starres, as rotten wood they shine.

6

Her sable mantle was embroydered gay
With silver beames, with spangles round beset:
Foure steedes her chariot drew, the first was gray,
The second blue, third browne, fourth blacke as jet.
The hollowing Owle her Post prepares the way,
And winged dreames (as gnat-swarms) fluttring, let
  Sad sleep, who faine his eies in rest would steep.
  Why then at death doe weary mortals weep?
Sleep's but a shorter death, death's but a longer sleep.

4.7 sav'd: i.e., from Guy Fawkes' Catholic plot of 1605 to destroy the English government.

5.7 tine: light.

5.8 Sunne: Son of God.

5.9 Hence: else (apparently a nonce meaning).

6.1 Her: Night's.

6.3 Foure steedes: Spenser describes them as being "two blacke as pitch,/ And two were browne, yet each to each unlich," *FQ* 1. 5. 28. Cf. *Æneid* 5. 721.

6.6 let: hindered.

7

And now the world, & dreames themselves were drown'd
In deadly sleep; the Labourer snorteth fast,
His brawny armes unbent, his limbs unbound,
As dead, forget all toyle to come, or past,
Onely sad Guilt, and troubled Greatnes crown'd
With heavy gold and care, no rest can tast.
    Goe then vaine man, goe pill the live and dead,
    Buy, sell, fawne, flatter, rise, then couch thy head
In proud, but dangerous gold: in silke, but restlesse bed.

8

When loe a sudden noyse breakes th' empty aire;
A dreadfull noyse, which every creature daunts,
Frights home the blood, shoots up the limber haire.
For through the silent heaven hells pursuivants
Cutting their way, command foule spirits repaire
With hast to Pluto, who their counsell wants.
    Their hoarse base-hornes like fenny Bittours sound;
    Th' earth shakes, dogs howle, & heaven it selfe astound
Shuts all his eies; the stars in clouds their candles drown'd.

9

Meane time Hels yron gates by fiends beneath
Are open flung; which fram'd with wondrous art
To every guilty soule yeelds entrance eath;
But never wight, but He, could thence depart,
Who dying once was death to endlesse death.
So where the livers channell to the heart
    Payes purple tribute, with their three-fork't mace
    Three Tritons stand, and speed his flowing race,
But stop the ebbing streame, if once it back would pace.

7.7 pill: rob.

8.7 Bittours: bitterns, birds noted for the booming sounds they make in their marshy breeding areas.

9.3 eath: easy.

9.4 He: Christ, who "descended into hell," according to the Apostle's Creed, between his death and resurrection.

9.6 channell: the inferior vena cava, a vein leading to the heart where the tricuspid valve ("Three Tritons") directs the flow of blood.

10

The Porter to th' infernall gate is Sin,
A shapelesse shape, a foule deformed thing,
Nor nothing, nor a substance: as those thin
And empty formes, which through the ayer fling
Their wandring shapes, at length they'r fastned in
The Chrystall sight. It serves, yet reignes as King:
    It lives, yet's death: it pleases, full of paine:
    Monster! ah who, who can thy beeing faigne?
Thou shapelesse shape, live death, paine pleasing, servile raigne.

11

Of that first woman, and th' old serpent bred,
By lust and custome nurst; whom when her mother
Saw so deform'd, how faine would she have fled
Her birth, and selfe? But she her damme would smother,
And all her brood, had not He rescued
Who was his mothers sire, his childrens brother;
    Eternitie, who yet was borne and dy'de:
    His owne Creatour, earths scorne, heavens pride,
Who th' Deitie inflesht, and mans flesh deifi'de.

12

Her former parts her mother seemes resemble,
Yet onely seemes to flesh and weaker sight;
For she with art and paint could fine dissemble
Her loathsome face: her back parts (blacke as night)
Like to her horride Sire would force to tremble
The boldest heart; to th' eye that meetes her right
    She seemes a lovely sweet, of beauty rare;
    But at the parting, he that shall compare,
Hell will more lovely deeme, the divel's selfe more faire.

10.3ff. The theory of vision here derives from Lucretius' discussion, *De Rerum Natura* 4. 25ff.

10.6 It: Sin.

11.1 first woman: Eve.

11.7 Eternitie: i.e., eternal.

12.1 Her former: Sin's forward.

12.6 right: directly.

13

Her rosie cheeke, quicke eye, her naked brest,
And whatsoe're loose fancie might entice,
She bare expos'd to sight, all lovely drest
Is beauties livery, and quaint devise:
Thus she bewitches many a boy unblest,
Who drench't in hell, dreames all of Paradise:
    Her brests his spheares, her armes his circling skie;
    Her pleasures heav'n, her love eternitie:
For her he longs to live, with her he longs to die.

14

But he, that gave a stone power to descry
'Twixt natures hid, and checke that mettals pride,
That dares aspire to golds faire puritie,
Hath left a touch-stone, erring eyes to guide,
Which cleares their sight, and strips hypocrisie.
They see, they loath, they curse her painted hide;
    Her, as a crawling carrion, they esteeme:
    Her worst of ills, and worse then that they deeme;
Yet know her worse, then they can think, or she can seem.

15

Close by her sat Despaire, sad ghastly Spright,
With staring lookes, unmoov'd, fast nayl'd to Sinne;
Her body all of earth, her soule of fright,
About her thousand deaths, but more within:
Pale, pined cheeks, black hayre, torne, rudely dight;
Short breath, long nayles, dull eyes, sharp-pointed chin:
    Light, life, heaven, earth, her selfe, and all shee fled.
    Fayne would she die, but could not: yet halfe dead,
A breathing corse she seem'd, wrap't up in living lead.

13.9 die: with the pun, to have intercourse.

14.1 stone: the touchstone, used for testing the quality of gold and silver alloys.

14.4 touch-stone: divine grace; cf. Ithuriel's "Touch of Celestial temper" which reveals Satan's true form when he is discovered at Eve's ear, *PL* 4. 812.

15.9 lead: Corpses were wrapped in lead before being placed in coffins.

16

In th' entrance Sicknes, and faint Languour dwelt,
Who with sad grones tolle out their passing knell:
Late feare, fright, horrour, that already felt
The Torturers clawes, preventing death, and hell.
Within loud Greife, and roaring Pangs (that swelt
In sulphure flames) did weep, and houle, and yell.
    And thousand soules in endles dolours lie,
    Who burne, frie, hizze, and never cease to crie,
Oh that I ne're had liv'd, Oh that I once could die!

17

And now th' Infernal Powers through th' ayer driving,
For speed their leather pineons broad display;
Now at eternall Deaths wide gate arriving,
Sinne gives them passage; still they cut their way,
Till to the bottome of hells palace diving,
They enter Dis deepe Conclave: there they stay,
    Waiting the rest, and now they all are met,
    A full foule Senate, now they all are set,
The horride Court, big swol'ne with th' hideous Counsel swet.

18

The mid'st, but lowest (in hells heraldry
The deepest is the highest roome) in state
Sat Lordly Lucifer: his fiery eye,
Much swol'ne with pride, but more with rage, and hate,
As Censour, muster'd all his company;
Who round about with awefull silence sate.
    This doe, this let rebellious Spirits gaine,
    Change God for Satan, heaven's for hells Sov'raigne:
O let him serve in hell, who scornes in heaven to raigne!

16.4 preventing: anticipating.

17.6 Dis: Pluto's.

17.9 swet: suite; followers.

18.5 Censour: attendance taker.

19

Ah wretch, who with ambitious cares opprest,
Long'st still for future, feel'st no present good:
Despising to be better, would'st be best,
Good never; who wilt serve thy lusting mood,
Yet all command: not he, who rais'd his crest,
But pull'd it downe, hath high and firmely stood.
    Foole, serve thy towring lusts, grow still, still crave,
    Rule, raigne, this comfort from thy greatnes have,
Now at thy top, Thou art a great commanding slave.

20

Thus fell this Prince of darknes, once a bright
And glorious starre: he wilfull turn'd away
His borrowed globe from that eternall light:
Himselfe he sought, so lost himselfe: his ray
Vanish't to smoke, his morning sunk in night,
And never more shall see the springing day:
    To be in heaven the second he disdaines:
    So now the first in hell, the flames he raignes,
Crown'd once with joy, and light: crown'd now with fire and paines.

21

As where the warlike Dane the scepter swayes,
They crowne Usurpers with a wreath of lead,
And with hot steele, while loud the Traitour brayes,
They melt, and drop it downe into his head.
Crown'd he would live, and crown'd he ends his dayes:
All so in heavens courts this Traitour sped.
    Who now (when he had overlook't his traine)
    Rising upon his throne, with bitter staine
Thus 'gan to whet their rage, & chide their frustrate paine.

22

See, see you Spirits (I know not whether more
Hated, or hating heaven) ah see the earth
Smiling in quiet peace, and plenteous store.
Men fearles live in ease, in love, and mirth:

19.5 rais'd his crest: challenged authority.

Where armes did rage, the drumme, & canon rore,
Where hate, strife, envy raign'd, and meagre dearth;
  Now lutes, and viols charme the ravish't eare.
  Men plow with swords, horse heels their armors weare.
Ah shortly scarce they'l know what warre, & armors were.

23

Under their sprowting vines they sporting sit.
Th' old tell of evils past: youth laugh, and play,
And to their wanton heads sweet garlands fit,
Roses with lillies, myrtles weav'd with Bay:
The world's at rest: Erinnys, forc't to quit
Her strongest holds, from earth is driven away.
  Even Turks forget their Empire to encrease:
  Warres selfe is slaine, and whips of Furies cease.
Wee, wee our selves I feare, will shortly live in peace.

24

Meane time (I burne, I broyle, I burst with spight)
In midst of peace that sharpe two edged sword
Cuts through our darknes, cleaves the misty night,
Discovers all our snares; that sacred word
(Loc'kt up by Rome) breakes prison, spreads the light,
Speakes every tongue, paints, and points out the Lord,
  His birth, life, death, and crosse: our guilded Stocks,
  Our Laymens bookes, the boy, and woman mocks:
They laugh, they fleer, and say, Blocks teach, and worship Blocks.

22.8 "They shall beat their swords into plowshares," Isa. 2:4.

22.9 were. : were 1627.

23.5 Erinnys: the Furies.

24.2 two edged sword: cf. Rev. 1:16, interpreted here as the Old and New Testaments.

24.5 breakes prison: Protestant translations of the Bible into the vernacular.

24.7 Stocks: religious images.

24.8 boy, and woman: i.e., even such inferior thinkers.

24.9 fleer: jeer.

25

Spring-tides of light divine the ayre suround,
And bring downe heaven to earth; deafe Ignoraunce,
Vext with the day, her head in hell hath drow'nd:
Fond Superstition, frighted with the glaunce
Of suddaine beames, in vaine hath crost her round.
Truth and Religion every where advaunce
    Their conqu'ring standards: Errour's lost and fled:
    Earth burnes in love to heaven: heaven yeelds her bed
To earth; and common growne, smiles to be ravished.

26

That little swimming Isle above the rest,
Spight of our spight, and all our plots, remaines
And growes in happines: but late our nest,
Where wee and Rome, and blood, and all our traines,
Monks, Nuns, dead, and live idols, safe did rest:
Now there (next th' Oath of God) that Wrastler raignes,
    Who fills the land and world with peace, his speare
    Is but a pen, with which he downe doth beare
Blind Ignoraunce, false gods, and superstitious feare.

27

There God hath fram'd another Paradise,
Fat Olives dropping peace, victorious palmes,
Nor in the midst, but every where doth rise
That hated tree of life, whose precious balmes
Cure every sinfull wound: give light to th' eyes,
Unlock the eare, recover fainting qualmes.
    There richly growes what makes a people blest;
    A garden planted by himselfe and drest:
Where he himselfe doth walke, where he himselfe doth rest.

28

There every starre sheds his sweet influence,
And radiant beames: great, little, old, and new

25.9 to : ro 1627.

26.6 Wrastler: James I, who prided himself on his pious wisdom and exercised it in many books.

Their glittering rayes, and frequent confluence
The milky path to Gods high palace strew:
Th' unwearied Pastors with steel'd confidence,
Conquer'd, and conquering fresh their fight renew.
 Our strongest holds that thundring ordinaunce
 Beats downe, and makes our proudest turrets daunce,
Yoking mens iron necks in his sweet governaunce.

29

Nor can th' old world content ambitious Light,
Virginia our soile, our seat, and throne,
(To which so long possession gives us right,
As long as hells) Virginia's selfe is gone:
That stormy Ile which th' Ile of Devills hight,
Peopled with faith, truth, grace, religion.
 What's next but hell? That now alone remaines,
 And that subdu'de, even here he rules and raignes,
And mortals gin to dreame of long, but endles paines.

30

While we (good harmeles creatures) sleep, or play,
Forget our former losse, and following paine:
Earth sweats for heaven, but hell keeps holy-day.
Shall we repent good soules? or shall we plaine?
Shall we groane, sigh, weep, mourne, for mercy pray?
Lay downe our spight, wash out our sinfull staine?
 May be hee'l yeeld, forget, and use us well,
 Forgive, joyne hands, restore us whence we fell:
May be hee'l yeeld us heaven, and fall himselfe to hell.

31

But me, oh never let me, Spirits, forget
That glorious day, when I your standard bore,
And scorning in the second place to sit,

28.7 thundring: i.e., from the pulpit.

29.2 Virginia, settled by the English, who are redeeming it from Satan. The New World Indians were supposedly devils.

29.5 Ile of Devills: Bermuda.

30.4 plaine: complain.

With you assaulted heaven, his yoke forswore.
My dauntlesse heart yet longs to bleed, and swet
In such a fray: the more I burne, the more
I hate: should he yet offer grace, and ease,
If subject we our armes, and spight surcease,
Such offer should I hate, and scorne so base a peace.

32

Where are those spirits? Where that haughty rage,
That durst with me invade eternall light?
What? Are our hearts falne too? Droope we with age?
Can we yet fall from hell, and hellish spight?
Can smart our wrath, can griefe our hate asswage?
Dare we with heaven, and not with earth to fight?
Your armes, allies, your selves as strong as ever,
Your foes, their weapons, numbers weaker never.
For shame tread downe this earth: what wants but your endeavour?

33

Now by your selves, and thunder-danted armes,
But never danted hate, I you implore,
Command, adjure, reinforce your fierce alarmes:
Kindle, I pray, who never prayed before,
Kindle your darts, treble repay our harmes.
Oh our short time, too short, stands at the dore,
Double your rage: if now we doe not ply,
We 'lone in hell, without due company,
And worse, without desert, without revenge shall ly.

34

He, Spirits, (ah that, that's our maine torment) He
Can feele no wounds, laughs at the sword, and dart,
Himselfe from griefe, from suff'ring wholly free:
His simple nature cannot tast of smart,
Yet in his members wee him grieved see;
For, and in them, he suffers; where his heart
Lies bare, and nak't, there dart your fiery steele,
Cut, wound, burne, seare, if not the head, the heele.
Let him in every part some paine, and torment feele.

34.5 members: i.e., followers.

35

That light comes posting on, that cursed light,
When they as he, all glorious, all divine,
(Their flesh cloth'd with the sun, and much more bright,
Yet brighter spirits) shall in his image shine,
And see him as hee is: there no despight,
No force, no art their state can undermine.
    Full of unmeasur'd blisse, yet still receiving,
    Their soules still childing joy, yet still conceiving,
Delights beyond the wish, beyond quick thoughts perceiving.

36

But we fast pineon'd with darke firy chaines,
Shall suffer every ill, but doe no more,
The guilty spirit there feeles extreamest paines,
Yet feares worse then it feeles: and finding store
Of present deaths, deaths absence sore complaines:
Oceans of ills without or ebbe, or shore,
    A life that ever dies, a death that lives,
    And, worst of all, Gods absent presence gives
A thousand living woes, a thousand dying griefes.

37

But when he summes his time, and turnes his eye
First to the past, then future pangs, past dayes
(And every day's an age of misery)
In torment spent, by thousands downe he layes,
Future by millions, yet eternity
Growes nothing lesse, nor past to come allayes.
    Through every pang, and griefe he wild doth runne,
    And challenge coward death, doth nothing shunne,
That he may nothing be; does all to be undone.

38

O let our worke equall our wages, let
Our Judge fall short, and when his plagues are spent,
Owe more then he hath paid, live in our debt:

35 The description of the saved comes from a conflation of Rev. 12:1, interpreted as the Virgin Mary, and Rev. 22:5.

Let heaven want vengeance, hell want punishment
To give our dues: when wee with flames beset
Still dying live in endles languishment.
    This be our comfort, we did get and win
    The fires, and tortures we are whelmed in:
We have kept pace, outrun his justice with our sin.

39

And now you States of hell give your advise,
And to these ruines lend your helping hand.
This said, and ceas't; straight humming murmures rise:
Some chafe, some fret, some sad and thoughtfull stand,
Some chat, and some new stratagems devise,
And every one heavens stronger powers ban'd,
    And teare for madnesse their uncombed snakes,
    And every one his fiery weapon shakes,
And every one expects who first the answer makes.

40

So when the falling Sunne hangs o're the maine,
Ready to droppe into the Westerne wave,
By yellow Chame, where all the Muses raigne,
And with their towres his reedy head embrave;
The warlike Gnat their flutt'ring armies traine,
All have sharpe speares, and all shrill trumpets have:
    Their files they double, loud their cornets sound,
    Now march at length, their troopes now gather round:
The bankes, the broken noise, and turrets faire rebound.

CANTO II.

1

What care, what watch need guard that tot'ring State
Which mighty foes besiege, false friends betray,
Where enemies strong, and subtile swol'ne with hate,
Catch all occasions; wake, watch night and day?

40.3 Chame: the River Cam (and Cambridge).

40.4 embrave: ornament (by reflection in the water).

The towne divided, even the wall and gate
Proove traitours, and the Councill' selfe takes pay
  Of forraigne States, the Prince is overswai'd
  By underminers, puts off friendly aid,
His wit by will, his strength by weakenes over-laid?

2

Thus men: the never seene, quicke-seeing-fiends:
Feirce, craftie, strong; and world conspire our fall:
And we (worse foes) unto our selves false friends:
Our flesh, and sense a trait'rous gate, and wall:
The spirit, and flesh man in two factions rends:
The inward senses are corrupted all,
  The soule weake, wilfull, swai'd with flatteries,
  Seekes not his helpe, who works by contraries,
By folly makes him wise, strong by infirmities.

3

See drousie soule, thy foe ne're shuts his eyes,
See, carelesse soule, thy foe in councell sits:
Thou prayer restrain'st, thy sin for vengeance cries,
Thou laugh'st, vaine soule, while justice vengeance fits.
Wake by his light, with wisedomes selfe advise:
What rigorous Justice damnes, sweet Mercy quits.
  Watch, pray, he in one instant helps and heares:
  Let him not see thy sins, but through thy teares,
Let him not heare their cries, but through thy groning feares.

4

As when the angry winds with seas conspire,
The white-plum'd hilles marching in set array
Invade the earth, and seeme with rage on fire,
While waves with thundring drummes whet on the fray,
And blasts with whistling fifes new rage inspire:
Yet soone as breathles ayres their spight allay,
  A silent calme insues: the hilly maine

2.8 his: Christ's.

3.6 quits: acquits.

3.7 he: Christ (as merciful).

Sinks in it selfe, and drummes unbrac't refraine
Their thundring noyse, while Seas sleep on the even plaine.

5

All so the raging storme of cursed fiends
Blowne up with sharp reproach, and bitter spight
First rose in loud uprore, then falling, ends,
And ebbes in silence: when a wily spright
To give an answere for the rest intends:
Once Proteus, now Equivocus he hight,
Father of cheaters, spring of cunning lies,
Of slie deceite, and refin'd perjuries,
That hardly hell it selfe can trust his forgeries.

6

To every shape his changing shape is drest,
Oft seemes a Lambe and bleates, a Wolfe and houles:
Now like a Dove appeares with candide brest,
Then like a Falcon, preyes on weaker foules:
A Badger neat, that flies his 'filed nest:
But most a Fox, with stinke his cabin foules:
A Courtier, Priest, transform'd to thousand fashions,
His matter fram'd of slight equivocations,
His very forme was form'd of mentall reservations.

7

And now more practicke growne with use and art,
Oft times in heavenly shapes he fooles the sight:
So that his schollers selves have learn't his part,
Though wormes, to glow in dark, like Angels bright.
To sinfull slime such glosse can they impart,

4.8 unbrac't: released from tension.

5.6 Proteus: a sea-god noted for the various shapes which he could assume; hence his new name Equivocus: equivocation. He will be titled Apollyon in stanza 9. Henry Garnet, leader of the English Jesuits, wrote *A Treatise of Equivocation* to defend Robert Southwell from charges of Catholicism. The treatise was interpreted as defending equivocation — lying or making statements with "mentall reservations" (6. 9) — in a good cause and was a part of the charges made against Garnet after the exposure of the Gunpowder Plot.

6.5 neat: clean. 'filed: polluted.

That, like the virgine Mother, crown'd in light,
    They glitter faire in glorious purity,
    And rayes divine: meane time the cheated eye
Is finely mock't into an heavenly ecstasy.

8

Now is he Generall of those new stamp't Friers,
Which have their root in that lame souldier Saint,
Who takes his ominous name from *Strife, and Fires,
Themselves with idle vaunt that name attaint,
Which all the world adores: These Master lyers
With trueth, Abaddonists, with Jesus paint
    Their lying title. Fooles, who think with light
    To hide their filth, thus lie they naked quite:
That who loves Jesus most, most hates the Jesuite.

* *Ignatius.*

9

Soone as this Spirit (in hell Apollyon,
On earth Equivocus) stood singled out,
Their Speaker there, but here their Champion,
Whom lesser States, and all the vulgar rout
In dangerous times admire and gaze upon,
The silly Commons circle him about,
    And first with loud applause they usher in
    Their Oratour, then hushing all their din,
With silence they attend, and wooe him to begin.

10

Great Monarch, ayers, earths, hells Soveraigne,
True, ah too true you plaine, and we lament,
In vaine our labour, all our art's in vaine;
Our care, watch, darts, assaults are all mispent.
He, whose command we hate, detest, disdaine,

8.1 Friers: the Jesuits, named for Jesus; their founder was Ignatius Loyola. Fletcher derives his first name (l. 3) from *igneus*, meaning "Strife, and Fires."

8.6 Abaddonists: from Rev. 9:11, hell's angels.

9.1 Apollyon: a name derived from Rev. 9:3–11.

10.2 plaine: complain.

Works all our thoughts and workes to his intent:
Our spight his pleasure makes, our ill his good,
Light out of night he brings, peace out of blood:
What fell which he upheld? what stood which he withstood?

11

As when from mores some firie constellation
Drawes up wet cloudes with strong attractive ray,
The captiv'd seas forc't from their seat and nation,
Begin to mutinie, put out the day,
And pris'ning close the hot drie exhalation,
Threat earth, and heaven, and steale the Sunne away:
Till th' angry Captive (fir'd with fetters cold)
With thundring Cannons teares the limber mould,
And downe in fruitfull teares the broken vapour's roul'd.

12

So our rebellion, so our spightfull threat
All molten falls; he (which my heart disdaines)
Waters heavens plants with our hell-flaming heat,
Husband's his graces with our sinfull paines:
When most against him, for him most we sweat,
We in our Kingdome serve, he in it raignes:
Oh blame us not, we strive, mine, wrastle, fight;
He breakes our troopes: yet thus, we still delight,
Though all our spight's in vain, in vain to shew our spight.

13

Our fogs lie scatt'red by his piercing light,
Our subtilties his wisedome overswaies,
His gracious love weighs downe our ranck'rous spight,
His Word our sleights, his truth our lyes displayes,
Our ill confin'd, his goodnesse infinite,
Our greatest strength his weaknesse overlaies.
He will, and oh he must, be Emperour,
That heaven, and earth's unconquer'd at this houre,
Nor let him thanke, nor do you blame our wil, but pow'r.

11.1 mores: moors.

11.5 hot drie exhalation: lightning.

14

Nay, earthly Gods that wont in luxury,
In maskes, and daliance spend their peacefull daies,
Or else invade their neighbours liberty,
And swimme through Christian blood to heathen praise,
Subdue our armes with peace; us bold defie,
Arm'd all with letters, crown'd with learned bayes:
    With them whole swarmes of Muses take the field;
    And by heavens aide enforce us way to yield;
The Goose lends them a speare, and every ragge a shield.

15

But are our hearts fal'ne too; shall wee repent,
Sue, pray, with teares wash out our sinfull spot?
Or can our rage with greife, and smart relent?
Shall wee lay downe our armes? Ah, feare us not;
Not such thou found'st us, when with thee we bent
Our armes 'gainst heaven, when scorning that faire lot
    Of glorious blisse (when we might still have raign'd)
    With him in borrowed light, and joyes unstain'd,
We hated subject crownes, and guiltlesse blisse disdain'd.

16

Nor are we changelings: finde, oh finde but one,
But one in all thy troopes, whose lofty pride
Begins to stoope with opposition:
But, as when stubborn winds with earth ralli'de
(Their Mother earth) she ayded by her sonne
Confronts the Seas, beates of the angry tide:
    The more with curl'd-head waves, the furious maine
    Renues his spite, and swells with high disdaine,
Oft broke, and chac't, as oft turnes, & makes head againe:

17

So rise we by our fall: that divine science
Planted belowe, grafted in humane stocke,
Heavens with frayle earth combines in strong alliance:

14.9 speare: goosequill pen. shield: i.e., paper.
16.6 of: off.

While he, their Lion, leads that sheepish flock,
Each sheepe, each lambe dares give us bold defiance:
But yet our forces broken 'gainst the rocke
We strongly reinforce, and every man
Though cannot what he will's, will's what he can,
And where wee cannot hurt, there we can curse, and banne.

18

See here in broken force, a heart unbroke,
Which neither hell can daunt, nor heaven appease:
See here a heart, which scornes that gentle yoke,
And with it life, and light, and peace, and ease:
A heart not cool'd, but fir'd with thundring stroke,
Which heaven it selfe, but conquer'd cannot please:
To drawe one blessed soule from's heavenly Cell,
Let me in thousand paines and tortures dwell:
Heaven without guilt to me is worse then guilty hell.

19

Feare then no change: such I, such are we all:
Flaming in vengeance, more then Stygian fire,
When hee shall leave his throne, and starry hall,
Forsake his deare-bought Saints, and Angells quire,
When he from heaven into our hell shall fall,
Our nature take, and for our life expire;
Then we perhaps (as man) may waver light,
Our hatred turne to peace, to love our spight,
Then heaven shall turne to hell, and day shall chaunge to night.

20

But if with forces new to take the feild
Thou long'st, looke here, we prest, and ready stand:
See all that power, and Wiles that hell can yeeld
Expect no watchword, but thy first command:
Which given, without or feare, or sword, or sheild
Wee'le fly in heavens face, I and my band
Will draw whole worlds, leave here no rome to dwell.

19.3 When: at the Incarnation.

20.2 prest: prepared.

Stale arts we scorne, our plots become black hell,
Which no heart will beleeve, nor any tongue dare tell.

21

Nor shall I need to spurre the lazy Monke,
Who never sweats but in his meale, or bed,
Whose forward paunch ushers his uselesse truncke,
He barrels darkenes in his empty head:
To eate, drinke, void what he hath eat and drunke,
Then purge his reines; thus these Saints merited:
They fast with holy fish, and flowing wine
Not common, but (with fits such Saints) *Divine:
Poore soules, they dare not soile their hands with precious mine!

* Hence called *Vinum Theologicum.*

22

While th' earth with night and mists was overswai'd,
And all the world in clouds was laid a steep,
Their sluggish trade did lend us friendly aid,
They rock't and hush't the world in deadly sleep,
Cloyst'red the Sunne, the Moone they overlaid,
And prison'd every starre in dungeon deep.
And when the light put forth his morning ray,
My famous Dominicke tooke the light away,
And let in seas of blood to quench the early day.

23

But oh, that recreant Frier, who long in night
Had slept, his oath to me his Captaine brake,
Uncloyst'red with himselfe the hated light;
Those piercing beames forc't drowsie earth awake,
Nor could we all resist: our flatt'rie, spight,
Arts, armes, his victorie more famous make.
Down cloysters fall; the Monkes chac't from their sty
Lie ope, and all their loathsome company;
Hypocrisie, rape, blood, theft, whooredome, Sodomy.

21.9 mine: i.e., gold.

22.1 While: during the Middle Ages.

22.2 a steep: steeping.

22.8 Dominicke: St. Dominic (1170–1221), who established the Dominican Order to combat heresy. The order was later an agent of the Inquisition.

23.1 Frier: Martin Luther.

24

Those troupes I soone disband now useles quite;
And with new musters fill my companies;
And presse the crafty wrangling Jesuite:
Nor traine I him as Monks, his squinted eyes
Take in and view ascaunce the hatefull light:
So stores his head with shifts and subtilties.
    Thus being arm'd with arts, his turning braines
    All overturne. Oh with what easy paines
Light he confounds with light, and truth with truth distaines.

25

The world is rent in doubt: some gazing stay,
Few step aright, but most goe with the croud.
So when the golden Sun with sparkling ray
Imprints his stamp upon an adverse cloud,
The watry glasse so shines, that's hard to say
Which is the true, which is the falser proud.
    The silly people gape, and whisp'ring cry
    That some strange innovation is ny,
And fearefull wisard sings of parted tyranny.

26

These have I train'd to scorne their contraries,
Out-face the truth, out-stare the open light:
And what with seeming truths and cunning lies
Confute they cannot, with a scoffe to sleight.
Then after losse to crowe their victories,
And get by forging what they lost by fight.
    And now so well they ply them, that by heart
    They all have got my counterfeiting part,
That to my schollers I turne scholler in mine art.

27

Follow'd by these brave spirits, I nothing feare
To conquer earth, or heaven it selfe assayle,

24.7 turning: changeful.

24.9 distaines: stains.

25.9 parted: shared, or doubled.

To shake the starres, as thick from fixed spheare,
As when a rustick arme with stubborne flayle
Beates out his harvest from the swelling eare;
T' eclipse the Moone, and Sun himselfe injayle.
    Had all our army such another band,
    Nor earth, nor heaven could long unconquer'd stand:
But hell should heaven, and they, I feare, would hell command.

28

What Country, City, Towne, what family,
In which they have not some intelligence,
And party, some that love their company?
Courts, Councells, hearts of Kings find no defence,
No guard to barre them out: by flattery
They worme and scrue into their conscience;
    Or with steel, poyson, dagges dislodge the sprite.
    If any quench or dampe this Orient light,
Or foile great Jesus name, it is the Jesuite.

29

When late our whore of Rome was disaray'd,
Strip't of her pall, and skarlet ornaments,
And all her hidden filth lay broad displayd,
Her putride pendant bagges, her mouth that sents
As this of hell, her hands with scabbes array'd,
Her pust'led skin with ulcer'd excrements;
    Her friends fall off; and those that lov'd her best,
    Grow sicke to think of such a stinking beast:
And her, and every limbe that touch't her, much detest.

30

Who help't us then? Who then her case did rue?
These, onely these their care, and art appli'de

28.7 dagges: pistols.

29-30 describes the Catholic activities of the Counter Reformation, following the Council of Trent.

29.4 bagges: breasts. sents: smells.

29.6 pust'led: broken out in pustules.

30.2 These: the Jesuits.

To hide her shame with tires, and dressing new:
They blew her bagges, they blanch't her leprous hide,
And on her face a lovely picture drew.
But most the head they pranck't in all his pride
    With borrowed plumes, stolne from antiquitie:
    Him with blasphemous names they dignifie;
Him they enthrone, adore, they crowne, they deifie.

31

As when an image gnawne with wormes, hath lost
His beautie, forme, respect, and lofty place,
Some cunning hand new trimmes the rotten post,
Filles up the worme-holes, paints the soyled face
With choicest colours, spares no art, or cost
With precious robes the putride trunck to grace.
    Circles the head with golden beames, that shine
    Like rising Sun: the Vulgar low incline;
And give away their soules unto the block divine.

32

So doe these Dedale workmen plaster over,
And smooth that Stale with labour'd polishing;
So her defects with art they finely cover,
Cloth her, dresse, paint with curious colouring:
So every friend againe, and every lover
Returnes, and doates through their neate pandaring:
    They fill her cup, on knees drinke healths to th' whore;
    The drunken nations pledge it o're and o're;
So spue, and spuing fall, and falling rise no more.

33

Had not these troopes with their new forged armes
Strook in, even ayre, earth too, and all were lost:
Their fresh assaultes, and importune alarmes

30.4 blew her bagges: inflated her breasts.

30.6 head: the pope. pranck't: decorated.

32.1 Dedale: skillful (from Dædalus).

32.2 Stale: decoy.

32.9 spue: vomit.

Have truth repell'd, and her full conquest crost:
Or these, or none must recompence our harmes.
If they had fail'd wee must have sought a coast
    I'th' Moone (the Florentines new world) to dwell,
    And, as from heaven, from earth should now have fell
To hell confin'd, nor could we safe abide in hell.

34

Nor shall that little Isle (our envy, spight,
His paradise) escape: even there they long
Have shrowded close their heads from dang'rous light,
But now more free dare presse in open throng:
Nor then were idle, but with practicke slight
Crept into houses great: their sugred tongue
    Made easy way into the lapsed brest
    Of weaker sexe, where lust had built her nest,
There layd they Cuckoe eggs, and hatch't their brood unblest.

35

There sowe they traytrous seed with wicked hand
'Gainst God, and man; well thinks their silly sonne
To merit heaven by breaking Gods command,
To be a Patriot by rebellion.
And when his hopes are lost, his life and land,
And he, and wife, and child are all undone,
    Then calls for heaven and Angells, in step I,
    And waft him quick to hel; thus thousands die,
Yet still their children doat: so fine their forgerie.

36

But now that stormy season's layd, their spring,
And warmer Sunnes call them from wintry cell;
These better times will fruits much better bring,
Their labours soone will fill the barnes of hell
With plenteous store; serpents, if warm'd, will sting:

33.7 Florentines: Galileo's, as revealed by his telescope.

34.1 Isle: England.

35.2 sonne: Guy Fawkes.

And even now they meet, and hisse, and swell.
Thinke not of falling, in the name of all
This dare I promise, and make good I shall,
While they thus firmely stand, wee cannot wholly fall.

37

And shall these mortals creep, fawne, flatter, ly,
Coyne into thousand arts their fruitfull braine,
Venter life, limbe, through earth, and water fly
To winne us Proselytes? Scorne ease, and paine,
To purchase grace in their whore-mistres eye?
Shall they spend, spill their dearest blood, to staine
Romes Calendar, and paint their glorious name
In hers, and our Saint-Rubrick? Get them fame,
Where Saints are fiends, gaine losse, grace disgrace, glory shame?

38

And shall wee, (Spirits) shall we (whose life and death
Are both immortall) shall we, can we faile?
Great Prince o' th' lower world, in vaine we breath
Our spight in Councell; free us this our jayle:
Wee doe but loose our little time beneath;
All to their charge: why sit we here to waile?
Kindle your darts, and rage; renew your fight:
We are dismist: breake out upon the light,
Fill th' earth with sin, and blood; heaven with stormes, and fright.

39

With that the bold black Spirit invades the day,
And heav'n, and light, and Lord of both defies.
All hell run out, and sooty flagges display,
A foule deformed rout: heav'n shuts his eyes;
The starres looke pale, and early mornings ray
Layes downe her head againe, and dares not rise:
A second night of Spirits the ayre possest;
The wakefull cocke that late forsooke his nest,
Maz'd how he was deceav'd, flies to his roost, and rest.

40

So when the South (dipping his sable wings
In humid seas) sweeps with his dropping beard
The ayer, earth, and Ocean, downe he flings
The laden trees, the Plowmans hopes new-eard
Swimme on the playne: his lippes loud thunderings,
And flashing eyes make all the world afeard:
    Light with darke cloudes, waters with fires are met,
    The Sunne but now is rising, now is set,
And finds West-shades in East, and seas in ayers wet.

CANTO III.

1

False world how doest thou witch dimme reasons eies?
I see thy painted face, thy changing fashion:
Thy treasures, honours all are vanities,
Thy comforts, pleasures, joyes all are vexation,
Thy words are lyes, thy oaths foule perjuries,
Thy wages, care, greife, begg'ry, death, damnation:
    All this I know: I know thou doest deceive me,
    Yet cannot as thou art, but seem'st, conceave thee:
I know I should, I must, yet oh I would not leave thee.

2

Looke as in dreames, where th' idle fancie playes,
One thinkes that fortune high his head advances:
Another spends in woe his weary dayes;
A third seekes sport in love, and courtly daunces;
This grones, and weeps, that chants his merry laies;
A sixt to finde some glitt'ring treasure chaunces:
    Soon as they wake, they see their thoughts were vaine,
    And quite forget, and mocke their idle braine,
This sighs, that laugh's to see how true false dreames can faine.

1.8 The familiar Platonic distinction between appearance and reality, developed in the following stanzas by the contrast between objects of fantasy (dreams) and true perception.

2.4 seekes : seemes 1627.

3

Such is the world, such lifes short acted play:
This base, and scorn'd; this high in great esteeming,
This poore, & patched seemes, this rich, and gay;
This sick, that strong: yet all is onely seeming:
Soone as their parts are done, all slip away;
So like, that waking, oft wee feare w'are dreaming,
    And dreaming hope we wake. Wake, watch mine eies:
    What can be in the world, but flatteries,
Dreams, cheats, deceits, whose Prince is King of night and lies?

4

Whose hellish troopes fill thee with sinne, and blood;
With envie, malice, mischiefs infinite:
Thus now that numerous, black, infernall brood
O're-spread thee round; th' earth struck with trembling fright
Felt their approach, and all-amazed stood,
So suddain got with child, & big with spight.
    The damned Spirits fly round, and spread their seede:
    Straight hate, pride, strife, warres, and seditions breed,
Get up, grow ripe: How soone prospers the vicious weed!

5

Soone in the North their hellish poyson shed,
Where seldome warres, dissention never cease:
Where Volga's streames are sail'd with horse and sled,
Pris'ning in Chrystal walls his frozen seas:
Where Tartar, Russe, the Pole, and prospering Swed

4.4 O're : Or'e 1627.

5.1 The North was well established in demonology as the dwelling place of witches and demons, and hence the Jesuits of 6. 2.

5.5 Tartar . . . Swed: After the death of Stephen, king of Sweden, in 1586, the Poles considered various foreign successors, including Fedor or Theodore, emperor of Russia. But the nobles finally chose Sigismund, son and heir of the king of Sweden, a fervent Roman Catholic. In Russia, Boris Godunov, the emperor's brother-in-law, was responsible for the apparent murder of the emperor's half-brother Dimitri, who should have succeeded him. Fletcher's father Giles had witnessed in Moscow the rising power of Boris (see his *Of the Russe Common Wealth*, London, 1591, pp. 21r–v), who instead was crowned emperor in 1598. In the summer of 1603 a man claiming to be Dimitri appeared in Poland, where the Catholic Sigismund promised him aid in establishing his

Nor know the sweet, nor heare the name of peace:
    Where sleeping Sunnes in winter quench their light,
    And never shut their eyes in Summer bright;
Where many moneths make up one onely day, and night:

6

There lie they cloyst'red in their wonted Cell:
The sacred nurseries of the Societie:
They finde them ope, swept, deck't: so there they dwell,
Teaching, and learning more and more impietie.
There blow their fires, and tine another hell,
There make their Magazine, with all varietie
    Of fiery darts; the Jesuites helpe their friends:
    And hard to say, which in their spightfull ends
More vexe the Christian world, the Jesuites, or the Fiends.

7

The Fiends finde matter, Jesuites forme; those bring
Into the mint fowle hearts, sear'd conscience,
Lust-wandring eyes, cares fil'd with whispering,
Feet swift to blood, hands gilt with great expence,
Millions of tongues made soft for hammering,
And fit for every stampe, but truths defence:
    These (for Romes use, on Spanish anvile) frame
    The pliant matter; treasons hence diflame,
Lusts, lies, blood, thousand griefes set all the world on flame.

8

But none so fits the Polish Jesuite,
As Russia's change, where exil'd *Grecian Priest
Late sold his Patriarchal chaire, and right;

** Hierom Patriarch of the Greeke Church came unto Mosco in the yeare* 1588. *sold to Theodore Ivanovich Emperour of Russia his Patriarchal right; who presently installed into it the Metropolitane of Mosco.*

claim to the throne if he would be converted. The Jesuits were especially supportive, for if a Catholic returned to rule Russia the entire country might be converted.

7.1 matter . . . forme: the Aristotelian constituents of real existence.

7.8 diflame: spread flames (? not recorded in NED).

8.2 gloss: Giles Fletcher (pp. 79v–81v) reports how in 1588 Theodore welcomed Hieronimo, Patriarch of the Greek Church, and convinced him that Russia should have a Patriarch too. Accordingly Job of Rostov was elevated from Metropolitan to Patriarch, the highest position in the Greek Church.

That now proud Mosko vants her lofty crest
Equall with Rome: Romes head full swolne with spight,
Scorning a fellow head, or Peer, but Christ,
  Straines all his wits, & friends; they worke, they plod
  With double yoke the Russian necks to load;
To crowne the Polish Prince their King, the Pope their God.

9

The fiends, and times yeeld them a fit occasion
To further their designes: for late a * Beast
Of salvage breed, of straunge and monsterous fashion,
Before a Fox, an Asse behind, the rest
A ravenous Wolfe, with fierce, but slie invasion
Enters the Russian court, the Lyons nest,
  Worries the Lions selfe, and all his brood:
  And having gorg'd his mawe with royall blood,
Would sleepe. Ah short the rest, that streames from such a food!

* Borrise Federowich *brother to the Empresse of Russia, having by the simplicitie of that Emperour aspired to that kingdome, by murther of the chiefe Nobility, & extirpation of the royall seed; entred as subtily as he ruled cruelly, & died foolishly, killing himselfe when his treasures were yet untoucht & great, & the chiefe City might have beene won to have stood to him.*

10

Ah silly man, who dream'st, that honour stands
In ruling others, not thy selfe! Thy slaves
Serve thee, and thou thy slaves: in iron bands
Thy servile spirit prest with wild passions raves.
Base state, where but one Tyrant realmes commands:
Worse, where one single heart serves thousand knaves.
  Would'st thou live honoured? Clip ambitious wing,
  To reasons yoke thy furious passions bring.
Thrice noble is the man, who of himselfe is King.

11

With mimicke skill, they trayne a * caged beast,
And teach him play a royall Lyons part:

* Griskey Strepey *a Mosique, & sometime Chorister at Precheste in Mosko, and from thence with an Embassadour passing into Polonia, and there cloystered, was taught by the Jesuites to play the King, and usurping the name of Demetrius (slaine by Borrise Federowich) under that mask with the Polonian forces, and by the revolt of the Russes was crowned Emperour.*

9.2 gloss: Borrise Federowich: Boris Godunov. All witnesses testify to Theodore's incapacities. Giles Fletcher (p. 110r) described him as not "greatly apt for matter of pollicie, very superstitious."

9.9 sleepe. : sleepe, 1627.

11.1 gloss: This is Dimitri, supported in Poland against Boris by the Jesuits and King Sigismund. After Dimitri's murder the conspirators who had overthrown him circulated "a writing . . . to justify the killing of Demetrius, a runnagate Fryer called Grishka, or Gregorie Strepy, professed in the Monasterie

Then in the Lyons hide, and titles drest
They bring him forth: he Master in his art,
Soone winnes the Vulgar Russe. who hopes for rest
In chaunge; and if not ease, yet lesser smart:
    All hunt that monster, he soone melts his pride
    In abject feare; and life himselfe envi'de:
So whelp't a Fox, a Wolfe he liv'd, an Asse he di'de.

12

Proud of his easy crowne and straunge successe,
The *second beast (sprung of a baser brood)
Comes on the stage, and with great seemelinesse
Acts his first scenes; now strong gins chaunge his mood,
And melts in pleasure, lust, and wantonnesse:
Then swimmes in other, sinkes in his owne blood.
    With blood, and warres the ice and liquid snowes
    Are thaw'd; the earth a red sea overflowes.
Quarrells by falling rise, and strife by cutting growes.

** At his first entry the counterfeit Demetrius, wan the applause and good opinion of many, and very politickly behaved himselfe: but when he conceaved himselfe to be setled on the throne; he grew lascivious, and insolent, and bloody: and by a conspiracy was slaine, and his dead corps exposed to all shame and contempt.*

13

Some fiends to Grece their hellish firebrands bring,
And wake the sleeping sparks of Turkish rage;
Where once the lovely Muses us'd to sing,

in the Castle [in Moscow] (which therefore hee would never enter lest hee should bee knowne) with other aspersions of Heresie, Sorcerie, affectation of inducing Popery . . . to give the Jesuits Temples, Colledges, and other necessaries." It goes on to emphasize his lasciviousness and other crimes. Samuel Purchas, *Purchas His Pilgrimes* (reprint, Glasgow: James MacLose, 1906), 14:180. Purchas cautiously evaluated the charge as propaganda to serve the restoration of the Russian Church over the Roman in Moscow, but it serves Fletcher's purposes better to accept it as truth. Likewise Fletcher questions the legitimacy of Dimitri's claims to be the heir supposedly murdered by Boris.

12.1 easy crowne: Boris either died suddenly or committed suicide in the spring of 1605 as Dimitri was beginning his invasion.

12.2 *second : second 1627.

12.2 gloss: himselfe : himsefe 1627. The year after his easy and popular victory Dimitri married a Catholic Polish princess, an event, celebrated for days, which opposed Russians against Polish visitors and supporters of the emperor. Thus the conspiracy to murder him was successful.

12.4 gins: begins.

13.1 Grece: a revolt in Epirus, led by Dionysios, archbishop of Larissa, against the ruling Turks, which failed in 1611.

And chant th' Heroes of that golden age;
Where since more sacred Graces learn'd to string
That heav'nly lyre, and with their canzons sage
    Inspirit flesh, and quicken stinking graves,
    There (ah for pitty!) Muses now are slaves,
Graces are fled to heav'n, and hellish Mahomet raves.

14

But Lucifers proud band in prouder Spaine
Disperse their troopes: some with unquench't ambition
Inflame those Moorish Grandes, and fill their braine
With subtile plots; some learne of th' Inquisition
To finde new torments, and unused paines:
Some traine the Princes with their lewd tuition,
    That now of Kings they scorne to be the first,
    But onely: deep with Kingly dropsies pierc't
Their thirst drinkes kingdomes downe, their drinking fires their thirst.

15

Æquivocus, remembring well his taske,
And promise, enters Rome; there soone he eyes
Waters of life tunn'd up in stinking caske
Of deadly errours poyson'd truth with lies:
There that stale purple Whore in glorious maske
Of holy Mother Church he mumming spies,
    Dismounted from her seven headed beast,
    Inviting all with her bare painted breast,
They suck, steep, swell, and burst with that envenom'd feast.

16

Nor stayes, till now the stately Court appeares,
Where sits that Priest-King, all the Alls Soveraigne:
Three mitred crownes the proud Impostor weares,
For he in earth, in hell, in heav'n will raigne:
And in his hand two golden keyes he beares,

13.5 more sacred Graces: i.e., of Christianity.

16.5 keyes: claimed by the Pope on the basis of Matt. 16:19 and Rev. 1:18. Cf. Isa. 22:22.

To open heav'n and hell, and shut againe.
    But late his keyes are marr'd, or lost; for hell
    He cannot shut, but opes, and enters well:
Nor heav'n can ope, but shut; nor heav'n will buy, but sell.

17

Say Muses, say; who now in those rich fields
Where silver Tibris swimmes in golden sands,
Who now, ye Muses, that great scepter wields,
Which once sway'd all the earth with servile bands?
Who now those Babel towres, once fallen, builds?
Say, say, how first it fell, how now it stands?
    How, and by what degrees that Citie sunk?
    Oh are those haughty spirits so basely shrunk?
Cesars to chaunge for Friers, a Monarch for a Monk?

18

Th' Assyrian Lyon deck't in golden hide, *Dan.* 7. 4.
Once grasp't the Nations in his Lordly paw:
But him the Persian silver Beare defi'd, *Dan.* 7. 5.
Tore, kill'd, and swallowed up with ravenous jaw;
Whom that Greeke Leopard no sooner spi'de, *Dan.* 7. 6.
But slue, devour'd, and fill'd his empty maw:
    But with his raven'd prey his bowells broke;
    So into foure divides his brasen yoke.
Stol'ne bits, thrust downe in hast, doe seldome feed, but choke.

19

Meane time in Tybris fen a dreadfull Beast *Dan.* 7. 7.
With monstrous breadth, and length seven hills o're-spreads:
And nurst with dayly spoyles and bloody Feast
Grew up to wondrous strength: with seven heads,
Arm'd all with iron teeth, he rends the rest,
And with proud feet to clay and morter treads.
    And now all earth subdu'de, high heav'n he braves,

18 glosses: Daniel's vision of the four beasts has had various historical interpretations. The last beast (19.1) is today usually thought to represent Greece, but its ten horns equate it for Fletcher with the beast of Rev. 17, already identified with Rome. It is disguised (20.7) as the lamb of Rev. 13:11 — that is, as Christ's representative — but "he spake as a dragon" as the same verse testifies.

The head he kills, then 'gainst the body raves:
With Saintly flesh he swells, with bones his den he paves.

20

Apoc. 17. 10.

At length five heads were fall'ne; the sixt retir'd
By absence yeelds an easy way of rising
To th' next, and last: who with ambition fir'd,
In humble weeds his haughty pride disguising,
By slow, sly growth unto the top aspir'd:
Unlike the rest he veiles his tyrannising
With that Lambs head, & horns: both which he claimes;
Thence double raigne, within, without hee frames:
His head the Lamb, his tongue the Dragon loud proclames.

Apoc. 13. 11.

21

Those Fisher Swaynes, whome by full Jordans wave
The Seas great Soveraigne his art had taught,
To still loud stormes when windes and waters rave,
To sink their laden boats with heavenly fraught,
To free the fish with nets, with hookes to save:
For while the fish they catch, themselves were caught:
And as the scaly nation they invade,
Were snar'd themselves. Ah much more blessed trade
That of free Fisher swaines were captive fishes made!

22

Long since those Fisher swains had chang'd their dwelling;
Their spirits (while bodies slept in honour'd toombes)
Heavens joyes enjoy, all excellence excelling;
And in their stead a crue of idle groomes
By night into the ship with ladders stealing,
Fearles succeed, and fill their empty roomes.
The fishers trade they praise, the paynes deride:
Their narrow bottomes strech they large & wide,
And make broad roomes for pomp, for luxury, and pride.

19.8 the body : tbe body 1627.

21.2 Soveraigne: Christ, addressing Peter and Andrew, who were fishing, promised, "I will make you fishers of men" (Matt. 4:19). For the storm see Luke 8:23–25.

22.1-3 i.e., had suffered martyrdom. Following these true fishermen are the false ones, "idle groomes" of the Church of Rome.

23

Some from their skiffs to crownes and scepters creep,
Heavens selfe for earth, and God for man rejecting:
Some snorting in their hulks supinely sleep,
Seasons in vaine recall'd, and winds neglecting:
Some nets, and hookes, and baits in poyson steep,
With deathfull drugges the guiltles seas infecting:
  The fish their life and death together drink;
  And dead pollute the seas with venom'd stink:
So downe to deepest hell, both fish and fishers sink.

24

While thus they swimme in ease, with plenty flowe,
Each losel gets a boat, and will to sea:
Some teach to work, but have no hands to rowe;
Some will be lights, but have no eyes to see;
Some will be guides, but have no feete to goe;
Some deafe, yet ears; some dumbe, yet tongues will bee;
  Some will bee seasoning salt, yet drown'd in gall:
  Dumbe, deafe, blinde, lame, and maime; yet fishers all,
Fit for no other use but 'store an Hospitall.

25

Mean time the Fisher, which by Tibers bankes
Rul'd leasser boates, casts to enlarge his See:
His ship (even then too great) with stollen plankes
Length'ning, he makes a monstrous Argosie;
And stretches wide the sides with out-growne flankes:
Peter, and Paul his badge, this' sword, that's key
  His feyned armes: with these he much prevailes,
  To him each fisher boy his bonnet veyles,
And as the Lord of seas adores with strooken sayles:

24.2 losel: scoundrel.

25.1 Fisher: the pope.

25.6 sword: "the sword of the Spirit, which is the word of God" (Eph. 6:17). For Peter's key see 16.5.

25.8 veyles: removes (?) This meaning is not recorded in NED.

26

Nor could all Seas fill up his empty mawe;
For earth he thirsts; the earth invades, subdues:
And now all earthly Gods with servile awe
Are highly grac't to kisse his holy shooes:
Augustus selfe stoops to his soveraigne lawe,
And at his stirrop close to lacky sues:
    Then heavens scepter claymes, then hell and all.
    Strange turne of chaunges! To be lowe, and thrall
Brings honour, honour strength, strength pride, and pride a fall.

27

Upon the ruines of those marble towres,
Founded, and rays'd with skill, and great expence
Of auncient Kings, great Lords, and Emperours,
He built his Babel up to heav'n, and thence
Thunders through all the world: On sandy floores
The ground-worke slightly floats, the walls to sense
    Seeme Porphyr faire, which blood of Martyrs taints;
    But was base lome, mixed with strawy Saints;
Daub'd with untemper'd lime, which glistering tinfoyle paints.

28

The Portall seemes (farre off) a lightsome frame;
But all the lights are false; the Chrystall glasse
Pack't with a thick mud-wall beates off the flame,
Nor suffers any sparke of day to passe.
There sits dull Ignoraunce, a loathly dame,
Two eyes, both blind; two eares, both deafe shee has;
    Yet quick of sense they to her selfe appeare.
    Oh who can hope to cure that eye, and eare,
Which being blind, & deafe, bragges best to see, & heare!

29

Close by her children two; of each side one,
A Sonne and Daughter sate: he Errour hight,
A crooked swaine; shee Superstition.

27.7 Porphyr: a white stone with red or purple veins in it. The Greek root means purple. taints: colors.

Him Hate of Truth begot in Stygian night;
Her Feare, and falsely call'd, Devotion;
And as in birth, so joyn'd in loose delight,
They store the world with an incestuous breed,
A bastard, foule, deform'd, but num'rous seed;
All monsters; who in parts, or growth, want, or exceed.

30

Her Sonne invites the wandring passengers
And calls aloud, Ho, every simple swaine
Come, buy crownes, scepters, miters, crosiers,
Buy thefts, blood, incests, oaths, buy all for gaine:
With gold buy out all Purgatory feares,
With gold buy heaven and heavens Soveraigne.
Then through an hundred Labyrinths he leads
The silly soule, and with vaine shadowes feeds:
The poore stray wretch admires old formes, and anticke deeds.

31

The daughter leads him forth in Pilgrims guise
To visite holy shrines, the Lady Hales;
The Doves, and Gabriels plumes in purple dyes,
Cartloads of Crosse, and straunge-engendring nayles:
The simple man adores the sottish lyes:
Then with false wonders his frayle sense assayles,
Saint *Fulbert nurst with milke of Virgine pure,
Saint Dominicks* bookes like fish in rivers dure;
Saint Francis birds, & wounds; & Bellarmines breeches cure.

** Saint Fulbert sucked the brests of the blessed Virgine, so saith Baronius,* *Annal.* 1028. n. 5.

** Dominicks books lay dry a whole night in a river. Antoninus Sum.*

30.1 passengers: passers-by.

31.2 Hales: Chaucer's Pardonner swears "By the blood of Crist that is in Hayles" — at an abbey in Gloucestershire. Anyone in a state of mortal sin supposedly could not see the blood.

31.7 gloss: Baronius : Baranius 1627. The reference is to Cardinal Cæsar Baronius, *Annales Ecclesiastici*, epitomes of which were published in 1614, 1618, and 1623.

31.8 gloss: The reference is to Antoninus' *Chronicorum Opus*, available most recently to Fletcher in an edition of 1586.

31.9 St. Francis traditionally preached to the birds and suffered from the stigmata of Christ. Cardinal Bellarmine (1542–1621) was one of the most vigorous Jesuit controversialists.

32

The Hall is vastly built for large dispence;
Where freely ushers loosest Libertie,
The waiters Lusts, the Caterer vaine Expence,
Steward of th' house wide panched Gluttonie;
Bed-makers ease, sloth, and soft wanton sense;
High Chamberlaine perfumed Lecherie:
    The outward Courtes with Wrong, and Bribery stink,
    That holy *Catherine smelt the loathsome sink
From French Avinions towers, to Tuscan Siens brinke.

** This is affirmed by Antonine hist.*

33

The stately presence Princely spoyles adorne
Of vassal Kings: there sits the man of pride,
And with his dusty *feete (oh hellish scorne!)
Crownes and uncrownes men by God deifi'de.
*He is that seeing, and proud-speaking Horne,
Who stiles himselfe Spouse of that glorious Bride;
    The *Churches Head, and Monarch; Jesses rod;
    The precious corner stone; supreame Vice-God;
The Light, the Sunne, the Rock, the Christ, the Lord our God.

** Celestine* 3 *thus delt with Henry* 6 *Emperour.*

** Dan.* 7. 8.

** All these titles & many more are given to the Popes by their vassals, and by them accepted and justified.*

34

There stand the Pillars of the Papacie;
Stout Champions of Romes Almighty power,

32.4 panched: paunched.

32.8 gloss: again referring to the *Chronicorum.*

32.9 Avinions: Avignon's.

33.3 gloss: Celestine III, pope from 1191 to 1198. When he crowned Henry VI Roman Emperor, Philippe de Mornay reports that, "sitting down in his pontificall Chaire, [he] holdeth the imperiall Crowne betweene his feet, and the Emperour bowing downe his head, and likewise the Empresse, receive it from his feet." *The Mysterie of Iniquitie,* Englished by Samson Lennard (London, 1612), p. 337.

33.5 gloss: Amidst the horns which Daniel has already described (see above, stanzas 18–19), a little horn appears "speaking great things."

33.6 Spouse . . . Bride: Christianity has long interpreted the love songs of the Song of Songs as referring to Christ and his bride, the church.

33.7 Jesses rod: See Rom. 15:12 which interprets Isa. 11:10 as prophecying the Christian church.

Carv'd out as patterns to that holy See.
First was that Boniface, the cheifest flower — *Boniface* 3.
In Papal Paradise, who climb'd to bee
First universall Bishop-governour.
Then he, that would be Pope and Emperour too: — *Boniface* 8.
And close by them, that monstrous Prelate, who
Trampled great Fredericks necke with his proud durty shooe. — *Alexander* 3.

35

Above the rest stood famous Hildebrand,
The Father of our Popish chastitie:
Who forc't brave Henry with bare feet to stand,
And beg for entrance, and his amitie.
Finely the workman with his Dedal hand
Had drawne disdaine sparkling in's fiery eie,
His face all red with shame and angry scorne,
To heare his sonne lament, his Empresse mourne,
While this chast Father makes poore Asto weare the horn.

34.4 gloss: pope in 605 who obtained from the emperor Phocas recognition that the pope headed the Church at Rome (in opposition to the Patriarch of Constantinople). See Mornay, p. 117.

34.7 gloss: pope from 1294 to 1303 who asserted his authority in temporal as well as spiritual matters. Mornay reports that he appeared one day "in his Pontificalibus, bestowing upon [everyone] his Apostolicall benediction; but the day after he presented himselfe in imperiall habit," p. 429. He later published a decretal "That both the materiall and spirituall sword, was in the Churches power."

34.9 gloss: pope from 1159 to 1181. He excommunicated Frederick Barbarossa, Roman Emperor who opposed him but was forced to do obeisance: "the Emperour being prostrate before him, Alexander [put] his foot upon his necke," Mornay, p. 326.

35.1 Hildebrand: Gregory VII, pope from 1072 to 1085. His opposition to the emperor Henry IV came to a head at a council called in Worms when Henry tried to depose him but was in turn excommunicated; in time he forced Henry to do the penance described. See Mornay, p. 253, who adds that it was "in the coldest time of Winter." Gregory also enforced celibacy among the clergy; Mornay, pp. 248–49.

35.5 Dedal: cunningly fashioning.

35.9 Mornay reports that the pope cuckolded Azo, marquesse of Este, who had married Mathilda, an Italian countess (p. 257).

36

Alexand. 6.

There stood Lucretia's Father, Husband, Brother,
The monster Borgia, cas'd in lust and blood:

Paul 3.

And he that fil'd his child, and quell'd his Mother:

Pius 4.

He, that was borne, liv'd, died in lust: there stood

John 8, *or rather Joan.*

The female Pope, Romes shame, and many other
Kindled for hell on earth in lustfull flood.
These Saints accurse the married chastity,
A wife defiles: oh deep hypocrisy!
Yet use, reward, and praise twice burning Sodomy.

37

And with those fleshly stood the spirituall Bauds:
They choose, and frame a goodly stone, or stock,
Then trimme their puppet god with costly gauds.
Ah who can tell which is the verier block,
His god, or he? Such lyes are godly frauds.
Some whips adore, the crosse, the seamelesse frock,
Nayles, speare, reed, spunge; some needing no partaker,
Nor using any help, but of the Baker,
(Oh more then power divine!) make, chew, and voide their Maker.

36.1 gloss: Rodrigo Borgia, pope from 1492 to 1503. Mornay reports that one of Rodrigo's sons killed another for his illicit love of his sister Lucretia, and "That in the love of Lucretia not onely the two brethren did concurre, but the father also" (p. 612).

36.3 gloss: pope from 1534 to 1549 who approved the establishment of the Jesuit society (1540) and the opening of the Council of Trent. filed: defiled.

36.4 gloss: pope from 1559 to 1565 under whom the Council of Trent was concluded.

36.5 gloss: mythical female pope, c. 854. Mornay, pp. 165–66, cites the church historian Platina as identifying her with John VIII, who actually was pope from 872 to 882.

36.8 defiles: because of the requirements of chastity in the priesthood.

37.3 puppet god: religious statues, anathema to Protestants.

37.6 whips: Flagellation has occasionally been practiced by Christian extremists.

37.7 Nayles . . . spunge: articles all associated with the Crucifixion.

37.8 Baker, : Baker; 1627.

37.9 referring to the Catholic dogma of transubstantiation.

38

By these were plac'd those dire incarnate fiends
Studied in that black art, and that alone:
One leagu'd himselfe to hell t' effect his ends,
In Romes Bee-hive to live the Soveraigne Drone:
Another musters all the Divels his friends
To pull his Lord out of his rightfull throne;
And worse then any fiend, with magicke rite
He casts into the fire the Lord of light:
So sacrific'd his God to an infernall spright.

Silvester 2 and many others.

Gregory 7.

39

But who can summe this holy rablement?
This prais'd the Gospel as a gainfull tale;
That questions heav'ns reward, hels punishment;
This for his dish in spight of God doth call;
That heaven taints, infects the Sacrament;

Leo 10.

John 23, and 24.

Henry Emperour was poysoned in the Sacrament given by a Preist, set on by Robert King of Naples, and Robert by Clement 5. Avent.

38.3 gloss: pope from 999 to 1003. Mornay (p. 226) reports "that his studies extended to Nigromancie it selfe, by helpe whereof he made his way to the Popedome."

38.5 gloss: See stanza 35 above. "As touching his Magick, all writers display him to be skillfull in this art" (Mornay, p. 259); "even in the Popedome, [he] was the chiefe instrument and companion of all their [the devils'] wickednesse" (p. 260). His "Lord" in the next line was Henry; "he consulted the Sacrament it selfe, as it had beene an Oracle, against the Emperour; and the Cardinals withstanding him, cast it into the fire" (p. 260).

39.2 gloss: John de Medici, pope from 1513 to 1521, during whose time the Protestant movement had its beginning. Mornay reports him to have said to Cardinal Bembo, his secretary, "It is sufficiently knowne to all ages, how greatly that fable of Christ hath profited us and ours" (p. 635).

39.3 gloss: Pisan anti-pope from 1410 to 1415, deposed by the Council of Constance, which charged him among other things (Mornay, pp. 521–22) with affirming that "the Soule of man dyeth and is extinct together with the humane bodie." Mornay interprets John XXIV (p. 535) as "*alias*, the three and twentieth."

39.5 gloss: Clement V, pope from 1305 to 1314, who moved the Papal Court to Avignon, beginning its "Babylonian captivity." When Henry of Luxemburg went to Rome to be crowned emperor, Mornay reports that "a few days after[ward] he was poysoned, whereof he died." The poison "was administred to him, by one *Bernard* a Dominican, who was *Henries* confessor, in the Hoast," p. 438; he then traces the crime loosely back through Robert of Naples to Clement.

The bread, and seale of life perpetuall:
    And pois'ning Christ, poisons with him his King;
    He life and death in one draught swallowing,
Wash't off his sinfull staines in that Lifes deadly spring.

CANTO IIII.

1

Looke as a goodly Pile, whose ayrie towres
Thrust up their golden heads to th' azure sky,
But loosely leanes his weight on sandy floores:
Such is that mans estate, who looking high,
Grounds not his sinking trust on heavenly powres:
His tott'ring hopes no sooner live, but die.
    How can that frame be right, whose ground is wrong?
    Who stands upon his owne legges, stands not long:
For man's most weake in strength, in weaknes only strong.

2

Thus Rome (when drench't in seas of Martyrs blood,
And tost with stormes, yet rooted fast on Christ)
Deep grounded on that rocke most firmely stood:
But when, with pride and worldly pompe entic't
She sought her selfe, sunke in her rising flood.
So when of late that boasted Jesuite Priest *Drury.*
    Gath'red his flocke, and now the house 'gan swell,
    And every eare drew in the sugred spell,
Their house, and rising hopes, swole, burst, and head-long fell.

3

Through this knowne entraunce past that subtile Spright:
There thundring Paul retir'd he sullen found,

2.1 Like all other Protestants, Fletcher endorses the primitive church at Rome.

2.6 gloss: Robert Drury (1587–1623), Jesuit priest who with nearly a hundred others was killed by the collapse of the building in Blackfriars where he was conducting a religious service.

3.1 Spright: Equivocus.

3.2 Paul: Paul V, pope from 1605 to 1621. From 1605 to 1607 he was involved in controversy and nearly at war with Venice. At issue was the pope's

Boyling his restles heart in envious spight,
Gall'd with old sores, and new Venetian wound:
His thoughtfull head lean'd downe his carefull weight
Upon a chayre, farre fetch't from Dodon ground.
Thence without feare of errour they define;
For there the Spirit his presence must confine.
Oh more then God, who makes his bread, blocks, chayres divine!

4

But that true Spirit's want this false supplies:
He folds that Scorners chayre in's cloudy wings,
And paints, and gilds it fayre with colour'd lies.
But now from's damned head a snake he flings
Burning in flames: the subtile Serpent flies
To th' aymed marke, and fills with firy stings
The Papal brest; his holy bosome swells
With pride & rage; straight cals for books, lights, bells,
Frets, fumes, fomes, curses, chafes, and threatens thousand hells.

5

So when cold waters wall'd with brasen wreath
Are sieg'd with crackling flames, their common foe,
The angry seas 'gin fome and hotly breath,
Then swell, rise, rave, and still more furious grow:
Nor can be held; but, prest with fires beneath,

temporal power and the Venetian expulsion of all Jesuits. Fletcher's authority seems to be Paolo Sarpi, *Interdicti Veneti Historia* (see gloss below at 14. 9), translated from Italian into Latin by William Bedell (Cambridge, 1626) and into English as *History of the Quarrels of Pope Paul V, with the State of Venice* by Christopher Potter (London, 1626). Sarpi says, "more Monitories and Citations were thundered out by him, during the five years of his office, than had beene in any fiftie yeares before," *History*, p. 2. For a full treatment of Sarpi's importance in seventeenth-century England see John Lievsay, *Venetian Phœnix: Paolo Sarpi* (Lawrence, Kans.: University Press of Kansas, 1973).

3.6 Dodon: Dodona, situation of the ancient oracle of Zeus.

3.7 The doctrine of papal infallibility.

3.9 Sanctification of various religious articles has been widely practiced.

4.8 Cursing him by the formula, "with bell, book, and candle."

5.1-6 That is, the pot begins to boil.

Tossing their waves breake out, and all o'reflow.
In hast he calls a Senate; thither runne
The blood-red Cardinalls, Friers white, and dunne,
And with, and 'bove the rest Ignatius' eldest sonne.

6

The conclave fills apace; now all are met:
Each knowes his stall, and takes his wonted place.
So downe they sit; and now they all are set:
Æquivocus, with his bat-wing'd embrace,
Clucks, broods his chickens, while they sadly treat;
Their eyes all met in th' holy Fathers face,
There first foresee his speech: a dusky cloud
Hangs on his brow; his eyes fierce lightnings shroud,
At length they heare it breake, and rore in thunders loud.

7

Thrice-glorious founders of Romes Hierarchy,
Whose towring thoughts and more then manly spirit
Beyond the spheares have ray'sd our Monarchy,
Nor earth, nor heaven can pay your boundlesse merit.
Oh let your soules above the loftiest sky
Your purchast crownes and scepters just inherit.
Here in your pourtraits may you ever live;
While wee (poore shadowes of your pictures) grieve
Our sloth should basely spend, what your high vertues give.

8

I blush to view you: see Priest-kings, oh see
Their lively shades our life as shades upbrayd:
See how his face sparkles in majesty,
Who that first stone of our vast Kingdome layd, *Boniface* 3.
Spous'd the whole Church, and made the world his See:
With what brave anger is his cheek arrayd,
Who Peters useles keyes in Tiber flings?

5.9 sonne: Cardinal Bellarmine.

8.4 See note to 3. 34. 4 gloss.

How high he lookes that treades on Basilisks stings,
And findes for's lordly foot no stool, but necks of Kings?

Julius 2.
Alexander 3.

9

See where among the rest great Clement stands,
Lifting his head 'bove heaven, who Angels cites
And bids them lowly stoop at his commands,
And waft tir'd soules to those eternall lights.
But what they wonne, we loose; Townes, Cities, Lands
Revolt: our Buls each petty Lamb-kin slights:
We storme and thunder death, they laugh, and gren.
How have we lost our selves? Oh where, and when
Were we thus chang'd? Sure they were more, we lesse then men.

Clement 5.

10

Can that uncloist'red Frier with those light armes,
That sword and shield, which we mocke, scorne, defie,
Wake all the sleeping world with loud alarmes,
And ever conqu'ring live, then quiet die?
And live, and dead load us with losse and harmes?
A single simple Frier? And oh shall I,
Christ, God on earth, so many losses beare
With peace and patience? Who then Rome will feare?
Who then to th' Romane God his heart and hands will reare?

Luther.

11

Belgia is wholy lost, and rather chuses
Warres, flame, and blood, then peace with Rome & Spain.
Fraunce halfe fal'ne off, all truce and parl' refuses:

8.8 gloss: *Julius 2* : *Julius 8* 1627. Julius II, pope from 1503 to 1513; Mornay, p. 630, recounts his casting "Peters keyes" into the Tiber.

8.9 See note to 3. 34. 9 gloss.

9.1 See note to 3. 39. 5 gloss.

9.7 gren: grin.

11.1 Catholic Spain had tried for a generation to subdue the Protestant Low Countries, which were tacitly aided by England and France. A peace agreement to last for twelve years was signed in 1609.

11.3 In April 1598 Henry IV had signed the Edict of Nantes, which ratified the privileges of Calvinists and promised liberty of conscience.

Edicts, massacres, leagues, threats, all are vaine.
Their King with painted shew our hope abuses,
And beares our forced yoke with scorne, and paine.
So Lyons (bound) stoop, crouch with fained awe,
But (loos'd) their Keeper seize with Lordly paw,
Drag, rend, & with his flesh full gorge their greedy maw.

12

** Dandalus Duke of Venice was compeld by the Pope Clement the* 5. *to crouch under the table chained like a dogge, before he could obtain peace for the Venetians.*

See where proud Dandal chain'd, some scraps expecting,
Lies cur-like under boord, and begs releife:
But now their Corno our three crownes neglecting
Censures our sacred Censures, scornes our Briefe.
Our English plots some adverse power detecting
Doubles their joy, trebles our shame and griefe.
What have we reap't of all our paines and seed?
Seditions, murthers, poysons, treasons breed
To us more spight and scorne; in them more hate & heed.

13

That fleet, which with the Moone for vastnesse stood,
Which all the earth, which all the sea admires,
Amaz'd to see on waves a Moone of wood,
Blest by our hands, frighted with suddaine fires
And Panicke feares, sunke in the gaping flood:
Some split, some yeeld, scarce one (that torne) retires.
That long wish't houre, when Cynthia set i' th' maine,
What hath it brought at length, what change, what gain?
One bright star fell, the Sun is ris'ne, and all his traine.

12.1 gloss: The story is told by Mornay, p. 441.

12.3 Corno: i.e., the Venetian leader. Perhaps Corno represents *Coron(a)*, "crown."

12.4 Briefe: The war was carried on mostly by written communications, "breves."

12.5 the contemporary plot by Guy Fawkes in November 1605.

13.1 fleet: the Armada. Its comparison with the moon has been discussed by Leslie Hotson, *Shakespeare's Sonnets Dated* (New York: R. Hart-Davis, 1949), pp. 4ff.

14

But Fates decree our fall: high swelling *names
Of Monarch, Spouse, Christ, God, breed much debate,
And heape disdaine, hate, envy, thousand blames:
And shall I yeeld to envy, feare their hate,
Lay downe my titles, quit my justest claimes?
Shall I, earths God, yeeld to uncertaine fate?
Sure I were best with cap in hand to pray
My sheepe be rul'd: I scorne that begging way;
*I will, I must command; they must, they shall obay.

** The Card. Giure made a motion in the holy office concerning the moderating the Popes titles. But the Pope would give no way to it: as beeing no greater then the authority of Peters successour did require.*

** Paul* 5. *in all his conferences with the Venetians had that continually in his mouth I must be obeyed.* Hist. Inter. Ven. *It was the saying of Paul* 5 *that he was purposely set to maintaine the churches authoritie, and that hee would account it a part of his happines to dye for it Hist. Interd. Ven.*

15

Shall I, the worlds bright Sunne, heavens Oracle,
The onely tongue of Gods owne mouth, shall I,
Of men, of faith the Judge infallible,
The rule of good, bad, wrong, and equitie,
Shall I, Almighty, Rock invincible,
Stoop to my servants, beg authoritie?
Rome is the worlds, I Romes Head: it shall raigne:
Which to effect, I live, rule, this to gaine
Is here my heaven; to loose is hells tormenting paine.

16

So said, and ceas'd: while all the Priestly Round
In sullen greife, and stupide silence sat:
This bit his lip, that nayl'd his eye to th' ground,
Some cloud their flaming eyes with scarlet hat,
Some gnash't their spightfull teeth, some lowr'd, and frown'd:

14.1 gloss: At the Council of Constance (1414–18) Cardinal Jean Gerson had maintained the superiority of the Council to the Pope; he also wrote *De excommunicationis valore* which Sarpi employed to support his argument for Venetian as against Papal authority in 1607. See his *Apology . . . unto the Exceptions and Objections of Cardinall Bellarmine, against certaine Treatises and Resolutions of John Gerson* (London, 1607).

14.9 gloss: Cf. Sarpi, *History*: "if any one did reply against him [Paul V] with reason, or contradict his discourses upon this subject, his ordinary answer was (as if it had been a forme of speech or a lesson given him) here I am *Pope*, and I will be obeyed," p. 5. Later Paul tells the Venetians that he "had beene placed in that Chaire for to sustaine the Jurisdiction *Ecclesiasticall*, in defence whereof hee would esteem himselfe happy to spill his bloud," p. 22.

15.9 loose: lose.

Till (greife and care driven out by spight and hate)
  Soft murmurs first gan creep along the croud:
  At length they storm'd, and chaf't, & thundred loud,
And all sad vengeance swore, and all dire mischeife vow'd.

17

So when a sable cloud with swelling sayle
Comes swimming through calme skies, the silent ayre
(While fierce winds sleepe in Æol's rocky jayle)
With spangled beames embroydred, glitters faire:
But soone 'gins lowre and grone; straight clatt'ring hayle
Fills all with noyse: Light hides his golden hayre;
  Earth with untimely winter's silvered.
  Then Loiol's eldest Sonne lifts up his head,
Whom all with great applause, and silence ushered.

18

Pope Innocent the 3 dreamed that the Lateran church at Rome was falling, but that Saint Dominick setting to his shoulders under-propt it, wherupon he confirmed his order.

Most holy Father, Priests, Kings Soveraigne,
Who equal'st th' highest, makest lesser Gods,
Though Dominick, and Loiola now sustaine
The Lateran Church, with age it stoopes, and noddes:
Nor have we cause to rest, or time to plaine:
Rebellious earth (with heaven it selfe to oddes)
  Conspires to ruine our high envi'de state:
  Yet may wee by those artes prolong our date,
Whereby wee stand; and if not chaunge, yet stay our fate.

19

When captaines strive a fort or towne to winne,
They lay their batt'ry to the weakest side;
Not where the wall, and guard stands thicke, but thinne:
So that wise Serpent his assault appli'de,

17.3 Æol's rocky jayle: the Cave of the Winds.

17.8 Sonne: Supporting Paul V, Bellarmine wrote three rejoinders against the Venetians.

18.1 gloss: Mornay tells the story about Innocent, pope from 1198 to 1216, on p. 355.

18.5 plaine: complain.

And with the weaker vessell would beginne:
He first the woman with distrust and pride,
    Then shee the man subdues with flatt'ring lies;
    So in one battaile gets two victories:
Our foe will teach us fight, our fall will teach us rise.

20

Our Cheife who every slight and engine knowes, *Bellarmine.*
While on th' old troupes he spent his restles paines,
With equall armes assaulting equall foes,
What hath he got, or wee? What fruite, what gaines
Ensu'de? we beare the losse, and he the blowes:
And while each part their wit, and learning straines,
    The breach repaires, and (foil'd) new force assumes:
    Their hard encounters, and hot angry fumes
Strike out the sparkling fire, which lights them, us consumes.

21

In stead of heavy armes hence use we slight:
Trade we with those, which train'd in ignorance
Have small acquaintance with that heavenly light;
Those who disgrac't by some misgovernance
(Their owne, or others) swell with griefe or spight.
But nothing more our Kingdome must advance,
    Or further our designes, then to comply
    With that weake sexe, and by fine forgerie
To worme in womens hearts, chiefly the rich and high.

22

Nor let the stronger scorne these weaker powres;
The labour's lesse with them, the harvest more:
They easier yeeld, and win; so fewer houres
Are spent: for women sooner drinke our lore,
Men sooner sippe it from their lippes, then ours:
Sweetly they learne, and sweetly teach: with store
    Of teares, smiles, kisses, and ten thousand arts
    They lay close batt'ry to mens frayler parts:
So finely steale themselves, and us into their hearts.

19.5 weaker vessell: Eve.

23

That strongest Champion, who with naked hands
A Lyon tore, who all unarm'd and bound
Heap't mounts of armed foes on bloody sands;
By womans art, without or force or wound
Subdu'de, now in a mill blind grinding stands.
That Sunne of wisedome, which the Preacher crown'd
    Great King of arts, bewitch't with womens smiles,
    Fell deepe in seas of folly by their wiles.
Wit, strength, and grace it selfe yeeld to their flatt'ring guiles.

24

This be our skirmish: for the maine, release
The Spanish forces, free strong Belgia
From feare of warre, let armes and armies cease.
What got our Alva, John of Austria?
Our Captaine, Guile; our weapons ease, and peace:
These more prevaile then Parma, Spinola.
    The Dutch shall yeeld us armes, and men; there dwell
    Arminians, who from heaven halfe way fell:
A doubtfull sect, which hang 'tween truth, lies, heaven and hell.

25

These Epicens have sowne their subtile brayne
With thorny difference, and neat illusion:
Proud, fierce, the adverse part they much disdaine.

23.1 Champion: Samson.

23.6 Sunne of wisedome: Solomon; the Preacher is the author of Ecclesiastes.

24.4 got: achieved. The Spanish Duke of Alva was governor of the Netherlands and enforced extremely oppressive measures there. He was followed by Don John of Austria. Neither was effective in stopping the Dutch movement for independence.

24.6 The Duke of Parma, Alessandro Farnese, nephew of John of Austria, succeeded him as governor of the Netherlands. Ambrogio Spinola, an Italian general, led the Spanish forces there prior to the peace of 1609.

24.8 Arminians: dissenters from Calvinism who remonstrated against it and were condemned in 1619 by the Synod of Dort. Fletcher's point is that religious dissention in the Netherlands has achieved more for Catholicism than the Spanish conquest did.

25.1 Epicens: those having the characteristics of either sex.

These must be handled soft with fine collusion,
For Calvins hate to side with Rome and Spaine,
To worke their owne, and their owne-homes confusion.
    And by large summes, more hopes, wee must bring in
    Wise Barnevelt to lay our plotted gin:
So where the Lyon fayles, the Fox shall eas'ly win.

26

The flowres of Fraunce, those faire delicious flowres,
Which late are imp't in stemme of proud Navar,
With ease wee may transferre to Castile bowres.
Feare not that sleeping Lyon: this I dare,
And will make good spight of all envious powres,
When that great bough most threats the neighb'ring ayre,
    Then shall he fall: when now his thoughts worke high,
    And in their pitch their towring projects fly,
Then shall he stoop; his hopes shall droop, and drop, & dy.

27

Wee have not yet forgot the shamefull day,
When forc't from Fraunce and our new holds to fly
(Hooted, and chac't as owles) we ran away.
That Pillar of our lasting infamy
Though raz'd, yet in our minds doth freshly stay.
Hence love wee that great King so heartily,

25.8 Barnevelt: John Oldenbarnevelt, Dutch leader who supported the Arminians. He was executed for alleged treason in 1619.

26.1 flowres of Fraunce: fleurs de lis.

26.2 imp't: grafted. Navar: Henry IV, followed by his minor son Louis XIII in 1610.

26.3 Castile: Louis' mother, Marie de Medici, ruled as regent; she soon moved to a rapprochement with Spain.

26.6-7 Henry was moving to war against Rudolph II of Austria when he was assassinated by Ravaillac, a demented Catholic.

26.7 thoughts : thonghts 1627.

26.8 projects : ptojects 1627.

27.1 Perhaps with reference to the mission of Bellarmine to Paris in 1589 after the murder of Henry III. The capital city was besieged while he was there by the Protestant forces of Henry IV.

27.6 King: an ironic reference to Henry IV.

That but his heart nought can our hearts content:
His bleeding heart from crazy body rent,
Shrin'd in bright gold shall stand our Jesuite monument.

28

This be our taske: the aged truncke wee'l lop,
And force the sprigges forget their former kind:
Wee'l graft the tender twigges on Spanish top,
And with fast knots Fraunce unto Spaine wee'l bind,
With crosse, and double knotts: wee'l still, and drop
The Romane sap into their empty mind:
Wee'l hold their heart, wee'l porter at their eare,
The head, the feet, the hands wee'l wholy steare:
That at our nod the head the heart it selfe shall teare.

29

All this a Prologue to our Tragedy:
My head's in travaile of an hideous
And fearfull birth; such as may fright the sky,
Turne back the Sun: helpe, helpe Ignatius.
And in this act proove thy new Deity.
I have a plot worthy of Rome and us,
Which with amazement heaven, and earth shall fill:
Nor care I whether right, wrong, good, or ill:
Church-profit is our law, our onely rule thy will.

30

That blessed Isle, so often curst in vaine,
Triumphing in our losse and idle spight,
Of force shall shortly stoop to Rome and Spayne:
I'le take a way ne're knowne to man or spright.
To kill a King is stale, and I disdaine:
That fits a Secular, not a Jesuite.
Kings, Nobles, Clergy, Commons high and low,

28.2 sprigges: Marie married her son Louis to Anne of Austria and her daughter Elizabeth to the son of Phillip III of Spain.

28.5 double knotts: two marriage ceremonies, one held in each country. still: distill.

29.5 new Deity: Loyola was canonized in 1622.

30.7 the objects of the Gunpowder Plot.

The Flowre of England in one houre I'le mow,
And head all th' Isle with one unseen, unfenced blow.

31

A goodly frame, rays'd high with carved stones,
Leaning his lofty head on marble stands
Close by that Temple, where the honour'd bones
Of Britaine Kings and many Princely Grands
Adorned rest with golden scutcheons:
Garnish't with curious worke of Dedal hands.
Low at his base the swelling Thamis falls,
And sliding downe along those stately halls,
Doth that chiefe Citie wash, and fence with liquid walls.

32

Here all the States in full assembly meet,
And every order rank't in fit array,
Cloth'd with rich robes fill up the crowded street.
Next 'fore the King his Heier leades the way,
Glitt'ring with gemmes, and royall Coronet:
So golden Phosphor ushers in the day.
And all the while the trumpets triumphs sound,
And all the while the peoples votes resound:
Their shoutes and tramplings shake the ayre and dauncing ground.

33

There in Astrea's ballaunce doe they weigh
The right and wrong, reward and punishment;
And rigour with soft equitie allay,
Curbe lawles lust, and stablish government;
There Rome it selfe, and us they dare affray
With bloody lawes, and threatnings violent:

31.1 frame: the Houses of Parliament.
31.3 Temple: Westminster Abbey.
32.4 Heier: heir, Prince Henry.
32.6 Phosphor: the morning star.
33.1 Astrea: goddess of justice.
33.3 rigour: i.e., common law.

** The printed lies concerning the torments of their Romane Martyrs which I sawe in the study of that learned Knight Sir* Thomas Hutchinson *priviledged by the Pope are for their monstrous impudency incredible.*

Hence all our suff'rings, *torments exquisite,
Varied in thousand formes, appli'de to fright
The harmeles yet (alas!) and spotles Jesuite.

34

But Cellars large, and savernes vaulted deep
With bending arches borne, and columnes strong
Under that stately building slyly creep:
Here Bacchus lyes, conceal'd from Juno's wrong,
Whom those cold vaults from hot-breath'd ayers keep.
In place of these wee'l other barrels throng,
Stuf't with those firy sands, and black dry mould,
Which from blue Phlegetons shores that Frier bold
Stole with dire hand, and yet hells force and colour hold.

35

And when with numbers just the house gins swell,
And every state hath fill'd his station,
When now the King mounted on lofty sell,
With honyed speech and comb'd oration
Charm's every eare, midst of that sugred spell
I'le teare the walls, blow up the nation,
Bullet to heaven the stones with thunders loud,
Equall to th' earth the courts, and turrets proud,
And fire the shaking towne, & quench't with royall blood.

36

Oh how my dauncing heart leapes in my breast
But to fore-thinke that noble tragedie!
I thirst, I long for that blood-royall feast.
See where their lawes, see, Holy Father, see
Where lawes and Makers, and above the rest
Kings marshal'd in due place through th' ayer flee:

33.7 gloss: *are for their* : *for their are* 1627. Sir Thomas (1589–1643) was a member of the Long Parliament.

34.4 Bacchus: i.e., wine casks. Jupiter had begotten him by Semele; the jealous Juno tried to kill him, but Jupiter kept him carefully hidden.

34.8 Frier: Roger Bacon, fabled as inventor of gunpowder.

35.3 sell: seat.

There goes the heart, there th' head, there sindged bones:
Heark, Father, heark; hear'st not those musicke tones?
Some rore, some houle, some shriek; earth, hell, and ayer grones.

37

Thus sang, and downe he sat; while all the Quire
Attune their ecchoing voices to his layes:
Some Jesuite Pietie, and zealous fire,
Some his deepe reaching wit, and judgement praise:
And all the plot commend, and all admire,
But most great Paul himselfe: a while he stayes,
Then suddaine rising, with embraces long
He hugges his sonne, while yet the passion strong
Wanting due vent, makes teares his words, and eyes his tongue.

38

At length the heart too full his joy dispers't,
Which mounting on the tongue, thus overflowes:
You Romane Saints, to whose deare reliques herst
In golden shrines every true Catholike bowes,
And thou of lesser gods the best and first,
Great English Thomas, ushering our vowes, *Thomas Becket.*
Who giv'st heaven by thy blood, and precious merit,
I see we still your love and helpe inherit,
Who in our need rayse up so true a Romane spirit.

39

What meed (my Sonne) can Christ, or he above,
Or I beneath, to thy deservings weigh?
What heaven can recompence thy pious love?
In Lateran Church thy statue crown'd with bay
In gold shall mounted stand next highest Jove:
To thee wee'l humbly kneele, and vowe, and pray:
Haile Romes great Patron, ease our restles cares,
Possesse thy heaven, and prosper our affayres,
Even now inure thine eare to our religious prayers.

38.3 herst: entombed.

38.6 gloss: Thomas (1118?–1170), Archbishop of Canterbury who opposed Henry II, supporting instead the authority of the pope. He was not a popular martyr with the Tudors and Stuarts.

40

So up they rose as full of hope, as spight,
And every one his charge with care applies.
Equivocus with heart, and pinions light
Downe posting to th' Infernall shadowes flies;
Fills them with joyes, such joyes as Sonnes of night
Enjoy, such as from sinne and mischiefe rise.
    With all they envy, greive, and inly grone
    To see themselves out-sinn'd: and every one
Wish't he the Jesuit were, and that dire plot his owne.

CANTO V.

1

Looke as a wayward child would something have,
Yet flings away, wralls, spurn's, his Nurse abuses:
So froward man, what most his longings crave,
(Likenes to God) profer'd by God refuses:
But will be rather sinnes base drudge and slave.
The shade by Satan promis'd greed'ly chuses,
    And with it death and hell. Oh wretched state,
    Where not the eyes, but feete direct the gate!
So misse what most we wish, and have what most we hate.

2

Thus will this man of sinne be like to Christ,
A King, yet not in heaven, but earth that raignes;
That murthers, saves not Christians; th' highest Preist,
Yet not to wait his course, (that he disdaines)
But to advaunce aloft his mitred crest;
That Christ himselfe may wait upon his traynes.
    Straunge Priest, oft heaven he sells, but never buyes:
    Straunge Doctor, hating truth, enforcing lyes:
Thus Satan is indeed, and Christ by contraryes.

1.2 wralls: squalls.

2.4 course: turn.

3

And such his Ministers all glist'ring bright
In night and shades, and yet but rotten wood,
And fleshly Devils: such this Jesuite,
Who (Loiol's Ensigne) thirsts for English blood.
He culs choice soules (soules vow'd to th' Prince of night,
And Priest of Rome) sweares them (an English brood,
    But hatch't in Rome for Spaine) close to conceale,
    And execute what he should then reveale:
Binds them to hell in sin, & makes heavens Lord the seale.

4

Now are they met; this armed with a spade,
That with a mattocke, voide of shame and feare:
The earth (their Grandame Earth) they fierce invade,
And all her bowels search, and rent, and teare,
Then by her ruines flesh't, much bolder made,
They ply their worke; and now neere hell, they heare
    Soft voices, murmurs, doubtfull whisperings:
    The fearfull conscience prick't with guilty stings,
A thousand hellish formes into their fancy brings.

5

This like a statue stands; cold fright congeales
His marble limbes; to th' earth another falling,
Creeping behind a barrell softly steales:
A third into an empty hogshead cralling,
Locks up his eyes, drawes in his stragling heeles:
A fourth, in vaine for succour loudly calling,
    Flies through the aire as swift as gliding starre;
    Pale, ghastly, like infernall sprites afarre
Each to his fellow seemes: and so, or worse they are.

6

So when in sleep's soft grave dead senses rest,
An earthly vapour clamb'ring up the braine
Brings in a meagre ghost, whose launched brest

3.2 rotten wood: will-o'-the-wisp.

6.3 launched: pierced.

Showres downe his naked corps a bloody raine:
A dull-blue-burning torch about his crest
He ghastly waves; halfe dead with frightfull paine
    The leaden foot faine would, but cannot fly;
    The gaping mouth faine would, but cannot cry:
And now awake still dreames, nor trusts his open eye:

7

At length those streames of life, which ebbing low
Were all retir'd into the frighted heart,
Backe to their wonted chanels gan to flow:
So peeping out, yet trembling every part,
And list'ning now with better heed, they know
Those next adjoyning roomes hollow'd by art
    To lie for cellerage: which glad they hire,
    And cramme with powder, and unkindled fire:
Slacke aged Time with plaints and praires they daily tire.

8

Slow Time, which every houre grow'st old and young,
Which every minute dy'st, and liv'st againe;
Which mak'st the strong man weak, the weak man strong:
Sad time which fly'st in joy, but creep'st in paine,
Thy steppes uneven are still too short or long:
Devouring Time, who bear'st a fruitfull traine,
    And eat'st what er'e thou bear'st, why dost not flee,
    Why do'st not post to view a Tragedie,
Which never time yet saw, which never time shall see?

9

Among them all none so impatient
Of stay, as firy Faux, whose grisly feature
Adorn'd with colours of hells regiment
(Soot black, and fiery red) betrayd his nature.
His frighted Mother, when her time shee went,
Oft dream't she bore a straunge, & monstrous creature,
    A brand of hell sweltring in fire and smoke,
    Who all, and's Mother's selfe would burne and choke:
So dream't she in her sleep, so found she when she woke.

10

Rome was his Nurse, and Spaine his Tutour; she
With wolvish milk flesh't him in deadly lyes,
In hate of Truth, and stubborn errour: he
Fats him with humane blood, inures his eyes
Dash't braines, torne guts, and trembling hearts to see,
And tun'de his eare with grones and shrieking cryes.
    Thus nurst, bred, growne a Canniball, now prest
    To be the leader of this troup, he blest
His bloody maw with thought of such a royall feast.

11

Meane time the Eye, which needs no light to see,
That wakefull Eye, which never winks or sleepes,
That purest Eye, which hates iniquitie,
That carefull Eye, which safe his Israel keepes,
From which no word, or thought can hidden bee,
Look's from his heaven, and piercing through the deepes,
    With hate, and scorne viewes the dire Jesuite
    Weary his hand, and quintessentiall wit,
To weave himselfe a snare, and dig himselfe a pit.

12

That Mounting Eagle, which beneath his throne
(His Saphire throne) fixed on Chrystall base,
Broadly dispreds his heaven-wide pineon,
On whome, when sinfull earth he strikes with 'maze,
He wide displayes his black pavilion,
And thundring, fires high towres with flashing blaze:
    Darke waters draw their sable curtaines o're him,
    With flaming wings the burning Angels shore him,
The cloudes, & guilty heavens for feare fly fast before him:

11.1 Eye: i.e., of God, an idea frequent in the Old Testament, e.g., Prov. 15:3. Cf. "He that keepeth Israel shall neither slumber nor sleep" (Ps. 121:4), which Fletcher understands as applying to righteous England.

12.1-2 Eagle . . . Saphire throne: Ezekiel's chariot was interpreted as God's throne. It had four eagle faces (Ezek. 1:10).

13

That mounting Eagle forth he suddaine calls,
Fly, winged Herald, to that Citie fly,
Whose towres my love, truth, wisedome builds and walls:
There to the Councell this foule plot descry:
And while thy doubtfull writ their wit appalls,
That great Peace-makers sense Ile open, I
 Will cleere his mind, and plaine those ridling folds.
 So said, so done: no place or time with-holds
His instant course, the towne he thinks, he sees, and holds.

14

There in another shape to that wise Peer
(That wisest Peer) he gives a darksome spell:
He was the states Treasure, and Treasurer,
Spaines feare, but Englands earthly oracle;
He Patron to my Mother Cambridge, where
Thousand sweet Muses, thousand Graces dwell:
 But neither hee, nor humane wit could find
 The riddles sense, till that learn'd royall mind,
Lighted from heaven, soone the knot, and plot untwin'd.

15

And now the fatall Morne approached neare:
The Sunne, and every starre had quench't their light,
Loathing so black a deed: the Articke Beare
Enjoyn'd to stay, trembling at such a sight,
Though drench't in ayrie seas, yet wink't for feare.
But hellish Faux laught at blinde heavens affright.
 What? Such a deed not seen? In vaine (saith he)
 You drowne your lights; if heaven envious be,
I'le bring hell fires for light, that all the world may see.

13.6 Peace-makers: James'.

13.7 plaine: explain.

14.3 Treasurer: Robert Cecil, made Earl of Salisbury in 1605, to whom the Plot was first disclosed by Lord Monteagle, one of the threatened victims. But Cecil was not elevated to Lord Treasurer until 1608.

16

So entring in, reviewes th' infernall mines;
Marshals his casks anew, and ord'ring right
The tragicke Scene, his hellish worke refines:
And now return'd, booted, and drest for flight,
A watchfull Swaine the Miner undermines,
Holds, binds, brings out the Plot to view the light;
    The world amaz'd, hel yawn'd, earth gap't, heaven star'd,
    Rome howl'd to see long hopes so sudden mar'd:
The net was set, the fowle escap't, the fowler snar'd.

17

Oh thou great Shepheard, Earths, Heavens Soveraigne,
Whom we thy pasture-sheep admire, adore;
See all thy flocks prostrate on Britaine plaine,
Pluck't from the slaughter; fill their mouthes with store
Of incens't praise: oh see, see every swaine
'Maz'd with thy workes; much 'maz'd, but ravish't more:
    Powre out their hearts thy glorious name to raise;
    Fire thou our zealous lippes with thankfull laies;
Make this sav'd Isle to burne in love, to smoke in praise.

18

Teach me thy groome, here dull'd in fenny mire,
In these sweet layes, oh teach me beare a part:
Oh thou dread Spirit shed thy heavenly fire,
Thy holy flame into this frozen heart:
Teach thou my creeping Muse to heaven aspire,
Learne my rude brest, learne me that sacred art,
    Which once thou taught'st thy Israels shepheard-King:
    O raise my soft veine to high thundering;
Tune thou my lofty song, thy glory would I sing.

16.5 Swaine: Thomas Knyvett, a magistrate in Westminster, who discovered the gunpowder and arrested Fawkes, who confessed.

17.9 smoke: as an Old Testament altar to God.

18.7 shepheard-King: David as author of psalms.

19

Thou liv'dst before, beyond, without all time;
Art held in none, yet fillest every place:
Ah, how (alas!) how then shall mortall slime
With sinfull eyes view that eternall space,
Or comprehend thy name in measur'd rime?
To see forth-right the eie was set i' th' face,
    Hence, infinite to come I wel descry,
    Past infinite no creature sees with eie:
Onely th' Eternall's selfe measures eternitie.

20

And yet by thee, to thee all live and move;
Thou without place or time giv'st times and places:
The heavens (thy throne) thou liftest all above,
Which folded in their mixt, but pure embraces
Teach us in their conjunctions chastest love,
Next to the Earth the Moone performes her races;
    Then Mercury; beyond, the Phosphor bright:
    These with their friendly heat, and kindly might,
Warme pallid Cynthia's cold, and draine her watry light.

21

Farre thou remoov'st slow Saturn's frosty drythe,
And thaw'st his yce with Mars his flaming ire:
Betwixt them Jove by thy appointment fly'th;
Who part's, and temper's well his Sonne and Sire;
His moist flames dull the edge of Saturnes sithe,
And ayry moisture softens Mars his fire.
    The Heart of heaven midst of heavens bodie rides,
    From whose full sea of light and springing tides
The lesser streames of light fill up their empty sides.

20.7 Phosphor: Venus.

21.1 drythe: dryness.

21.3 Jove: temperate Jupiter as the planet situated between his hot son (Mars) and cold father (Saturn).

21.7 Heart of heaven: the Sun.

22

The Virgin Earth, all in green-silken weed
(Embroyder'd fayre with thousand flowres) arrayd:
Whose wombe untill'd knew yet nor plough, nor seed,
Nor midwifry of man, nor heavens ayd,
Amaz'd to see her num'rous Virgin breed,
Her fruit even fruitfull, yet her selfe a mayd:
  The earth of all the low'st, yet middle lies;
  Nor sinks, though loosely hang'd in liquid skies:
For rising were her fall; and falling were her rise.

23

Next Earth the Sea a testy neighbour raves,
Which casting mounts, and many a churlish hill,
Discharges 'gainst her walles his thundring waves,
Which all the shores with noyse and tumult fill:
But all in vaine; thou beat'st downe all his braves;
When thee he heares commanding, Peace, be still,
  Downe straight he lowly falls, disbands his traynes,
  Sinks in himselfe, and all his mountaines playnes,
Soft peace in all the shores, and quiet stillnes raygnes.

24

Thou mad'st the circling ayre aloft to fly,
And all this Round infold at thy command;
So thinne, it never could be seen with eye,
So grosse, it may be felt with every hand.
Next to the horned Moon and neighbour sky,
The fire thou highest bad'st, but farthest stand.
  Straungely thou temper'st their adverse affection:
  Though still they hate and fight, by thy direction
Their strife maintaines their owne, and all the worlds perfection.

25

For Earth's cold arme cold Winter friendly holds;
But with his dry the others wet defies:

22.1 Earth: Fletcher now moves to the sub-lunar elements, earth, water, air, and fire.

23.6 The command by Jesus is from Mark 4:39.

25 Each of the four qualities, moist cold, dry cold, moist heat, and dry heat, pertains to an element.

The Ayer's warmth detests the Water's colds;
But both a common moisture joyntly ties:
Warme Ayre with mutuall love hot Fire infolds;
As moist, his drythe abhorres: drythe Earth allies
    To Fire, but heats with cold new warres addresse:
    Thus by their peacefull fight, and fighting peace
All creatures grow, and dye, and dying still increase.

26

Above them all thou sit'st, who gav'st all being,
All every where, in all, and over all:
Thou their great Umpire, all their strife agreeing,
Bend'st their stiffe natures to thy soveraigne call:
Thine eye their law: their steppes by overseeing
Thou overrul'st, and keep'st from slipp'ry fall.
    Oh if thy steady hand should not maintaine
    What first it made, all straight would fall againe,
And nothing of this All, save nothing would remaine.

27

Thou bid'st the Sunne piece out the ling'ring day,
Glitt'ring in golden fleece: The lovely Spring
Comes dauncing on; the Primrose strewes her way,
And satten Violet: Lambs wantoning
Bound o're the hillocks in their sportfull play:
The wood-musicians chant and cheerely sing;
    The World seemes new, yet old by youths accruing.
    Ah wretched men, so wretched world pursuing,
Which still growes worse with age, and older by renuing!

28

At thy command th' Earth travailes of her fruit;
The Sunne yeelds longer labour, shorter sleep;
Out-runnes the Lyon in his hot pursuit;
Then of the golden Crab learnes backe to creep:

26.4 their : rheir 1627.

27.4 wantoning : wantoniug 1627.

28.3, 4 Lyon, Crab: in the Zodiac.

Thou Autumne bid'st (drest in straw-yellow suit)
To presse, tunne, hide his grapes in cellars deep:
    Thou cloth'st the Earth with freez in stead of grasse,
    While keen-breath'd winter steeles her furrow'd face,
And vials rivers up, and seas in Chrystall glasse.

29

What, but thy love and thou, which feele no change?
Seas fill, and want: their waters fall, and grow;
The windy aire each houre can wildly range;
Earth lives, and dies; heavens lights can ebbe, and flow:
Thy Spowse her selfe, while yet a Pilgrim strange,
Treading this weary world (like Cynthia's bow)
    Now full of glorious beames, and sparkling light;
    Then soone oppos'd, eclips't with earthly spight
Seemes drown'd in sable clouds, buried in endles night.

30

See, Lord, ah see thy rancorous enemies
Blowne up with envious spight, but more with hate,
Like boisterous windes, and Seas high-working, rise:
So earthly fires, wrapt up in watry night,
With dire approach invade the glistring skies.
And bid the Sunne put out his sparkling light;
    See Lord, unles thy right hand even steares
    Oh if thou anchour not these threatning feares,
Thy Ark will sayle as deepe in blood, as now in teares.

31

That cursed Beast, (which with thy Princely hornes,
With all thy stiles, and high prerogatives
His carrion cor's and Serpents head adornes)
His croaking Frogges to every quarter drives:

28.6 tunne: put into casks.

29.5 Spowse: the moon.

31.1 Beast: John "saw a beast rise up out of the sea, having seven heads and ten horns . . . and upon his heads the name of blasphemy" (Rev. 13:1, interpreted by Protestants as the Roman Church).

31.2 With : with 1627.

See how the key of that deep pit he tournes,
And cluck's his Locusts from their smoky hives:
    See how they rise, and with their numerous swarmes
    Filling the world with fogges, and fierce alarmes,
Bury the earth with bloodles corps, and bloody armes.

32

The bastard Sonne of that old Dragon (red
With blood of Saints) and all his petty states;
That triple monster, Geryon, who bred,
Nurs't, flesh't in blood thy servants deadly hates,
And that seduced Prince who hath his head
Eyes, eares, and tongue all in the Jesuite pates;
    All these, and hundred Kings, and nations, drunk
    With whorish Cup of that dire witch and punk,
Have sworne to see thy Church in death for ever sunk.

33

Now from those hel-hounds turne thy glorious eyes;
See, see thy fainting Spouse swimme, sinke in teares:
Heare Lord, oh heare her grones, and shrieking cries:
Those eyes long wait for thee: Lord to thine eares
She brings heart, lips, a Turtle sacrifice.
Thy cursed foe that Pro-Christ trophies reares:
    How long (just Lord) how long wilt thou delay
    That drunken whore with blood and fire to pay?
Thy Saints, thy truth, thy name's blasphem'd; how canst thou stay?

31.5-6 key . . . Locusts: In Rev. 9:1 a star falls, "and to him was given the key of the bottomless pit." He opened it and smoke came out together with locusts which attacked "only those men which have not the seal of God in their foreheads."

32.3 Geryon: mythical three-headed monster killed by Hercules. The three heads Fletcher identifies with the triple crown of the popes.

32.5 Prince: perhaps Henry IV of France.

32.8 punk: prostitute.

32.9 Church: the true (Protestant) church.

33.2 Spouse: the true church.

33.5 Turtle: dove.

33.9 stay: delay.

34

Oh is not this the time, when mounted high
Upon thy Pegasus of heavenly breed,
With bloody armes, white armies, flaming eye,
Thou vow'st in blood to swimme thy snowy steed;
And staine thy bridle with a purple dye?
This, this thy time; come then, oh come with speed,
    Such as thy Israel saw thee, when the maine
    Pil'd up his waves on heapes; the liquid plaine
Ran up, and with his hill safe wall'd that wandring traine.

Revel. 19. 11. 12. 13. 14. *Revel.* 14. 20

35

Such as we saw thee late, when spanish braves
(Preventing fight with printed victorie)
Full fraught with brands, whips, gyves for English slaves,
Blest by their Lord God Pope, thine enemie,
Turn'd seas to woods; thou arm'd with fires, winds, waves,
Fround'st on their pride: they feare, they faint, they fly:
    Some sink in drinking seas, or drunken sand,
    Some yeeld, some dash on rocks; the Spanish Grand
Banquets the fish in seas, or foules, and dogs on land.

36

Oh when wilt thou unlock the seeled eyes
Of those ten hornes, and Kings, which with the Beast
(Yet by thy hand) 'gan first to swell and rise?
How long shall they (charm'd with her drunken feast)
Give her their crownes? Bewitch't with painted lies,
They dreame thy spirit breathes from her sug'red breast,
    Thy Sun burnes with her eye-reflected beames,

Revel. 17. 12 13. 16.

34.2 Pegasus: the white horse of Rev. 19:11, the Word of God.

34.7-9 The Israelites' crossing of the Red Sea.

35.1 late: in 1588.

35.2 Preventing: anticipating. The Spanish had publicly boasted of the victory of the Armada before it left.

35.8 Grand: grandee.

36.2 The ten horns represent ten kings who will be defeated by the Lamb (the Son of God). They give their kingdoms to the Beast (i.e., for Fletcher, the papacy) "until the words of God shall be fulfilled" (Rev. 17:17).

From her life, light, all grace, and glory streames.
Wake these enchaunted sleepes, shake out these hellish dreames.

37

Wake lesser Gods, you sacred Deputies
Of heavens King, awake: see, see the light
Bares that foule whore, dispells her sorceries,
Blanch't skin, dead lippes, sowre breath, splay foot, owl-sight.
Ah can you dote on such deformities?
While you will serve in crownes, and beg your right,
Pray, give, fill up her never fill'd desire,
You her white Sonnes: else knives, dags, death your hire.
Scorne this base yoke; strip, eat, and burne her flesh in fire.

Revel. 17. 16.

38

But thou, Greate Prince, in whose successefull raigne,
Thy Britanes 'gin renue their Martiall fame,
Our Soveraigne Lord, our joy more Soveraigne,
Our onely Charles, under whose ominous name
Rome wounded first, still pines in ling'ring paine;
Thou who hast seen, and loath'd Romes whorish shame,
Rouge those brave Sparkes, which in thy bosome swell,
Cast downe this second Lucifer to hell:
So shalt thou all thy Sires, so shalt' thy selfe excell.

39

'Tis not in vaine, that Christ hath girt thy head
With three fayre peacefull Crownes: 'tis not in vaine,
That in thy Realmes such spirits are dayly bred,
Which thirst, and long to tug with Rome, and Spayne:
Thy royall Sire to Kings this lecture red;

37.8 dags: pistols.

38.4 Charles as Charlemagne who first "wounded Rome" by exercising undisputed authority over it.

38.7 Rouge: kindle.

39.2 three: of England, Scotland, and Ireland.

39.5 this lecture: James wrote several treatises against Rome. Perhaps Fletcher refers to his *Pro Jure Regio adversus Card. Perronii* (London, 1616) or to his *Triplici nodo, Triplex Curceus* (London, 1607), which Bellarmine answered in 1610.

This, this deserv'd his pen, and learned veine:
    Here, noble Charles, enter thy chevalrie;
    The Eagle scornes at lesser game to flie;
Onely this warre's a match worthy thy Realmes, & Thee.

40

Ah happy man, that lives to see that day!
Ah happy man, who in that warre shall bleed!
Happy who beares the standard in that fray!
Happy who quells that rising Babel seed!
Thrice happy who that whore shall doubly pay!
This (royall Charles) this be thy happy meed.
    Mayst thou that triple diademe trample downe,
    This shall thy name in earth, and heaven renowne,
And adde to these three here there a thrice triple crowne.

FINIS.

To my beloved Cousin *W. R.* Esquire.

Calend. Januar.

Cousin, day-birds are silenc't, and those fowl
Yet onely sing, which hate warm *Phœbus* light;
Th' unlucky Parrat, and death-boding Owl,
Which ush'ring in to heav'n their mistresse Night,
Hollow their mates, triumphing o're the quick-spent light.

The wronged *Philomel* hath left to plain
Tereus constraint and cruel ravishment:
Seems the poore bird hath lost her tongue again.
Progne long since is gone to banishment;
And the loud-tuned Thrush leaves all her merriment. 10

All so my frozen Muse, hid in my breast,
To come into the open aire refuses;
And dragg'd at length from hence, doth oft protest,
This is no time for *Phœbus*-loving Muses;
When the farre-distant sunne our frozen coast disuses.

Then till the sunne, which yet in fishes hasks,
Or watry urn, impounds his fainting head,
'Twixt Taurus horns his warmer beam unmasks,
And sooner rises, later goes to bed;
Calling back all the flowers, now to their mother fled: 20

Till *Philomel* resumes her tongue again,
And *Progne* fierce returns from long exiling;

Title: The *Dictionary of National Biography* entry for Fletcher speculates that W.R. may be one of his neighbors, a Walter Robarts. *Calend. Januar.*: January 1.

3 The parrot seems to be unlucky — for others — in repeating their secrets.

6 left to plain: stopped bewailing.

16 fishes hasks: containers for fish, with reference to the zodiacal sign of Pisces, the location of the sun in late February and March.

17 watry urn: Aquarius, the water bearer, the constellation which precedes Pisces as the sun's location.

18 Taurus: the Bull, in which the sun is located in late April and May.

Till the shrill Blackbird chants his merry vein;
And the day-birds the long-liv'd sunne beguiling,
Renew their mirth, and the yeares pleasant smiling:

Here must I stay, in sullen study pent,
Among our *Cambridge* fennes my time misspending;
But then revisit our long-long'd-for *Kent.*
Till then live happy, the time ever mending:
30 Happy the first o' th' yeare, thrice happy be the ending.

To *Thomalin.*

Thomalin, since *Thirsil* nothing ha's to leave thee,
And leave thee must; pardon me (gentle friend)
If nothing but my love I onely give thee;
Yet see how great this *Nothing* is, I send:
For though this love of thine I sweetest prove,
Nothing's more sweet then is this sweetest love.

The souldier *Nothing* like his prey esteems;
Nothing toss'd sailers equal with the shore:
Nothing before his health the sick man deems;
10 The pilgrim hugges his countrey; *Nothing* more:
The miser hoording up his golden wares,
This *Nothing* with his precious wealth compares.

Our thoughts ambition onely *Nothing* ends;
Nothing fills up the golden-dropsied minde:
The prodigall, that all so lavish spends,
Yet *Nothing* cannot; *Nothing* stayes behinde:
The King, that with his life a kingdome buyes,
Then life or crown doth *Nothing* higher prize.

28 Fletcher was born and spent his early life in Cranbrook, Kent, where his grandfather was rector.

1 *Thomalin*: From Fletcher's *Piscatory Eclogues* one discovers that he is a friend, John Tomkins. *Thirsil*: Fletcher's pastoral name for himself.

Who all enjoyes, yet *Nothing* now desires;
Nothing is greater then the highest *Jove*: 20
Who dwells in heav'n, (then) *Nothing* more requires;
Love, more then honey; *Nothing* more sweet then love:
    Nothing is onely better then the best;
    Nothing is sure: *Nothing* is ever blest.

I love my health, my life, my books, my friends,
Thee; (dearest *Thomalin*) *Nothing* above thee:
For when my books, friends, health, life, fainting ends,
When thy love fails, yet *Nothing* still will love me:
    When heav'n, and aire, the earth, and floating mains
    Are gone, yet *Nothing* still untoucht remains. 30

Since then to other streams I must betake me,
And spitefull *Chame* of all ha's quite bereft me;
Since Muses selves (false Muses) will forsake me,
And but this *Nothing*, nothing els is left me;
    Take thou my love, and keep it still in store:
    That given, *Nothing* now remaineth more.

A reply upon the fair *M.S.*

A Daintie maid, that drawes her double name
From bitter sweetnesse, (with sweet bitternesse)
Did late my skill and faulty verses blame,
And to her loving friend did plain confesse,
That I my former credit foul did shame,
And might no more a poets name professe:
    The cause that with my verse she was offended,
    For womens levitie I discommended.

32 *Chame*: the river Cam and its University. The context clearly shows that Fletcher left it in a mood of profound hostility.

Title: As line 2 makes clear, her name, perhaps from etymology, means *bitter-sweet*. The bitter-sweet is a kind of apple; Fletcher returns to the meaning in the fourth stanza.

Too true you said, that poet I was never,
10 And I confesse it (fair) if that content ye,
That then I playd the poet lesse then ever;
Not, for of such a verse I now repent me,
(Poets to feigne, and make fine lies endeavour)
But I the truth, truth (ah!) too certain sent ye:
Then that I am no poet I denie not;
For when their lightnesse I condemne, I ly not.

But if my verse had ly'd against my minde,
And praised that which truth cannot approve,
And falsly said, they were as fair as kinde,
20 As true as sweet, their faith could never move,
But sure is linkt where constant love they finde,
That with sweet braving they vie truth and love;
If thus I write, it cannot be deni'd
But I a poet were, so foul I ly'd.

But give me leave to write as I have found:
Like ruddy apples are their outsides bright,
Whose skin is fair, the core or heart unsound;
Whose cherry-cheek the eye doth much delight,
But inward rottennesse the taste doth wound:
30 Ah! were the taste so good as is the sight,
To pluck such apples (lost with self same price)
Would back restore us part of paradise.

But truth hath said it, (truth who dare denie?)
Men seldome are, more seldome women sure:
But if (fair-sweet) thy truth and constancie
To better faith thy thoughts and minde procure,
If thy firm truth could give firm truth the lie,
If thy first love will first and last endure;
Thou more then woman art, if time so proves thee,
40 And he more then a man, that loved loves thee.

22 braving: show. vie: equal. The word is taken from the popular card game primero and means to bid.

[Vast Ocean of light.]

Vast Ocean of light, whose rayes surround
The Universe, who know'st nor ebb, nor shore,
Who lend'st the Sun his sparkling drop, to store
With overflowing beams Heav'n, ayer, ground,
Whose depths beneath the Centre none can sound,
Whose heights 'bove heav'n, and thoughts so lofty soar,
Whose breadth no feet, no lines, no chains, no eyes survey,
    Whose length no thoughts can reach, no worlds can bound,
    What cloud can mask thy face? where can thy ray
Find an Eclipse? what night can hide Eternal Day? 10

Our Seas (a drop of thine) with arms dispread
Through all the earth make drunk the thirsty plains;
Our Sun (a spark of thine) dark shadows drains,
Guilds all the world, paints earth, revives the dead;
Seas (through earth pipes distill'd) in Cisterns shed,
And power their liver springs in river veins.
The Sun peeps through jet clouds, and when his face, and gleams
    Are maskt, his eyes their light through ayers spread;
    Shall dullard earth bury life-giving streams?
Earths foggs impound heav'ns light? hell quench heav'n-kindling beams? 20

How miss I then? in bed I sought by night,
But found not him in rest, nor rest without him.
I sought in Towns, in broadest streets I sought him,
But found not him where all are lost: dull sight
Thou canst not see him in himself: his light
Is maskt in light: brightness his cloud about him.
Where, when, how he'l be found, there, then, thus seek thy love:
    Thy Lamb in flocks, thy Food with appetite,
    Thy Rest on resting dayes, thy Turtle Dove
Seek on his cross: there, then, thus Love stands nail'd with love. 30

16 This kind of image, based upon the analogy between the body and the earth, is the basis of Fletcher's *Purple Island*.

18 spread; : spread, 1670.

[How is't, my soul.]

I.

How is't, my soul, that thou giv'st eyes their sight
  To view their objects, yet hast none
    To see thine own?
Earths, ayers, Heav'ns beauties they discern; their light
  Fair flowers admires; their several dresses,
    Their golden tresses;
The Lilly, Rose, the various Tulip, scorning
The pride of Princes in their choice adorning.

II.

They joy to view the ayers painted Nations;
  The Peacocks train, which th' head out vies
    With fairer eyes,
And emulats the heav'nly constellations;
  The Ostrich, whose fair plume embraves
    Kings, Captains, Slaves;
The Halcions, whose Triton-bills appease
Curl'd waves, and with their Eggs lay stormy seas.

III.

Pilots fixt eyes observe the Artick Bear,
  With all her unwasht Starry trains
    In Heav'nly plains.
Night-Travellers behold the Moon to steer
  Her Ship, sailing (while *Eol* raves)
    Through cloudy waves:
Our less Worlds sunns with pleasure view the light
Which gives all beauties beauty, them their sight.

2.1 ayers painted Nations: clouds.

2.5 embraves: makes showy.

2.7-8 Halcions: Traditionally these birds nested on the ocean in mid-winter; like the sea-god Triton they then stilled the waves.

3.2 unwasht: because the constellation Ursa Minor does not set in northern latitudes.

3.5 *Eol*: Æolus, god of the winds.

3.7 sunns: i.e., the eyes.

IV.

Thou that giv'st sight to clay, to blackness light
How art so dull, so dimm in duty
To view his beauty,
Who quickens every life, lights every light?
His height those Eagles eyes surpasses;
Thou wants thy glasses:
Take up that Perspective, and view those streams
Of light, and fill thy waning Orb with beams.

V.

Then see the flowers clad in his Liveries,
And from his cheek, and lovely face
Steal all their grace.
See Fouls from him borrow their braveries,
And all their feather-painted dresses
From his fair tresses:
See Starrs, and Moon, the Sun, and all perfection
Beg light, and life from his bright eyes reflection.

VI.

Look on his lipps; heav'ns gate there open lies:
Thence that grace-breathing Spirit blows,
Thence honey flowes.
Look on his hands, the Worlds full treasuries;
Fix all thy looks his heart upon,
Loves highest Throne.
And when thy sight that radiant beauty blears,
And dazels thy weak eyes; see with thine ears.

4.7 Perspective: telescope, but also with its modern meaning.

5.4 Fouls: Fowls.

Sadducismus Triumphatus.

Henry More

The life of Henry More is the simple one, quickly told, of a Cambridge don. He was born in Grantham, Lincolnshire, in 1614 and grew up there. Through the assistance of an uncle he attended Eton and in 1631 matriculated at Christ's College, Cambridge, just as Milton completed his M.A. there. Following the granting of his own B.A. in the spring of 1636 More seems to have undergone some kind of extended spiritual crisis which endured until about 1640, when he found himself again and began writing the poetry which appeared in 1642 as *Psychodia Platonica* (see C. C. Brown, *Review of English Studies*, 20 [1969]: 445–54). In 1639 he had earned the M.A. and was ordained, becoming in time a Fellow and a Tutor in his college, where he remained for the rest of his life despite family encouragement toward a worldly career and offers of clerical advancement elsewhere. In 1647 he reprinted an enlarged edition of his poetry as *Philosophicall Poems* but thenceforth turned to prose, becoming for a time a vigorous proponent of the philosophy of Descartes and later an opponent of the "materialistic" or "atheistic" philosophy represented in England by Hobbes. An especially attractive feature of his later years is his correspondence with Anne, Viscountess Conway, which Marjorie Nicolson has edited (New Haven: Yale University Press, 1930). The fact that he kept his university post through the political and religious tumult of the mid-century is testimony to his good sense and moderation at a time when both were rare. It is small wonder that he is recognized as the leader of the Cambridge "Latitudinarians." He died in 1687 and was buried in the college chapel.

Despite the rather uncomplimentary depiction of him in John Barth's *The Sotweed Factor*, More is recognized today as he was by contemporaries as enunciator of some of the major intellectual ideas of the seventeenth century (see, e.g., Basil Willey, *Seventeenth Century Background* [London: Chatto and Windus, 1934] and, for texts as well as its introduction, C. A. Patrides, *The Cambridge Platonists* [London: Edward Arnold, 1970]). His poetry is of a piece with his prose, providing early expression of beliefs which he was later to formulate at greater length. The list of these later efforts is very large; for a good treatment of his ideas see Ahron Lichtenstein, *Henry More* (Cambridge: Harvard University Press, 1962), with its accompanying bibliography.

The Præexistency of the Soul, which is printed here, was first appended in 1647 to More's *The Sleep of the Soul*, itself the third part of *A Platonick Song of the Soul* of which the first part was *The Life of the Soul* and the second *The Immortality of the Soul*. More prefaces the first part with a philosophical essay in prose, "To the Reader," which equates the "Platonic" trinity of Ahad–Æon–Psyche (meaning, as the "Interpretation Generall" appended to the collection asserts, One–Eternity–Soul) with the Christian Trinity (for further discussion of this Christian–pagan analogue see W. B. Hunter, *Bright Essence* [Salt Lake City: University of Utah Press, 1971], pp. 44–51). More believed that the Platonists, especially Plotinus, whose philosophy he does not distinguish from Plato's, had expressed the Christian dogma in their pagan writings, if sometimes rather darkly, and thus support his belief in the universality of the divine message. The earlier parts of the *Platonick Song* present this thesis at length (see Geoffrey Bullough's excellent annotated edition, *Philosophical Poems* [Manchester: University of Manchester, 1931]). In them More tries to prove that the soul or spirit does exist, that it is immortal, and that at death it does not die (or sleep). Supporting this last tenet is an argument for its existence prior to conception or birth, the section printed here. This belief has never been widely held by Christians except by Origen and some of his followers. Its best-known exposition is in Plato's *Phædo*, where Socrates assumes the pre-existence of the soul to prove the origin of what seems to be innate knowledge. Learning, in this dialogue, is argued to be remembrance of information which the soul had known in some previous state, a hypothesis accepted for poetic purposes by More's contemporary Henry Vaughan in his "Retreat."

More argues his case, however, for a very different reason: to prove the existence of the soul, which he defines as an incorporeal substance (the issue is by no means dead today as the morality of abortion is debated). For him, as he writes in *Sadducismus Triumphatus* (4th ed. [1726], p. 119), the general term *substance* relates to the more specific term *matter* as genus does to species. There are, that is, two kinds of substance, material and immaterial or incorporeal. To the former belong all physical objects, to the latter all spiritual natures, including the soul, angels, and God himself. Unlike the monist Milton, who believed that body could become spirit (*PL*, 5. 478), More is a thorough-going dualist at this point in his system. He spent much of his life trying to prove in scientific and experimental terms the real existence of the soul as a substance separate from the physical body. One way to do this, an indirect one, is to argue for its pre-existence. Another, much more direct, is to prove the existence of witches, whose souls leave their bodies to wreak all manner of evil. If witches exist, that is, the reality of incorporeal substance would be demonstrated; and if incorporeal substance exists, then so does man's incorporeal soul. Thus the interrelated subjects of the pre-existent soul and the disembodied witch appear together as mutually supportive arguments in More's poem. To deny witches then is to deny spirits and thus man's own soul and even God himself, and is a form of atheism. As Sir Thomas Browne confessed in a famous passage of *Religio Medici*, "I have ever believed and do now know, that there are Witches: they that doubt of these, do not onely deny *them*, but Spirits; and are obliquely and upon consequence a sort not of Infidels, but Atheists." This is exactly More's position.

Thus he argues for a pre-existent soul which, like other spirits, exists in what More calls its "aery vehicle," for he views it still as a substance, however attenuated, in which various attributes may inhere. In this disembodied condition its senses are not differentiated: it is "all ear" or "all eye" (see stanza 14). Governed by its phantasy-imagination, the soul may alter the airy vehicle so as to appear in any shape whatsoever, and to change it at will, as stanzas 23–34 argue. Existing between the divine world and the created world (stanzas 8–9), it may move in either direction and thus exhibits free will. But whenever the immense orb of such unutilized vitality is exposed to "matter right-prepar'd" (stanza 96), it will impart soul to it just as the sun does to "matter fit" in the *Faerie Queene* (3. 6. 9).

Following the abstract argument is the empirical proof, furnished primarily from witchcraft in a long series of examples taken from More's reading. It is not surprising that this kind of research, in More's hands, never led to personal hysteria and charges against anyone. Indeed, for More to have been bewitched (as he apparently never was) would have provided his most rapturous moment: experimental proof of the existence of disembodied soul and even of God. Failing his own experience, he collected that of others, a pursuit which occupied him for much of the rest of his life, as is attested by large parts of his *Antidote Against Atheisme* (1652), his *Immortality of the Soul* (1659), and his contributions to *Sadducismus Triumphatus* by his friend Joseph Glanvil. The witch provides objectively what the mystic intuits, but More was not a mystic, at least in this sense.

Inevitably one must question whether this kind of subject is suited to poetic expression. More's concern is always for content; as he asks at the end of the poem "To the Reader" prefixed to the whole collection,

> Nor do thou, Reader, rashly brand
> My rhythmes 'fore thou them understand.

And he believes that the true expression of his own insights is the sole criterion:

> Possest with living sense I inly rave,
> Carelesse how outward words do from me flow,
> So be the image of my mind they have
> Truly exprest.
>
> ["Ad Paronem," ll. 25–28]

To us, such standards obviously are not sufficient, and the poetic inadequacy of much of More's work proves it.

It is odd, however, to see him adopting all of the external trappings from Spenser: the complicated stanza, the archaic vocabulary, the old-fashioned syntax. But he unfortunately ignores his model in his omission of both characters and narrative. Perhaps the Mutability Cantos of the *Faerie Queene* were primarily his model in these respects, but they have a setting, speaking (if purely allegorical) characters, and some sense of conflict, even though their intellectual content, exploring the concept of mutability, outweighs almost any other aspect of the poem. Spenserianism, that is, is More's "aery vehicle," and he later found prose a better one; in "Ad Paronem" he recognizes some of his difficulties:

> A rude confused heap of ashes dead
> My verses seem, when that cælestiall flame
> That sacred spirit of life's extinguished
> In my cold brest. Then gin I rashly blame
>   My rugged lines: This word is obsolete;
>   That boldly coynd, a third too oft doth beat
>
> Mine humourous ears.
>
> [ll. 13–19]

On the other hand, his ideas are sufficiently interesting and provocative in themselves to carry his lines and he is sometimes vivid, as when he observes that one soul can no more beget another than a man can "presse the Sunne beams in his fist/And squeez out drops of light" (*Præexistency*, 87. 2–3). The description of finding one's way home through "slabby streets" by means of a lantern (stanza 101) is memorable, as is his observation that for those (like Milton) who believe that body can become spirit,

> grosse Pie-crust will grow wise,
> And pickled Cucumbers sans doubt Philosophize.
> [90. 8–9]

Indeed, the similarities between More and Milton were overstated by Marjorie Nicolson in a series of articles published in the 1920s, as W. R. Lowery has argued in his Northwestern University Ph.D. dissertation, "John Milton, Henry More and Ralph Cudworth" (1970). Rather, they represent divergent tendencies from a common educational background.

Finally, one must observe that in his shorter pieces More could be more effective as poet than as philosopher. "Devotion" is not the equal of Herbert's lyrics but shares something of the same feeling and form. "Exorcismus" shows remarkable control of a long and elaborate stanza with real religious feeling. Its approximate rhymes e.g., *confind–command*) are unusual. And last, in "The Philosophers Devotion" and "Charitie and Humilitie" More for once voices his faith in simple, direct statements.

The texts of all of the poems are taken from the *Philosophicall Poems* of 1647. They have been reproduced in an unannotated edition by Alexander Grosart (1878) and more recently in a Scolar Press facsimile (Menston, England, 1969).

To the Reader.

Reader, sith it is the fashion
To bestow some salutation,
I greet thee; give free leave to look
And nearly view my opened Book.
But see then that thine eyes be clear
If ought thou wouldst discover there.
Expect from me no Teian strain,
No light wanton Lesbian vein:
Though well I wot the vulgar spright
Such Harmony doth more strongly smite. 10
Silent Secesse, wast Solitude
Deep searching thoughts often renew'd,
Stiffe conflict 'gainst importunate vice,
That daily doth the Soul entice
From her high throne of circuling light
To plunge her in Infernall Night:
Collection of the mind from stroke
Of this worlds Magick, that doth choke
Her with foul smothering mists and stench,
And in Lethæn waves her drench: 20
A daily Death, drad Agony,
Privation, dry Sterility;
Who is well entred in those wayes
Fitt'st man to read my lofty layes.
But whom lust, wrath and fear controule,
Scarce know their body from their soul.
If any such chance hear my verse,
Dark numerous Nothings I rehearse
To them; measure out an idle sound,
In which no inward sense is found. 30
Thus sing I to cragg'd clifts, and hils,
To sighing winds, to murmuring rills,

4 nearly: closely.

7 Teian: Teos was the Greek city in which Anacreon was born.

8 Lesbian: Lesbos was sacred to Venus.

11 Secesse: retirement.

32 winds, : winds 1647.

To wastefull woods, to empty groves,
Such things as my dear mind most loves.
But they heed not my heavenly passion,
Fast fixt on their own operation.
On chalky rocks hard by the Sea,
Safe guided by fair Cynthia,
I strike my silver-sounded lyre,
40 First struck my self by some strong fire;
And all the while her wavering ray,
Reflected from fluid glasse doth play
On the white banks. But all are deaf
Unto my Muse, that is most lief
To mine own self. So they nor blame
My pleasant notes, nor praise the same.
Nor do thou, Reader, rashly brand
My rhythmes 'fore thou them understand.

H. M.

33 groves, : groves. 1647.

38 Cynthia: Diana, here as goddess of chastity.

The Præexistency of the Soul.

The Preface to the Reader.

Although the opinion of the Præexistency of the Soul be made so probable and passable in the Canto it self, that none can sleight and contemn it, that do not ordinarily approve themselves men by Derision more then by Reason; yet so heavie prejudice lying upon us both from Naturall diffidence in so high Points, and from our common Education, I thought it fit, for securing my self, from suspicion of overmuch lightnesse, to premize thus much: That that which I have taken the pains and boldnesse to present to the free judgement of others, hath been already judged of old, very sound and orthodox, by the wisest and most learned of preceding ages. 10

Which R. Menasseh Ben-Israel, *doth abundantly attest in his 15.* Problem. De Creatione*; Avouching that it is the common Opinion of all the Hebrews, and that it was never called into controversie, but approved of, by the common consent and suffrage of all wise men.*

And himself doth by severall places out of the Old Testament (as pat for his purpose, I think, as any can be brought against it) endeavour to make it good; but might I confesse, have been more fitly furnished, could his Religion have reached into the New. For Philip. *2.* v. *6, 7, 8.* John *9.* v. *1, 2, 3.* John *17.* v. *4, 5.* Mark *8.* v. *27, 28. all those places do seem so naturally to favour this Probability, that* 20 *if it had pleas'd the Church to have concluded it for a standing Truth; He that would not have been fully convinc'd upon the evidence of these passages of Scripture, would undoubtedly, have been held a man of a very timorous & Scepticall constitution, if not something worse.*

Nor is the feeblenesse and miserable ineptnesse of Infancy any greater damp to the belief of this Præexistency then the dotage and debility of old Age, to the hope of the Souls future subsistency after death.

Nor, if we would fetch an argument from Theologie, is Gods Justice, and the divine Nemesis lesse set out, by supposing that the Souls 30 *of men, thorough their own revolting from God before they came into the body, have thus in severall measures engaged themselves in the*

11 Rabbi Manasseh (1604–57) published *De Creatione. Problemata XXX* at Amsterdam in 1635.

28 death. : death, 1647.

sad, dangerous, and almost fatall entanglements of this Corporeall World; then it is, by conceiving that they must needs survive the Body, that the judgement of the Almighty may passe upon them, for what they have committed in the flesh.

Nor lastly, is it harder to phansie, how these Prææxistent Souls insinuate into seed, Embryos, or Infants, then how Created ones are 40 *insinuated; nor yet so hard, to determine of their condition if they depart in Infancy, as of the condition of these.*

But mistake me not, Reader; I do not contend (in thus arguing) that this opinion of the Prææxistency of the Soul, is true, but that it is not such a self-condemned Falsity, but that I might without justly incurring the censure of any Vainnesse or Levity, deem it worthy the canvase and discussion of sober and considerate men.

Yours H. M.

The Prææxistency of the Soul.

The Argument:

Of the Souls Prææxistency
Her Orb of Fire and Aire,
Of Ghosts, of Goblins, of Sorcery,
This Canto doth declare.

1

Rise then *Aristo's* son! assist my Muse.
Let that hie spright which did inrich thy brains
With choice conceits, some worthy thoughts infuse
Worthy thy title and the Readers pains.
And thou, O *Lycian* Sage! whose pen contains
Treasures of heavenly light with gentle fire,
Give leave a while to warm me at thy flames
That I may also kindle sweet desire
In holy minds that unto highest things aspire.

1.1 *Aristo's*: Ariosto's; the "son" is Spenser, whose *Faerie Queene* is to some extent modeled upon *Orlando Furioso*. Muse. : Muse 1647.

1.5 *Lycian* Sage: apparently Apollo, so named because of a shrine to him in Lycia. Virgil mentions the utterances of its oracle, the *Lyciæ sortæ*.

2

For I would sing the Præexistency
Of humane souls, and live once ore again
By recollection and quick memory
All what is past since first we all began.
But all too shallow be my wits to scan
So deep a point and mind too dull to clear
So dark a matter, but Thou, O more then man!
Aread thou sacred Soul of *Plotin* deare
Tell what we mortalls are, tell what of old we were.

3

A spark or ray of the Divinity
Clouded in earthy fogs, yclad in clay,
A precious drop sunk from Æternitie,
Spilt on the ground, or rather slunk away.
For then we fell when we gan first t' assay
By stealth, of our own selves something to been,
Uncentring our selves from our great stay.
Which fondly we new liberty did ween
And from that prank right jolly wights our selves did deem.

4

For then forthwith some thing beside our God
We did conceive our parted selves to be,
And loosened, first from that simple Good,
Then from great *Æon*, then from *Psyche* free,
We after fell into low phantasie,

2.8 Aread: declare.

3.7 stay: support.

4.4 *Æon . . . Psyche*: Eternity and soul or spirit. In his notes on *Psychozoia* More defines the former as "a life exhibiting all things at once, and in one." The latter is the "life of time." In the Neoplatonic system, which More is following, everything proceeds from an eternal, changeless One ("that simple Good," 4.3) into temporal, changing multiplicity, the intermediary to it being Psyche, the "Soul of the world" and mother of all beings. Here More is asserting that man has turned away from God, from Eternity, and from the World Soul to self-interest and a supposed new liberty (3.8) which leads to ignorance, plurality, and a meaningless existence. Or one moves down the chain of being from rational freedom to the fanciful (a lower mental state), to physical sensations, and finally to the merely vegetative ("embarkd as in a tree").

And after that into corporeall sense,
And after sense embarkd as in a tree,
(First sown in earthly slime, then sprung from thence)
A fading life we lead in deadly influence.

5

Thus groping after our own Centres near
And proper substance, we grew dark, contract,
Swallow'd up of earthly life, ne what we were
Of old, through ignorance can we detect.
Like noble babe by fate or friends neglect
Left to the care of sorry salvage wight,
Grown up to manly years cannot conject
His own true parentage, nor read aright
What Father him begot, what womb him brought to light:

6

So we as stranger Infants elsewhere born
Can not divine from what spring we did flow
Ne dare these base alliances to scorn,
Nor lift our selves a whit from hence below,
Ne strive our Parentage again to know;
Ne dream we once of any other stock,
Since foster'd upon *Rheas* knees we grow,
In Satyres arms with many a mow and mock
Oft danc'd, and hairy *Pan* our cradle oft hath rock'd.

7

But *Pan* nor *Rhea* be our Parentage;
We been the Of-spring of all-seeing *Jove*
Though now, whether through our own miscariage
Or secret force of fate, that all doth move
We be cast low; for why? the sportfull love
Of our great Maker (like as mothers dear
In pleasance from them do their children shove

6.7 *Rheas*: She was the benevolent wife of Saturn, the "mother goddess."

7.1 Parentage; : Parentage 1647.

7.5 low; : low, 1647.

That back again they may recoyl more near)
Shoves of our soules a while, the more them to endear.

8

Or whether Justice and due Equity
Expects the truth of our affection,
And therefore sets us 'twixt the Deitie
And the created world, that thereupon
We may with a free resignation
Give up our selves to him deserves us best.
That love is none that's by coaction.
Hence he our soules from his own self releast
And left us free to follow what the most us pleas'd.

9

And for this purpose did enrich our choice
By framing of the outward Universe.
The framing of this world a meet devise
Whereby Gods wisedome thorough all may pierce,
From hight to depth. In depth is vengeance fierce,
Whereby transgressing souls are sorely scourged
And back again are forced to reverse
By *Nemesis* deep-biting whips well urged,
And in sad sorrows bath well drench'd and soundly purged.

10

Thus nothing's lost of Gods fecundity.
But stretching out himself in all degrees
His wisedome, goodnesse and due equity
Are rightly rank'd, in all the soul them sees.
O holy lamps of God! O sacred eyes
Filled with love and wonder every where!
Ye wandring tapers to whom God descryes
His secret paths, great *Psyches* darlings dear!
Behold her works, but see your hearts close not too near.

7.9 of: off, away.

8.2 expects: awaits.

8.7 coaction: coercion.

11

But they so soon as vitall Orbs were made
That rolled round about each starry fire
Forth-with pursue, and strive them to invade;
Like evening flies that busily conspire
Following a Jade that travail long doth tire,
To seize his nodding head and suck his sweat.
But they suck'd in into the vitall mire
First died and then again reviv'd by heat,
Did people all the Orbs by this audacious feat.

12

But infinite Myriads undipt as yet
Did still attend each vitall moveing sphear,
And wait their turnes for generation fit
In airy bodies wafted here and there,
As sight and sympathy away did bear.
These corporate with bloud, but the first flight
Of fallen souls, ymeint with slimy gear
Rose from their earth, breaking their filmes slight:
As Storyes say, *Nile* living shapes sends forth to sight.

13

Here their third chariot cleep'd terrestiall
Great *Psyches* brood did enter; for before
They rode more light; first in cœlestiall
Or fiery chariots, wherein with *Uranore*
The care and thought of all the world they bore.
This is the Orb of pure quick life and sense
Which the thrice mighty *Mercury* of yore

11.1 they: the yet-unborn souls. vitall Orbs: worlds that can support life. In *Democritus Platonissans* More argues for a plurality of habitable worlds.

12.7 ymeint: mixed.

12.9 The idea of life (flies) being bred by the sun upon mud such as that of the Nile was traditional.

13.4 *Uranore*: defined in More's "Interpretation Generall" appended to his collection of poetry as "the light or beauty of heaven." The unborn souls first exist in the region of fire, the highest order of nature. The soul there is purely rational.

13.7 thrice mighty *Mercury*: Hermes Trismegistus, who describes this experience at the beginning of his *Poimandres*.

Ascending, held with Angels conference
And of their comely shapes had perfect cognoscence.

14

In this the famous *Tyanean* swain,
Lifted above the deadly charming might
Of the dull Carkasse could discover plain
From seven-hill'd *Rome* with speedy piercing sight
What they in *Egypt* did as Stories write.
This is that nimble quick vivacious Orb
All ear, all eye, with rayes round shining bright;
Sphear of pure sense with noe perpessions curb
Nor uncouth shapen Spectres ever can disturb.

15

Next this is that light Vehicle of air,
Where likewise all sense is in each part pight.
This is more grosse subject to grief and fear
And most-what soil'd with bodily delight;
Sometimes with vengeance, envie, anger, spight.
This Orb is ever passive in sensation.
But the third wagon of the soul that hight
The terrene Vehicle, beside this passion
Hath organized sense, distinct by limitation.

16

These last be but the souls live sepulchres
Where least of all she acts, but afterward
Rose from this tomb, she free and lively fares
And upward goes if she be not debar'd
By *Adrastias* law nor strength empar'd

14.1 *Tyanean* swain: Apollonius, born in Tyane in Cappadocia. A Pythagorean, he supposedly worked miracles and could see happenings at great distances.

14.8 perpessions: endurances of suffering.

15.2 pight: lodged. Descending from the sphere of fire to that of air, the soul becomes subject to passions.

15.9 Finally descending to the sphere of the earth, the soul develops the different senses, limited by the organs in which they are placed.

16.5 *Adrastias*: that of Nemesis.

By too long bondage, in this Cave below.
The purged souls ascent nought may retard;
But earthly-mindednesse may eath foreslow
Their flight, then near the ground in airy weeds they go;

17

Awak'd to life more ample then before,
If they their fortune good could then pursue.
But sith unwillingly they were ytore
From their dear carkasses their fate they rue,
And terrene thoughts their troubled minds embue:
So that in languishment they linger near
Their wonted homes and oft themselves they shew;
Sometimes on purpose, sometimes unaware
That wak'd by hasty call they streightway disappear.

18

For men that wont to wander in their sleep
By the fixt light of inward phantasie,
Though a short fit of death fast bounden keep
Their outward sense and all their Organes tye;
Yet forth they fare steared right steddily
By that internall guide: even so the ghosts
Of men deceas'd bedewed with the sky
And nights cold influence, in sleep yclos'd
Awake within, and walk in their forewonted coast.

19

In shape they walk much like to what they bore
Upon the earth: For that light Orb of air
Which they inact must yielden evermore
To phansies beck, so when the souls appear
To their own selves alive as once they were,

16.8 eath: easily.

17ff. This commonplace idea derives ultimately from Plato's *Phædo* 81 as well as from popular superstition. Its literary use can be seen in *Comus* 464ff. and in the sylphs of the *Rape of the Lock*.

18.4 tye: tied.

19.3 inact: activate.

So cloath'd and conversant in such a place,
The inward eyes of phansie thither stear
Their gliding vehicle, that bears the face
Of him that liv'd, that men may reade what wight it was.

20

And often ask'd what would they, they descry
Some secret wealth, or hidden injury.
That first they broach that over oft doth ly
Within their minds: but vanish suddenly
Disturb'd by bold mans importunity.
But those that on set purpose do appear
To holden talk with frail mortality
Make longer stay. So that there is no fear
That when we leave this earthly husk we perish clear.

21

Or what is like to perfect perishing,
That inert deadlinesse our souls shall seize,
That neither sense nor phansies fountains spring,
But ever close in dull unactive ease.
For though that Death our spirits doth release
From this distinguish'd organizate sense,
Yet we may hear and see, what, where we please,
And walk at large when we are gone from hence
And with both men and ghosts hold friendly conference;

22

And all in virtue of that airy Waine
In which we ride when that of earth is gone,
Unlesse no terrene tinctures do us stein,
For then forthwith to heaven we be yflone,
In our swift fiery chariot thither drawn.
But least men deem me airy notions feigne:
All stories this sure truth do seem to own.
Wherefore my Muse! some few do not disdain,
Of many, to relate, more firm assent to gain.

20.3 over oft: most often.

22.1 Waine: wagon, vehicle.

23

But first lay out the treasures of the Air
That immense womb from whence all bodies spring;
And then the force of Phantasie declare.
Of Witches wonnes a while then maist thou sing
Their Stygian rites, and nightly revelling.
Then to the wished port to draw more near
Als tell of the untimely wandering
Of the sad ghosts of men that oft appear,
All which to the hard search of truth, joynt light do bear;

24

Shew fitly how the præexistent soul
Inacts and enters bodies here below,
And then entire, unhurt, can leave this moul
And thence her airy Vehicle can draw,
In which by sense and motion they may know
Better then we what things transacted be
Upon the Earth; and when they list, may show
Themselves to friend or foe, their phantasie
Moulding their airy Orb to grosse consistency.

25

For sooth to sayn, all things of Air consist
And easly back again return to air.
Witnesse the carkases of man and beast
Which wast though teeth of Wolves them never tear,
Nor Crow nor Vulture do their flesh empare,
Yet all is wast and gone, no reliques seen
Of former shape, saving the bones bare,
And the bare bones by Time and Art, I ween,
First into liquour melt to air ychanged been.

23.4 wonnes: dwellings.

23.7 Als: also.

23.8 appear, : appear 1647.

24.3 moul: mold.

25.4 wast: waste, decay.

25.9 melt: melted.

26

Besides experience doth maken plain
How clouds be but the crudling of the air.
Take a round glasse, let 't nought but air contain,
Close it with Hermes seal, then cover it over
With cinders warm, onely the top discover;
The gentle fire hard at the bottome pight
Thins the low air, which got above doth hover
Like a white fume embodying in the hight
With cooler parts, then turns to drops all crystall bright.

27

Not much unlike to the experiment
That learned Leech professes to have seen
Amongst the *Alps*, where the wind violent
Hammered out clouds with his strong blustring keen
'Gainst a steep rock, which streight themselves did teem
Upon the Earth and wet the verdant Plain,
Dissolved by the sight of Phœbus sheen.
But sometimes clouds afford, not onely rain
But bloud, stones, milk, corn, frogs, fire, earth and all contain.

28

Wherefore all bodies be of air compos'd,
Great Natures all-complying Mercury,
Unto ten thousand shapes and forms dispos'd:
Like nimble quick-silver that doth agree

26.2 crudling: curdling.

26.3 glasse, : glasse 1647.

26.4 Hermes seal: one of mercury. More is describing an experiment with the metal in an inverted glass vessel, hot at the bottom and cold at the top. The vaporized metal appears first as a cloud, then condenses into liquid drops.

27.2 Leech: David Leech (d. 1653), *Philosophia Lachrymans* (1637), p. Cr.

27.4 keen: i.e., keenness.

27.5 teem: rain.

27.7 Phœbus sheen: the sun's light.

28.1 compos'd, : compos'd 1647.

28.4 agree: unite.

With gold, with brasse, or with what ere it be
Amalgamate, but brought unto the fire
Into an airy fume it all doth flie,
Though you before might turn to earth and mire
What into ancient air so quickly doth retire.

29

Wherefore the soul possest of matter meet
If she hath power to operate thereon
Can eath transform this Vehicle to sight,
Dight with due colour, figuration.
Can speak, can walk, and then dispear anon
Spreading her self in the dispersed air;
Then if she please recall again what's gone.
Those th' uncouth mysteries of phansie are
Then thunder farre more strong, more quick then lightning far.

30

Some heavings toward this strange activity
We may observe even in this mortall state.
Here health and sicknesse of the phantasie
Often proceed, which working minds create,
And pox and pestilence do malleate,
Their thoughts still beating on those objects ill,
Which doth the mastered bloud contaminate,
And with foul poysonous impressions fill
And last the precious life with deadly dolour kill.

31

And if't be true that learned Clerks do sayen
His phantasie whom a mad dog hath bit
With shapes of dogs doth all his Urine stain.
Women with child, if in their longing fit
They be differ'd, their eager appetite

28.5 gold, : gold 1647. brasse, : brasse 1647.

29.1 meet: suitable.

29.5 dispear: disappear.

30.5 malleate, : malleate 1647. It means to hammer.

31.5 differ'd: deferred, put off.

So sharply edges the quick phantasie
That it the Signature doth carve and write
Of what she long'd for, on the Infants body,
Imprinting it so plain that all the world may see.

32

Those streaked rods plac'd by that *Syrian* swain
Before the sheep when they receiv'd the ramme,
(Whence the best part of *Labans* flock became
All spotted or'e, whereby his shepheard wan
The greater wages,) show what phansie can.
And boyes ore night when they went to their rest
By dreams grown up to th' stature of a man
And bony shapes in mens sad hearts exprest
Dear image of their love, and wrought by loves unrest:

33

Things farre more wonderfull then *Cippus* horn
Who in the field with so much earnestnesse
Viewing the fight of bulls rose in the Morn
With forked front: for though the fight did cease
Amongst th' enraged heards, yet ne're the lesse
His working phansie did the war revive.
Which on the bloud did make so strong impresse
In dewy sleep that humours did arrive
His knobby head and a fair pair of horns contrive:

34

All these declare the force of phantasie
Though working here upon this stubborn clay.
But th' airy Vehicle yields more easily,
Unto her beck more nimbly doth obey.
Which truth the joynt confessions bewray
Of damned Hags and Masters of bold skill

32.1-5 The story of how Jacob tricked his father-in-law is told in Genesis 30.

33.1 In mythology *Cippus* grew horns after watching a bullfight.

33.8 arrive: reach.

34.3 easily, : easily 1647.

34.5 bewray: reveal.

Whose hellish mysteries fully to display
With pitchy darknesse would the Heavens fill,
The earth would grone, trees sigh, and horrour all ore spill.

35

But he that out of darknesse giveth light
May guide my steps in this so uncouth way
And ill done deeds by children of the Night
Convert to good, while I shall thence assay
The noble souls conditions ope to lay,
And show her empyre on her ayry sphear
By what of sprights and specters Stories say.
For sprights and spectres that by night appear
Be or all one with souls or of a nature near.

36

Up then renowned Wizard, Hermite sage!
That twice ten years didst in the desert wonne,
Convers'dst with sprights in thy hid Hermitage
Since thou of mortals didst the commerce shun,
Well seen in these bad arts that have foredone
Many a bold wit; Up *Marcus*; tell again
That story of thy *Thrax*, who has thee wonne
To Christian faith, the guise and haunts explain
Of all air-trampling ghosts that in the world remain.

34.8 fill, : fill 1647.

35.2 May : He 1647.

35.9 or all one with: either the same as.

36.1 The "Hermite sage" More identifies in the *Immortality of the Soul*, vol. 2, chap. 17 (*Works* [London, 1662], p. 135), as "*Marcus* the Eremite," who, according to a dialogue written by the Neoplatonist Michael Psellus, had described the nature of Dæmons "as being throughout *Spirit* and *Aire*; whence they hear and see and feel in every part of their Body" (see above at stanza 15). More seems to have consulted the Greek original of Psellus' *De operatione demonum dialogus*, printed with a Latin translation in 1577 and again in 1615 and 1618 (it had earlier been translated by Marsilio Ficino). "Thrax," 36.7, one of the participants in Psellus' dialogue, had converted Marcus to Christianity.

36.6 wit; : wit, 1647.

36.7 wonne : wonne, 1647.

37

There be six sorts of sprights. *Lelurion*
Is the first kind, the next are nam'd from Air;
The first aloft, yet farre beneath the Moon,
The other in this lower region fare.
The third Terrestriall, the fourth Watery are,
The fift be Subterranean, the last
And worst, Light-hating ghosts more cruel farre
Then Bear or Wolf with hunger hard opprest,
But doltish yet and dull like an unweildy beast.

38

If this sort once possesse the arteries
Of forlorn man: Madnesse and stupor seize
His salvag'd heart, and death dwels in his eyes.
Ne is there remedy for this sad disease.
For that unworthy guest so senselesse is
And deaf, no Exorcist can make him hear,
But would in vain with Magick words chastise.
Others the thundering threats of *Tartar* fear
And the drad names of Angels that this office bear.

39

For they been all subject to passion.
Some been so grosse they hunger after food,
And send out seed of which worms spring anon,
And love to liggen warm in living bloud,

37.1ff. This classification of demons and its details derive from Psellus. See *Dialogue on the Operation of Dæmons*, trans. Marcus Collison (Sidney, Australia, 1848), pp. 31ff.

37.2 Air; : Air 1647.

37.3 Moon, : Moon 1647.

37.8 opprest, : opprest 1647.

38.3 salvag'd: rendered savage.

39 In the *Antidote against Atheisme* (*Works*, p. 132), More traces this idea to Hermes Trismegistus. He recurs to it below at 71.1-2.

39.3 Psellus, p. 30, holds that worms arise from the sperm of demons.

39.4 liggen: lie.

Whence they into the veins do often crowd
Of beasts as well as men, wherein they bathe
Themselves, and sponge-like suck that vitall flood,
As they done also in their aery path
Drink in each unctuous steam, which their dire thirst allayth.

40

Such be the four last kinds, foul, dull, impure
Whose inward life and phansy's more inert
And therefore usually in one shape endure.
But those of aire can easily convert
Into new forms and then again revert,
One while a man, after a comely maid,
And then all suddenly to make the stert,
Like leaping Leopard he'll thee invade,
Then made a man again he'll comfort thee afraid.

41

Then straight more quick then thought or cast of eye
A snarling Dog, or brisled Boar he'll be;
Anon a jugge of milk if thou be dry,
So easily's turned that aire-consistency
Through inward sport and power of phantasie.
For all things virtually are containd in aire.
And like the sunne, that fiery spirit free
Th' internall soul, at once the seed doth rear
Waken and ripe at once as if full ag'd they were.

42

Cameleon like thus they their colour change
And size contract, and then dilate again:
Like the soft earthworm hurt by heedlesse chance
Shrinks in her self to shun or ease her pain.
Nor done they onely thus themselves constrain

40.7 the: thee.

41.6 virtually: a term from scholastic philosophy meaning that one thing contains another more completely than mere formal possession requires.

42 The details are all from Psellus. For analogous beliefs in Milton's writing see Robert H. West, *Milton's Angelology* (Athens, Ga.: University of Georgia Press, 1955), especially pp. 103ff.

Into lesse bulk, but if with courage bold
And flaming brond thou strike these shades in twain,
A sudden smart they feel that cannot hold,
Close quick as cloven aire. So sang that Wizzard old.

43

And truth he said what ever he has told,
As even the present Age may verifie,
If any lists its stories to unfold
Of Hags, of Hobgoblings, of Incubi,
Abhorred dugs by devils sucken dry,
Of leaping lamps and of fierce-flying stones,
Of living wool, and such like witchery,
Or prov'd by sight or self confessions,
Which things much credence gain to past traditions.

44

Wherefore with boldnesse we will now relate
Some few in breif, as of th' *Astorgan* lad,
Whose peevish mother in fell ire and hate
Quite drunk with passion, through quick cholar mad
With execrations bold the devil bad,
Take him alive, which mood the boy no'te bear
But quits the room, walks out with spirit sad
Into the court, where, Lo! by night appear
Tall Giants with grim looks, rough limbs, black grizely hair.

45

These in a moment hoist him into th' air,
Away him bear more swift then bird can fly,
Straight to the destin'd place arrived are
Mongst craggy rocks, and bushy Mountains high,
Where up and down they drag the sorry boy;

43.4 Hags, : Hags 1647. Hobgoblings, : Hobgoblings 1647.

43.6 stones, : stones 1647.

44ff. The collection of relations which follows is a regular feature of witchcraft texts, perhaps its most interesting one today. Not all of More's sources have been identified.

44.6 no'te: could not.

His tender skin and goary flesh they tear
Till he gan on his Maker call and cry.
Which forc'd the villains home again him bear,
Where he the story told, restor'd by Parents care.

46

The walking Skeleton in *Bolonia*
Laden with rattling chains, that showd his grave
To th' watchfull Student, who without dismay
Bid tell his wants, and speak what he would have:
Thus cleared he the house by courage brave.
Nor may I passe the fair *Cerdinian* maid
Whose love a jolly swain did kindly crave,
And oft with mutuall solace with her stay'd;
Yet was no jolly swain but a deceitful shade.

47

More harmlesse mirth may that mad spright commend
Who in an honest widows house did won
At *Salamanca*, who whole showers would send
Of stones that swifter then a whirlwind come
And yet where ere they hit no hurt is done.
But cursed cruell be those wicked Hags
Whom poysonous spight, envy and hate have won
T' abhorred sorcery, whose writhled bags
Fould feinds oft suck and nestle in their loathsome rags.

48

Such as the Devil woes in homely form
Of swarthy man, or some black shaggy Curre,
Or vermine base, and in sad case forlorn
Them male-content to evil motions stirre,
Proffer their service, adding a quick spurre

47.8 writhled: wrinkled.

48 "The devil is president of the Assembly and sits on a throne in some terrible shape, as of a goat or a dog; and they [the witches] approach him to adore him. . . . and kiss him upon the buttocks in sign of homage." Francisco Guazzo, *Compendium Maleficarum* (1608, 1626) as edited by Montague Summers and translated by E. A. Ashwin (London: J. Rodker, 1929), p. 35.

To meditated vengance, and fell teen.
Whose hellish voice they heare without demur,
Abjure God and his Sonne, who did redeem
The world, give up themselves to Satan and foul sinne.

49

Thus 'bodyed into that *Stygian* crue
Of damned wights made fast by their own bloud
To their bad Master, do his service due,
Frequent the assemblies, dance as they were wood
Around an huge black Goat, in loansome wood
By shady night, farre from or house or town,
And kisse with driveling lips in frantick mood
His sacred breech. Catch that catch may anon
Each Feind has got his Hag for copulation.

50

O loathsome law! O filthy fond embrace!
The other root of cursed sorcery.
For if the streams of this bad art we trace
They lead to two foul springs, th' one Venerie
And coarsest Lust, the other near doth lie
And is ycleeped Vengeance, Malice, Hate,
Or restlesse Envy that would all destroy.
But both but from one seed do germinate
Hight uncurb'd Will, or strong Desire inordinate.

51

Wherefore I needs must humbly here adore
Him whose chaste soul enwombd in Virgin chast,
As chast a body amongst mortals wore,
Who never woman knew, ne once did taste
Of Hymens pleasures while this life did last.
Ah! my dear Lord! dread Sovereigne of souls
Who with thy life and lore so warmed hast

48.6 teen: injury.

49.7 frantick : frantcik 1647.

51-55 Here at the midpoint of the poem More pauses for an apostrophe to Christ.

My wounded heart, that when thy Storie's told,
Sweet Love, methinks, in 's silver wings me all infolds.

52

How do I hang upon thy sacred lips
More sweet then Manna or the hony-dew!
Thy speech, like rosie drops doth cool my wits
And calme my fierce affections untrue,
And winne my heart unto obeisance due.
Blest O thrice blessed be that holy hill
Whereon thou did'st instruct thy faithfull crue
In wayes of peace, of patience and good-will
Forbidding base self-love, revenge and speeches ill.

53

Meek Lambe of God! the worlds both scourge and scorn!
How done th' infernall feinds thy face envy!
Thou light, they darknesse, they Night, thou the Morn!
Mild chariot of Gods lovely Majesty!
Exalted Throne of the Divinitie!
As thou with thine mak'st through the yielding aire
How do thy frighted foes before thee fly!
And grin and gnash their teeth for spight and fear
To see such awfull strength quite to themselves contraire.

54

Ho! you vain men that follow filthy lust
And swallow down revenge like pleasant wine.
Base earthly spirits! fly this sinfull dust.
See with what hellish Comrades you combine,
Als see whose lovely friendship you decline.
Even his whose love to you more strong then death
Did death abide, foul shame and evil tine,
But if sweet love your hearts may move uneath
Think how one fatall flame, shall burn all underneath.

52.6 holy hill: that of Matthew 5, where Jesus uttered the Beatitudes.

53.2 done: do.

54.7 tine: teen, affliction.

54.8 uneath: with difficulty.

55

Pans pipe shall then be mute, and Satyrs heel
Shall cease to dance ybrent in scorching fire;
For pleasure then each earthly spright shall feel
Deep searching pain; Revenge and base desire
Shall bear due vengeance, reap their worthy hire;
From thee, great Prince of souls! shall be their doome.
Then thou and thy dear Saints ascending higher
Shalt fly the fate, and quit this stinking room
With smouldry smoak, fierce fire, and loathsome stench o'rerun.

56

Go now you cursed Hags, salute your Goat
Whether with driveling lips or taper end,
Whereby at last you fire his hispide coat,
And then the deadly dust on mischief spend
As your Liege Lord these ashes doth commend
For wicked use, thundring this precept drad,
Revenge, revenge, or I shall on you send
Due vengeance: Thus dismist th' Assembly bad
Hoyst up into the Air, fly home through clammy shade.

57

Which stories all to us do plainly prove
That airy sprights both speak, and hear, and see.
Why do not then the souls of mortalls move
In airy Chariots but stupid lie
Lock'd up in sloth and senselesse Lethargie.
Certes our soul's as well proportionate
To this aeriall weed as spirits free:
For neither can our souls incorporate
With naked Earth, the Air must ever mediate.

56 In his *Demonomanie des Sorciers* (Anvers, 1593, p. 176), which More often cites from its Latin version in his *Antidote against Atheism*, Jean Bodin writes that witches dance about a great black goat and kiss him as More describes; then "the goat is consumed with fire and each takes some of its ashes to kill an enemy's cattle, horse," and so on. "At the end the Devil tells them in a fearful voice, 'Avenge or die.' "

56.3 hispide: shaggy.

57.8-9 In *Immortality of the Soul*, bk. 2, chap. 14 (*Works*, pp. 118–19), More argues this conclusion from Aristotle's *Generation of Animals*. Later he

58

Which that bold Art which Necromancy hight
Doth know too well, and therefore doth prepare
A vap'rous vehicle for th' intended spright,
With reek of oyl, meal, milk, and such like gear,
Wine, water, hony; Thus souls fitted are
A grosser Carkas for to reassume.
And though *Thessalian* Hags their pains do spare
Sometimes they enter without Magick fume;
Witnesse ye *Cretick* wives, who felt their fruitlesse spume.

59

And therefore to prevent such hellish lust
They did by laws Municipall provide
That he that dar'd to rise out of his dust
And thus infest his wife, a stake should gride
His stubborn heart and 's body burn beside.
Hereto belongs that story of the spright
Of fell Asuitus noted far and wide,
And of his faithfull comrade Asmund hight;
Twixt whom this law was made, as Danish Records write:

60

Which of them two the other did survive
Must be intomb'd with 's fellow in one grave.
Dead *Asuit* therefore with his friend alive
His dog and horse all in one mighty Cave
Be shut together, yet this eare they have,
That faithfull Asmund, be not lost for meat:
Wherefore he was well stor'd his life to save
And liv'd sometime in that infernall seat,
Till *Errick* King of Sweads the door did open break.

states that "the nature of the Soul is such, as that she cannot act but in dependence on *Matter*," p. 146. See also stanza 15 above.

58.9 In *Immortality of the Soul*, bk. 2, chap. 14 (*Works*, p. 131), More relates from Cornelius Agrippa how the spirits of their dead husbands tried to lie with Cretan widows.

59.2 Municipall: local.

59.4 gride: pierce.

59.6ff. The story is from Saxo, *Gesta Danorum*, bk. 5, sec. 49 a–b.

61

For well he ween'd there was some treasure hid
Which might enrich himself, or 's Army pay.
But when he had broke ope the brasen lid
Nought but a sory wight they finden may,
Whom out of darknesse brought to open day
The King beheld, dight with most deadly hue,
His cheek all gore, his ear quite bit away.
Then gan the King command the cause to shew,
To which Asmundus answers, as doth here ensue:

62

Why gaze you thus on my sad squalid face,
Th' alive needs languish must amongst the dead,
But this sore wound that further doth deface
My wasted looks, Asuitus (who first fed
On 's horse and dog, and then with courage dred,
At me let fly), *Asuit* this wound me gave,
But well I quit my self, took off his head
With this same blade, his heart nayl'd to the Cave:
Thus I my self by force did from the monster save.

63

The soul of *Naboth* lies to *Ahab* told,
As done the learned Hebrew Doctours write,
His foe in mischief thereby to infold.
Go up to *Ramoth Gilead* and fight,
Go up and prosper, said the lying spright,
The angry ghost of *Naboth* whom he slew
Unjustly, and possest his ancient right.
Hence his revengefull soul with speech untrue
Sat on his Prophets lips, and did with lies embue.

62 As Saxo states more clearly, Asmund, buried alive with the dead Aswid and the latter's horse and dog, was attacked by the ghost of his friend after it had eaten both animals. In the struggle the spirit bit off Asmund's ear, but Asmund cut off its head and impaled the body on a stake.

62.2 Th': That.

63 In 1 Kings 21 King Ahab seized the vineyard, hereditary property of Naboth, after Ahab's Queen, Jezebel, had had Naboth killed. In the next chapter a ghost, interpreted to be that of Naboth, put a "lying spirit" into the mouths

64

Ne may I passe that story sad of *Saul*
And *Samuels* ghost, whom he in great distresse
Consulted, was foretold his finall fall
By that old man whom *Endors* sorceresse
Awak'd from pleasant vision and sweet ease,
Straitning a while his wonted liberty
By clammy air more close and thick compresse,
Then gan the mantled Sage *Sauls* destiny
To reade, and thine with his, dear *Jonathan*! to tye.

65

That lovely lasse *Pausanias* did kill
Through ill surmise she ment him treachery;
How did her angry spirit haunt him still
That he could no where rest, nor quiet ly:
Her wronged ghost was ever in his eye.
And he that in his anger slew his wife,
And was exempt by Law from penalty,
Poore sorry man he led a weary life:
Each night the Shrow him beat with buffes and boxes rife.

66

And love as well as hate the dead doth reach,
As may be seen by what *Albumaron*
Did once befall, that learnd *Arabian* Leach.
He of a late-deceas'd Physition
Upon his bed by dream or vision

of the prophets whom Ahab consulted about attacking Ramoth Gilead. Following their advice, he attacked and was killed.

64 In 1 Samuel 28 Saul consults the Witch of Endor, who at his request calls up the spirit of the dead prophet Samuel to advise him. He prophesies disaster at the hands of the Philistines, including the death of Saul's son Jonathan. The episode was often cited as biblical proof of witchcraft.

65 Bodin (p. 151) tells the story of this king of Lacedæmonia and traces it to Plutarch.

65.8 life: : life 1647.

66.2 In his *Immortality of the Soul* (*Works*, p. 129), More tells the story of *Albumaron*, citing as his source Marsilio Ficino's *Theologica Platonica*. A few lines later he traces the story of *Simonides* (l. 7) to the same source.

Receiv'd a soveraign salve for his sore eye,
And just *Simonides* compassion
Unto the dead that did unburied ly
On washed shore, him sav'd from jaws of destinie.

67

For he had perish'd in th' unruly waves,
And sudden storm, but lo! the thankfull spright
Of the interr'd by timely counsell saves,
Warning him of the danger he would meet
In his intended voyage,
Simonides desists by 's counsell won:
The rest for want of faith or due foresight,
A prey to the devouring Seas become,
Their dashed bodies welter in the weedy scum.

68

In Artick Climes, an Isle that *Thule* hight
Famous for snowy monts, whose hoary head's
Sure signe of cold, yet from their fiery feet
They strike out burning stones with thunders dread,
And all the Land with smoak, and ashes spread:
Here wandring Ghosts themselves have often shown,
As if it were the region of the dead.
And men departed met with whom they've known,
In seemly sort shake hands, and ancient friendship own.

69

A world of wonders hither might be thrown,
Of Sprights and spectres, as that frequent noise
Oft heard upon the Plane of *Marathon*,
Of neighing horses and of Martiall boyes.
The Greek, the Persian, nightly here destroyes
In hot assault, embroyl'd in a long war.
Foure hundred years did last these dreadfull toyes,
As doth by *Attick* Records plain appear,
The seeds of hate, by death so little slaked are.

68.1 *Thule*: a mythical land in the far North. The Arctic was notorious as the haunt of witches. See 83.9.

70

Nor lists me speak of *Remus* Lemures,
Nor haunted house of slain *Caligula*,
Nor *Julius* stern Ghost, who will, with ease
May for himself of old or new purvey.
Thousand such stories in mens mouths do stray.
But sith it much perplexeth slower minds
To think our souls unhurt can passe away
From their dear corps so close thereto confin'd,
From this unweildy thought let's now their wits unbind.

71

For if that spirits can possesse our veins
And arteries (as usuall stories tell)
Use all our Organes, aċt our nerves and brains,
And by our tongue can future things foretell,
And safely yet keep close in this warme cell
For many years and not themselves impare
Nor lose ymeint with the bloud where they dwel,
But come out clever when they conjured are
And nimbly passe away soft-gliding through the air:

72

Why scape not then the souls of men as clear
Since to this body they're no better joyn'd
Then thorough it to feel, to see, to hear
And to impart the passions of the mind?
All which done by th' usurping spright we find.
As witnesse may that maid in *Saxony*,

70.1 *Remus* Lemures: After his death the ghost of Remus appeared one day and asked that that day be named for him. It was, as Remuria, but later by change of pronunciation it became Lemuria. So writes Ovid in *Fasti*, 5. 445ff.

70.2 Suetonius, in the *Life of Caligula*, sec. 59, tells the story. Bodin also mentions it, p. 152.

70.3 The story of Cæsar's ghost as it appeared to Brutus is, of course, most familiar in Shakespeare's retelling of Plutarch. who: whoever.

71.3 Organes, : Organes 1647. aċt: influence, stimulate. brains, : brains 1647.

71.7 ymeint: mixed.

72.6 More repeats her story in *Antidote against Atheism* (*Works*, p. 100), where he traces it to Bodin.

Who meanly born of rude unlearned kind,
Not taught to reade, yet Greek and Latine she
Could roundly speak and in those tongues did prophesie.

73

Timotheus sister down in childbed laid
Disturb'd, all phrantick thorough deadly pain
Tearing the clothes, which much her friends dismai'd,
Mumbling strange words as confus'd as her brain
At last was prov'd to speak *Armenian.*
For an old man that was by chance in town
And from his native soyle *Armenia* came,
The woman having heard of his renown
Sent to this aged Sire to this sick wight to come.

74

Lo! now has entred the *Armenian* Sage
With scalp all bald, and skin all brown and brent,
The number of his wrinkles told his age:
A naked sword in his dry hand he hent.
Thus standing near her bed strong threats he sent
In his own language, and her fiercely chid.
But she well understanding what he meant
Unto his threats did bold defiance bid.
Ne could his vaunts as yet the sturdy spirit rid.

75

Then gan he sternely speak and heave his hond
And feign'd himself enrag'd with hasty ire
As ready for to strike with flaming brond,
But she for fear shrunk back and did retire
Into her bed and gently did respire,
Muttering few easie words in sleepy wise.
So now whom erst tumultuous thoughts did tire

73 Timotheus, the interlocutor in Psellus' dialogue, narrates this story of his sister-in-law, pp. 39ff.

73.2 Disturb'd : Distur'b 1647.

74.2 brent: burnt.

74.4 hent: held.

Compos'd to rest doth sweetly close her eyes,
Then wak'd, what her befell, in sober mood descryes.

76

Now, *Thrax!* thy Story adde of *Alytas*
Who got his freind into a Mountain high
Where he with him the loansome night did passe
In Stygian rites and hellish mystery.
First twiches up an herb that grew thereby,
Gives him to taste, then doth his eyes besmear
With uncouth salves, wherewith all suddenly
Legions of spirits flying here and there
Around their cursed heads do visibly appear.

77

Lastly into his mouth with filthy spaul
He spot, which done, a spirit like a Daw
His mouth did enter, and possessed all
His inward parts. From that time he gan know
Many secret things, and could events foreshow.
This was his guerdon, this his wicked wage
From the inwoning of that Stygian Crow.
But who can think this bird did so engage
With flesh that he no'te scape the ruin of the cage.

78

No more do souls of men. For stories sayen
Well known 'mongst countrey folk, our spirits fly,
From twixt our lips, and thither back again,
Sometimes like Doves, sometime like to a Bee,
And sometime in their bodyes shape they be;
But all this while their carkase lyes asleep
Drownd in dull rest, son of mortality;

76.1 In Psellus' dialogue, pp. 37–38, the speaker describes this episode from his own experience in Elason.

77.1 spaul: spit.

77.2 spot: spat.

77.6 guerdon, : guerdon 1647.

78.7 rest, : rest 1647.

At last these shapes return'd do slily creep
Into their mouth, then the dead clouds away they wipe.

79

Nor been these stories all but Countrey fictions,
For such like things even learned Clerks do write,
Of brasen sleep and bodi's derelictions.
That *Proconnesian* Sage that *Atheus* hight
Did oft himself of this dull body quit,
His soul then wandring in the easie aire.
But as to smoking lamp but lately light
The flame catch'd by the reek descends from farre,
So would his soul at last to his warm blood repair.

80

And *Hermotime* the *Clasomenian*
Would in like sort his body leave alone,
And view with naked soul both Hill and Plain
And secret Groves and every Region,
That he could tell what far and near was done:
But his curs'd foes the fell *Cantharidæ*
Assault his house when he was far from home,
Burn down to ashes his forsaken clay:
So may his wandring ghost for ever freely stray.

81

And 'tis an art well known to Wizards old
And wily Hags, who oft for fear and shame
Of the coarse halter, do themselves with-hold
From bodily assisting their night game:
Wherefore their carkasses at home retain,
But with their soules at those bad feasts they are,

79.3 brasen: brazen, sound.

79.4 *Proconnesian*: of the island Marmora.

80.1 *Hermotime*: a famous prophet of Clazomenæ, who as More says was fabled to leave his body.

80.8 clay: : clay. 1647.

80.9 stray. : stray: 1647.

81.5 retain, : retain. 1647.

And see their friends and call them by their name
And dance around the Goat and sing, har, har,
And kisse the Devils breech, and taste his deadly chear.

82

A many stories to this purpose might
Be brought of men that in this Ecstacy
So senselesse ly, that coales laid to their feet
Nor nips nor whips can make them ope their eye.
Then of a sudden when this fit's gone by,
They up and with great confidence declare
What things they heard and saw both far and nie,
Professing that their soules unbodied were
And roam'd about the earth in Countries here and there.

83

And to confirm the truth of this strange flight
They oft bring home a letter or a ring
At their return, from some far distant wight
Well known to friends that have the ordering
Of their forsaken corps, that no live thing
Do tread or touch't, so safely may their spright
Spend three whole dayes in airy wandering.
A feat that's often done through Magick might,
By the *Norvegian* Hags as learned Authors write.

84

But now well-wearied with our too long stay
In these Cimmerian fogs and hatefull mists
Of Ghosts, of Goblins, and drad sorcery,
From nicer allegations we'll desist.
Enough is said to prove that souls dismist
From these grosse bodies may be cloth'd in air,
Scape free (although they did not præexist,)

81.8 More refers to such animalism again in *Antidote against Atheism* (*Works*, p. 120), citing Bodin as authority, according to whom (p. 178) "har, har" is part of the song sung by witches at such dances.

84.2 Cimmerian: people fabled to live in perpetual darkness.

84.3 Ghosts, : Ghosts 1647. Goblins, : Goblins 1647.

And in these airy orbs feel, see, and hear
And moven as they list as did by proof appear.

85

But that in some sort souls do præexist
Seems to right reason nothing dissonant
Sith all souls both of trees, of men and beast
Been indivisible; And all do grant
Of humane souls though not of beast and plant:
But I elsewhere, I think, do gainly prove
That souls of beasts, by reasons nothing scant,
Be individuous, ne care to move
This question of a new, mens patiences to prove.

86

But if mens souls be individuous
How can they ought from their own substance shed?
In generation there's nought flows from us
Saving grosse sperm yspent in Nuptiall bed
Drain'd from all parts throughout the body spred,
And well concocted where me list not name.
But no conveyances there be that lead
To the souls substance, whereby her they drain
Of loosened parts, a young babe-soul from thence to gain.

87

Wherefore who thinks from souls new souls to bring
The same let presse the Sunne beams in his fist
And squeez out drops of light, or strongly wring
The Rainbow, till it die his hands, well-prest.
Or with uncessant industry persist
Th' intentionall species to mash and bray

85.3 all souls: The several life principles, also called souls, were traditionally classified as vegetative, sensitive, and rational.

85.6 elsewhere: More returns to the subject a number of times. See, for instance, book 1, canto 2 of his poem *Psychathanasia* and the *Appendix* to the *Antidote against Atheism*, chapter 10. gainly: satisfactorily.

87.1 The idea of the begetting of souls this way is called traducianism. See 91.9.

87.6 intentionall: conceptual. bray: crush to a powder.

In marble morter, till he has exprest
A sovereigne eye-salve to discern a Fay.
As easily as the first all these effect you may.

88

Ne may queint similies this fury damp
Which say that our souls propagation
Is as when lamp we lighten from a lamp.
Which done withouten diminution
Of the first light, shows how the soul of man
Though indivisible may another rear,
Imparting life. But if we rightly scan
This argument, it cometh nothing near.
To light the lamp's to kindle the sulphurious gear.

89

No substance new that act doth then produce;
Onely the oyly atomes 't doth excite
And wake into a flame, but no such use
There is of humane sperm. For our free sprite
Is not the kindled seed, but substance quite
Distinct therefrom. If not, then bodies may
So changed be by nature and stiff fight
Of hungry stomacks, that what erst was clay,
Then herbs, in time itself in sense may well display.

90

For then our soul can nothing be but bloud
Or nerves or brains, or body modifide.
Whence it will follow that cold stopping crud,
Hard moldy cheese, dry nuts, when they have rid
Due circuits through the heart, at last shall speed
Of life and sense, look thorough our thin eyes
And view the Close wherein the Cow did feed

88.6 rear, : rear 1647.
89.1 produce; : produce 1647.
89.8 clay, : clay 1647.
90.3 crud: curd.

Whence they were milk'd, grosse Pie-crust will grow wise,
And pickled Cucumbers sans doubt Philosophize.

91

This all will follow if the soul be nought
But the live body. For mens bodies feed
Of such grosse meat, and if more fine be brought,
Suppose Snipes heads, Larks heels for Ladies meet,
The broth of Barly, or that oily Sweet
Of th' unctious Grape, yet all men must confesse
These be as little capable of wit
And sense, nor can be so transform'd, I wisse:
Therefore no soul of man from seed traducted is.

92

Ne been they by th' high God then first create
When in this earthly mansion they appear.
For why should he so soon contaminate
So unspotted beauties as mens spirits are,
Flinging them naked into dunghills here?
Soyl them with guilt and foul contagion?
When as in his own hand they spotlesse were
Till by an uncouth strange infusion
He plung'd them in the deep of Malediction.

93

Besides unworthily he doth surmise
Of Gods pure being and bright Majesty
Who unto such base offices him ties,
That He must wait on lawlesse Venery;
Not onely by that large Causality
Of generall influence (for Creation
More speciall concourse all men deem to be)
But on set purpose He must come anon,
And ratifie the act which oft men wish undone.

92 This theory of the origin of the soul is called creationism.

92.4 are, : are 1647.

93.4 Venery; : Venery 1647. Milton, who was a traducian, employs the same argument in his *Christian Doctrine*.

94

Which is a rash and shamelesse bad conceit,
So might they name the brat *Adeodatus*,
Whatever they in lawlesse love beget.
Again, what's still far more prodigious
When men are stung with fury poysonous
And burn with flames of lust toward brute beasts,
And overcome into conjunction rush,
He then from that foul act is not releast,
Creates a soul, misplacing the unhappy guest.

95

Wherefore mans soul's not by Creation.
Nor is it generate, as I prov'd before.
Wherefore let 't be by emanation
(If fully it did not præexist of yore)
By flowing forth from that eternall store
Of Lives and souls ycleep'd the World of life,
Which was, and shall endure for evermore.
Hence done all bodies vitall fire derive
And matter never lost catch life and still revive.

96

And what has once sprout out doth never cease
If it enjoy itself, a spray to be
Distinct and actuall, though if God please
He can command it into th' ancient tree.
This immense Orb of wast vitality
With all its Lives and Souls is every where,
And do's, where matter right prepar'd doth lie.
Impart a soul, as done the sunne beams clear
Insinuate themselves, where filth doth not debarre.

97

Thus may the souls in long succession
Leap out into distinct activity:
But sooth to say though this opinion
May seem right fair and plausible to be

94.2 *Adeodatus*: given by God.

Yet toils it under an hard difficulty.
Each where this Orb of life's with every soul;
Which doth imply the souls ubiquity.
Or if the whole Extent of Nature's full
Of severall souls thick set, what may the furthest pull?

98

What may engage them to descend so low,
Remov'd farre from the steam of earthly mire?
My wits been here too scant and faith too slow.
Ne longer lists my wearied thoughts to tire.
Let bolder spirits to such hight aspire.
But well I wote, if there admitted were
A præexistency of souls entire,
And due Returns in courses circular
This course all difficulties with ease away would bear.

99

For then suppose they wore an airy sphear
Which choice or *Nemesis* suck'd lower down,
Thus without doubt they'll leave their carcase clear;
Like dispossessed spright when death doth come
And by rude exorcisme bids quit the room.
Ne let these intricacies perplex our mind
That we forget that ere we saw the sunne
Before this life. For who can call to mind
Where first he here saw sunne or felt the gentle wind.

100

Besides what wonder is 't, when fierce disease
Can so empair the strongest memory
That so full change should make our spirits leese
What 'fore they had impress'd in phantasie.
Nor doth it follow thence that when we die
We nought retain of what pass'd in these dayes,
For Birth is Death, Death Life and Liberty.

100.3 leese: lose.

100.6 dayes, : dayes. 1647.

The soul's not thence contract but there displayes
Her loosened self, doth higher all her powers raise.

101

Like to a light fast lock'd in lanthorn dark,
Whereby, by night our wary steps we guide
In slabby streets, and dirty channels mark,
Some weaker rayes through the black top do glide,
And flusher streams perhaps from horny side.
But when we've past the perill of the way
Arriv'd at home, and laid that case aside,
The naked light how clearly doth it ray
And spread its joyfull beams as bright as Summers day.

102

Even so the soul in this contracted state
Confin'd to these strait instruments of sense
More dull and narrowly doth operate.
At this hole hears, the sight must ray from thence,
Here tasts, there smels; But when she's gone from hence,
Like naked lamp she is one shining sphear.
And round about has perfect cognoscence
What ere in her Horizon doth appear:
She is one Orb of sense, all eye, all airy ear.

103

Now have I well establish'd the fourth way
The souls of men from stupid sleep to save,
First Light, next Night, the third the soules Self-ray,
Fourth the souls Chariot we named have
Whether moist air or fire all sparkling brave
Or temper mixt. Now how these foure agree,
And how the soul her self may dip and lave
In each by turns; how no redundancy
Ther's in them, might we tell, nor scant deficiency.

101-2 are quoted in *Antidote against Atheism* (*Works,* p. 131).

101.3 slabby: miry.

103.1 fourth: The previous three were argued in the three cantos of *Antipsychopannychia*, to which this poem is appended.

104

But cease my restlesse Muse, be not too free;
Thy chiefest end thou hast accomplished
Long since, shak'd of the *Psychopannychie*
And rouz'd the soul from her dull drowsiehed.
So nothing now in death is to be dred
Of him that wakes to truth and righteousnesse.
The corps lies here, the soul aloft is fled
Unto the fount of perfect happinesse
Full freedome, joy and peace she lively doth possesse.

104.1 Muse, : Muse 1647. free; : free, 1647.

104.3 of: off. *Psychopannychie*: sleep of the soul. John Calvin's second publication, attacking this Anabaptist teaching, had this as title.

104.9 freedome, : freedome 1647.

Devotion.

Good God! when thou thy inward grace dost shower
Into my brest,
How full of light and lively power
Is then my soul!
How am I blest!
How can I then all difficulties devour!
Thy might
Thy spright
With ease my combrous enemy controll.

If thou once turn away thy face and hide 10
Thy chearfull look,
My feeble flesh may not abide
That dreadfull stound,
I cannot brook
Thy absence. My heart with care and grief then gride
Doth fail,
Doth quail,
My life steals from me, at that hidden wound.

My phansie's then a burden to my mind,
Mine anxious thought 20
Betrayes my reason, makes me blind:
Near dangers drad
Make me distraught.
Supriz'd with fear, my senses all I find.
In hell
I dwell
Opprest with horrour, pain and sorrow sad.

My former Resolutions all are fled,
Slip't over my tongue,
My Faith, my Hope, and Joy, are dead. 30

13 stound: time.
15 gride: wounded.
22 drad: dread.
24 find: lose the use of (?).

Assist my heart
Rather then my song
My God! my Saviour! when I'm ill bested
Stand by,
And I
Shall bear with courage, undeserved smart.

Ad Paronem.

Right well I wot, my rhymes seem rudely drest
In the nice judgement of thy shallow mind
That mark'st expressions more then what's exprest,
Busily billing the rough outward rinde,
But reaching not the pith. Such surface skill's
Unmeet to measure the profounder quill.

Yea I alas! my self too often feel
Thy indispos'dnesse; when my weakened soul
Unstedfast, into this Outworld doth reel,
10 And lyes immerse in my low vitall mold.
For then my mind, from th'inward spright estrang'd,
My Muse into an uncouth hew hath chang'd.

A rude confused heap of ashes dead
My verses seem, when that cælestiall flame
That sacred spirit of life's extinguished
In my cold brest. Then gin I rashly blame
My rugged lines: This word is obsolete;
That boldly coynd, a third too oft doth beat

Mine humourous ears. Thus fondly curious
20 Is the faint Reader, that doth want that fire

Title: To Paro (named in l. 48), Latin for a shallow vessel.

4 billing: pecking.

9 Outworld: Bullough reads Outward.

19 humourous: capricious, hard to please. fondly curious: foolishly hard to satisfy.

And inward vigour heavenly furious
That made my enrag'd spirit in strong desire
  Break through such tender cob-web niceties,
  That oft intangle these blind buzzing flies.

Possest with living sense I inly rave,
Carelesse how outward words do from me flow,
So be the image of my mind they have
Truly exprest, and do my visage show;
  As doth each river deckt with Phebus beams
  Fairly reflect the viewer of his streams. 30

Who can discern the Moons asperity
From of this earth, or could this earths discover
If from the earth he raised were on high
Among the starrs and in the sky did hover?
  The Hills and Valleyes would together flow
  And the rough Earth, one smooth-fac'd Round would show.

Nor can the lofty soul snatch'd into Heven
Busied above in th'Intellectuall world
At such a distance see my lines uneven,
At such a distance was my spirit hurld, 40
  And to my trembling quill thence did endite,
  What he from thence must reade, who would read right.

Fair Fields and rich Enclosures, shady Woods,
Large populous Towns, with strong and stately Towers,
Long crawling Rivers, far distended Flouds,
What ever's great, its shape these eyes of ours
  And due proportions from high distance see
  The best; And *Paro*! such my Rhyme's to thee.

Thy groveling mind and moping poreblind eye,
That to move up unmeet, this to see farre, 50

31 asperity: uneven surface.

32 of: off.

49 poreblind: purblind, blind.

The worth or weaknesse never can descry
Of my large winged Muse. But not to spare
Till thou canst well disprove, proves well enough
Thou art rash and rude how ere my rhymes are rough.

Exorcismus.

What's this that in my brest thus grieves and groanes,
Rives my close-straitned heart, distends my sides
With deep fetch'd sighs, while th'other in fell pride
Resists and choaks? O hear the dreadfull moanes
Of thy dear son, if so him cleep I may.
If there be any sense 'twixt Heven and Earth,
If any mutuall feeling sure this birth
May challenge speed, and break off all delay.
You Winged people of the unseen sky
10 That bear that living Name in your pure brest,
Chariots of God in whom the Lord of rest
Doth sit triumphant, can not you espy
The self same Being in such jeopardy?
Make haste, make haste if you Gods army been,
Rescue his son, wreak your revengefull teen
On his fast holding Enemy.
Hath Nature onely sympathy?

What? may I deem you self-exulting sprights
Lock'd up in your own selves, whose inward life
20 Is self-contenting joy, withouten strife
Of doing good and helping wofull wights?

1 groanes, : groanes 1647.

3 With : with 1647. th'other: his sinful nature.

11 More has in mind the description in Ezekiel 1 of God's chariot spirited with angels.

14 haste, make : haste make 1647.

15 teen: rage.

17 onely: alone.

18-21 More describes the life of ethereal spirits which he elaborates more fully elsewhere, as in *Præexistency of the Soul.*

21 wights? : wights. 1647.

Then were you empty carres and not the throne
Of that thrice-beautious sun, the god of love,
The Soul of souls and heart of highest Jove,
If you to others good were not most prone.
    Open thou Earth; unclose thou fast-bound ball
Of smoring darknesse! The black jawes of Hell
Shall issue forth their dead, that direfull cell
Of miscreant Lives that strive still to enthrall,
Shall let him go at last, and he ore all — 30
Shall triumph. Then the gladsome Progeny
Of the bright Morning star shining on high,
    Shall fill the Round ætheriall
    With sound of voices musicall.

Nor yet this breath's quite spent. Swift flight of wing
Hath shot my soul from th'hight to th'depth again
And from th'depth to th'height. The glistring Main
Of flowing light and darknesses curs'd spring
I've mov'd with sacred words: (the extreme worlds
In holy rage assaulted with my spell) — 40
I'll at the middle Movable as well
As those, and powerfull magick gainst it hurle.
    You waving aires! and you more boistrous winds!
Dark *Zaphons* sons, who with your swelling blasts
Thrust out the ribs of heaven, and that orepast
Leave Nature languid to her wont confind,
Suppresse your spright and be at his command
Who on the troubled *Galilean* lake

23 sun, : sun 1647. love, : love 1647.

27 smoring: suffocating.

28 issue forth: release.

29 miscreant: depraved.

30 him: Christ.

41 middle Movable: the observable world, existing between heaven and hell.

44 *Zaphon*, according to "The Interpretation Generall," is "*Aquilo*. The North," i.e., the wind. Winds represent passions which must be reduced to obedience to Christ, who commanded them on Galilee (l. 48) as Mark 4:35–41 relates.

Did wind and storm to him obedient make.
50 Let still serenity the land
Inclose about with steddy hand.

And you heaven-threatning rocks, whose tops be crown'd
With wreaths of woolly clouds, fall into dust.
And thou, O *Ida* hill! thy glory must
Consume, and thou lye equall with the ground.
O're quick-ey'd *Ida*! thou which seest the Sun
Before day spring? those Eastern spatterd lights
And broad spread shinings purpling the gay Night,
And that swoln-glowing ball; they'll all be gone.
60 You summer neezings when the Sun is set
That fill the air with a quick fading fire,
Cease from your flashings, and thou Self-desire
The worst of meteors, curs'd Voraginet!
The wind of God shall rend thee into nought
And thou shalt vanish into empty air,
Nor shall thy rending out leave any scarre.
Thy place shall not be found though sought;
So perish shall all humane thought.

The Philosophers Devotion.

Sing aloud His praise rehearse
Who hath made the Universe.
He the boundlesse Heavens has spread
All the vitall orbs has kned;
He that on *Olympus* high

54 *Ida* hill: in *Psychozoia* 3. 10, a hill of half-truths where the soul may sometimes cease its search for God.

60 neezings: sneezes, i.e., heat lightning.

63 Voraginet: whirlpool or gulf.

67 sought; : sought 1647.

4 kned: kneaded.

5-8 As in *Democritus Platonnisans* More supports the idea of a plurality of worlds.

Tends his flocks with watchfull eye,
And this eye has multiplide
Midst each flock for to reside.
Thus as round about they stray
Toucheth each with out-stretch'd ray, 10
Nimble they hold on their way,
Shaping out their Night and Day.
Summer, Winter, Autumne, Spring,
Their inclined Axes bring.
Never slack they; none respires,
Dancing round their Centrall fires.
    In due order as they move
Echo's sweet be gently drove
Thorough Heavens vast Hollownesse,
Which unto all corners presse: 20
Musick that the heart of *Jove*
Moves to joy and sportfull love;
Fills the listning saylers eares
Riding on the wandring Sphears.
Neither Speech nor Language is
Where their voice is not transmisse.
    God is good, is Wise, is Strong,
Witnesse all the creature-throng,
Is confess'd by every Tongue.
All things back from whence they sprong, 30
As the thankfull Rivers pay
What they borrowed of the Sea.
    Now my self I do resigne,
Take me whole; I all am thine.
Save me, God! from Self-desire,
Deaths pit, dark Hells raging fire,
Envy, Hatred, Vengeance, Ire.

11-14 A very long note to these lines, omitted here, argues, with diagrams, the truth of the Copernican hypothesis.

15 respires: takes a rest.

23 saylers: inhabitants of planets.

25-26 echoing Ps. 19:3.

26 transmisse: transmitted.

34 whole; : whole 1647.

Let not Lust my soul bemire.
    Quit from these thy praise I'll sing,
40 Loudly sweep the trembling string.
Bear a part, O Wisdomes sonnes!
Free'd from vain Religions.
Lo! from farre I you salute,
Sweetly warbling on my Lute.
Indie, *Egypt*, *Arabie*,
Asia, *Greece*, and *Tartarie*,
Carmel-tracts, and *Lebanon*
With the *Mountains* of the *Moon*,
From whence muddie *Nile* doth runne
50 Or where ever else you wonne;
Breathing in one vitall air,
One we are though distant farre.
    Rise at once; let's sacrifice.
Odours sweet perfume the skies.
See how Heavenly lightning fires
Hearts inflam'd with high aspires!
All the substance of our souls
Up in clouds of Incense rolls.
Leave we nothing to our selves
60 Save a voice, what need we els!
Or an hand to wear and tire
On the thankfull Lute or Lyre.
    Sing aloud His praise rehearse
Who hath made the Universe.

Charitie and Humilitie.

Farre have I clambred in my mind
But nought so great as love I find:
Deep-searching wit, mount-moving might

42 vain: empty. More welcomes pagans who have come to recognize a universal God.

50 wonne: dwell.

53 once; : once 1647. sacrifice. : sacrifice 1647.

3 More is thinking of 1 Cor. 13:2.

Are nought compar'd to that good spright.
Light of delight and soul of blisse!
Sure source of lasting happinesse!
Higher then Heaven! lower then hell!
What is thy tent? where maist thou dwell?
    My mansion hight humilitie,
Heavens vastest capabilitie. 10
The further it doth downward tend
The higher up it doth ascend;
If it go down to utmost nought
It shall return with that it sought.
    Lord stretch thy tent in my strait breast,
Enlarge it downward, that sure rest
May there be pight; for that pure fire
Wherewith thou wontest to inspire
All self dead souls. My life is gone,
Sad solitude's my irksome wonne. 20
Cut off from men and all this world
In Lethes lonesome ditch I'm hurld.
Nor might nor sight doth ought me move,
Nor do I care to be above.
O feeble rayes of mentall light!
That best be seen in this dark night,
What are you? what is any strength
If it be not laid in one length
With pride or love? I nought desire
But a new life or quite t'expire. 30
Could I demolish with mine eye
Strong towers, stop the fleet stars in skie,
Bring down to earth the pale-fac'd Moon,
Or turn black midnight to bright Noon:
Though all things were put in my hand,
As parch'd as dry as th'Libyan sand
Would be my life if Charity
Were wanting. But Humility
Is more then my poore soul durst crave

9 My: i.e., Charity's.

15 tent: i.e., tabernacle or shrine.

17 pight: pitched.

40 That lies intombd in lowly grave.
But if't were lawfull up to send
My voice to Heaven, this should it rend.
    Lord thrust me deeper into dust
That thou maist raise me with the just.

Index

Authors' names are printed in small capitals, titles of poems in italics, and first lines of poems in roman.

THE ENGLISH SPENSERIANS was set in Intertype Baskerville
with handset foundry Baskerville display type.
Typography by Donald M. Henriksen.
Printed by the University of Utah Printing Service
on Warren's 1854 Offset paper.
Bound by Mountain States Bindery in Holliston Zeppelin cloth.